George Washington and
the Virginia Backcountry

George Washington

AND THE

Virginia Backcountry

EDITED BY WARREN R. HOFSTRA

Madison House

MADISON 1998

Hofstra, Warren R.
George Washington and the Virginia Backcountry

Copyright © 1998 by Madison House Publishers, Inc.
All rights reserved.

LIBRARY OF CONGRESS CATALOGING-IN-PUBLICATION DATA

George Washington and the Virginia backcountry / edited by Warren R. Hofstra. —
1st ed.
p. cm.
Includes bibliographical references and index.
ISBN 0-945612-50-8 (acid-free paper)
1. Washington, George, 1732-1799.   2. Washington, George, 1732-1799—Political
and social views.   3. Regionalism—Virginia—History—18th century.
4. Land settlement—Virginia—History—18th century.   5. Virginia—Historical
geography.   6. Virginia—History—Colonial period, ca. 1600-1775.   I. Hofstra,
Warren R., 1947–   .
E312.2G47 1996

975.5'02'092—DC20   96-16602
[B]   CIP
                                                                 REV.

Printed in the United States of America
on acid-free paper

Published by Madison House Publishers, Inc.
P.O. Box 3100, Madison, Wisconsin, 53704

FIRST EDITION

Contents

To friends and mentors,
Stewart Bell Jr. and W. W. Abbot

Preface

$\mathcal{D}$URING THE SAME SPRING OF 1732 when George Washington was born to a middling-class, planter family in Virginia's Northern Neck, a German immigrant, Jost Hite, led between fifteen and twenty families to new lands in Virginia's Shenandoah Valley. Although scattered European settlements already existed in this backcountry region of the colony, the peoples of German, Scotch-Irish, and English backgrounds accompanying Hite would establish one of the first sustained communities there. For the next sixteen years the Tidewater youth would grow into a young man increasingly enamored with the lifestyle and outlook of Virginia's wealthy and well-born tobacco planters. Meanwhile the people of the backcountry would clear the land and establish the farms that would sustain the independence of their own families and communities.

In 1748 the young man and the region would encounter one another for the first time. During the next decade this encounter would deepen as Washington assumed key roles in the development of the backcountry—first as surveyor defining property holdings that for settler families meant the means of survival and sustenance, then as commander of the Virginia Regiment charged with the responsibility of maintaining the safety of these families and thus the security of the colony during the exceedingly dangerous years of the French and Indian or Seven Years' War, and finally as the region's delegate to the Virginia House of Burgesses representing its concerns in the governing body of the colony.

During these same ten years, the backcountry also developed in ways that made Washington's expanding role possible. More land was surveyed and granted than in any earlier or later period. Scattered settlements of the pioneer era matured and grew together. Towns were established that assumed increasingly important governing and market functions. And although the Seven Years' War profoundly disrupted life in rural communities, it stimulated the growth of towns, generated commercial ties between the backcountry and the major port cities of British America, and joined the West more fully to the governing structures of both colony and empire.

George Washington left the backcountry to take up residence at Mount Vernon in 1758, his ambitions for social and political preferment largely fulfilled. As one of Virginia's wealthiest men—a position gained not least through the acquisition of backcountry lands—he could now assume a rightful role among the elite of the colony's Tidewater. He was also in possession of a reputation, attained through military service, that not only made him one of the most talked-about men in Virginia but brought mention of his name in both colonial capitals and European courts. Through wealth and reputation he had also achieved a political position consonant with his class.

This book, however, is about more than how the region helped make the man. It is, in fact, an examination of the deeper, more perplexing and certainly more ambiguous influences on the great man during his formative years. In his experiences as a surveyor, George Washington no doubt saw the intimate connection between the appropriation of property and the conquest of territory by one people over another. As colonel of the Virginia Regiment, Washington learned the nature of command—how to lead in the most trying circumstances, how to accept defeat without demise, and how to inspire both loyalty and fear. These were all qualities that would stand him and an unfolding nation well two, three, and four decades later. Washington also found that command meant assuming responsibility for people he did not always like. In fact, his encounters with the men and women of the backcountry—Hite's settlers and others like them and Native American peoples—revealed the ugliness of prejudice and what we would call racism within him. Throughout his long sojourn west of the Blue Ridge, George Washington made plain his distaste, if not disdain, for all these people. But in his criticisms, denunciations, confusions, and misapprehensions, Americans of the twentieth century can see how these peoples and their lifeways varied from the expectations that not only Washington had about a proper social order but also we have about a properly ordered past that produced great men. From this messiness, nonetheless, came a man who could overcome his dislike for others and otherness if a greater good was to result.

So this book is first of all about the impact of a region on a young man whose career was of incalculable importance to the history of a new nation, but it is also about that region itself and the diversity of its peoples and cultures. It is a book about the backcountry and how its character was revealed through an encounter with an extraordinary representative of an equally distinctive region. Thus, it is a book about a particular social world that has become the object of increasing historical attention as being perhaps more expressive than Chesapeake plantations or New England towns of how British colonists became an American people during the nineteenth century.

This project began as a conference held in 1989, the year of the bicentennial of the presidency, at Shenandoah University in Winchester, Virginia. Winchester was the headquarters of the Virginia Regiment and the scene of some of Washington's most significant activities. Most of the papers included in this volume were originally presented at the conference, although some were prepared later for the sake of rounding out the record of Washington in the backcountry. The book is divided into three parts. In part one Dorothy Twohig surveys the full scope of Washington's career to provide a context for his particular experiences as a young man on the Virginia frontier. Bruce A. Ragsdale follows with a review of what we now know about the society and economy of Chesapeake planters after several decades of new and innovative research into the world that gave rise to a Washington and turned his ambitions westward.

Part two shifts attention from the lowcountry to the backcountry. Robert D. Mitchell begins with a historical geographer's account of the movement of European peoples into the eighteenth-century Virginia frontier, a discussion of the communities they created, and an explanation of the transformation these communities experienced during the years of Washington's contact with them. The following two articles focus on what Washington's experiences reveal about the peoples of the backcountry. Warren R. Hofstra examines Washington's frustrations with German, Scotch-Irish, English, and Anglo-American transplants to the region west of the Blue Ridge as their aspirations for a better, less dependent life thwarted his own social and political ambitions. The encounter between Washington and the Native American peoples of the Ohio Country forms the setting for J. Frederick Fausz's investigation into the failure of eighteenth-century British colonists to comprehend Indian cultures very different from their own.

In the final section of the book, three historians assess the meaning of Washington's backcountry years for the emerging Tidewater planter, Revolutionary War commander, and president. Philander D. Chase looks at Washington's career in frontier surveying and landowning as a means of acquiring a stake in the West that not only placed him prominently within the world of Chesapeake planters but also shaped his vision for the extent and purpose of the nation he would lead as first president. For John E. Ferling the lessons Washington learned under trying circumstances—partly of his own making—as colonel of the Virginia Regiment formed the basis of his successful command during the American Revolution and his deepening understanding of the proper relationship between civilian and military authority in a republic. In the anchor to all the essays, Don Higginbotham explores the revolutionary in Washington and concludes that backcountry experiences may have helped unhinge him from loyalties to king, but it was love for his own country, Virginia—and especially the deferential world of Chesapeake planters—that prompted Washington to rise up in rebellion during the 1770s and then willingly to surrender power for the good of the nation once in the 1780s and again in the 1790s to return to home and family. Collectively these final essays, then, evaluate the contributions made by the backcountry to the emerging political order of republican America through one of its most remarkable leaders.

$\mathcal{A}$N ENTERPRISE BEGINNING IN A conference and concluding years later inevitably assumes many debts along the way. Although I took on the burden of organizing the conference, I owe its inspiration and whatever vision it embodied to Stewart Bell, Jr., retired councilman, mayor, teacher, and farmer of Winchester, Virginia. A man whose great grandfather lived in the town at a time in which he could have met George Washington, Stewart Bell understood that great things can happen in the little communities of America and that the legacy of the nation's leaders is held in trust by those places where ordinary events can have incalculable and unforeseeable consequences.

Stewart Bell's personal admiration for Washington was sufficient motivation for me to search out those historians, biographers, geographers, and anthropologists—social scientists as well as humanists—who knew the most about Washington, his times, and especially his early years and invite them to gather for two days of deliberations at Shenandoah University two hundred years to the month after George Washington was inaugurated as first president of the United States. This search would never have achieved success without the thoughtful guidance and wise counsel of William W. Abbot, editor in chief of the Washington Papers. Well-entrenched in the Alderman Library of the University of Virginia, this project, under his expert hand, has been turning out volume after widely respected volume of Washington's letters, papers, and other writings as an endowment upon which all future Washington scholarship will inevitably draw. To my unending gratitude, the Washington Papers was to join the conference effort as cosponsor and soon the wisdom and experience of Mr. Abbot's collaborators, Dorothy Twohig, Philander D. Chase, and Beverly H. Runge were brought to bear on inviting participants, shaping sessions, and giving life and public meaning to a scholarly conference.

No less helpful at this critical time was the support of the Virginia Commission on the Bicentennial of the United States Constitution and its chairman A. E. Dick Howard. Timothy G. O'Rourke, executive director of the commission, and his staff housed in the Center for Public Service at the University of Virginia turned over the resources of the commission to the conference and convinced many participants and much of the audience to journey to Winchester and spend two days discussing George Washington's formative years.

Without the Virginia Foundation for the Humanities and Public Policy, however, none of these first steps could have been taken. Not only did the many excellent conferences and humanities programs sponsored throughout Virginia by the foundation furnish the model and inspiration for the Washington project, but funds provided by a foundation grant ultimately covered most of the conference expenses. The broad experience of Robert Vaughan, president of the foundation, and associate director David Bearinger and their willingness to share their knowledge of how to open humanities scholarship to public audiences made my job of foreseeing and meeting the challenges of organizing a conference measurably easier. So did the willing assistance of members of the Advisory Council for the Community History Project at Shenandoah University. Juliette Armer, Ilona Benham, William W. Hassler, Alvin Perlman, and Sarah P. Trumbower lent their years of experience in planning events, shepherding academics in practical causes, engaging the public through the press, and leading historical societies in worthwhile causes to the task of transforming a rigorous schedule of scholarly deliberations into many productive opportunities for people of varying backgrounds to engage each other over mutual interests. Rebecca Ebert and Theodora Rezba planned exhibits in conjunction with the conference, and Shenandoah University students Rose Anderson and Eric Michael did whatever small job was needed to make the event a success. The members of the Clarke-Frederick-Winchester Bicentennial of the Constitution Commission under the able direction of Anna G. Thomson lent additional help and guidance as did other members of the university and local community including Ned Burks, Karen Clay, Malinda Feathers, Lisa Frye, Nancy Melton, Pat Patterson, Katie Rockwood, Richard Shickle, Laura Sirbaugh, and Patricia Wrinkle.

Perhaps my greatest obligation is to Shenandoah University and the support faculty, students, and administration have given to the Community History Project since its inception in 1987. Devoted to seeking common ground among the needs and enthusiasms of students, the skills and interests of scholars, and the local community's intense concern and high standards for historical preservation and interpretation, the project often leads me as director into activities many academics would wisely avoid. Most of these activities, however, have yielded benefits beyond expectation but not without backing and guidance from such individuals as James A. Davis, university president; Joel S. Stegall, academic vice-president; deans Warren DeArment and Catherine Tisinger; chief development officer John Warren; John Stevens, director of auxiliary services; and my friend and colleague in the history department, Brandon Beck.

The conference itself was a success only because of the immense effort that participants put into it. More of these fine scholars than I had a right to expect invested the extra effort required to transform conference papers into essays for this volume. Their good grace in the face of my attempts to be useful as volume editor and their unflagging willingness to make minor changes in their manuscripts for the sake of balance and cohesion in the volume is deeply appreciated. So are all the unrecognized contributions of other participants, session chairs, and commenters, especially those of Steven L. Cooksey, Ryan Fletcher, William M. Gardner, Clarence R. Geier, Sarah S. Hughes, Jim Morrison, Charles Royster, Lorena S. Walsh, Joseph W. A. Whitehorne, and Edwin M. Yoder.

The preparation of the manuscript also benefitted from the experience of others. Don Higginbotham served as mentor to the final product giving key bits of advice about its organization and disposition at critical times. A discretionary grant from the Virginia Foundation for the Humanities helped with expenses. The maps are owing to the careful cartographic attention of Robert D. Mitchell and collaborators, Geoffrey Buckley, Jasper Rubin, and Joseph B. Thomas. Ann Grogg freely lent her years of experience as an editor of scholarly volumes to serve as general counsel to this one. That the manuscript found so happy a home at Madison House, however, is owing to the quick read John Kaminski gave it and his long support for it. Gregory M. Britton, director of Madison House, adopted the manuscript and in many ways created the nurturing environment in which it could grow into a book. Christopher Hill's extremely competent copyediting gave it style and consistency.

From the conception of the conference to the publication of the book consumed the better part of a decade—an overly long lapse of time, which is my responsibility alone. My wife Mary saw more clearly than I did the tensions and pressures of organizing a conference and sticking to the project until it emerged as a book. Her many reminders about overwork and the cautions she raised when persistence became doggedness helped see the effort through. So did the numerous distractions of my children, Andrew and Kate. The cherry tree in our yard has so far survived their youthful adventures, but my fondest hope for them and their generation is that the experiences of a young man in the Virginia backcountry two hundred and fifty years ago will help guide them through a world in which the encounter of more cultures than George Washington ever knew is yet fraught with both great peril and immeasurable opportunity.

Warren R. Hofstra
Berryville, Virginia
January 9, 1996

Part One

The Making of
George Washington

DOROTHY TWOHIG

ON APRIL 16, 1789, WASHINGTON
began his journey to New York City to assume the presidency. He went
"to the chair of government," as he wrote Henry Knox, with "feelings
not unlike those of a culprit who is going to the place of his execution:
so unwilling am I, in the evening of a life nearly consumed in public
cares, to quit a peaceful abode for an Ocean of difficulties. . . . Integrity
& firmness is all I can promise—these, be the voyage long or short;
never shall foresake me although I may be deserted by all men."[1]
Everywhere along his route to the capital Washington encountered unprecedented adulation. At the apex of his career, he seemed to the people
who saw him pass the very embodiment of Bolingbroke's Patriot King.
He even looked the part. Physically he was overpowering. In a nation
where the height of the average man was perhaps five feet, four inches,
he towered at six feet, two. Benjamin Rush observed that "there is not a
king in Europe that would not look like a valet de chambre by his side."[2]
No other man of his time evoked the kind of tribute that Washington
did on the eve of his inaugural journey. From the vortex of the Revolution, he had acquired an immense reputation for integrity, disinterest-
edness, and service to the state, and by the end of the war his image,
both in the United States and abroad, as the great man of his century
was unrivaled.

In a nation obsessed with fears of a standing army, of disunion,
and of the restoration of monarchy, its greatest military leader had
angrily repudiated proposals to create a kingship with himself at its
head. His skillful diffusing of the Newburgh mutiny had allayed fears
that the military would supplant civilian authority. In the summer of

1783 Washington's closing circular to the governors of the states—except for the Farewell Address probably his best known public document and soon to be known as his legacy to the nation—not only presented his hopes for the new nation but indicated that his sole role would be as a citizen of the republic. As Gary Wills has observed, Washington was a virtuoso of resignations and his abdication of power at the moment of triumph in 1783 enhanced his reputation as no military feat could have done. "Scarce had the solemn scene passed over," the citizens of Philadelphia assured Washington, "when a triumphant Victor returned his sword to the Hands of the civil Rulers of his country." Washington had acquired the symbolic status of Cincinnatus, the soldier who left his farm to defend Rome and when the danger had passed returned to his plow. Indeed, Jefferson probably echoed the views of most Americans when he said at the close of the war that "the moderation and virtue of a single character has probably prevented this revolution from being closed as most others have been by a subversion of that liberty it was intended to establish."[3]

When Washington accepted command of the Continental army in June 1775 he had already acquired much of the intellectual baggage that was to accompany him for the rest of his public career. If the war years brought a wealth of experience that carried over into the presidency and later, it only confirmed the qualities that were to elevate him to the American pantheon; qualities acquired in his early youth, during his military service on the Virginia frontier, and especially during his pre-war years as a Virginia planter

WASHINGTON CAME FROM A FAMILY of the middling rank in the colony, and as he later admitted, he knew next to nothing about his ancestry, although he used the family coat of arms. When in December 1791 Sir Isaac Heard of the College of Heraldry in London wrote him asking for genealogical information about the family, he replied that it was "a subject to which I confess I have paid very little attention. My mind has been so much occupied in the busy and active scenes of life from an early period of it that but a small portion of it could have been devoted to researches of this nature, even if my inclination or particular circumstances should have prompted the enquiry."[4] He lost no time, however, in sending Heard a genealogi-

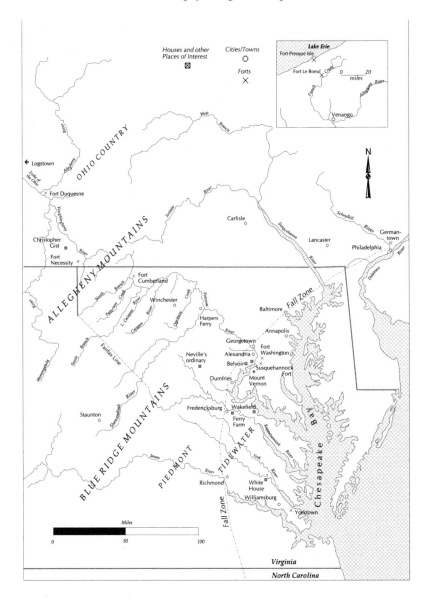

cal chart, taking the trouble to verify it, and seeking additional information from a family connection.[5]

The English Washingtons had been prosperous clergymen, merchants, and minor landholders. The twenty-five-year-old John Washington, who came to Virginia in 1657 aboard the ketch *Sea Horse of*

London, was the son of Lawrence Washington, an Oxford-educated cleric whose brushes with the Puritans during the Commonwealth had left him professionally and financially ruined.[6] Like many families that came to America in similar circumstances, the Virginia branch married well and acquired modest landholdings, though they never rose to the class of the colony's great landowners. Washington's father, Augustine Washington, was a reasonably prosperous planter involved also in a number of other business enterprises. The family lived first at Wakefield on Pope's Creek, a tributary of the Potomac in Virginia's Northern Neck, where George was born, but some time before November 1735 Augustine moved to the land that was eventually to become Mount Vernon.[7] Augustine died in 1743, leaving his second wife, Mary Ball Washington, two surviving sons of his first marriage, and the four sons and one daughter of his second. Young George's portion of his father's estate was not impressive—the 280-acre farm on the Rappahannock on which Augustine had lived, a share in other small holdings, three lots in Fredericksburg, and a few slaves.[8]

Not enough is known of Washington's youth to reconstruct his family life with any degree of certainty. His father apparently left little impression on his young son, and his two half-brothers, Augustine and Lawrence, were still at school in England. Among his own siblings, Washington was exceedingly fond of his brother John Augustine, "the intimate companion of my youth and the friend of my ripened age."[9] What is apparent is that the nuclear household headed by Mary Ball Washington after Augustine's death belonged more to the authoritarian, paternalistic family of the late seventeenth century than to the open, affectionate, and child-oriented family unit that was developing by the mid-eighteenth century in the Chesapeake.[10]

There is singularly little documentary evidence for the traditions that have come down concerning Washington's relationship with his mother. What little we know of the relationship indicates in Washington's youth a struggle between an overly possessive woman with a strong inclination to keep her eldest son perpetually in her service—her objections kept him from going to sea in 1746—and a young man endeavoring to escape from parental bondage. When Augustine died she was living at Ferry Farm, bequeathed to Washington in his father's will. It took many years and her own failing health to dislodge her from it. She seems never to have been satisfied with either her possessions or the attentions of her family. Washington's biographers have frequently commented on how seldom her name appears in contemporary literature in connection with that of her famous son. It was not until the nineteenth century that she was canonized as "Mary, mother of Washington." For much of her life Washington seems to have kept her, as much as possible, at a distance from his residence and his affairs. He supplied her with money to the best of his ability and was enraged when she encouraged a plan in the Virginia legislature to give her a pension during the Revolution.[11]

When it became evident in the late 1780s that his mother was no longer able to live alone, Washington urged her to leave her plantation near Fredericksburg and live with one of her children, although, he hastened to add, not with him. "Candour requires me to say," he wrote her, that moving to Mount Vernon "will never answer your purposes, in any shape whatsoever—for in truth it may be compared to a well resorted tavern, scarcely any strangers who are going from north to south, or from south to north, do not spend a day or two at it . . . nor indeed could you be retired in any room in my house; for what with the sitting up of Company, the noise and bustle of servants—and many other things you would not be able to enjoy that calmness and serenity of mind, which in my opinion you ought now to prefer to every other consideration in life." In contrast, his invitation to his wife's mother was considerably more cordial, proposing that she make Mount Vernon "her entire and absolute home . . . it might suit her well, and be agreeable, both to herself and my Wife, to me most assuredly it would."[12]

His father's early death and his incompatibility with his mother undoubtedly fostered young Washington's independence and self-reliance, but he still sought the emotional support of a surrogate family. He soon exhibited considerable skill in building his own network of relationships, notably with his half-brother Lawrence and Lawrence's connections. Lawrence Washington was fourteen years George's senior, proprietor of Mount Vernon, and veteran of the abortive campaign against Cartagena in 1740–1741. Partly through his marriage in 1743 to Ann Fairfax, daughter of William Fairfax of nearby Belvoir, and partly through his own abilities, Lawrence had, by the time the eleven-year-old George began to spend a considerable amount of his time with him in the early 1740s, established himself in the first rank of the colony's social strata. Much has been made of Lawrence's influence as a role model to young George. Douglas Southall Freeman described his "genial approachability and a capacity for making friends. One thinks of him as the person to whom, in a crowd, a stranger would go to make an inquiry."[13] Lawrence's virtual adoption of his younger half-brother was not unusual in colonial Virginia, where ties between brothers were frequently very close and where older brothers often assumed parental duties in matters of education and economic support.[14]

Young George flourished in the new environment of his brother's connections. In 1749 he qualified as a surveyor for Culpeper County, and within a year he had saved enough to buy almost fifteen hundred acres on Bullskin Creek in the Shenandoah Valley. Surveying, he believed, was something of a gentleman's accomplishment as well as a way to earn his living, and it played a part in his anticipated role as a great planter. "Nothing can be more essentially necessary to any man possessed of a large landed Estate," he wrote some years later, "the bounds of some part or other of which are always in controversy."[15]

Washington was serving the kind of apprenticeship not uncommon in Chesapeake society, particularly for younger sons who needed a marketable skill. But, probably inspired by Lawrence's adventures in the Cartagena campaign, he early appears to have acquired a sense that military activity would provide a quick path for advancement. He deliberately sought mentors from among Virginia's social and political elite. Through his Belvoir connections he quickly found favor with the group of older men, prominent in the colony, who were instrumental in his advancement—George Corbin; John Robinson, treasurer of the colony and Speaker of the House of Burgesses; Thomas, Lord Fairfax, who encouraged his advancement and sent him on his first surveying mission in 1748; and above all William Fairfax, his brother's father-in-law. Landon Carter was free with advice; Lord Fairfax's estate at Greenway Court helped form Washington's conception of the role of a great landowner; William Fairfax played the role of surrogate father. And there were friends closer to his own age. George William Fairfax, William's son, was his close companion, and his wife Sally's relationship with Washington during his French and Indian War military career has been the subject of curious examination for the last two centuries.[16] At Belvoir there were the wives and daughters of the colony's first families, towards whom young George learned to display a labored gallantry. To these connections, perhaps more than to his own incipient abilities, he owed his first opportunities for prominence—the chance to take a message from the governor to the commander of the French forces on the frontier in 1753 and his command during the Fort Necessity campaign the next year. And they were the friends who continued to defend and support him in his controversies with the colonial government in Williamsburg while he was in command of the Virginia Regiment, from 1755 to 1759. In spite of his youth, he was well aware of the importance of the proper connections. As he wrote his brother in May 1755 from the frontier: "I shoud be glad to hear that you live in perfect Harmony and good fellowship with the family at Belvoir, as it is in their power to be very serviceable upon many occasion's to us as young beginner's: I woud advise your visiting there often, as one Step towards the rest."[17] Washington was already very much a young man in pursuit of social advancement. And in view of the warm support of his friends and mentors, if he lacked polish he must have had considerable charm.

We know very little of Washington's schooling, but he lacked a formal education and what little instruction he received seems to have stressed such practical skills as surveying.[18] Had his father lived, George undoubtedly would have followed his two half-brothers to school in England. As it was, he and his brothers probably had at least some tutoring and may have attended a local school. "Endowed with the blood and instincts of a gentleman," historian Samuel E. Morison observed, "he was not given a gentleman's education."[19] But even in his teens what was soon to become an obsession with self-improvement was evident. Sometime before he was sixteen Washington copied a series of "Rules of Civility and Decent Behaviour in Company and Conversation" from a seventeenth-century English translation of the maxims of a fifteenth-century French Jesuit.[20] Some of the rules for social conduct that caught Washington's eye—to the extent that he chose to copy them—reflected the timidity of a young man moving out of a ruder rural society into the more elegant surroundings of his brother's world. "Kill no vermin as Fleas, lice, ticks &c in the Sight of others," the author warned. "Spit not in the Fire." "Put not your meat to your Mouth with your Knife in your hand neither Spit forth the Stones of any fruit Pye upon a dish nor Cast anything under the table." "Cleanse not your Teeth with the Table Cloth Napkin Fork or Knife but if Others do it let it be done wt a Pick Tooth." All were designed to keep the reader from disgrace in the dining room at Mount Vernon. But there were other less pragmatic maxims dealing with respect for one's superiors and one's god, with honesty in business, and with moderation in behavior. So much, indeed, did many of the rules correspond with Washington's later standards of conduct, for many years it was assumed that he had composed rather than copied the maxims.

Although he may have been shy and awkward in the first years of his residence at Mount Vernon, when he fell under the sway of the Fairfax family and their friends, he was not completely the country bumpkin. He was familiar enough with the amenities of life and the qualities required of a gentleman to know what attributes he sought to add to his own repertoire. Washington was well aware of his lack of formal education, and it troubled him throughout his life—there are frequent disparaging references to it in his correspondence, and no doubt it contributed to the trepidation with which he always responded to calls on him for public service. His biographers have occasionally suggested that his uneasiness concerning his educational background may have accounted for his reserve in the presence of men he considered his superiors in learning. It was universally observed that he had, as John Adams said, "the gift of silence." If so, this was a quality that added immensely, if accidentally, to his reputation for wisdom.

It is almost a cliché to consider Washington in terms of the eighteenth century's definition of classical philosophy. But the Stoic ideas of fame and honor and glory, and of public service, were an important part of the intellectual assumptions that shaped his views of his leadership during the Revolution and even more his conception of his presidential role. This was a legacy that he brought with him from his youth. In the eighteenth century the words *fame* and *honor* were common intellectual catchwords, but the concepts they represented were not used in any pejorative sense. To disciples of the Enlightenment, fame was not simply for personal aggrandizement or a pursuit of celebrity. Rather the goal was to elevate oneself above the crowd, to acquire a reputation for virtue and integrity that would become an inspiration for future generations. And accompaniments to fame were honor and prestige in the eyes of one's contemporaries. Stoicism was predicated on courage, a reverence for duty, and simplicity in life. In the age of the Enlightenment the pursuit of glory was part of the path of virtue. It was a path chosen not for personal advantage but because it was the function of a citizen of the state. "The love of fame," Hamilton wrote in *Federalist* 72, "[is] the ruling passion of the noblest minds." One did not choose public life casually or automatically or for the sake of celebrity or personal advantage; one chose it because it was the function proper to a good man. Where Washington acquired a knowledge of the classical precepts of public virtue is uncertain, but from the time he moved to Mount Vernon he associated with men mostly, like his half-brothers, educated in England and immersed in classical philosophy and literature—men who gave at least lip service to Stoic ideals.

It has often been suggested—not least by such of Washington's contemporaries as John Adams, Timothy Pickering, and Benjamin Rush—that Washington's reading was not extensive. Indeed, Adams, always a jealous observer, remarked that it was beyond dispute that Washington was "too illiterate, unlearned, unread for his station."[21] But by the close of his career Washington had collected an impressive private library, and recent biographers have argued that it is probable that he may have read in it much more widely and at an earlier stage of his life than has been generally appreciated.[22] As Peter Gay has pointed out, classical literature was in the eighteenth century "the common possession of educated men, not the preserve of the specialist." Classical influences may, in fact, have had even more impact in America than in Europe, where there was competing diversity in local intellectual resources.[23] In Virginia, where planters were eager to imitate the lifestyle of the English gentry, classical education, architecture, and ideas held a special attraction. From his own comments it is evident that a few books of his youth influenced Washington deeply, and one of these was Joseph Addison's play *The Tragedy of Cato*, which Washington saw on the stage, read and reread, and he occasionally quoted.[24] The Cato of Plutarch's *Lives* and of Addison's play expressed what came to be Washington's own idea of the ultimate public leader. More than once he quoted Cato's famous lines "'Tis not in mortals to command success, But we'll do better . . . we'll deserve it." But for Washington the application of the tenets of Stoic philosophy to the creation of his own character came only with maturity and experience.

IN LIGHT OF HIS LATER MILITARY career, it is easy to underestimate the value of his years on the Virginia frontier. The skills he acquired during the French and Indian War in dealing with the Virginia Burgesses were to stand him in good stead later in his relations with Congress and the state governments during the Revolution and during his presidency. Washington's greatest political strength during the Revolutionary War—the ability to convince civilians that he subordinated military power to civil authority—he learned on the frontier. His letters to Dinwiddie and Fauquier complaining of deficiencies in men, supplies, and support, with their implicit criticism of the political establishment, mirror in fact, if not in tone, his later reports to the Continental Congress. In fact, Washington's frontier experiences provided a microcosm for the problems he faced as commander in chief during the Revolution. But the young commander of the Virginia Regiment bears little resemblance to the Washington of the Revolution or the presidency. In his official correspondence he seems brash, argumentative, impatient, greedy for land and possessions, in hot pursuit of a commission in the British army, often unlikable but very human—in fact, very much a young man on the make. If he was at all interested in projecting an image of the Cato ideal at this stage of his career, he was more concerned with the form than the substance.[25]

Washington became increasingly sensitive to any criticism that he felt threatened his growing reputation and struck without mercy when censure hit a vulnerable point—a trait he carried with him for the rest of his career. And as a young officer on the frontier he did receive criticism—for his precipitate behavior in firing on the French mission in 1754, for his surrender of Fort Necessity, for his frank and unending complaints to the governor on his military situation, and for the behavior of his officers during several of his campaigns. His military correspondence with officials in Williamsburg very quickly declined from deferential acknowledgments of his gratitude for his appointment to imperious expressions of his views and demands, punctuated with threats to resign. "If you think me capable of holding a commission," he wrote William Fitzhugh, "that has neither rank nor emolument annexed to it, you must entertain a very contemptible opinion of my weakness, and believe me to be more empty than the commission itself."[26] Disputes over precedence and pay occupied almost as much of his correspondence as military matters. His often arrogant letters to his civilian superiors seemed to evidence an overweening self-confidence, but in fact his underlying misgivings concerning his ability to succeed in his new role were painfully apparent. His reply to reports of criticism in the assembly concerning the regiment is typical of his response: "I find that my own character must of necessity be involved in the general censure: for which reason I can not help observing, that if the country think they have cause to condemn my conduct, and have a person in view that will act; that he may do. But who will endeavour to *act more* for her Interests than I have done? It will give me the greatest pleasure to resign a command, which I solemnly declare I accepted against my will." Washington called on his friends in Williamsburg not only for constant reassurance but also for advice.[27] Indeed, he had an instinct for seeking advice in the right quarters. And there was a positive side to his diffidence. In his military correspondence during the French and Indian War with his officers and with friends in high places in Williamsburg, it is possible to see the beginning of what later became one of his established policies—to seek counsel from friends and subordinates on substantive decisions. Washington was not indecisive, but throughout his life he maintained a healthy doubt of his own infallibility. During the Revolution, councils of war with his general officers preceded major strategic decisions; during the presidency he invariably turned to his cabinet for advice on critical policy decisions. But always he reserved much of his soul-searching for decisions that he felt would affect his reputation. Even on relatively minor matters—but ones he felt might reflect on his public reputation—he turned to friends for counsel.[28]

Washington carried his exaggerated reaction to criticism into his retirement after he left the Virginia Regiment in 1759. When a small storm of protest arose in the early 1770s over the surveying of bounty land sponsored by Washington on behalf of the regiment, he was outraged. There is reason to believe that there was some justification for the veterans' complaints. Washington later admitted that the landholdings he had acquired through the survey were "the cream of the Country."[29] But his reaction to a now-missing letter from Maj. George Muse displays a typical response to adverse comment on his actions:

> Your impertinent Letter of the 24th ulto, was delivered to me yesterday . . . as I am not accustomed to receive such from any Man, nor would have taken the same language from you personally, without letting you feel some marks of my resentment. . . . For though I understand you were drunk when you did it, yet give me leave to tell you, that drunkness is no excuse for rudeness; & that, but for your stupidity & sottishness you might have known, by attending to the public Gazettes . . . that you had your full quantity of ten thousand acres of Land allow'd you; . . . do you think your superlative merit entitles you to greater indulgences than others? or that I was to make it good to you, if it did? . . . all my concern is, that I ever engag'd in behalf of so ungrateful & dirty a fellow as you are.[30]

$\mathcal{A}$T NO OTHER TIME IN HIS CAREER was Washington to come so close to that amorphous and disparate group known as *the people* as he did during his early military service on the Virginia frontier. It left a lasting impression. During his later years of public service he was sheltered by his rank. But on the frontier there was no buffer, and he encountered ordinary men in all their foibles and inconsistencies. He was not favorably impressed. Washington's first impressions—sometimes prejudices—concerning people and places could be indelible. In his 1748 surveying diary he described with amused tolerance the party's encounter with about thirty Indians. Local settlers, however, who must have viewed the surveying party with all the apprehension of people whose land is threatened by authority, evoked contempt. "A great Company of People Men Women & Children," he wrote, "attended us through the Woods as we went, shewing there Antick tricks. I really think they seem to be as Ignorant a Set of People as the Indians. They would never speak English, but when spoken to, they speak all Dutch."[31]

Older images of a crude frontier society composed of lower-class, poorly-educated immigrants recently arrived from Europe have not survived close examination. In the 1750s settlers were moving into the Virginia frontier at a rapid pace, and Robert D. Mitchell has estimated that by 1760 the vast majority of the eighteen thousand Europeans in the Shenandoah Valley were from other colonies. The frontier settlers were a diverse lot, of varied ethnic, religious, and social backgrounds, often men who had farmed in other colonies and brought with them the political and economic ideas characteristic of an upwardly mobile society. The fact that these ideas included a strong sense of independence and a marked lack of reverence for leadership from east of the mountains did not endear them to the Tidewater establishment.[32]

While Washington often admired and respected the men of his own rank whom he met during his frontier service, the lower orders—the settlers who flocked into the forts to escape Indian attacks, the local officials, the petty contractors, the rank and file in the regiment—all too often failed to fit his ideas of a responsible citizenry. Generally he shared the Tidewater planter's disdain for the quality and lifestyle of the frontier settler. His objectives, even as a young colonel in the regiment, were fundamentally different from those of the residents of the frontier. He had little understanding of or interest in the local concerns and ambitions of the settlers and even less in the West's transient population, except in their relationship to the larger concerns of the eastern establishment. In justice to Washington, it must be observed that he was equally critical of the dilatory tactics of the government in Williamsburg in the struggle against the French. He could and did plead movingly on many occasions for supplies and pay for his soldiers and for protection for the frontier inhabitants—those "miserable, undone people." As he wrote Gov. Robert Dinwiddie in April 1756, "I see their situation, *know* their danger, and participate their *Sufferings*; without having it in my power to give them further relief, than uncertain promises. . . . The supplicating tears of the women; and moving petitions from the men, melt me into such deadly sorrow, that I solemnly declare, if I know my own mind—I could offer myself a willing Sacrifice to the butchering Enemy, provided that would contribute to the peoples ease."[33]

But Washington also tended to forget that frontiersmen lived on the thin edge of survival. For the most part he agreed with John Robinson that the state of the backcountry was owing "in my Opinion in a great Measure to the obstanctcy and dasturdlyness of the People themselves."[34] In general, Washington found them "very selfish, every person expects forces at his own door, and is angry to see them at his neighbours."[35] These "infatuated people" consistently failed to behave as he thought they should. "The timidity of the Inhabitants of this Country," he complained to Robinson, "is to be equalled by nothing but their perverseness." The local small businessmen outraged him. "Were it not too tedious," he wrote Governor Dinwiddie in October 1757, "I cou'd give your Honor such instances of the villainous Behaviour of those Tipling-house keeper's, as wou'd astonish any person. . . . it is impossible to maintain that discipline and do that Service with a Garrison thus corrupted by a sett of people, whose conduct looks like the effect of a combination to obstruct the Service, and frustrate the methods pointed out for their own preservation."[36] The local professionals did not escape his ire. "The Country has great objections," he complained to Robert Stewart of certain medical men, "these occasional Quacks—whose only study is to swell their Bills, and to make their profit of the Country." Militiamen were "obstinate, self-willed, perverse; of little or no service to the people, and very burthensome of the Country. Every mean individual has his own crude notion of things, and must undertake to direct. If his advice is neglected, he thinks himself slighted, abused and injured; and to redress his wrongs, will depart for

[15]

home." By the end of his service on the frontier, Washington came fairly close to echoing William Byrd II in regarding the Scotch-Irish settlers as comparable to "the Goths and Vandals of old."[37] On their part the settlers seem not to have reciprocated Washington's poor opinion of them, although his considerable popularity appears to have stemmed not so much from personal esteem as from the conviction that he was committed to their protection in a struggle understood poorly by the government in Williamsburg and not at all by the commanders sent by London.

Although he retained his suspicion of frontiersmen for the rest of his life, Washington soon lost the patronizing tone of his early diary entries regarding Indians as he gained experience with them and developed skill in Indian diplomacy. A lasting legacy that Washington brought with him from his frontier service to his Revolutionary and presidential career was an understanding, unusual for his time, of Indians and ways of dealing with them. He quickly realized the importance of Indian allies, repeatedly pointing out that the Indians were a strong asset to frontier defense. "Those Indians who are now coming, should be shewed all possible respect, and the greatest care taken of them, as upon them much depends. . . . they are very humoursome, and their assistance very necessary. One *false* step might not only lose us *that,* but even turn them against us." As early as 1756 he issued orders for all "Soldiers & Towns people to use the Indians civilly and kindly; to avoid giving them liquor; and to be cautious what they speak before them: as all of them understand english and ought not to be affronted."[38]

Washington sought ways of attaching the Indians to the colonies and later to the new national government and strongly advocated integrity in dealing with them. In general, he maintained that Indian problems were as much the fault of recalcitrant frontiersmen as of the tribes. As he wrote Edmund Pendleton in 1795, the Indians "are not without serious causes of complaint, from the encroachments which are made on their lands by our people; who are not to be restrained by any law now in being, or likely to be enacted. They, poor wretches, have no Press thro' which their grievances are related." During his presidency he constantly harangued Congress to "make fair treaties with the Savage tribes (by this I mean that they shall *perfectly* understand every article and clause of them . . . that these treaties shall be held sacred, and the infractors on either side punished exemplarily." And he retained from his Virginia days a deep and abiding suspicion of frontiersmen and frontier lawlessness as the cause of Indian troubles. What hope existed of living in "tranquillity" with the Indians, "so long as a spirit of land jobbing prevails, and our frontier Settlers entertain the opinion that there is not the same crime (or indeed no crime at all) in killing an Indian as in killing a white man."[39]

WASHINGTON'S MILITARY CAREER on the frontier had given him a background different from that of most Virginians of his class. But in spite of the acclaim his years in the Virginia Regiment brought, he was still not without doubts of his place in the colonial hierarchy. He had inherited the English concept that no one except a member of the clergy could attain gentry status without land, and to his mind both land and money were necessary to consolidate his position. Whatever he thought of the people of the frontier, he coveted the rich acreage he saw on his western travels, and his conviction of the value of western lands was reinforced by the scarcity of good land east of the Piedmont. Indeed as Thomas Slaughter has correctly pointed out, Washington's desire for transmontane land probably influenced him at least as much as patriotism or a hope of furthering his reputation. He felt that the lure of profit was the most potent means of encouraging western development. "What inducements have men to explore uninhabited wilds," he contended, "but the prospects of getting good lands?"[40]

Eventually he would own more than sixty thousand acres in the West, but unlike some of his contemporaries who moved to the frontier, settled there, and began careers and families, Washington never seems to have been tempted to relocate, although he advised others to go west to make their fortunes. The frontier remained for him in his early years primarily a tool for furthering his ambitions in the Tidewater.[41] Virginia's involvement in the French and Indian War was largely over by the beginning of 1760, and Washington had had enough of military life. He had acquired possession of Mount Vernon after his brother's death in 1752 and had already during his military service begun to put together other landholdings, a few hundred acres at a time. After his return from the war Washington turned his main attention to the estate and his ambition to become a planter on a scale worthy of his new status. The plantation had been seriously neglected during the war. More slaves and additional buildings were needed, provisions had to be purchased, and much of the land reclaimed. Mount Vernon was becoming his passion. He had unending plans for its improvement; to adorn it he purchased furniture and ornaments he could often ill afford; he avidly acquired surrounding properties to add to its size.[42] During the Revolution he was forced to leave the plantation to the care of managers—he returned only once in the eight years of the war— but during his presidency this was a sacrifice he was not prepared to make. For the course of both terms he remained deeply immersed in the management of his Virginia estate. In effect, he ran Mount Vernon from New York and later from Philadelphia. In reply to his managers' weekly reports, he sent detailed instructions on planting and construction, on the profits and losses of the mill and, fisheries, and on the use of the plantations' slave labor.

Washington's marriage in 1759 to Martha Dandridge Custis, the wealthy young widow of Daniel Parke Custis, brought him control of a fortune of the first rank accompanied by greatly increased social status and a ready-made family of two stepchildren. He found himself cushioned in a stable and happy domestic life, and in the fall of 1759, shortly after his marriage, he wrote one of his London agents from Mount Vernon, "I am now I beleive fixd at this Seat with an agreable Consort for Life and hope to find more happiness in retirement than I ever experiencd amidst a wide and bustling World."[43] If the Custis fortune made him independent, he still continued to broaden his holdings through speculation in land and in various business enterprises. Appealing as retirement may have been intellectually, it was never really part of his game plan. Washington had chosen the military as a path for advancement, an unusual choice in Virginia, and he now began to pay his political dues in terms of the civilian service mandated for men of substance in the colony. An earlier attempt at the House of Burgesses from Frederick had failed, but in 1758 he was elected, pursuing the usual campaign practices of providing his frontier constituency with copious food and drink.

Washington proved a dutiful, if not particularly articulate, member of the legislature, and he tried to serve his Frederick constituency— indeed the first bill he brought in addressed a petition from Winchester's citizens to prevent hogs from running wild in the streets of the town.[44] In 1766 he went to the House of Burgesses for Fairfax County and represented his home county until 1775. He served for many years as a member of the Fairfax County Court, which not only exercised judicial power but had a wide range of administrative duties as well. Although his own interest in religion appears always to have been perfunctory, Washington served from 1762 as a member of the Truro vestry, which dealt not only with ecclesiastical matters but temporal ones as well, including the care of the local poor. Being a vestryman was a public duty for a Virginia gentleman of Washington's status. Although he carried out his duties conscientiously, there is nothing in his service to indicate any particular religious commitment.[45]

As valuable as the practical aspects of his military experience were during his years on the frontier, the qualities that later so set Washington apart from his peers were hardly discernible in the young man. After his return from the war he had for the first time, in spite of the demands of his plantation, at least some leisure to contemplate the creation of his own character. Indeed, Washington himself may not have much liked the young man he had become. In any case, with increasing maturity he undertook to remedy the defects in the young commander of the Virginia Regiment. What he now did, consciously or not, was to model his character in the image of the classical figures admired by his society. After all, Richard Steele had observed that Cato had rather be than appear to be good. Washington's pre-Revolutionary years at Mount Vernon were a nursery for his later conceptions of public and private responsibility and reputation. His diaries and correspondence reveal how much the self-control and iron self-discipline he grew to demand of himself during these years contributed to the mature Washington.

For Washington, as for most successful planters, his daily life on the plantation was one of strenuous labor, but there were pleasures as well—occasional trips to Alexandria and Williamsburg and other towns, where he was able to attend the theater and keep up with local politics. There were barbecues and balls, and although he occasionally grumbled, he enjoyed the frequent guests who graced Mount Vernon. Fox hunting was one of his passions, and his diaries are filled with the details of hunts and of the ancestry, breeding, and amorous behavior of his horses and hunting dogs. Like most planters he developed a strong sense of noblesse oblige, writing Lund Washington in 1775 when he left for the war that the "Hospitality of the House, with respect to the poor" should be kept up, "Let no one go hungry away."[46] In these years Washington sought the planter's ideal of an independent paternalistic environment over which he presided in every aspect—the seasonal planting, the workers' activities, the fisheries, and the mill. He yearned for a utopian world that satisfied his need for organization, one where, as in George Washington Parke Custis's description of Mount Vernon, "all was order."[47] Washington, like other planters, could cherish the ideal while facing the reality of falling tobacco prices, a frequently inefficient labor force, and the everyday problems of running a plantation.

Unlike many of his peers, Washington had a substantial dread of falling into debt. His return to Mount Vernon in 1759 coincided with a rising tide of personal debt among Virginia's great tobacco planters. Tempted by the increasing demands of an opulent lifestyle and the easy credit extended by British merchants, many planters found themselves entangled in a web of debt not only with their correspondents abroad but with other planters as well.[48] Although he was not always able to follow his own precepts, Washington cautioned his British agents against allowing him to overdraw his accounts, although "my own aversion to running in Debt will always secure me against a Step of this Nature." With the example of planters like John Mercer and Ralph Wormeley sinking into a morass of unfulfillable commitments, Washington ran his plantations as much as possible in accordance with his resolution "not to incumber myself with Debt," although he was not actually free of substantial obligations until 1773 when his young stepdaughter's death brought him additional funds.[49]

Washington was an enthusiastic and innovative planter, in constant touch through books and correspondence with new methods of farming and production, and after his decision to diversify from a tobacco-dominated agriculture, he was a tireless experimenter in new crops. He abandoned tobacco reluctantly and with a sense of personal failure. As historian Timothy H. Breen has pointed out, the growing of fine tobacco had a psychological significance to southern planters beyond the financial importance of the crop itself, and it is evident that Washington, too, felt the production of superior leaf was inextricably connected with the image he hoped to portray to his peers.[50] After he abandoned tobacco, he shipped wheat to the West Indies; he kept fisheries; he built several mills and explored new uses for his slave labor.

Like all large plantations, Mount Vernon as a separate hierarchical world was bolstered by the slave system. Before the Revolution, Washington was a typical Virginia slaveholder of his time and place, more conscious perhaps than some of his slaves' welfare but still principally concerned that they live up to his exacting criteria in their work on the plantation. Motivated no doubt by self-interest as well as humanitarianism, he exhibited considerable concern for their welfare. "It is foremost in my thoughts," he wrote his Mount Vernon manager in 1792, "to desire you will be particularly attentive to my Negros in their sickness; and to order every Overseer *positively* to be so likewise; for I am sorry to observe that the generality of them, view these poor creatures in scarecely any other light than they do a draughthorse or Ox; neglecting them as much when they are unable to work; instead of comforting & nursing them when they lye on a sick bed." As a matter of plantation policy, slaves were not worked when they were ill, and competent medical care was provided; they were furnished with adequate food, housing, and clothing; families might work on separate plantations, but they were not generally separated by sale or purchase. Except for his long absences during the war and the presidency, Washington managed his own plantations and was well acquainted with the strengths and weaknesses of individual slaves. He was not impressed by their efficiency as a work force. Washington commented frequently in his correspondence with his managers on their laziness and irresponsibility, although he tended to blame the institution rather than the slaves. Slavery was, he felt, a system that hindered agricultural progress and prevented the best use of new farming methods and machinery.

Although he was well aware of the institution's inefficiencies, there is little evidence that the moral and ethical considerations of slavery troubled Washington to any considerable degree before 1775. The rhetoric of the Revolution, with its emphasis on the rights and responsibilities of man, convinced Washington of the inherent evils of the system. As he wrote John Francis Mercer in September 1786, "I never mean (unless some particular circumstance should compel me to it) to possess another slave by purchase; it being among my first wishes to see some plan adopted, by which slavery in this country may be abolished by slow, sure, and imperceptible degrees." In his will Washington arranged for the emancipation of his own slaves after Martha Washington's death.[51]

Washington always found almost irresistibly appealing the English country party's regard for a pastoral life independent of outside corrupting influences. The concept, culled primarily from Horace and

Virgil, of the peaceful and leisurely rural life of the Roman farm, held great appeal for Virginians who idealized their own plantation life. But there were elements of fiction in country party ideals as practiced in Virginia even in Washington's youth. The slave system augmented the planter's freedom to pursue roles in colonial politics, and the growing patron-client relationship between planter and yeoman farmers gave them a substantial base for political authority.[52] Virginia gentry had no intention of abdicating political power; indeed with a few exceptions they eagerly sought it. Nor did they share the view that government, in which so many of them participated, was necessarily corrupt. And in an economy dependent on English trade goods and the international tobacco market, the personal autonomy sought by many planters who entertained country party views became increasingly chimerical. Washington was deeply immersed in the attitudes of the Virginia gentry on the responsibility of their class to provide political leadership, a commitment that gave him a powerful incentive to accept the command of the army and election to the presidency. As he wrote in 1775, "it was utterly out of my power to refuse this appointment without exposing my Character to such censures as would have reflected dishonour upon myself, and given pain to my friends." But he was also reported to have said to Patrick Henry, "from the day that I enter upon the command of the American armies, I date my fall and the ruin of my reputation."[53]

*I*N 1788 AND 1789, WHEN HE WAS pressed to accept the presidency, Washington was torn between his desire to remain in the pastoral peace of his plantation, "under my vine and fig tree," and the demands and attractions of public service. He greatly feared that if he accepted the office the enormous reputation he hoped to leave to succeeding generations would not survive the difficulties facing the new nation. "I walk on untrodden ground," he wrote Catharine Macaulay Graham. Perhaps even more he feared accepting the office would be viewed as a violation of his role as Cincinnatus. Because so many of his peers subscribed to classical and English country party values, Washington feared any implication of lusting after power or even of being particularly concerned with rewards and emoluments for public service. Indeed, this disavowal of a desire for power was a convention among American elite in the eighteenth century.[54] No doubt it contributed to Washington's reluctance to accept the offers for public office extended to him. He felt he *should* prefer his vine and fig tree above the tumult and strife of public life.

In the triumphs of his first presidential term, Washington had very little reason to question that his reputation had survived intact the return to public life. He worked tirelessly to attach the citizens of the new nation to their country. Deliberately and through exceedingly skillful appeals to public opinion, he presented himself and his administration as part of the symbols the new nation needed. If he would not have understood the term *charisma,* he had a thoroughly modern comprehension of its function. As John Adams said, "if he was not the greatest President, he was the greatest actor of the presidency we have ever had."[55] His second administration succeeded in many spheres—in maintaining neutrality, in establishing peace on the frontiers, and in the negotiation of the Jay Treaty. But for these successes Washington paid a heavy price in public support and popularity. The events of 1793, beginning with the outbreak of war between Britain and France in January, provided a concrete issue for divisions among Federalists and Republicans that were no less real because they were amorphous. Britain and France became the symbols for a political division already perceived, but not well articulated, in the United States. To the Federalists, Britain represented the forces of stability and a bulwark against anarchy. France was viewed by Republican supporters as the bellwether of freedom and the logical culmination of the American Revolution. By temperament and background Washington identified more with the habits, lifestyle, and role models of Britain's eighteenth-century elite than with the brave new world of the French Revolution. He was appalled at the excesses of the Revolution, but his concern was for the impact it had on the United States. Although party spirit, he maintained, existed in some form in all governments, "in those of the popular form it is seen in its greatest rankness and is truly their worst enemy." To Washington partisanship was what the new republic had most to fear. The neutrality crisis, the fight over the Jay Treaty, and Washington's own quick and stringent actions to suppress the Whiskey Rebellion resulted in a storm of public criticism to which he was quite unaccustomed and which appeared to him to threaten the principles on which he had constructed his public life. The activities of the Democratic societies formed in the mid-1790s in support of the principles of the French Revolution—those "self-created societies," as he called them—enraged him.[56] As a politician Washington retained one serious flaw he had brought with him from his youth—he was extraordinarily thin-skinned. Press invective aimed at him grew so virulent and, as he said, was "couched in such exagerated & indecent terms as could scarcely be applied to a Nero, a serious defaulter; or even to a common pick-pocket."[57] Catapulted from his deliberately cultivated stance above political fray into the party infighting he most abhorred, policies and views after 1793 that tended to mirror those of the Federalists.

If Washington's reaction to the disorder of the 1790s seems exaggerated, it must be viewed in the light of the classical conceptions of public virtue acquired in his youth and his obsession with his own reputation. Even on a private level, deviations from what he considered due demands had always troubled him. He had a very long memory for unpleasant incidents, especially when they reflected on his reputation or the respect he felt was due to him and to the public positions he occupied. He very often forgave, but he rarely forgot, either public or private slights. If he was given to expressions of appreciation and satisfaction to friends and subordinates who were involved in his public and private affairs, it is not a quality that emerges in his correspondence.

A perfectionist himself, Washington found few people able to measure up to his high expectations. His colonial correspondence abounds with complaints about the services and shipments of his London agents. After the war, squatters who had the temerity to settle on his Pennsylvania lands were summarily ejected. Subordinates who managed his western holdings were the subjects of constant carping. His overseers and workers rarely pleased him. His cousin Lund Washington, manager of Mount Vernon during the war, labored mightily and with considerable success on the plantation's behalf in the face of the enormous economic and military difficulties of wartime. But for five years after he returned in 1784, Washington constantly bemoaned the fact that the plantation had been allowed to fall into ruin in his absence. Relatives did not escape. The feckless financial maneuverings of his stepson John Parke Custis, of whom he was very fond, filled him with consternation, and the behavior of other members of the family often appalled him. "In God's name," he wrote John Augustine Washington in 1783, "how did my brother Saml contrive to get himself so enormously in Debt? Was it by purchases? By misfortunes? or shear indolence and inattention to business?"[58] Many of these people were indeed incompetent or worse, and Washington's problems in dealing with them were certainly great. But Washington often set the same impossibly high standards for his subordinates that he set for himself, he failed to appreciate their difficulties, and he felt betrayed when their achievements fell short of his expectations.

Washington's approach to dealing with his political and social inferiors was essentially paternalistic, but he expected that on their parts, singly or in groups, they should do what was required of them, from showing up as militiamen when they were needed to paying their rent when they were his tenants. Acquired during his early days on the frontier, this was an attitude he carried with him into the political arena, where he applied many of the same standards to his views of public behavior. With his almost obsessive fear of factions, the "death knell of republics," Washington had little conception of a loyal opposition. Disorder, whatever the cause, he viewed as a threat to the stability of the new nation, as "diabolical attempts to destroy the best fabric of human government and happiness, that has ever been presented for the acceptance of mankind." During Shays's Rebellion in 1786 he wrote to Benjamin Lincoln: "Are your people getting mad? Are we to have the goodly fabrick we were nine years raising, pulled over our heads? What is the cause of all this? When and where is it to end?" When Kentucky citizens protested against the Jay Treaty, he was, he said, surprised to find such disaffection in Kentucky. "There must exist a pre-disposition among them to be dissatisfied under any circumstances, and under every exertion of government." The rebellious citizens of Pennsylvania's western counties in 1794 represented "a daring and factious spirit which . . . ought to be subdued. If this is not done . . . we may bid adieu to all government in this Country, except Mob and Club Govt."[59]

For a time during his presidency, perhaps continuing through the successes of his first administration, Washington seems briefly to have held a hope, foreign to many of his Federalist contemporaries, not only of the boundless possibilities open to the new republic but of the perfectibility of its citizens. What he had in mind when he spoke of the promise of the future was the development of a responsible citizenry, replete with republican virtues, free of party faction, and dedicated to his own classical ideals. What he feared had taken its place by the middle of his second administration was a nation with different aspirations, with a taste for political struggles, and with a passion for luxury. He came to believe his worst fears had been confirmed. He had devoted his life to the service of the people and believed very firmly that he governed for and in their name, but he had never, from his days on the frontier, been convinced of their political wisdom. And he had very little faith that they could govern for themselves.

Throughout much of his public life Washington judged his achievements in light of his contributions to the creation of what he referred to as a *national character*. He was careful to give the impression that his ambition was for his offices and not for himself since he shared the view of most Americans on the ease of a popular leader's metamorphosis into a demagogue. He deliberately projected the image of aloofness. If he has seemed stiff and unapproachable to posterity, it is because, at least partially, this was his intention. Keeping his own counsel and remaining aloof from competing positions on issues was part of the image he intended to project.

The political squabbles, the Jacobin Clubs, the newspaper attacks all signaled to Washington that he had failed to create his dream of a citizenry free from those political factions that he considered the death knell of republics. The kind of republic Washington visualized was essentially an eighteenth-century utopia, much of it based on the political education of his early years and much of it having very little to do with the democratization of politics in the United States and the private aspirations of its citizens in the last decade of the eighteenth century. He was mistaken in thinking he had lost the regard of his fellow citizens—his place in the forefront of the American pantheon was still secure—and by the end of the century he had become a canonized icon in the American mythos. Indeed, it has been suggested that the eulogies commemorating Washington's death created something of a national religion.[60] But what had become obsolete were many of the political assumptions he had brought with him from his youth. As he wrote, sadly, to Henry Knox in 1795: "If any power on earth could, or the great power above would, erect the standard of infallibility in political opinions, there is no being that inhabits this terrestrial globe that would resort to it with more eagerness than myself. But as I have found no better guide hitherto than upright intentions, and close investigation, I shall adhere to these maxims while I keep the watch; leaving it to those who will come after me to explore new ways, if they like; or think them better."[61]

NOTES

1. George Washington to Henry Knox, April 1, 1789, *The Papers of George Washington*, Presidential Series, ed. W. W. Abbot et al., 6 vols. to date (Charlottesville: University Press of Virginia, 1987–), 2:2–3.

2. Benjamin Rush to Thomas Ruston, October 29, 1775, *Letters of Benjamin Rush,* ed. L. H. Butterfield, 2 vols. (Princeton: Princeton University Press, 1951), 2:91–94.

3. Garry Wills, *Cincinnatus: George Washington and the Enlightenment* (Garden City: Doubleday, 1984), 3; Address from Philadelphia Officials, ca. April 20, 1789, Washington Papers, Library of Congress, Washington, D.C.; Thomas Jefferson to Washington, April 16, 1784, in *The Papers of Thomas Jefferson,* ed. Julian P. Boyd et al., 26 vols. to date (Princeton: Princeton University Press, 1950–), 7:105–10. For Washington's symbolic importance, see Peter Karsten, *Patriot-Heroes in England and America: Political Symbolism and Changing Values over Three Centuries* (Madison: University of Wisconsin Press, 1978), 1–12, 86.

4. Washington to Sir Isaac Heard, May 2, 1792, Huntington Library, San Marino, Calif.

5. Washington to Hannah Fairfax Washington, March 24, 1792, and her reply, April 9, 1792, Washington Papers, Library of Congress.

6. For Washington's English ancestors, see Charles A. Hoppin, *The Washington Ancestry and Records of the McClain, Johnson, and Forty Other Colonial American Families,* 3 vols. (Greenfield, Ohio: privately printed, 1932), 1:1–138; Douglas Southall Freeman, *George Washington: A Biography,* 7 vols. (New York: Charles Scribner's Sons, 1948–1957), 1:15–47; Charles H. Callahan, *Washington: The Man and the Mason* (Washington, D.C.: National Capital Press, 1913), 3–28. For controversy over the immigrant, see Charles H. Browning, "The Washington Pedigree: Corigenda and Addenda," *Pennsylvania Magazine of History and Biography* 45 (1921): 320–63, and Charles A. Hoppin's "The Good Name and Fame of the Washingtons," *Tyler's Quarterly Historical and Genealogical Magazine* 4 (January 1923): 315–52. There are intriguing parallels between the immigrant John Washington, in his attempts to establish himself in Virginia, and the young George Washington. The immigrant's career is discussed in Martin H. Quitt, "The English Cleric and the Virginia Adventurer: The Washingtons, Father and Son," *Virginia Magazine of History and Biography* 97 (January 1989): 163–84.

7. Truro Vestry Book, November 18, 1735, Library of Congress.

8. 2 King George Orders, 333 (1743), in microfilm of Virginia county

records, Library of Virginia, Richmond. A copy of Augustine Washington's will is in the Washington Papers, Library of Congress.

9. Washington to Knox, April 27, 1787, Washington Papers, Library of Congress.

10. See Daniel Smith, *Inside the Great House* (Ithaca: Cornell University Press, 1980), 284–85; Philip Slater, "Parental Role Differentiation," in *The Family: Its Structures and Functions*, ed. Rose L. Coser (New York: St. Martin's Press, 1974), 270.

11. Robert Jackson to Lawrence Washington, September 18, 1746, Lloyd W. Smith Collection, Morristown National Historical Park, Morristown, N.J.; Joseph Ball to Mary Ball Washington, May 19, 1747, Joseph Ball Papers, Library of Congress. For the pension proposal and Washington's exasperated reply, see his exchange of letters with Benjamin Harrison, February 25 and March 21, 1781, Washington Papers, Library of Congress.

12. Washington to Mary Ball Washington, February 15, 1787, Washington Papers, Library of Congress; Washington to Burwell Bassett, June 20, 1773, *The Papers of George Washington*, Colonial Series, ed. W. W. Abbot et al., 10 vols. (Charlottesville: University Press of Virginia, 1983–1995), 9:243–44.

13. Freeman, *Washington*, 1:57–58, 70–71, 76–77. For a discussion of a scandal involving his wife and the Rev. Charles Green and revealing a darker side of Lawrence's character, see Peter R. Henriques, "Major Lawrence Washington versus The Reverend Charles Green: A Case Study of the Squire and the Parson," *Virginia Magazine of History and Biography* 100 (April 1992): 233–64.

14. Smith, *Great House*, 178–82.

15. Washington to Jonathan Boucher, July 9, 1771, *Washington Papers*, Col. Ser., 8:494–98.

16. See Freeman, *Washington*, 2:336–39; *Washington Papers*, Col. Ser., 6:10–13.

17. Washington to John Augustine Washington, May 28, 1755, *Washington Papers*, Col. Ser., 1:289–93.

18. For the suggestion by John Parke Custis's tutor, Jonathan Boucher, that Washington was taught by a convict tutor, see Boucher's *Reminiscences of an American Loyalist, 1737–1789: Being the Autobiography of the Rev. Jonathan Boucher* (Boston and New York: Houghton Mifflin, 1925), 49.

19. Samuel E. Morison, *The Young Man Washington* (Cambridge: Harvard University Press, 1932), 13. Washington's correspondence with young relatives abounds with references to the importance of education to the development of the individual. Washington offered money for the education of the children of family and friends on numerous occasions. To advance public education he lent his name and more concrete financial aid to such institutions as the Alexandria Academy, Washington College, and Liberty Hall. He advocated a national military academy, and to further his dream of a national university "to educate our youth in the science of Government," he left his holdings in

the Potomac Company for its establishment; see Washington to Alexander Hamilton, December 12, 1799, Eighth Annual Address to Congress, December 7, 1796, Washington to John Adams, November 15, 1794, Washington to William Ramsay, January 29, 1769, all in the Washington Papers, Library of Congress; Will, July 9, 1799, Fairfax County Courthouse, Fairfax, Va.

20. Moncure D. Conway, ed., *George Washington's Rules of Civility* (New York: United States Book Company, 1890); Ann Rausher, ed., *George Washington's Rules of Civility & Decent Behaviour in Company and Conversation* (Mount Vernon, Va.: Mount Vernon Ladies' Association of the Union, 1989).

21. Quoted in Marcus Cunliffe, *George Washington: Man and Monument* (Boston: Little, Brown, 1958), 34. Adams, who "sometimes amused myself with inquiring where Washington got his system," suspected that he had derived his principles of behavior from characters in Charles Rollins's *Ancient History*, although "our beloved Washington was but very superficially read in history of any age, nation, or country"; see Adams to Benjamin Rush, September 1807, Adams Family Papers, Massachusetts Historical Society, Boston.

22. For a detailed account of Washington's early reading and his access to books, see Paul K. Longmore, *The Invention of George Washington* (Berkeley: University of California Press, 1988), 213–26. See also, Appleton P. C. Griffin, *A Catalogue of the Washington Collection in the Boston Athenaeum* (Boston: J. Wilson and Son, 1897); Frances Laverne Carroll and Mary Meacham, *The Library at Mount Vernon* (Pittsburgh: Beta Phi Mu, 1977), 85–129.

23. Peter Gay, *The Enlightenment: An Interpretation*, 2 vols. (New York: Alfred A. Knopf, 1966–1969), 1:39, 44; Albert Furtwangler, *American Silhouettes: Rhetorical Identities of the Founders* (New Haven: Yale University Press, 1987), 70–84.

24. For a brief discussion of *Cato* and its significance to eighteenth-century Americans, see Furtwangler, *American Silhouettes*, 72–73.

25. The portrait might be different if more of Washington's early personal correspondence with friends and family had survived. As he wrote William Peachey in 1757, "I keep no copies of Epistles to my friends"; see Washington to Peachey, September 18, 1757, *Washington Papers*, Col. Ser., 4:414–15. It was not until the Revolutionary War years that he began to take extraordinary pains to preserve his correspondence.

26. Washington to William Fitzhugh, November 15, 1754, *Washington Papers*, Col. Ser., 1:225–27.

27. Washington to John Robinson, c. April 18, 1756, *Washington Papers*, Col. Ser., 3:15–17. For examples of his friends' reassurances, see letters to Washington from Landon Carter, April 21, 1756, from William Fairfax, April 26, 1756, from Charles Carter, April 27, 1756, from Augustine Washington, October 16, 1756, and from William Ramsay, September 3, 1758, all in *Washington Papers*, Col. Ser., 2:30–32, 56–58, 64–65, 3:435–38, 5:454–56.

28. For Washington's fear his membership in the Society of the Cincinnati would be misinterpreted and his quest for advice on his membership, see his letter to Thomas Jefferson, April 8, 1784, and Jefferson's reply, April 16, 1784, *The Papers of George Washington*, Confederation Series, ed. W. W. Abbot et al., 5 vols. to date (Charlottesville: University Press of Virginia, 1992–), 1:275–77, 287–92. For similar requests for reassurance concerning his attendance at the Constitutional Convention, see his letters to James Madison, November 18, 1786, Washington Papers, Library of Congress, and December 16, 1786, Rosenbach Foundation; to David Stuart, November 19, 1786, Dreer Collection, Historical Society of Pennsylvania, Philadelphia; to David Humphreys, December 26, 1786, Washington Papers, Library of Congress; and to Henry Knox, February 3, 1787, Knox Papers, The Gilder Lehrman Collection on deposit at the Pierpont Morgan Library, New York City. For his concern over acceptance of the Potomac Company shares presented to him by the Virginia legislature, see his letters to William Grayson and to Benjamin Harrison, both January 22, 1785, *Washington Papers*, Conf. Ser., 2:280–84.

29. Washington to Presley Neville, June 16, 1794, Washington Papers, Library of Congress. For critical views of Washington's methods of acquiring land, see Bernard Knollenberg, *George Washington: The Virginia Period, 1732– 1775* (Durham: Duke University Press, 1964), 91–100; John E. Ferling, *The First of Men: A Life of George Washington* (Knoxville: University of Tennessee Press, 1988), 69–73; Robert F. Jones, *George Washington* (New York: Fordham University Press, 1986), 34–36.

30. Washington to George Muse, January 29, 1774, *Washington Papers*, Col. Ser., 9:460–62.

31. Washington, April 4, 1748, *The Diaries of George Washington*, ed. Donald Jackson and Dorothy Twohig, 6 vols. (Charlottesville: University Press of Virginia, 1976–1979), 1:18. In the case of the German settlers, time and experience mitigated Washington's disdain. Even before the Revolution he sought Germans avidly as settlers for his western lands; see, for example, his letter to Henry Riddell, February 22, 1774, Riddell to Washington, February 24, 1774, and John David Wilper to Washington, March 23, 1774, all in *Washington Papers*, Col. Ser., 9:493–96, 498–99; 10:3–7.

32. Robert D. Mitchell, "Content and Context: Tidewater Characteristics in the Early Shenandoah Valley," *Maryland Historian* 5 (Winter 1974), 82; Mitchell, *Commercialism and Frontier: Perspectives on the Early Shenandoah Valley* (Charlottesville: University Press of Virginia, 1977), 110, 131; James T. Lemon, *The Best Poor Man's Country: A Geographical Study of Early Southeastern Pennsylvania* (Baltimore: Johns Hopkins University Press, 1972), 1–13, 42–70; Emory Evans, "Trouble in the Backcountry, Disaffection in Southwest Virginia during the American Revolution," in *An Uncivil War: the Southern Backcountry during the American Revolution*, ed. Ronald Hoffman, Thad W.

Tate, and Peter J. Albert (Charlottesville: University Press of Virginia, 1985), 185. For a view that the contrast between the Tidewater and the frontier has been overemphasized, see Jack P. Greene, "Independence, Improvement, and Authority: Toward a Framework for Understanding the histor*ies* of the southern Backcountry during the Era of the American Revolution," in *An Uncivil War*, 9–10.

33. Washington to Dinwiddie, April 23, 1756, *Washington Papers*, Col. Ser., 3:33–34.

34. Robinson to Washington, April 17, 1756, *Washington Papers*, Col. Ser., 3:12–13. Washington's comments echoed the criticism leveled by other members of the eastern elite and their retainers against residents of the frontier; see Gregory H. Nobles, "Breaking into the Backcountry: New Approaches to the Early American Frontier, 1750–1800," *William and Mary Quarterly*, 3d ser., 46 (October 1989): 641–70; Richard J. Hooker, ed., *The Carolina Backcountry on the Eve of the Revolution: The Journal and Other Writings of Charles Woodmason, Anglican Itinerant* (Chapel Hill: University of North Carolina Press, 1953), 60, 101.

35. Washington to Dinwiddie, September 8, 1756, *Washington Papers*, Col. Ser., 3:396–401.

36. Washington to Robinson, April 16, 1756, *Washington Papers*, Col. Ser., 3:6–8; Washington to Dinwiddie, October 9, 1757, *Washington Papers*, Col. Ser., 5:10–13.

37. Washington to Robert Stewart, May 10, 1756, *Washington Papers*, Col. Ser., 3:112–13; Washington to Dinwiddie, November 9, 1756, *Washington Papers*, Col. Ser., 4:1–10. Byrd is quoted in Richard R. Beeman, *The Evolution of the Southern Backcountry: A Case Study of Lunenburg County, Virginia, 1746–1832* (Philadelphia: University of Pennsylvania Press, 1984), 22.

38. Washington to Dinwiddie, September 8, 1756, *Washington Papers*, Col. Ser., 3:396–401; Orders, October, 27, 28, 1756, *Washington Papers*, Col. Ser., 3:444–45.

39. Washington to Edmund Pendleton, January 22, 1795, Washburn Papers, Massachusetts Historical Society; Washington to David Humphreys, July 20, 1791, Washington Papers, Library of Congress.

40. Washington to George Mercer, November 7, 1771, *Washington Papers*, Col. Ser., 8:541–45; Thomas P. Slaughter, *The Whiskey Rebellion: Frontier Epilogue to the American Revolution* (New York: Oxford University Press, 1986), 79–80, 247–48.

41. Washington to John Posey, June 24, 1767, *Washington Papers*, Col. Ser., 8:1–4. For the migration of small planters from the Tidewater, see Mitchell, "Content and Context," 85–87; Mitchell, "Agricultural Change and the American Revolution: A Virginia Case Study," *Agricultural History* 47 (April 1973): 130–32; Joseph Clarke Robert, *The Tobacco Kingdom: Plantation, Market, and Factory in Virginia and North Carolina, 1800–1860* (Durham: Duke University

Press, 1938), 3–53; Lemon, *Poor Man's Country*, 46–49, 77–78, 222. For the suggestion that Virginia and Maryland attracted settlers of the "poorer sort," see Lemon, *Poor Man's Country*, 68.

Once Washington's career assumed national proportions, he carried with him his almost obsessive enchantment with the West and his conviction of its importance to the young nation. Except for the establishment of the new Federal City, probably no object more engaged his interest during his presidency. He supplemented the knowledge gained in his early military adventures with his own sources of information. Although in later life he could not often venture again into the region himself—he did make extended tours of the Ohio Valley in 1770 and western Pennsylvania in 1784—as early as the 1770s he began to construct an elaborate network of correspondents in the West. He found men who could give him information drawn from their own experience and observations—tables of distances, details of navigable streams and portages, and reports on Indian activities. After the war Washington stressed in a series of letters the importance of the West to the new nation and the necessity of preventing "the trade of the Western territory from settling into the hands, either of the Spaniards or British. If either of these happen, there is a line of separation at once drawn between the Eastern & Western Country. The consequences of which may be fatal," (Washington to Jacob Read, November 3, 1784, *Washington Papers*, Conf. Ser., 1:118–23). For Washington's comment that "the western settlers . . . stand as it were upon a pivot—the touch of a feather, would turn them any way," see Washington to Benjamin Harrison, October 10, 1784, *Washington Papers*, Conf. Ser., 1:86–98. During the pre-Revolutionary years Washington's principal informants were William and Valentine Crawford, who also acted as his land agents. After the war his correspondents on the frontier were legion. Among the most useful were Arthur St. Clair, Thomas Marshall, and Thomas Lewis. By the end of his life there was probably no man in America who knew more about the frontier than Washington or who was more aware of its significance to the future of the country.

42. For the gradual development of Mount Vernon to its eventual size of about 7,000 acres, see "The Growth of Mount Vernon, 1754–1786," map and notes, *Washington Diaries*, 1:240–43.

43. Washington to Richard Washington, September 20, 1759, *Washington Papers*, Col. Ser., 6:358–59.

44. H. R. McIlwaine, ed., *Journals of the House of Burgesses of Virginia, 1758–1761* (Richmond: The Colonial Press, 1908), 225, 228, 241; William W. Hening, ed., *The Statutes at Large; Being a Collection of All the Laws of Virginia . . .* , 13 vols. (Richmond: 1809–1823), 7:411–12.

45. Paul F. Boller, Jr., *George Washington and Religion* (Dallas: Southern Methodist University Press, 1963), 27.

46. Washington to Lund Washington, November 26, 1775, *The Papers of George Washington*, Revolutionary War Series, ed. W. W. Abbot et al., 7 vols. to date (Charlottesville: University Press of Virginia, 1985–), 2:431–33.

47. George Washington Parke Custis, *Recollections and Private Memoirs of Washington, by His Adopted Son, George Washington Parke Custis* (New York: Derby and Jackson, 1860), 455.

48. For a discussion of the significance of the growing planter debt in colonial Virginia, see Timothy H. Breen, *Tobacco Culture: The Mentality of the Great Tidewater Planters on the Eve of the Revolution* (Princeton: Princeton University Press, 1985), 160–75.

49. Washington to Robert Cary & Company, August 10, 1760, *Washington Papers*, Col. Ser., 6:448–51; Washington to Lund Washington, August 15, 1778, Washington Papers, Library of Congress.

50. Breen, *Tobacco Culture*, 75–83.

51. Washington to Anthony Whitting, October 14, 1792, Washington to John Francis Mercer, September 9, 1786, Washington to Tobias Lear, May 6, 1794, Washington to Robert Morris, April 12, 1786, all in Washington Papers, Library of Congress; Washington to Joseph Whipple, February 28, 1796, New York Public Library; Will, July 9, 1799, Fairfax County Courthouse.

52. Douglas L. Wilson, "The American *agricola*: Jefferson's Agrarianism and the Classical Tradition," *South Atlantic Quarterly* 80 (Summer 1981): 339–54. See also Leo Marx, *The Machine in the Garden: Technology and the Pastoral Ideal* (New York: Oxford University Press, 1964), 4, 23, 24; Allan Kulikoff, *Tobacco and Slaves: The Development of Southern Cultures in the Chesapeake, 1680–1800* (Chapel Hill: University of North Carolina Press, 1986), 262–63.

53. Washington to Martha Washington, June 16, 1775, *Washington Papers*, Rev. Ser., 1:3–6; George W. Corner, ed., *The Autobiography of Benjamin Rush* (Princeton: Princeton University Press, 1948), 113.

54. Gordon S. Wood, *The Creation of the American Republic, 1776–1787* (Chapel Hill: University of North Carolina Press, 1969), 21–23, 60; Washington to Catharine Macaulay Graham, January 9, 1790, Leicester City Museum and Art Gallery, Great Britain. For a discussion of Washington's disavowals of his fitness for public office as part of the "begging off" tradition in English and American rhetoric, see Walter Jozet Asonevich, "George Washington's Speeches and Addresses: Origins of an American Presidential Rhetoric" (Ph.D. diss., University of Delaware, 1987), 73–81.

55. Adams to Benjamin Rush, June 21, 1811, Adams Family Papers, Massachusetts Historical Society.

56. Washington to Congress, November 19, 1794, Record Group 46, Third Congress, Records of Legislative Proceedings, President's Messages, National Archives.

57. Washington to Thomas Jefferson, July 6, 1796, Jefferson Papers, Library of Congress.

58. Washington to John Augustine Washington, January 16, 1783, Washington Papers, Library of Congress.

59. Washington to Henry Lee, August 26, 1794, Washington to Benjamin Lincoln, November 7, 1786, Washington to Charles Mynn Thruston, August 10, 1794, Washington to Daniel Morgan, October 8, 1794, all in Washington Papers, Library of Congress.

60. Michael Gilmore, "Eulogy as Symbolic Biography," *Harvard English Studies* 8 (1978): 131. See also Barry Schwartz, "The Character of Washington: A Study in Republican Culture," *American Quarterly* 38 (Summer 1986): 204, 219–20.

61. Washington to Henry Knox, September 20, 1795, Henry Knox Papers, The Gilder Lehrman Collection on deposit at the Pierpont Morgan Library.

Young Washington's Virginia: Opportunity in the "Golden Age" of a Planter Society

BRUCE A. RAGSDALE

*A*S GEORGE WASHINGTON CAME OF age in the middle decades of the eighteenth century, Virginia enjoyed a combination of political stability and economic prosperity that was unique among the colonies of British North America and in contrast with much of the history of the Old Dominion. To the young Washington, the most obvious manifestation of Virginia's wealth and social order was the class of "great planters" that constituted the colony's gentry. By the year of his birth, 1732, this elite group of planters dominated the public life of Virginia and gained ever greater wealth from the colony's rich export trade and increasingly complex domestic economy.

Even as a boy, Washington was familiar with the planters who lived on the imposing estates throughout his native Northern Neck of Virginia. From this close-knit and frequently interrelated group of families he learned of the pattern of their political influence and the foundation of their wealth. The world of the great planters guided Washington's youthful ambition as he pursued the ideals of economic independence and public service that characterized success in the colony. His expectations for himself and for Virginia were largely defined by the imperatives of preserving and extending the reach of the planter society that had developed by the mid-eighteenth century.

The first thirty years of Washington's life coincided with the full development of the gentry class—a period that later generations would consider the golden age of colonial Virginia. At a time of economic growth and relative social harmony, the great planter families cultivated the British ideal of an independent landed class. They lived on Georgian estates furnished in the latest London fashion. They dressed in English clothes and filled their libraries with English books. In public life, the men of the gentry families adhered to a code of civic responsibility that enhanced the political effectiveness of provincial government and secured the deference of the yeomen.

This idealized concept of a golden age held great appeal when Virginia's economic fortunes vanished and its political influence waned in the following century. In the twentieth century, historians recovered the idea in an attempt to explain the remarkable quality of political leadership that emerged from Virginia in the era of the American Revolution. The very concept of a golden age, with its nostalgic overtones, its narrow definition of society, and whiggish celebration, would find few adherents today. Historical studies that focused exclusively on the accomplishments of gentry planters offered a distorted view of the diverse and complicated society of eighteenth-century Virginia. The reliance on slave labor and the demands of plantation management belie any analogy between the gentry planters and the leisured proprietors of English country estates. Stripped of its elitist assumptions, however, the notion that Washington's generation was distinct provides an understanding of his own ambitions and of the opportunities available to an aspiring planter. The concept of a golden age might well have been comprehensible to Washington and those of his contemporaries fortunate enough to benefit from Virginia's prosperity.

$\mathcal{T}$O VIRGINIANS OF THE MID-EIGHTeenth century who looked back at the colony's history, their own era appeared as exceptional as it would to later observers. The gentry that held dominion over provincial politics and the domestic economy emerged in the generation or two preceding Washington's and consolidated its position only at the time of his birth. The colony's internal order was of such recent development that few took it for granted or assumed its permanency.

Over the past two decades, a profusion of scholarship on the colonial Chesapeake has described a seventeenth-century Virginia sharply different from the world of Washington. To be sure, tobacco laid the foundation for a staple economy in the early years of settlement, and a plantation agriculture based on bound labor was well established in the seventeenth century. But demographic patterns, the structure of economic opportunity, and the political order in Virginia's first century bore little resemblance to the colony in the fifty years preceding the American Revolution.[1]

Through much of the seventeenth century, population grew largely in response to the labor requirements of a rapidly expanding tobacco economy. A majority of immigrants to the colony arrived as indentured servants answering the demand for new field laborers. They were overwhelmingly male and bound to serve an average of seven years before they received their freedom dues and a chance to establish their own plantation. Disease, climate, and working conditions killed many before they completed their terms. Mortality rates, particularly in the first half century of settlement, were high for seasoned residents as well. Unable to reproduce itself, the population of Virginia remained predominantly male, English-born, and young. Only in the 1670s did births equal deaths, and the creole population first became a majority in the 1690s.[2]

Although most servants survived their term and eventually purchased land, the obligations of servitude and the scarcity of women delayed marriage for many men. They established households later in life than was common in England or New England, and families were smaller. Under these conditions a relative equality persisted among landholders. While a few planters gained great wealth, small planters predominated among tobacco producers. As long as European demand for tobacco increased, Virginia planters devoted their resources to expanded production rather than the development of their estates. Standards of living were accordingly simple, with few material comforts and no great distinctions between households.[3]

Politics in seventeenth-century Virginia reflected the uncertainty of life as well as the opportunities for free white men. Former servants frequently achieved political office, particularly on the county level, but few could offer experience or leadership. Wealthy planters dominated the more important positions on the court bench and in the House of Burgesses, but these men also were of limited experience and served too briefly to form a political establishment. With little continuity in political service and with recurrent tensions between landholders and freed servants, factions plagued county government and the assembly.[4]

Some historians have been tempted to overstate the disorder of the seventeenth century, particularly when judged against contemporaneous standards of New England. Virginia, in fact, developed a wide variety of political and social institutions that marked a permanent settlement and an attempt to compensate for the disruptive effects of high mortality and a large population of unsettled young men. Yet by any measure this was not a society conducive to the formation of family estates or the development of political leadership, let alone the social confidence characteristic of the gentry in Washington's era.[5]

In the final quarter of the seventeenth century, as mortality declined, the sexes reached parity, and Virginia's population finally stabilized, a series of fortuitous economic developments set the stage for the emergence of a very different social order. As is typical of new staple commodities, tobacco culture expanded as long as productivity gains in the Chesapeake and expanding markets overseas offset falling prices for the leaf. Planters achieved most of their productivity gains before 1660, and within a decade faced higher land and labor costs. By the 1680s, tobacco had saturated the English market, and a series of European wars soon closed the Chesapeake crop to potential new consumers. For more than three decades beginning in the 1680s, tobacco planters, unable to reduce their own costs, faced low prices for all but the highest-grade tobacco in the colony and stagnant demand abroad. At the same time, the supply of servants from England declined and left a labor shortage in the colony. Wealthier Virginia planters, determined to increase production and compensate for lower prices, turned to the newly available slave labor from Africa and the West Indies.[6]

The ramifications of these economic shifts, particularly the transition to slave labor, were immense and established the contours of economic opportunity in Virginia through the eighteenth century. In the midst of a depressed tobacco market, success came only to those planters with the means to compensate for low prices by producing sweet-scented tobacco on the most fertile land. Slaves proved a profitable investment under these circumstances, but they were expensive and out of reach for many smaller households that previously relied on servants to make the family competitive in the export trade. Participation in an uncertain tobacco trade also required the margin of security provided by diversification and a measure of self-sufficiency. Again, most families were without sufficient labor to divert to the development of new crops and home manufactures while maintaining tobacco production. Many chose simply to abandon tobacco and produced for the domestic market, while others bore the full risks of an uncertain export market.[7]

Planters who could afford slaves bought them quickly and in great numbers. Between 1695 and 1700, three thousand slaves entered the colony—as many as in all the preceding years. Blacks made up 13 percent of the population in 1700, 20 percent by 1720, and 30 percent by the time of Washington's birth. By the second decade of the eighteenth century, slaves had become the most important source of labor in the cultivation of tobacco. Virginia continued to import slaves through the middle decades of the eighteenth century. These imports and a rate of natural increase unique among American slave populations raised the number of black slaves in the colony from thirty thousand in 1730 to around two hundred thousand in 1775. By 1770 more than half of the white families in Virginia owned slaves, and in many Tidewater counties two-thirds of the households held slaves.[8]

The wide-scale introduction of slavery exaggerated the advantages of the wealthier planters, who purchased a disproportionate share of the black slaves. Both slave women and slave men worked the fields, and their children joined the planters' labor force as well. Planters could divert the additional labor to other crops, and young and elderly slaves were productive in home manufactures. As chattel, the slaves became part of the planter's estate, transferable to the next generation of the master's family. At the same time that white Virginians began to live longer and families achieved a new stability, inheritance of land and labor took on an added significance for the accumulation of an estate.[9]

By the time tobacco markets began to recover after 1715, Virginia had become a more hierarchical and stratified society than in the seventeenth century. A recognizable elite, constituting no more than 5 percent of the population, dominated economic resources and provincial government. While no precise criteria distinguished the gentry planters, they all owned sufficient slaves to avoid working in their own fields and enough land to bequeath an estate to their children. The majority of the free population of eastern, settled areas consisted of small planter families who worked the land by themselves or with the help of a few slaves or servants. These yeoman planters also produced tobacco for export, but fewer and fewer found it possible to enter the highest ranks of planter society without inheritance or a favorable marriage.[10]

The new distinctions of wealth and the importance of inheritance contributed to the emergence of the family dynasties that dominated so much of Virginia life in the eighteenth century. These families were generally descended from seventeenth-century settlers who had the material advantages to prosper in hard times and the political connections to gain additional opportunities in land speculation and public service. By the early eighteenth century, they were in a position to provide valuable estates for all of their children, daughters as well as sons. Intermarriage among these families increased the value of estates and further cemented ties within this increasingly self-conscious elite.[11]

As the great planter families secured their own position in Virginia society, they imposed a new economic and political order on local communities. Drawing on their own estates and their access to English credit, the great planters became the principal source of credit for small planters intending to purchase a slave or improve their lands. As the largest tobacco producers, they also controlled access to export markets and the various services of merchants in the metropolitan center of London.[12]

Ironically, the same gentry families whose emergence restricted mobility for other Virginians subsequently provided the best opportunity for smaller planters to participate in tobacco markets and improve their status. In the early decades of the eighteenth century, small planters in the Tidewater came to accept the ascendancy of the great planters in return for a share of expanding economic opportunities that offered them a common interest, albeit on a different scale. The growing population of black slaves and the racial distinctions embodied in the legal code as well as the cultural assumptions of white Virginians further united the small planters and the gentry. Eighteenth-century Virginia consequently experienced few of the social and political conflicts characteristic of the colony's first century of settlement.[13]

A secure economic base, declining social tensions, and greater continuity in political service enabled the great planters and their allies to assert their authority over local and provincial government. By the eighteenth century, the sitting justices of the courts in each county, already governed by the wealthiest planters, nominated their own successors, whom the governor seldom failed to offer a commission. The planter-dominated House of Burgesses extended its prerogatives in the early decades of the eighteenth century until by the time of Washington's birth it was the most powerful lower house of any assembly in the British American colonies. Like the seats on the county benches, membership in the House of Burgesses was increasingly the perquisite of the wealthiest families in the colony and took on the appearance of a self-perpetuating governing elite.[14]

By 1732, everywhere in Tidewater Virginia, from the Northern Neck counties along the Potomac south to the James, was physical evidence of the hierarchical society that developed with the rise of the great planters. New forms of dwellings, ranging from brick mansions in the classical style to the rudest slave quarters, demarcated social distinctions and rank. Courthouses and churches, those most important centers of community in a colony with few towns, now stood as durable, brick reminders of the gentry's authority. The recent influx of British consumer goods through the tobacco trade provided an additional indicator of wealth and status.[15]

As the gentry coalesced and Virginia became a society measured by social rank and divided by race, the public display so characteristic of life in eighteenth-century Virginia provided frequent reminders of social gradations. An element of contest pervaded public life, as though all were determined to prove or reaffirm their social position. The rituals of court day, the assembling of the local militia, and the services of the Anglican church reaffirmed the great planters' influence in the colony and fostered the deference of the rest of white society. These and less-structured community gatherings were occasions for the great planters to demonstrate their command of the colony's resources and institutions and to acknowledge their obligations to the rest of society.[16]

The white master's near absolute dominion over black slaves was only the most exaggerated of the patriarchal relations that extended to every level of Virginia society. The Virginia of Washington's youth was a world in which each individual occupied a recognized place within the social order and was conscious of those of greater and lesser station. While this perception of rank limited mobility, it also permitted an easy commerce among the ranks of society, especially between the gentry and the small planters. On public occasions ranging from horse races and cockfights to formal political meetings, wealthy planters, secure in their status, regularly mixed with small planters and landless whites. Most notable were the election gatherings at which the great planters vied with one another for the votes of the smaller landowners, whose assent was so critical to the maintenance of social order. By the mid-eighteenth century, the great planters skillfully incorporated free-

holders in the political process, giving legitimacy to their own hegemony and mirroring the economic interdependence of great and small
planters.[17]

The degree of social mobility that persisted in eighteenth-century
Virginia followed closely the pattern established by the great planters
and their families. New wealth, whether accumulated in trade or speculation or through marriage into an established family, almost invariably supported the development of a landed estate complete with a
labor force of slaves and the material goods that marked the gentry
class. The limited merchant community that developed in Virginia
before the 1760s supported rather than competed with the interests of
the wealthy planters. In fact, most resident Virginians who might be
classified as merchants were also the active proprietors of landed estates. The prevailing ideal of the independent landed gentlemen was so
powerful among white Virginians that it served as the goal of most
yeoman farmers as well.[18]

GEORGE WASHINGTON WAS BORN
into a family that stood outside the first rank of gentry planters but
was accustomed to dealing with the more powerful and wealthier families in the Northern Neck. Immediate family members were quick to
seize opportunities that might advance their own wealth and status.
His father, Augustine, joined in the rush of land speculation in the 1720s,
albeit on a scale far more modest than that of such Northern Neck
planters as Robert Carter and Thomas Lee. Augustine Washington increased the size of his holdings from fewer than eighteen hundred acres
at the time of his first marriage around 1715 to more than ten thousand
acres at his death in 1743.[19]

Aware of the need to develop his various lands, Augustine Washington in 1735 moved his family from Westmoreland County to his tract
on Little Hunting Creek, in the growing area just south of the falls of
the Potomac. The family moved again three years later to the Ferry
Farm in King George County to be closer to the Principio Furnace so
that Augustine might oversee his investment in Virginia's infant, but
still promising, iron industry. In addition to his varied investments,
Augustine Washington followed in the footsteps of his father and grandfather by serving as a justice of the peace. If he failed to achieve great

wealth by the standards of the day, he nevertheless fulfilled the first duty of the gentry planters by providing each son with sufficient land and slaves to secure a livable income.[20]

Mary Ball Washington, Augustine's second wife and the mother of George, brought her eldest son fewer tangible advantages but conveyed a more thorough acquaintance with the leading gentry. The Balls were a prominent family from Lancaster County, and after Mary was orphaned at age twelve, she lived with the Bonum and Eskridge families in Westmoreland County. Her guardian, George Eskridge, was one of Westmoreland's most prominent planters and a long-time member of the House of Burgesses.[21]

Perhaps the most influential example for the young Washington was his eldest half-brother. Lawrence Washington provided a compelling model of a rising planter and public official. After inheriting the most valuable share of his father's estate, he enhanced his economic and social position with his marriage to Ann Fairfax. Ann's father was William Fairfax, agent for his cousin Lord Fairfax, the proprietor of Virginia's Northern Neck and one of the colony's largest landholders. Lawrence soon shared the Fairfax family's preoccupation with the West. He invested in unsettled lands and joined the fledgling Ohio Company, which sought to develop western territory for Virginia. Lawrence Washington matched his ambitious economic ventures with political service that surpassed his father's. In 1744, Lawrence became one of the first burgesses from the recently formed county of Fairfax and in 1749 served as a trustee of the new town of Alexandria. Following service in the Cartagena expedition of 1740–41, he won appointment as adjutant of the colonial militia. Before his death in 1752, Lawrence Washington provided for his brother the practical advantages of contact with the Fairfax family and other powerful gentry in the Northern Neck. Perhaps of even greater value for George Washington was Lawrence's example of an aspiring planter who found opportunity and influence through military service and political office.[22]

Throughout his early years, even as he dreamed of military service, George Washington understood that ownership of land, and more particularly the successful management of a plantation, was the most favorable foundation for success in colonial Virginia. As a surveyor eager to make his first land purchases, as a twenty-five-year-old bachelor sending to London for papier-mâché ceiling ornaments and fine English furniture, and in his stated intentions on returning to Mount Vernon from military service on the frontier, Washington made clear his ambition to join the planters of the first rank.[23]

Although his inheritance was smaller than Lawrence's, the Ferry Farm, the rights to the lands at Mount Vernon, and his recent purchases in the West allowed Washington to follow the course of management and investment set out by the great planters. With his marriage to the widow Martha Dandridge Custis in 1759, he gained control of one of the richest estates in Virginia and immediately was able to trade with the leading merchants in the Virginia trade.[24]

THE ASCENDANCY OF THE GREAT planters established certain outlines of estate management that Washington and almost all other wealthy planters followed in the years before the Revolution. Land and slaves remained the most important capital investments even as large plantations diversified to achieve a greater degree of self-sufficiency and take advantage of new markets. Investments in agricultural production far exceeded the speculative mercantile enterprises of wealthy planters. The limited development of home manufactures and industries such as iron furnaces never challenged the overwhelmingly agricultural character of the colonial economy.

The commitment to plantation agriculture was in part a rational response to the continued centrality of tobacco in Virginia's economy. The staple export remained the most important determinant of the direction and rate of growth throughout the colonial period. The shifting fortunes of the tobacco trade affected every aspect of the colony's economic life. An advancing market attracted credit to the colony and allowed planters, large and small, to improve their estates and invest in more land and slaves. When demand and prices for tobacco fell, as they did even during extended periods of prosperity, planters concentrated on self-sufficiency schemes to avoid going deeper in debt. East of the Blue Ridge, the rate of settlement paralleled the expansion of the tobacco trade, and migration into the Piedmont was concentrated in those areas favored by British tobacco traders. Tobacco continued to account for 60–70 percent of the value of Virginia's exports up to the Revolution and 85 percent of the value of exports to Great Britain. Even in the wake of diversification into grains and other crops, two-thirds of the households in the Chesapeake produced some tobacco for export.[25]

As long as British merchants offered generous credit services and commodities below the cost of colonial manufacture, Virginia planters focused on tobacco and the other agricultural commodities in demand throughout the Atlantic economy. The concentration of merchants in London and the British outports discouraged the development of commercial centers in Virginia, and the costs of competing with British merchants were beyond the means of almost all individual colonists. A native merchant community developed around the colony's grain trade but never replaced the essential services of the British tobacco merchants in the years before Independence.[26]

By the mid-eighteenth century, plantation agriculture and the predominance of slave labor were essential foundations of the social and political order as well as the economy of Virginia. As long as land and slaves were the principal sources of wealth in the colony, inheritance patterns ensured that the families of the great planters would perpetuate their advantages, and few would enter the ranks of the gentry except by marriage into an established family. Despite growing discrepancies in wealth, the widespread dependence on tobacco culture created a common interest between the largest estates and more modest households that participated in the export trade. A slave population defined by race created an additional bond among white planters of all ranks and eliminated the unrest associated with landless white laborers in the previous century. By the time of Washington's youth, the social and economic order wrought from the instability of the seventeenth century seemed to depend on the maintenance of the great planters' hegemony and their alliance with the smaller freeholders.[27]

Yet within the parameters of the plantation economy that developed by the time of Washington, a young planter could not thrive solely on the basis of inheritance, an advantageous marriage, or reliance on old patterns of management. The prosperity and stability of Virginia in the golden age was never indicative of a static economy. The plantation economy of the Tidewater was expanding too rapidly across the Piedmont and the trade of the colony was too closely intertwined with the broader Atlantic world for the pattern of economic opportunity to remain constant. In the forty years before the Revolution, the growth and shifts in Virginia's economy demanded frequent adjustments and reallocation of resources by any planter involved in export crops. Opportunities abounded for those with productive land, valuable slave labor, and the ability to manage an estate, but the risks of the tobacco trade in particular increased in proportion to the potentially greater rewards.

The exhaustive demands of tobacco culture and a growing population hastened a steady westward movement of plantation agriculture in the eighteenth century. Young men hoping to establish their own households moved into the Piedmont or Southside counties, where they could secure the minimum of fifty acres per laborer that was required for cultivation of tobacco and basic provisions. A natural increase in the colony's slave population and continued importations of Africans in the middle decades of the century helped satisfy the labor demands of recently settled areas and facilitated the progress of staple agriculture. As tobacco culture expanded west of the fall line, the process of settlement begun in Tidewater repeated itself until by the time of the Revolution the culture and political structure of the great planters reached to the Blue Ridge and beyond. Like Washington's father, many planters from Tidewater counties added new lands to their estates to gain the appreciation in value and to compensate for declining productivity on their old estates. For smaller planters, relocation to the Piedmont offered the best opportunity to compete in the production of tobacco and other export crops.[28]

The extension of staple agriculture into new areas was just one dimension of the revival of the tobacco trade in the mid-eighteenth century. Beginning in the 1720s and 1730s, tobacco exports from the Chesapeake entered a period of growth that extended into the early 1770s with only occasional interruption by poor markets and wars. The value of tobacco shipped from the region grew threefold between the 1720s and the 1770s. Driven by increased European consumption, both the expansion of the tobacco trade and the development of a marketing system to meet Continental demand presented new opportunities and challenges for Virginia's planters. The resultant economic growth increased the wealth of most households at the same time that it perpetuated the dependence on tobacco culture and strengthened the influence of British merchants in the colony.[29]

The great planters had since the seventeenth century favored the consignment trade, through which they shipped their crops to a merchant in London or another British port who then sold the cargo on the planter's account. The personal services of these merchants were especially valuable in the late seventeenth and early eighteenth centuries, when prices were low in the colony but high in Great Britain. Such merchants also served as the planter's metropolitan agents, overseeing purchases of English goods, advancing bills of exchange on a planter's account or on credit, and representing the Virginian in legal affairs.[30]

In the 1730s and 1740s the consignment system quickly gave way in importance to a new form of purchasing and marketing that was responsible for as much as four-fifths of Virginia's tobacco exports by the eve of the Revolution. Direct-trade merchants purchased tobacco from growers in the Chesapeake and sold their bulk cargoes on the reexport market in Great Britain. Beginning in the 1730s, Scottish traders led the transition to the direct trade and established chains of stores in Virginia where resident factors offered British goods for tobacco or on credit in expectation of future crops.

The Glasgow firms were the first with sufficient concentration of capital to develop the store trade, which required a high initial investment and a large stock of goods with which to attract the tobacco of planters throughout Virginia. As the demand for tobacco on the Continental market increased, English firms imitated the direct trade of the Scotsmen and concentrated their businesses to raise the necessary capital. The Britons' ability to mobilize credit and achieve economies of scale were in large measure responsible for the economic growth of Virginia during the mid-eighteenth century. The credit distributed through the store trade was particularly influential in the settlement of the Piedmont and the expansion of tobacco culture into the upper James River district.[31]

Large planters, who traditionally relied on the consignment trade, benefited from the general expansion of British credit and improved tobacco markets, but they gained few opportunities from the direct trade. Some direct trading firms ordered their factors not to deal with the "Great Men" or the "first crop masters," who were likely to be continually in debt. The direct traders focused on the yeoman planters who produced five or fewer hogsheads a year. Washington and other great planters, many of whom shipped fifty or even one hundred hogsheads a year, relied on the consignment merchants as long as they produced large crops of tobacco.[32]

Only the consignment merchants offered loans of the size and duration needed to develop a large estate such as Mount Vernon. The merchant, moreover, was an important cultural link with the center of the empire and a source for the fashionable goods that marked the great planters' standard of living. Even more essential were the merchants' shipments of coarse cloth for the slaves, common agricultural tools, and the various supplies on which the operation of the plantation depended. Such goods were available in local stores but not in the quantities or on the credit terms required by large estates.[33]

Planters with access to sufficient slaves and productive land continued to profit from the consignment of large crops during favorable markets, but the stagnant demand for quality tobacco on the British domestic market and the diminishing share of the trade controlled by consignment merchants restricted opportunities for new planters in this trade. As Washington and many others discovered, the services of the consignment trade remained expensive even as the trade slipped into the margin of tobacco commerce.

Planters maintained responsibility for all costs incurred in the shipping and handling of the tobacco to consignment merchants. These charges and the merchant's commission of 3 percent could eliminate a planter's profit if the tobacco did not sell well. When direct traders in Virginia began to offer higher prices in the colony than some planters received in London, the risks of consigning became more evident. In the 1760s, Washington found that buyers in Virginia offered more than the London market in four out of five years. Landon Carter echoed the comments of many planters when he declared, "it must be madness that can continue attached to such a trade and the favour or whatever it is that inclines a man to trade to London is very dearly purchased."[34]

While the rise of the direct trade isolated the great planters in a declining sector of the tobacco market, the store system threatened to supersede the gentry's role in local communities. The factors, who resided in the colony for a limited time and developed no attachment to local communities, offered small planters the same kind of credit and marketing services formerly delivered by large planters with access to merchants in Great Britain. By separating the interests of large and small producers, the influx of direct traders challenged one of the fundamental supports of the social structure that developed out of the seventeenth century.

Gentry planters were not the only ones to face the mixed effects of the revival of the tobacco trade after the 1720s. The advance of mercantile credit restricted the path of development at the same time that it stimulated economic growth and geographical expansion. Acceptance of credit from tobacco traders required the production of sufficient leaf to make remittances on the debt even in years when tobacco prices fell. Merchants, especially in newly settled areas of the Piedmont, were well aware that debt would perpetuate tobacco cultivation, and they generously extended loans and goods to secure future crops.[35]

The efficiency and economy of the trade in British goods enabled planters to raise their standard of living and devote more resources to the improvement of their estates, but the availability of inexpensive, imported merchandise discouraged the development of colonial manufactures. The dependence on imports, like the reliance on tobacco culture, limited the planters' options during the depressions in the tobacco market that recurred even during the generally prosperous years of the mid-eighteenth century. As the planters' debt grew with the increased value of Virginia's trade with Great Britain, it exacerbated the weaknesses of a staple economy and frustrated efforts to raise capital for diversification.[36]

After midcentury, British merchants threatened to make the planters' debt more onerous by demanding greater protection for their credit extensions in Virginia. An act of the Virginia Assembly passed in 1749 and permitting the discharge of sterling debts in local currency at a fixed exchange rate of 25 percent provoked British merchants to demand repeal. The assembly relented in 1755, but merchants in Great Britain and their factors in Virginia continued to insist on more regular and favorable proceedings for the collection of the full value of debts. By the 1760s, the assembly was reluctant to endorse any legislation that might limit the merchants' ability to recover debts. What measures it approved were likely to meet disallowance from a Privy Council quick to reaffirm the monopoly of credit services that developed in the tobacco trade.[37]

The influence of a centralized merchant community in Great Britain and imperial regulation of Virginia's economy were direct results of the continuation of tobacco culture and commercial dependence on the mother country. By the time Washington turned his attention to the development of his estate in the 1750s, more and more of the commerce and economy of the Chesapeake seemed to be beyond the influence of individual planters or of Virginia's provincial government. While they continued to trade with British tobacco merchants, planters, particularly the gentry with extensive obligations and fixed costs, recognized the need to diversify their estates and develop some immunity from the colony's endemic boom-and-bust cycles. Within the confines of an economy heavily reliant on British credit and committed to a plantation system of agriculture, Washington and his contemporaries set out to develop new crops, to seek new trading networks, to foster internal markets, and to develop western territory as a basis of greater economic independence.

At least since the prolonged depression of the late seventeenth century, Virginians had responded to poor tobacco markets with schemes to develop other staple crops and local manufactures that might lessen dependence on British trade. These diversification schemes coincided with various political attempts to limit tobacco production through stinting laws or restrictions on slave imports. In the 1720s, for instance, some planters joined in an effort to restrict production and to shift the burden of duties to consumers in Great Britain. One achievement of this movement was the Inspection Act of 1730, which required the destruction of trash tobacco at inspection warehouses located throughout the colony.[38]

The revival of the tobacco trade came at a time when the need to diversify and develop an integrated economy was more compelling as well as more feasible than ever. Population growth and the rapid settlement of the area east of the Blue Ridge combined with an exhaustive tobacco culture to create pressure on the land by the third quarter of the eighteenth century. With rising land prices in the Tidewater and settled parts of the Piedmont, middling or poorer planters found it difficult to gain any land except through inheritance. The declining ratio of land to labor and reduced yields from long-cultivated fields forced many young men to delay the establishment of independent households and convinced others to resettle in frontier counties. Those who remained behind, particularly large planters like Washington with sufficient labor to apply to various crops, devoted more and more of their existing land to the production of cereals and other crops less demanding of their resources than tobacco. The cultivation of grains provided employment for slaves and laborers who could not profitably be employed in tobacco production and compensated for losses in the tobacco trade during poor markets for that staple.[39]

Virginia had long been self-sufficient in grain and foodstuffs and produced sufficient surpluses to accommodate export markets. The cultivation of wheat and corn for export was easily incorporated into the plantation structure that developed in Virginia and was a logical alternative to tobacco. By midcentury, most large estates employed slaves in the commercial production of grain, which made a significant contribution to the planters' income and provided some protection from temporary depressions in tobacco prices.[40]

The markets for grain in the West Indies and southern Europe, however, did not provide the steady demand that might have allowed planters to abandon tobacco or replace the financial services of British merchants. Not until the 1760s did Virginia grain exports find a steady market, and even then they failed to offer planters the credit and goods that made the British tobacco trade so essential. Prior to the Revolution, only areas unsuited for tobacco cultivation and on the perimeter of the colony concentrated exclusively on grain production. Although these areas, such as the lower James and the Shenandoah Valley, never accumulated the wealth of tobacco-growing regions, they did achieve the type of integrated economies that eluded other areas of the colony.[41]

Despite the value of the colony's trade with Great Britain and other colonies, Virginia developed no trading centers comparable to the quickly growing port cities of the Middle Colonies or Charleston, South Carolina. As long as tobacco dominated the colony's export trade, no town served as a central shipping point. The costs of tobacco and the concentration of the crops in hogsheads encouraged shippers to collect the crop first at plantations and after 1730 at the local inspection warehouses scattered along Virginia's tidal rivers. The management of the tobacco trade always centered in London and British outports where crops were landed according to the Navigation Acts and merchants enjoyed proximity to both tobacco buyers and the commodity wholesalers who provided most of the credit and capital for the Chesapeake trade. The expense of collecting a cargo of tobacco, shipping English goods in return, and paying duties of 200 percent in Great Britain barred almost all colonists from the trade. Those like William Lee who ventured into the consignment business operated out of London.[42]

The requirements of the Inspection Act of 1730 and the stores of the British factors contributed to the rise of small trading centers near inspection warehouses throughout tobacco-producing regions of the colony. For the most part, however, these localities attracted few residents and failed to develop a supporting artisan population that would have hastened urban development. Only in the decade preceding independence did native merchants establish competing stores in these nascent towns. Drawing on the tremendous surpluses of British mercantile credit in the late 1760s and early 1770s, Virginia merchants opened stores that traded imported goods for tobacco and other crops, much as the factors did. These independent traders remained as dependent on British credit as any planter and were devastated by the withdrawal of credit in the aftermath of a British financial panic in 1772, but their businesses represented a promising mercantile development among native traders in the colonial period and laid a permanent foundation for centers of exchange in Virginia.[43]

The growth of the grain trade, erratic though it may have been, offered the likeliest opportunities for commercial development in this colony traditionally dominated by British merchants and capital. Native merchants, often with the backing of planters, organized grain ventures to the West Indies and in the coastwise trade, where they could afford to compete. The transportation, storage, and processing of the comparatively bulky wheat and other grains required far more support services in the colony than did tobacco. The shipping centers for grain, with their warehouses, mills, shipbuilding, and artisans, soon developed into the most prosperous towns in the Chesapeake. Norfolk and Baltimore, the Chesapeake's largest cities in the colonial period, owed their rise almost exclusively to trade in commodities other than tobacco. Smaller towns such as Alexandria also grew as they became shipping centers for wheat from interior regions.[44]

In the late colonial period, the rise of the port cities in grain-exporting areas and the expansion of trading centers around tobacco inspection warehouses demonstrated the potential for commercial growth and internal trade that lay in the development of Virginia's western territory. Long the center of interest for eastern speculators, the regions beyond the Blue Ridge and in the Ohio territory took on a new importance after midcentury as the objects of an expanding plantation economy and foundations for the growth of eastern towns. As tobacco culture extended into the Shenandoah Valley and Tidewater Virginians devised schemes to capture the trade from that area and farther west, the development of the backcountry increasingly seemed to offer opportunities for greater economic independence and the continued viability of the planter society.[45]

*T*HE YOUNG GEORGE WASHINGTON
learned of opportunities in Virginia from the perspective of the Northern Neck region, where he was born and lived most of his life. A geographical designation of the land between the Potomac and
Rappahannock rivers, the Northern Neck was also the area of a proprietary grant extended by Charles II to seven Royalists in 1649 and held
in the exclusive possession of the Fairfax family by the time of
Washington's birth. In the late seventeenth century the area attracted
settlers who established estates similar to those of the lower Tidewater
and followed the pattern of tobacco cultivation found along the York
and James rivers. By the eighteenth century, the great planters of the
Northern Neck assumed positions of leadership in the House of Burgesses, frequently served on the governor's Council, and generally shared
the political and economic assumptions of the gentry planters in older-
settled areas. The Carters, the Lees, the Fitzhughs—families that defined
the concept of a golden age—were among the prosperous residents of
the Northern Neck.[46]

While the proprietors of the Northern Neck declined the opportunity to develop the area as a manor, as they might have, the system of
land grants created several distinctions from the lower Tidewater. The
proprietors followed the freehold pattern common to the rest of Virginia by offering patents in free and common socage, but they did not
require settlement or improvement of minimum portions of each grant.
Although few grants in the rest of Virginia were revoked for failure to
settle or improve land, the policy of the proprietors encouraged large
land patents in the Northern Neck. When Robert Carter and Thomas
Lee served as resident agents for the proprietor, they patented enormous tracts—as much as two hundred thousand acres for Carter—
and encouraged their friends to do the same. The planters of the
Northern Neck stood out, even in land-hungry Virginia, for their
fixation on speculation and the development of new lands.[47]

The availability of concentrated landholdings in the Northern Neck
attracted wealthy families but restricted options for small planters and
landless young men. The consequent pressures on small planters may
have been responsible for the area's early reputation as a source of social unrest. The region was the center of opposition to the Inspection
Act of 1730, which threatened to force marginal producers out of the
tobacco market. The violence soon ceased, but the relative concentration of landholding in the Northern Neck continued to restrict oppor-

tunities for many. Tenancy was more common here than elsewhere in Virginia, as was the hiring out of slaves. Leasing land and slaves could be viable options for a young man hoping to produce surplus crops for market and accumulate money for the purchase of land in newly settled areas, but they were also indicative of a concentration of wealth that restricted opportunities in the Tidewater for those who did not inherit land and slaves.[48]

Large planters with more land than they personally could supervise encouraged tenancy as a means of improving land without the allocation of their own slaves and as a device for shifting the burden of a fluctuating commodity market onto the tenants. Robert Carter of Nomini Hall offered leases for land beyond his own plantations and attached detailed instructions for the cultivation of the land. Leases might have a broader social purpose as well. George Mason proposed legislation to encourage settling lands with tenants, a practice he thought "more beneficial to the Community than [the custom] of settling them with Slaves." Richard Henry Lee considered leasing a means to distribute the benefits of land to a broader group of Virginians. Lee turned over much of his land to tenants, who also hired out slaves. Washington followed this practice common to the Northern Neck and proposed to settle tenants on his western lands as well.[49]

The Northern Neck's location on the periphery of the consignment trade and the region's declining soil productivity further convinced great planters in the area to diversify production on their plantations. Although the Potomac River district maintained its proportional share of Virginia's tobacco exports throughout the eighteenth century, the consignment merchants steadily restricted purchases in this area where soil conditions had always been unfavorable for the cultivation of premium, sweet-scented tobacco. As Scottish purchasers such as William Cunninghame & Company and the Glassford Company absorbed much of the tobacco from the Northern Neck, large planters led the transition to grain cultivation. Washington went so far as to abandon all tobacco growing at his Potomac estates and turned to wheat and other provisions for the West Indies while concentrating on tobacco at his York River estates.[50]

The interest in diversification also focused attention on the western lands that always had been of special interest to wealthy planters in the Northern Neck. In 1745, the extension of the proprietary to include the area beyond the Blue Ridge enticed eastern planters to invest in the transmontane region. Two years later, Northern Neck residents, led by Thomas Lee, were the principal founders of the Ohio Company, which secured a grant for the land around the Forks of the Ohio, beyond the reach of the proprietary. For Washington as for others in the Northern Neck, the West was not just an object of speculation but a foundation for the agricultural and commercial development of the Potomac River area.

The interest in expansion and diversification did not separate the Northern Neck planters from the gentry of lower Tidewater so much as it put them at the forefront of the efforts to reduce dependence on staple agriculture and develop opportunities outside the imperial economy. Washington and others in the Northern Neck were among the earliest to confront the restrictions on Virginia's colonial economy that became apparent to planters throughout the colony during the sharp credit restriction of the early 1760s and the even more severe credit crisis of 1772. At the onset of the imperial crisis in 1765, Northern Neck planters, including Washington, George Mason, and Richard Henry Lee, drew on their diversification schemes to formulate a strategy of commercial resistance that sought to redirect the colony's economy at the same time that it applied political pressure to British merchants and members of Parliament. The politicization of what previously had been private frustrations with British trade and the persistence of a staple economy united the struggle for political rights with the search for economic autonomy.[51]

The commercial resistance of the 1760s and 1770s was one dimension of the broader search for economic independence that guided Washington and other great planters in the management of their estates, in their choice of investments, and in their vision for the expansion and development of Virginia. The diversification of agricultural production, the promotion of commerce, and the extension of settlement and trade into the backcountry, all offered means of enhancing the value of land and slaves while broadening the influence of the great planters. The opportunities pursued by Washington and his contemporaries also entailed the risks of investment in the far-flung economies of the Atlantic world and the frustrations of encountering societies distinct from the hierarchical, stable world of Tidewater Virginia in the mid-eighteenth century.

NOTES

1. For a review of the literature, see Thad W. Tate, "The Seventeenth-Century Chesapeake and Its Modern Historians," in *The Chesapeake in the Seventeenth Century: Essays on Anglo-American Society and Politics*, ed. Thad W. Tate and David L. Ammerman (New York: W.W. Norton, 1979), 3–50; Anita H. Rutman, "Still Planting the Seeds of Hope: The Recent Literature of the Early Chesapeake Region," *Virginia Magazine of History and Biography* 95 (January 1987): 3–24; and Lois Green Carr, Philip D. Morgan, and Jean B. Russo, eds., *Colonial Chesapeake Society* (Chapel Hill: University of North Carolina Press, 1988).

2. Wesley Frank Craven, *White, Red, and Black: The Seventeenth-Century Virginian* (Charlottesville: University Press of Virginia, 1971), 1–30; James Horn, "Servant Emigration to the Chesapeake in the Seventeenth Century," in *The Chesapeake in the Seventeenth Century*, 51–95; Edmund S. Morgan, *American Slavery, American Freedom: The Ordeal of Colonial Virginia* (New York: W. W. Norton, 1975), 395–432; Jack P. Greene, *Pursuits of Happiness: The Social Development of Early Modern British Colonies and the Formation of American Culture* (Chapel Hill: University of North Carolina Press, 1988), 82.

3. Allan Kulikoff, *Tobacco and Slaves: The Development of Southern Cultures in the Chesapeake, 1680–1800* (Chapel Hill: University of North Carolina Press, 1986), 23–44.

4. Morgan, *American Slavery, American Freedom*, 133–57; Bernard Bailyn, "Politics and Social Structure in Virginia," in *Seventeenth-Century Virginia*, ed. James Morton Smith (Chapel Hill: University of North Carolina Press, 1959), 90–115.

5. Morgan, *American Slavery, American Freedom*; T. H. Breen, "A Changing Labor Force and Race Relations in Virginia, 1660–1710," in *Shaping Southern Society: The Colonial Experience*, ed. T. H. Breen (New York: Oxford University Press, 1976), 116–34. For emphasis on political stability in the seventeenth century, see Jon Kukla, "Order and Chaos in Early America: Political and Social Stability in Pre-Restoration Virginia," *American Historical Review* 90 (April 1985): 275–98; Darrett B. and Anita H. Rutman, *A Place in Time: Middlesex County, Virginia, 1650–1750* (New York: W. W. Norton, 1984).

6. John J. McCusker and Russell R. Menard, *The Economy of British America, 1607–1789* (Chapel Hill: University of North Carolina Press, 1985), 122–26; Kulikoff, *Tobacco and Slaves*, 37–43, 79–92; Lorena Walsh, "Plantation Management in the Chesapeake, 1620–1820," *Journal of Economic History* 49 (June 1989): 393–97.

7. Kulikoff, *Tobacco and Slaves*, 37–44; Walsh, "Plantation Management."

8. Kulikoff, *Tobacco and Slaves*, 37–44; McCusker and Menard, *The Economy of British America*, 137–38.

9. Walsh, "Plantation Management"; Kulikoff, *Tobacco and Slaves*, 37–44; McCusker and Menard, *The Economy of British America*, 137–38.

10. Bailyn, "Politics and Social Structure in Virginia"; Kulikoff, *Tobacco and Slaves*, 9–10, 263–80; Greene, *Pursuits of Happiness*, 92–94.

11. Bailyn, "Politics and Social Structure in Virginia," 90–115.

12. Kulikoff, *Tobacco and Slaves*, 288–90; Rutman and Rutman, *A Place in Time*, 204–33; Aubrey C. Land, "Economic Behavior in a Plantation Society: The Eighteenth-Century Chesapeake," *Journal of Southern History* 33 (November 1967): 469–85.

13. Kulikoff, *Tobacco and Slaves*, 261–63, 280–82; Morgan, *American Slavery, American Freedom*, esp. chaps. 17, 18. For a general overview of the order of white society in the eighteenth century, see Charles S. Sydnor, *Gentlemen Freeholders: Political Practices in Washington's Virginia* (Chapel Hill: University of North Carolina Press, 1952).

14. Jack P. Greene, "Foundations of Political Power in the Virginia House of Burgesses, 1720–1776," *William and Mary Quarterly*, 3d ser., 16 (October 1959): 485–506.

15. Rhys Isaac, *The Transformation of Virginia, 1740–1790* (Chapel Hill: University of North Carolina Press, 1982), 18–42; Lorena S. Walsh, "Urban Amenities and Rural Sufficiency: Living Standards and Consumer Behavior in the Colonial Chesapeake, 1643–1777," *Journal of Economic History* 43 (March 1983): 109–17.

16. Walsh, "Urban Amenities," 88–114; T. H. Breen, "Horses and Gentlemen: The Cultural Significance of Gambling among the Gentry of Virginia," *William and Mary Quarterly*, 3d ser., 34 (April 1977): 239–57; A. G. Roeber, "Authority, Law, and Custom: The Rituals of Court Day in Tidewater Virginia, 1720 to 1750," *William and Mary Quarterly*, 3d ser., 37 (January 1980): 29–52.

17. Isaac, *Transformation of Virginia*, 88–114, 131–35; Sydnor, *Gentlemen Freeholders*; Breen, "Horses and Gentlemen."

18. Emory G. Evans, "The Rise and Decline of the Virginia Aristocracy in the Eighteenth Century: The Nelsons," in *The Old Dominion: Essays for Thomas Perkins Abernethy*, ed. Darrett B. Rutman (Charlottesville: University Press of Virginia, 1964), 62–78; Kulikoff, *Tobacco and Slaves*, 141–48.

19. Douglas Southall Freeman, *George Washington: A Biography*, 7 vols. (New York: Charles Scribner's Sons, 1948–57), 1:34–41, 73.

20. Freeman, *George Washington*, 1:48–74.

21. Freeman, *George Washington*, 1:42–47.

22. Freeman, *George Washington*, 1:66–78, 224–65.

23. Freeman, *George Washington*, 1:224–46; Invoice to Richard Washington, April 15, 1757, *The Papers of George Washington*, Colonial Series, ed. W. W. Abbot et al., 10 vols. (Charlottesville: University Press of Virginia, 1983–1995), 4:132–33; Invoice from Richard Washington, November 10, 1757, *Washington Papers*, Col. Ser., 5:49–51.

24. Bruce A. Ragsdale, "George Washington, the British Tobacco Trade, and Economic Opportunity in Pre-Revolutionary Virginia," *Virginia Magazine of History and Biography* 97 (April 1989): 133–62.

25. McCusker and Menard, *The Economy of British America*, 119–27; Kulikoff, *Tobacco and Slaves*, 118–31; Jacob M. Price, "Economic Function and the Growth of American Port Towns in the Eighteenth Century," *Perspectives in American History* 8 (1974): 165; Charles Wetherell, "'Boom and Bust' in the Colonial Chesapeake Economy," *Journal of Interdisciplinary History* 15 (Autumn 1984): 185–210.

26. Price, "Economic Function," 166–69; Carville Earle and Ronald Hoffman, "Urban Development in the Eighteenth-Century South," *Perspectives in American History* 10 (1976): 19–50.

27. Morgan, *American Slavery, American Freedom*, 338–62; Kulikoff, *Tobacco and Slaves*, 280–300.

28. Kulikoff, *Tobacco and Slaves*, 92–99, 131–57.

29. Allan Kulikoff, "The Colonial Chesapeake: Seedbed of Antebellum Southern Culture?," *Journal of Southern History* 45 (November 1979): 513–40; McCusker and Menard, *The Economy of British America*, 120–25; Jacob M. Price, "The Economic Growth of the Chesapeake and the European Market, 1677–1775," *Journal of Economic History* 24 (December 1964): 496–511.

30. Samuel M. Rosenblatt, "The Significance of Credit in the Tobacco Consignment Trade: A Study of John Norton & Sons, 1768–1775," *William and Mary Quarterly*, 3d ser., 19 (July 1962): 383–99; Robert P. Thomson, "The Merchant in Virginia, 1700–1775" (Ph.D. diss., University of Wisconsin, 1955), chap. 2.

31. The work of Jacob M. Price provides the most authoritative description of the rise of the direct trade: see *France and the Chesapeake: A History of the French Tobacco Monopoly 1674–1791, and Its Relationship to the British and American Tobacco Trades*, 2 vols. (Ann Arbor: University of Michigan Press, 1973); "The Rise of Glasgow in the Chesapeake Tobacco Trade, 1707–1775," *William and Mary Quarterly*, 3d ser., 11 (April 1954): 179–99; "Economic Function and the Growth of American Port Towns in the Eighteenth Century," *Perspectives in American History* 8 (1974), 123–86; *Capital and Credit in British Overseas Trade: The View from the Chesapeake, 1700–1776* (Cambridge: Harvard University Press, 1980). See also Robert P. Thomson, "The Tobacco Export of the Upper James River Naval District, 1773–1775," *William and Mary Quarterly*, 3d ser., 18 (July 1961): 393–407.

32. J. H. Soltow, "Scottish Traders in Virginia, 1750–1775," *Economic History Review*, 2d ser., 12 (August 1959): 83–98; William Cunninghame & Co. to James Robinson, May 16, 1772, Cunninghame of Lainshaw Muniments, 1761–1778, Scottish Record Office; Glassford Papers, Library of Congress.

33. Ragsdale, "George Washington," 133–62.

34. Landon Carter, *The Diary of Landon Carter of Sabine Hall, 1752–1775*, ed. Jack P. Greene, 2 vols. (Charlottesville: University Press of Virginia, 1965), 1:413.

35. Price, *Capital and Credit*, 10–16.

36. Kulikoff, *Tobacco and Slaves*, 118–19, 122–24; Walsh, "Urban Amenities"; Price, *Capital and Credit*, chaps. 4–6.

37. Lawrence Henry Gipson, "Virginia Planter Debts before the American Revolution," *Virginia Magazine of History and Biography* 69 (July 1961): 275; Joseph A. Ernst, "Genesis of the Currency Act of 1764: Virginia Paper Money and the Protection of British Investments," *William and Mary Quarterly*, 3d ser., 22 (January 1965): 33–74; Peter J. Coleman, *Debtors and Creditors in America: Insolvency, Imprisonment for Debt, and Bankruptcy, 1607–1900* (Madison: State Historical Society of Wisconsin, 1974), chap. 14.

38. Lorena S. Walsh, "Plantation Management," 393–406; McCusker and Menard, *The Economy of British America*, 126; John M. Hemphill II, *Virginia and the English Commercial System, 1689–1733; Studies in the Development and Fluctuations of a Colonial Economy under Imperial Control* (New York: Garland, 1985): chaps. 5–8.

39. Peter V. Bergstrom, *Markets and Merchants: Economic Diversification in Colonial Virginia, 1700–1775* (New York: Garland, 1985); Harold B. Gill Jr., "Wheat Culture in Colonial Virginia," *Agricultural History* 52 (July 1978): 380–93; Kulikoff, *Tobacco and Slaves*, 131–34; Walsh, "Plantation Management."

40. Walsh, "Plantation Management"; McCusker and Menard, *The Economy of British America*, 126.

41. Price, "Economic Function," 169–70.

42. Price, "Economic Function," 164–69; for the career of William Lee, see Bruce A. Ragsdale, *A Planters' Republic: The Search for Economic Independence in Revolutionary Virginia* (Madison: Madison House, 1996), 154–68.

43. Price, *Capital and Credit*, 127–30.

44. David C. Klingaman, *Colonial Virginia's Coastwise and Grain Trade* (New York: Arno Press, 1975); Price, "Economic Function," 169–73; Earle and Hoffman, "Staple Crops and Urban Development," 26–50.

45. For the extension of tobacco culture and the development of Shenandoah Valley, see Robert D. Mitchell, *Commercialism and Frontier: Perspectives on the Early Shenandoah Valley* (Charlottesville: University Press of Virginia, 1977).

46. History of the Northern Neck Proprietary in Freeman, *George Washington*, 1:447–513; see also, Fairfax Harrison, *Landmarks of Old Prince William;*

A Study of Origins in Northern Virginia, 2 vols. (Richmond: Old Dominion Press, 1924); Greene, "Foundations of Political Power," 491–92.

47. James Blaine Gouger III, "Agricultural Change in the Northern Neck of Virginia, 1700–1860: An Historical Geography" (Ph.D. diss., University of Florida, 1976), 15, 79–82; Freeman, *George Washington*, 1:493–500.

48. Willard Bliss, "The Rise of Tenancy in Virginia," *Virginia Magazine of History and Biography* 58 (October 1950): 427–41; Kulikoff, *Tobacco and Slaves*, 132–34.

49. Louis Morton, *Robert Carter of Nomini Hall: A Virginia Planter in the Eighteenth Century* (Williamsburg: Colonial Williamsburg, 1941; Charlottesville: University Press of Virginia, 1964): 71–76; "Scheme for Replevying Goods and Distress for Rent," December 23, 1765, *Papers of George Mason*, ed. Robert A. Rutland, 3 vols. (Chapel Hill: University of North Carolina Press, 1970), 1:61–62; *Rusticus* [Richard Henry Lee] to Rind, [176–], Lee Family Papers, microfilm, Alderman Library, University of Virginia, Charlottesville, Va.

50. Bergstrom, *Markets and Merchants*, 141; Thomson, "Tobacco Export," 393–407; Freeman, *George Washington*, 3:117; Walsh, "Plantation Management," 396–97.

51. Ragsdale, *A Planters' Republic*; Marc Egnal, *A Mighty Empire: The Origins of the American Revolution* (Ithaca: Cornell University Press, 1988), 87–101.

Part Two

"Over the Hills and Far Away": George Washington and the Changing Virginia Backcountry

ROBERT D. MITCHELL

𝐼N THE SPRING OF 1748, AT THE formative age of sixteen, George Washington made his first venture west of the Blue Ridge as a neophyte surveyor for Thomas, Lord Fairfax, proprietor of Virginia's Northern Neck. Though engaged in carving new properties out of the "wilderness," he was impressed by the agricultural qualities of the recently founded Frederick County. "The Land exceeding Rich & fertile," he noted, "all the way produces abundance of Grain Hemp and Tobacco &c."[1] Working in the central part of the county around the new village of Frederick Town (Winchester), he "took a Review of y[e] Town" and found fine lodgings with "a Good Feather bed with clean sheets."[2] Washington had entered a pioneer colonial landscape that was scarcely two years older than he was. Within five years, he had come to own parts of this landscape in the form of twenty-three hundred acres of land and a lot in Winchester, thus anointing the region as a formative influence in the life of America's first president.

Washington returned to the Shenandoah Valley in a very different capacity in the fall of 1755 as a colonel in command of the Virginia Regiment charged with the defense of the colony's western frontier. He supervised the construction of Fort Loudoun at the north end of Winchester and made the town his military headquarters until the fall of 1758, when he took up residence at Mount Vernon. The Virginia backcountry was then a much-changed place compared with the 1730s, one populated by a second generation of settlers more integrated into the expanding commercial world of the Atlantic. How and why this transformation occurred between 1730 and 1760, and what influence it may have had on Washington, are the subjects of this essay.

[63]

THE FIRST COLONIAL SETTLERS FIL-
tered into the Shenandoah Valley and the western foothills of the Blue
Ridge from the North during the early 1730s. Encountering no resident
Indian populations, their sustained occupancy set a new precedent in
Virginia's settlement history. Expansion in eastern Virginia barely had
made an impression on the Piedmont, and areas at the eastern foothills of the Blue Ridge would not be occupied for another two decades.
Virginia thus had two frontiers during Washington's youth. One expressed continuity with the tobacco plantation traditions of the Tidewater as young and middling planters moved westward to the Piedmont.
The other, west of the Blue Ridge, introduced a new frontier society to
the colony. It comprised middling farm families from diverse areas of
Europe, the province of Ulster, lowland Scotland, midland England,
and the Rhineland-Palatinate, as well as settlers from these areas who
had prior experience in Pennsylvania, New Jersey, or New York.[3]

Scholarly interpretations of these frontiers have undergone
significant reappraisals during the twentieth century. Frederick Jackson Turner's frontier thesis dominated approaches to westward expansion for more than a half century. His sweeping evaluation of the frontier
experience, both in his famous essay delivered in 1893, "The Significance
of the Frontier in American History," and in his later writings, portrayed the westward-moving frontiers of the eighteenth century as the
beginnings of the process of "Americanization." The encounter with
American environments and the increasing distance from European
centers of influence created opportunities for the formation of new
societies and the emergence of American democracy. Although he cap-
tured the essence of Virginia's two frontiers as "presenting contrasted
types of civilization," he viewed the frontier process as a set of inexo-
rable forces that repeated their imprint across the eastern United States
regardless of environment or culture.[4]

The influence of Turner's thought on younger scholars is
exemplified in the works of Charles H. Ambler and Thomas P.
Abernethy. Ambler was the first scholar to apply Turnerian ideas to the
settlement history of Virginia. In his revised dissertation, completed
under Turner at the University of Wisconsin, *Sectionalism in Virginia
from 1776 to 1861*, published in 1910, he combined Turner's concepts of
frontier and section. He argued persuasively for a clear distinction between the communities of eastern Virginia, the initial Tidewater settlement and the gradually assimilated Piedmont based on commercial

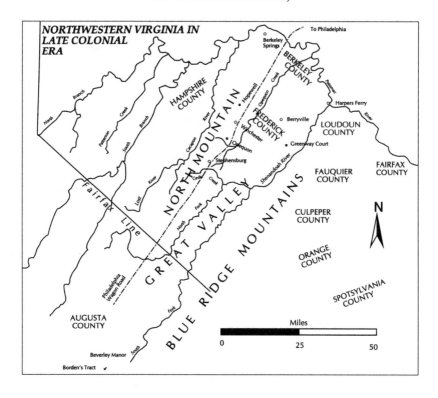

plantations and social and political elites, and the more democratic western frontier communities based on small farms, economic diversification, and ethnically mixed societies.[5] Thirty years later, Thomas Abernethy, a later student of Turner's at Harvard University, demonstrated the persistence of his mentor's ideas in his *Three Virginia Frontiers.* He interpreted greater Virginia's history as the product of three successive frontiers, Tidewater, Piedmont and Valley, and Kentucky. But he added a note of revisionism. In his estimation, "the Piedmont and Valley regions thus furnish another illustration of the fact that frontier conditions do not necessarily produce democratic institutions, even when the lands are easily accessible to independent small farmers."[6] By combining Piedmont and Valley into one frontier experience, however, he reduced the distinctiveness of Appalachian settlement west of the Blue Ridge.

It was not until the publication of Carl Bridenbaugh's *Myths and Realities* in 1952 that the backcountry was brought back into clear focus.[7] Bridenbaugh viewed the frontier South during the middle decades of the eighteenth century as "the back settlements" occupied by settlers whose timing of settlement and whose national origins he considered to be more important than the value assigned them in Turnerian thought. What was most striking about the backcountry was its topographic and ethnic diversity, which prevented the formation of a distinctive regional society until after the American Revolution. His ideas on the Virginia backcountry derived substantially from Freeman H. Hart's *The Valley of Virginia in the American Revolution,* published in 1942. This seminal work placed great emphasis on both the diversity and complexity of life west of the Blue Ridge during the second half of the eighteenth century.[8] Yet it was not until the late 1970s and early 1980s that more detailed studies of Virginia's backcountry communities, most notably my own examination of the Shenandoah Valley, *Commercialism and Frontier,* and Richard Beeman's study of Lunenburg County on the Piedmont entitled *The Evolution of the Southern Backcountry,* confirmed Hart's emphasis on diversity and complexity.[9] The possibility of a reappraisal of frontier communities based on more place-sensitive criteria, however, was swept away by the tide of synthesis that engulfed historical scholarship during the later 1980s.

The "new synthesis" was largely anti-Turnerian but much less in agreement about the characteristics of the Southern backcountry. Premised on the importance of continuity with the European past, its practitioners expressed their conclusions in diffusionist and derivative terms. Employing such ideas as "marchland," "transplanted seed," and "Greater Pennsylvania," they portrayed an interior region on the extreme periphery of the British imperial system, more dependent for its character on direct extensions of British or coastal colonial traditions than on innovative encounters with new environments. Thus, the Great Valley of Virginia was described as a southward extension of Pennsylvania's small-farm, ethnically diverse world or portrayed as a region where an initial distinctiveness was eroded by the penetration of Tidewater-based social, economic, and governmental institutions.[10] In another view the extreme instability of frontier conditions, the difficulties of pioneering, the high rates of population turnover, and the comparative weakness of governmental institutions precluded the formation of strong, distinct backcountry communities.[11] The Great Valley's diversity was also explained as a direct transplant from northern Britain, especially Ulster, and a distinctly different world from the Cavalier ethos of the Tidewater.[12] Even the one study that depicted the mountain interior more on its own terms, *The American Backwoods Frontier* by Terry Jordan and Matti Kaups, attributed the source of its distinctiveness to Europe, to the "preadapted" material culture of the heavily forested areas of central Europe and present-day Scandinavia.[13] Backcountry society was predominantly classless, decentralized, individualistic, dispersed, and ecologically adapted to forest environments but wasteful of their resources.

More recently, however, closer attention to the Southern backcountry itself has begun to lay the foundation for a more empirically sound interpretation of frontier communities. A notable feature of reviews of this trend is general agreement that interior backcountry areas exhibited a set of shared experiences that distinguished newer western settlements from those along the Atlantic seaboard.[14] These experiences included not only clearing forested environments and building in wood, generous land-grant policies, family migration, and ethnically mixed populations but also persistent localism and independence, the creation of new settlement systems dominated by market towns, and the rapid development of commercial life necessitating close trade links with Atlantic seaport cities. At this more locally based, community-oriented scale of analysis, the backcountry remained quite regionally distinctive, both from within and in comparison with the East.[15]

THE DISTINCTIVENESS OF THE Shenandoah Valley was apparent by the mid-1760s, a decade prior to the Revolution. As a result of two decades of local and regional scholarship, it is possible to identify two phases of frontier evolution. A pioneer phase of farm site selection and land-cover change took place in geographical isolation during the 1730s and 1740s, largely before Washington's involvement in the region. It included several critical events, however, that provided a context of opportunity for ambitious young men familiar with Virginia's newest frontier. This phase merged into a second, developmental phase of gradual social complexity with increasing population growth and settlement density, the first indications of agricultural specialization, and the appearance of county seat, market towns with commercial ties to Atlantic ports forged during the French and Indian War. George Washington was intimately involved in this process of regional development.

There has been considerable debate over the landscape characteristics of the Shenandoah Valley during the pioneer phase of European

[67]

settlement. In the conventional view, derived from settler recollections during the early nineteenth century, Indians had regularly burned the area for hunting purposes, producing extensive areas of virtually tree-less grassland.[16] These "prairies" and the absence of a resident Indian population then facilitated the rapid settlement of the Virginia backcountry. It is true that by the time of Washington's first visit to the Valley in 1748 approximately ten thousand settlers had staked out residency in the region. But a close examination of the 350 extant survey records for Frederick County between 1730 and 1753 suggests that the northern Valley was still covered with extensive deciduous forest during the initial contact period.[17] Analysis of the vegetation data from individual survey points and from surveyors' notations about land cover, within surveyed tracts and along the boundaries between tracts, reveals that the majority of boundary markers were trees, particularly white and red oaks and hickories, rather than stakes or stone piles, which would have been indicative of extensive areas of unforested land. Surviving records of Washington's own forty-five surveys recorded west of the Blue Ridge indicate his familiarity with a great variety of trees and no reference to other kinds of survey markers.[18]

The same analysis suggests, however, that the region was not an undisturbed, forested wilderness by the early eighteenth century. References by surveyors to open land through the use of terms like Long Meadow, Perkin's Marsh, "barren ground," or "a glade" indicate that such open areas were limited in extent and most likely distributed along stream channels. This would support the contention that most grassy openings were the result of natural, rather than social, processes. River erosion and deposition, storm-related flooding, the creation of marl-deposit obstructions along stream beds, and even beaver activities were likely contributors to stream-related open lands. Many early survey markers, moreover, included reference to tree saplings. The presence of such saplings even during the 1730s would indicate that at least some areas might have been covered with early successional forest as a consequence of recent Indian hunting activities.[19]

Colonial settlers were certainly cognizant of vegetation indicators in their selection of settlement sites. Pioneer families sought out promising agricultural land along stream channels or adjacent to springs but sited their farmsteads on land above flood level and within easy access to woodland for purposes of construction and fuelwood. Areas of previously cleared land, generally designated as "old fields," would have attracted the earliest attention but such areas rarely appeared on Frederick County surveys. More common were areas of light deciduous woodlands containing oaks and hickories with relatively little undergrowth. Settlers would have killed the larger trees by girdling them and cleared the underbrush to make way for house and field sites. Most of the floor of the northern Valley is comprised of limestone formations, which support productive loam soils for farming. Through the center of the Valley, however, is a north-south band of infertile shale lands that produced more pine woods and oak scrub. These lands were seldom claimed or settled before the Revolution.

Four sets of events set the tone for the elaboration of this colonial settlement. First, many of the first generation of settlers west of the Blue Ridge were attracted there more by the land policies of Governor William Gooch, who arrived in Virginia in 1727, than by prior knowledge of the region's physical geography.[20] Gooch's western policy focused on the need to secure eastern Virginia against threats from interior Indian populations allied with the French and on countering the proprietary claims of the Fairfaxes to lands west of the Blue Ridge. Gooch put into full operation Virginia's policy of granting large areas of western lands to reputable individuals or partners who were then required to certify the settlement of one family within two years for every one thousand acres granted. Each family in turn had to fulfill its claim by "improving" three acres of every fifty acres granted within a three-year period. At the same time, Robert "King" Carter, acting as Lord Fairfax's agent, was equally busy granting large acreages along the Shenandoah River in the northern Valley to prominent Tidewater planters mostly members of his own family.[21] The liberal land policies of both the colony and the proprietary created a brisk land market which ambitious men could exploit for both settlement and speculative purposes. In the central part of the northern Valley county of Frederick, most familiar to George Washington, four hundred of the one thousand land grants made during the eighteenth century were recorded between 1730 and 1755. The market was particularly active between 1746 and 1755 when thirty-six grants on average were recorded per year.[22] The 171 landholders identified in the county in 1746 held 84,700 acres of land; only 32 percent of the landholdings were for more than four hundred acres. By 1764, when the next most comprehensive record is available, the number of landholders had increased more than five fold to 938. They controlled almost 480,600 acres, and the number of holdings of more than four hundred acres had increased to 45 percent.[23] The most active period of land acquisition thus coincided with the time when Washington was most involved in the development of the backcountry.

Second, the remarkably rapid initial occupance of the Shenandoah Valley led to early requests by its settlers for the extension of the Virginia county system of government west of the Blue Ridge.[24] Governor Gooch was only too happy to respond since such requests seemed to vindicate his western land policies and ensure the orderly development of a buffer zone capable of resisting French and Indian threats. The Virginia government thus created Frederick and Augusta in 1738 as the first counties west of the Blue Ridge. Although most of Virginia's western land claims were encompassed within Augusta's vast size, in the Shenandoah Valley the east-west boundary between the two counties (the Fairfax Line) divided the Valley into two, almost equal sections. While Frederick County did not complete the construction of a courthouse and a jail until late in 1751, the institutions of Virginia local government, the court, vestry, and militia, were already in place and functioning when Washington began his surveying activities in 1748.[25]

Third, European settlement was facilitated by treaty negotiations between the Virginia government and the Iroquois concerning control of the Virginia backcountry. Unease over possible Indian allegiance to French territorial interests in the trans-Allegheny interior encouraged representatives of Governor Gooch and the governors of Maryland and Pennsylvania to meet Iroquois leaders at Lancaster, Pennsylvania, in late June 1744. In the resulting treaty, the Iroquois swore allegiance to the British and relinquished all claims to lands south of New York and east of the Alleghenies in exchange for rights of passage through the Great Valley.[26] Iroquois movements through Virginia were henceforth located mainly west of the Shenandoah Valley, thus leaving it free for uninterrupted settlement by American colonists and European immigrants. Colonization increased in volume during the late 1740s and early 1750s until arrested by the increasing tension between French and British forces in the upper Ohio Valley late in 1753. This situation brought Major George Washington back to Winchester on assignment intermittently between November 1753 and April 1754, prior to his defeat by the French and their Indian allies at Great Meadows in southwestern Pennsylvania during the first week of July 1754.[27] General Braddock's defeat south of Fort Duquesne almost exactly one year later provided the opportunity for Washington's second association with the northern Shenandoah Valley, one which was to link Washington and his family with the region for the rest of his life. Governor Dinwiddie appointed Washington as colonel of the recently constituted Virginia Regiment in August 1755, and the new colonel arrived in Winchester to set up his headquarters on September 14. By the time he returned to Mount Vernon in the fall of 1758, Washington had not only influenced the growth and shape of Winchester and acquired more land in the northern Valley to which some of his relatives were attracted after the Revolution, but he also had overcome his initial defeat for political office in Frederick County in 1757 by being elected to the House of Burgesses from the county a year later. Thus, it was in the backcountry that Washington initially combined his distinguished political and military careers.[28]

Fourth, Lord Fairfax's claims to extend his proprietorship west of the Blue Ridge to include the northern half of the Shenandoah Valley led to the infamous suit known as *Virginia* v. *Fairfax* presented to the Privy Council in London in 1744.[29] The Privy Council's confirmation of Fairfax's claim in April 1745 provided the basis for early regionalism within the Valley. First, it consolidated his control over the northern Valley, forcing the principal recipients of Governor Gooch's land policy to struggle to maintain their land rights under Fairfax. The resultant *Fairfax* v. *Hite* suit instituted in 1749 was not resolved fully until long after Lord Fairfax's death in 1781.[30] The geographical consequences of these competing land policies was apparent long before then. Proprietary grants for large acreages in the eastern third of Frederick County along or near the Shenandoah River to planter families from eastern Virginia with no specific settlement stipulations created an enclave of reserved lands to which Tidewater planters began to move in earnest only after the Revolution. Jost Hite and other settlers who had migrated to the Valley from more northern colonies brought a different set of settlement characteristics to the central and western parts of the county. There, the more rapid occupancy by settlers with no ties to the planter world created a landscape of small, diversified farms, open-country neighborhoods, and market towns that contrasted strongly with the planter-dominated East.[31] Second, the resurvey of the so-called Fairfax Line after 1745 forced a slight readjustment of the Frederick-Augusta boundary within the Shenandoah Valley in favor of Frederick. The new line became the de facto boundary between a northern section (Frederick), where Tidewater influences were strong, and a southern section (Augusta), where they were weak and replaced by influences more characteristic of the Middle Colonies.[32] Thus, the backcountry that George Washington knew by 1758 already was divided regionally on at last two levels, the east-west distinction within the northern Valley and the north-south distinction within the Shenandoah Valley as a whole.

*D*ISPERSAL AND DECENTRALIZATION were the key elements of the first two decades of colonial settlement. Pioneer settlers did not move southward through the Valley in contiguous, successive waves. Rather, they distributed themselves loosely along water courses with farmsteads one-half mile to one mile apart in "open-country neighborhoods." Neighborhood preceded county or region and formed the basis of pioneer rural society throughout the Valley. Such neighborhoods could involve areas of twenty-five to forty square miles in extent, within which families of very different ethnic origins carved out subsistence farms, cleared country paths and rudimentary roads, and by the late 1740s were likely to participate in shared service sites such as simple churches, meeting houses, and grain mills. In the Winchester area, for example, two such neighborhoods had emerged by 1748. They were Hopewell, arranged around a large Crown land grant and a Quaker meeting house eight miles north of the town, and Opequon, focused on the creek of that name six miles south of Winchester, where Ulster and German-speaking pioneers, who were often kin-related, shared the same space.[33]

These neighborhoods superficially resembled settlement patterns in eastern Virginia, but they differed from plantation neighborhoods in important respects. Backcountry neighborhoods, like those in the Tidewater and Piedmont, were composed of dispersed settlements, but their smaller landholding units meant that neighbors were less far apart. Farmsteads also had fewer outbuildings than on plantations, usually only a shed or, later, a barn. Backcountry neighborhoods also appear to have functioned as communities focused on log meeting houses and churches, which attracted early road patterns and brought in families within a radius of about eight miles several times a month. This social network placed a general boundary between one neighborhood and adjacent communities.[34]

Because such neighborhoods were founded on family-based, mixed farms, their level of economic self-sufficiency differed from that in plantation areas. On the one hand, they were more diversified agriculturally and less dependent on imported goods. Settlers were more likely to make their own utensils, furniture, and clothing and to use family labor to fulfill their farming needs. On the other hand, the limited ability of settlers to trade did not generate an immediate demand for local merchants or for country stores. Itinerant peddlers supplied the few required imports. Local government officials and institutions were virtually nonexistent in the backcountry for the first ten years of settlement except for land surveyors. This vacuum rendered neighborhoods virtually autonomous until the first meeting of the Frederick County Court in 1743. Yet, perhaps the most significant contrast between planter and backcountry neighborhoods was developmental. In most areas of the Tidewater and Piedmont, neighborhoods did not evolve into more concentrated forms such as villages and small towns but remained in a prolonged state of dispersal. As population and the demand for economic and governmental services increased in the backcountry, however, county towns were founded and grew into regional market centers, thus creating more complex and dynamic settlement systems.[35]

A similar process occurred in Augusta County, in the southern half of the Shenandoah Valley. Governor Gooch made two extremely generous grants that were to monopolize land available for settlers in the region and to become the focus of a series of rural neighborhoods. William Beverley, son of Virginia's historian Robert Beverley and one of Virginia's two negotiators at the Treaty of Lancaster in 1744, acquired a 118,491-acre tract in September 1736 known as Beverley Manor, which began seven miles south of Frederick County's southern boundary and stretched for twenty-two miles along the valley floor. Borden's Tract, a 92,100-acre grant to Benjamin Borden Sr., in November 1739, shared Beverley's southern boundary and extended another seventeen miles up the Valley.[36] Beverley Manor sprouted several open-country neighborhoods on and around the county seat of Staunton (laid out in 1746), while other neighborhoods emerged slowly at the southern end of Borden's Tract near present-day Lexington. Settlers of Scotch-Irish origins predominated in both grants, while German-speaking settlers and a few eastern Virginians acquired lands, particularly in Beverley Manor. Although settlement was sparse and neighborhoods were slower to form in Augusta County, rural neighborhood clusters stretched from the Potomac River one hundred miles southward to the headwaters of the

James River by the time George Washington first set foot in the Virginia backcountry.

These discrete neighborhoods and their spatially restricted communities formed the foundation of Valley society throughout the colonial era. But within the region, four processes induced significant changes between the early 1740s and the early 1760s. The emergence of agricultural specialization, the development of county government, the expansion of trade networks, and the militarization of frontier society associated with the French and Indian War all contributed to the transformation of the backcountry. The result, particularly in Frederick County, was a shift from a rural society based on dispersed farms in open-country neighborhoods to one organized around a primary town-country system focused on Winchester.

Pioneer agriculture throughout the backcountry reflected the mixed-farming traditions already established in southeastern Pennsylvania. Dispersed, subsistence farms, generally in tracts ranging in size from one to four hundred acres, concentrated on wheat, corn, rye, and flax, together with the raising of cattle and hogs in Frederick County and cattle and horses in Augusta County.[37] Hunting for deer, fox, and beaver was an important economic supplement, particularly in Augusta. Whatever surpluses small farms produced during the first twenty years of settlement could be sold to incoming settlers or to migrants passing through to frontier settlements farther south. Moravian missionaries traveling between Pennsylvania and the western Carolinas during the late 1740s and early 1750s, for example, had difficulty finding sufficient provisions in the Shenandoah Valley for themselves and their horses and complained about road conditions, particularly south of Staunton.[38] It is not surprising, therefore, that cattle on the hoof were the first important export from the region. By the early 1740s, drovers were collecting steers and driving them as far north as Philadelphia. This trade was interrupted by the increasingly tense military situation west of the Shenandoah Valley after 1753, and for the next five years surplus steers were slaughtered locally to help feed frontier militia.

The initial response to county government formation west of the Blue Ridge was significantly different from traditional developments in eastern Virginia. During the seventeenth and early eighteenth centuries, settlers in Tidewater and Piedmont regions had organized administrative life, as they had their social and economic affairs, by arranging government functions at dispersed locations. County seats generally consisted of little more than a courthouse, jail, and law office at sites that seldom attracted permanent economic activities. Trade occurred principally at country stores located on larger plantations or, after the Tobacco Inspection Act of 1730, at tobacco warehouses. Because tobacco was less bulky than grain and needed minimal processing, trade in the leaf required limited auxiliary services and created few opportunities for employment. With little demand for centralized services, county seats seldom evolved into villages or towns. As a result, towns in eastern Virginia, except for the colonial capital, the occasional Tidewater port, and a string of fall-zone settlements, were virtually absent.[39]

Although county justices in Frederick and Augusta originally met in private homes, concern over the provision of government services quickly led to the selection of sites for permanent governing functions. In Frederick County, James Wood, the first county clerk, volunteered late in 1743 to lay out two streets in twenty-six half-acre lots together with four public lots for a county seat on land that he owned between the Hopewell and Opequon neighborhoods. The plan aligned the prospective settlement along the main trail running south from Pennsylvania through the Valley. Loudoun Street was located on this trail with Cameron Street parallel to the east. Each was thirty-three feet wide and crossed by two narrower streets named Piccadilly and Water (later Boscawen). By April 1745 this show of private initiative encouraged at least sixteen people to acquire lots in the village that was later named Winchester.[40] It contained at least two stores and an ordinary on Loudoun Street, a score of houses, and the beginnings of a courthouse and jail on the public lots by the time of Washington's visit in 1748. A nucleated settlement was taking shape. Four years later, with the help of Lord Fairfax, who had taken up permanent residence in Frederick County in 1750, the county justices petitioned successfully to the House of Burgesses for a town charter that permitted Winchester to conduct semi-annual fairs to complement the periodic markets its storekeepers and artisans had already created.[41] The growing town was not self-governing, however, but remained under the jurisdiction of Frederick County court, most of whose members lived in the countryside.

In Augusta County, William Beverley himself took a similar initiative in 1746 by granting twenty-five acres of his Mill Tract in Beverley Manor to be laid out in half-acre lots with three lots reserved for a courthouse, jail, and public square.[42] Within a few years several merchants had acquired town lots and a courthouse and jail were under construction. Staunton's petition for town status was turned down in 1749, however, and it did not receive a charter until 1761, after both Winchester and Stephensburg in Frederick County.[43]

The creation of counties did not mean that local government functioned in the backcountry precisely as it had in eastern Virginia. Life in early Augusta County indicates the varied responses of backcountry settlers to the imposition of traditional power structures west of the Blue Ridge. Political leaders of the county were primarily members of large, landowning pioneer families, who filled the local offices of justice of the peace, county clerk, county surveyor, and militia captain. This elite class, however, clearly lacked the stature and pedigree of the Tidewater planter-gentry and failed to create the deferential political climate of eastern counties. Augusta leaders, therefore, offset such disparities by deliberately manipulating land acquisition and officeholding for their own benefit and that of their families to exclude enterprising newcomers. Meanwhile, the ordinary people of the backcountry created something of an "alternative political culture" to that formed in the East. Local leaders, nonetheless, by retaining close ties with neighbors of similar background, if not achievement, were able to create a more stable political environment than in the Carolina backcountry.[44] Even in Frederick County, where Lord Fairfax and a small cadre of planter families had taken up residence by the early 1760s, the local gentry remained largely unaffected by eastern influences.

Militia behavior was also different in the backcountry and demonstrates the nature of the popular political culture. Although members of the local gentry filled most officer positions, their views of frontier service were not always shared by ordinary militiamen. Frequent absences from public musters, relatively high rates of desertion, and bold refusals to perform military duties in the face of more pressing family and local needs compromised the ability of commanders to command. These patterns appear to reflect the close-knit social networks generated by open-country neighborhoods, in which family and local priorities took precedence over county and regional matters. In 1754, for example, Augusta County failed to raise its quota of militia for an expedition to the Ohio Valley. Ordinary settlers, moreover, were much more likely to show hostility to even friendly Indians than their officers were, reflecting particular concern for the safety of family, kin, and neighbor.[45]

Despite their status as county seats, neither Winchester nor Staunton grew rapidly. It was the French and Indian War that provided the first impetus to growth, particularly in Winchester, which emerged as a garrison town and military headquarters during the conflict. Three important consequences ensued from the war. First, Winchester, described as having about sixty houses in 1753, more than doubled in population by 1756 with the appearance of the Virginia Regiment and several score of farm families fleeing from unprotected areas immediately to the west. James Wood and Lord Fairfax together laid out 365 new half-acre lots in 1758, by which time Washington's men had completed Fort Loudoun at the north end of Loudoun Street. This boom period for population and construction continued through 1760, when the town was described as containing about two hundred houses supporting one thousand residents.[46]

Second, Winchester became a provisions center for militia and horses. This demand was a boon for local farmers, storekeepers, and tavern owners, who responded by producing and collecting additional supplies of wheat, corn, beef, pork, mutton, hay, oats, and liquor. So great was the need for provisions that Washington complained in 1756 that local farmers were selling steers to Pennsylvania butchers rather than providing them to Virginia forces.[47] And, local tavern owners seem to have been more interested in plying soldiers with liquor than with the immediate defense of the backcountry.

Third, the concentration of Virginia's war effort in the Winchester area not only stimulated local trade, it also attracted the attention of wholesale merchants, who were to become a resident feature of economic life in the backcountry. Five or six retailers were operating stores in Winchester by 1757. The most prominent merchants in Frederick County, however, between the French and Indian War and the outbreak of the Revolution were three individuals, Bryan Bruin, Philip Bush, and his brother Daniel, all of whom had left Philadelphia for Winchester about 1756 and acquired lots and stores there and in the newly chartered town of Stephensburg.[48] At the same time, they retained their links with Philadelphia and were instrumental in involving Philadelphia dry goods firms in the Virginia backcountry. Bruin used his lots in Winchester and his rural holdings in Frederick and Hampshire counties to develop a line of credit with the Philadelphia firms of Owen Jones and Jones and Wister. Philip Bush made his connections with Jones and with Henry Kepple, while the firm of Jeremiah

Warder was trading as far south as Staunton.[49] After 1760, Philadelphia became the Virginia backcountry's major entrepôt despite the region's ties with Alexandria, Fredericksburg, and Richmond and despite the recent emergence of the Chesapeake port of Baltimore. Retail trade in the backcountry thus was organized locally, in contrast to tobacco-producing areas, where the consignment system in the Tidewater and the factor-store system on the Piedmont were controlled by British mercantile firms. This meant that backcountry communities eventually exerted greater control over their trading practices and patterns while relying on the generous credit of wholesalers in port cities from Philadelphia to Richmond. Only the occasional planter in Frederick County could avoid the local retail network and trade directly through fall-zone merchants. In 1759, for example, George Washington sent sixteen thousand pounds of sweet-scented tobacco from his plantation near the Shenandoah River to accompany Lord Fairfax's tobacco output on consignment through Alexandria to England. Alexandria merchants operated as little more than freight agents in such circumstances.[50]

BY THE EARLY 1760S, THEREFORE, population and society in the Virginia backcountry had undergone considerable alteration. The ten thousand pioneer residents of 1748 had increased to about twenty-five thousand by 1760 despite the disruptions of the war. They were distributed more extensively throughout the backcountry, and they had begun to recolonize areas to the west and south of the Shenandoah Valley.[51] At the same time, war-related activities helped to consolidate the positions of the county-seat, market towns of Winchester and Staunton within the increasingly integrated town-and-country settlement systems that characterized the Valley by the end of the colonial era. In Winchester, for example, the number and frequency of lot transactions doubled between 1755 and 1760 over the previous five-year period. Among the new lot purchasers were George Washington, himself, and several of his officers from the Virginia Regiment, including Lt. Charles Smith, paymaster Alexander Boyd, and surgeon James Craik. Several eastern Virginia merchants also acquired lots, including Charles Dick and Fielding Lewis of Fredericksburg and James Wilson of Fairfax County.[52] Winchester merchant Thomas Lemon transferred a Winchester lot and seven hundred acres of land to the Glasgow firm of John Glassford and Company, thus ushering in a new phase of external contacts in the northern Valley.[53]

The Lemon-Glassford transaction was significant for two reasons. First, it was symptomatic of an increasing trend among local merchants in their credit dealings with eastern merchants, whereby local, rural, and urban real estate was used as collateral in acquiring favorable credit terms. Winchester's most prominent merchants, Bryan Bruin and the Bush brothers, incurred much larger debts with a number of merchants in Philadelphia, Baltimore, and Fredericksburg. Yet what this process of credit extension achieved was the primacy of Winchester as the preeminent trading center for the entire northern section of the Virginia backcountry. Long-distance trade in the backcountry was organized differently than in areas dependent on tobacco production.[54] The export of farm commodities, the provision trade, was highly decentralized. Farmers who had goods to sell did not market them through villages and towns but sent them directly to eastern markets from their farms, as in the case of live cattle, or from mills, as in the case of wheat and flour. They did not have the mercantile connections or the credit to import goods directly as planters did. They depended on town merchants to organize the import trade or dry goods trade, which became centralized in Winchester and Staunton.[55]

The second important aspect of the Lemon-Glassford transaction was what it indicated about the beginnings of agricultural specialization in the backcountry. Although farmers had planted occasional crops of tobacco in the Shenandoah Valley since the mid-1740s, tobacco never became a major commercial crop immediately west of the Blue Ridge. Its appearance in trade transactions from the late 1750s on, however, indicates its singular importance in the eastern section of the northern Valley where Fairfax and Washington had their largest holdings. The Dumfries ledgers of the Glassford Company show that tobacco was being exported from individual plantations in Frederick County at least as early as 1758.[56] Within the next two years, more than a dozen county residents and two Winchester merchants were trading regularly with the Dumfries store for a variety of household goods. Tobacco cultivation was to represent the influence of eastern Virginian agricultural practices in the backcountry, and it became associated as elsewhere with the institution of slavery. Although there were only 760 black tithables recorded in the backcountry in 1755, 90 percent were located in Frederick County.[57] This pattern, which was to continue for the rest of the eighteenth century, was one of the most significant features that distinguished Frederick from the rest of the Virginia backcountry.

The backcountry's development of agricultural specialties, however, came not in tobacco but in the cattle, hemp, and wheat trades. It was this combination of exports that defined western Virginia's contribution to the growth of the American economy during the last third of the eighteenth century. By 1760, cattle droving was again underway on a regular basis from Augusta at the southern end of the Valley through Frederick County. This development demonstrated the particular initiative of William Crow, a merchant in Staunton, who was shipping steers to Carlisle and Philadelphia.[58] Cattle raising also emerged along the South Branch of the Potomac west of the Shenandoah Valley. This frontier area had been severely depopulated during the French and Indian War, but it had developed into a major supply center for cattle droves through the Shenandoah Valley by the early 1760s.[59]

Commercial hemp production was the result of more direct governmental intervention. Virginia governments began to encourage the cultivation of hemp during the 1720s as a means of inducing pioneer settlement on the Piedmont, but production was modest before the 1750s and planters viewed it as a partial supplement to tobacco cultivation. The frontier war and a decline in tobacco prices began to alter this situation during the late 1750s. Even before the inauguration of a new government bounty on hemp production in 1764, a few farmers in the backcountry had recognized the economic possibilities of the fiber plant. In the southern Shenandoah Valley the first hemp certificates were issued in 1759, but regular production was well established by 1762.[60] Augusta County remained the principal focus of hemp production in the backcountry for the remainder of the colonial period, with Frederick farmers showing much less interest in its commercial possibilities. It was the demand on labor by hemp cultivation and processing, rather than that of tobacco, that encouraged the first appearance of slaves in Augusta County.

Wheat, on the other hand, was a common feature of subsistence agriculture throughout the backcountry, and its emergence as the most important commercial crop west of the Blue Ridge was not yet evident in 1760. Indeed, during the pioneer phase in the Shenandoah Valley, wheat seems to have been no more important than corn or rye. While the number of mills in the Valley had increased from about eighty in 1750 to more than 140 by 1760, most millers were engaged in supplying local needs.[61] Wheat and flour prices had been on the increase in the colonies since the late 1740s, but not until the late 1760s did the wholesale price of wheat overcome the costs of transporting flour from the Valley. The French and Indian War had induced an increased demand for backcountry wheat, but that demand had abated by 1760. The first evidence of wheat exports appeared in the Alexandria ledgers of John Glassford and Company in 1765, and it was to that port that Valley farmers began to send regular shipments of flour.[62] The Shenandoah Valley, and particularly Frederick County, had become a major wheat-producing region by the outbreak of the Revolution.

IN EXAMINING GEORGE WASHINGTON's association with the Virginia backcountry, we can appreciate the opportunities that "growing up with the country" presented to enterprising men interested in land acquisition, commercial farming and trade, and public service on the frontier. If the maturing of Washington occurred between 1748 and 1758, then most of this growth came while Washington was operating in the backcountry.[63] When he first visited the northern Shenandoah Valley, it was a sparsely settled, isolated frontier zone that as yet lacked strong regional character and place differentiation. It was, indeed, for most Virginians "over the hills and far away." Life was simple, subsistent, dispersed, decentralized, and isolated from the rest of the colony. Yet there were signs of civility and growth, as Washington's experiences in the fledgling settlement of Winchester testify. It was, ironically, strategic upheaval in the backcountry and the outbreak of war during the mid-1750s that broke the isolation of the region and encouraged a reciprocal relationship between Washington and Frederick County. Washington and his soldiers gave an immediate boost to the county's economy and to the growth of Winchester in particular. In turn, the county's residents first elected him to political office and thus launched him on a career culminating in the presidency of the United States.

Washington never made the bold commitment that his initial benefactor, Lord Fairfax, did in settling permanently in this mountain environment. But his long association with the region as surveyor, landowner, soldier, lot owner, absentee planter, and politician was to be a formative influence on his career and on his western outlook for America's future. During his brief liaisons with the backcountry between 1748 and 1758, he was witness to the transformation of the region from an isolated frontier into the beginnings of one of Virginia's most productive regions. It was, however, a different region from his native Tidewater, one whose settlers were more ethnically varied and religiously pluralistic, whose settlements were more town-based, whose society was less aristocratic and more equal and independent, and whose economy was more diversified and ultimately more resilient than the tobacco-dependent world to the east. His participation in this transformation testified both to the opportunities that emerging backcountries could provide enterprising young men as residents and as sojourners and to the formative influences such experiences had on the first generation of American leaders. By the time Washington took up residence in Mount Vernon late in 1758 his former haunts in the Valley may still have been over the hills, but they were no longer quite so far away.

NOTES

1. Washington, March 14, 1748, *The Diaries of George Washington*, ed. Donald Jackson and Dorothy Twohig, 6 vols. (Charlottesville: University Press of Virginia, 1976–1979), 1:7.

2. Washington, March 16, 1748, *Washington Diaries*, 1:11.

3. Robert D. Mitchell, *Commercialism and Frontier: Perspectives on the Early Shenandoah Valley* (Charlottesville: University Press of Virginia, 1977), 15–55; Charles H. Ambler, *George Washington and the West* (Chapel Hill: University of North Carolina Press, 1936), 18–25.

4. Frederick Jackson Turner, *The Frontier in American History* (New York: Holt, Rinehart and Winston, 1920), 1–38, 89–94.

5. Charles H. Ambler, *Sectionalism in Virginia from 1776 to 1861* (Glendale, Calif.: Arthur H. Clark, 1910), 3–23.

6. Thomas Perkins Abernethy, *Three Virginia Frontiers* (Baton Rouge: Louisiana State University Press, 1940), 60. See also Abernethy, "The First Transmountain Advance," in *Humanistic Studies in Honor of John Calvin Metcalf*, University of Virginia Studies, vol. 1 (Charlottesville: University Press of Virginia, 1941), 120–38.

7. Carl Bridenbaugh, *Myths and Realities: Societies of the Colonial South* (Baton Rouge: Louisiana State University Press, 1952), 119–96.

8. Freeman H. Hart, *The Valley of Virginia in the American Revolution, 1763–1789* (Chapel Hill: University of North Carolina Press, 1942).

9. Mitchell, *Commercialism and Frontier;* Richard R. Beeman, *The Evolution of the Southern Backcountry: A Case Study of Lunenburg County, Virginia, 1746–1832* (Philadelphia: University of Pennsylvania Press, 1984). See also, Beeman, "The Political Response to Social Conflict in the Southern Backcountry: A Comparative View of Virginia and the Carolinas during the Revolution," in *An Uncivil War: The Southern Backcountry during the American Revolution,* ed. Ronald Hoffman, Thad W. Tate, and Peter J. Albert (Charlottesville: University Press of Virginia, 1985), 213–39.

10. D. W. Meinig, *The Shaping of America,* vol. 1, *Atlantic America, 1492–1800* (New Haven: Yale University Press, 1986), 158–60; Jack P. Greene, "Independence, Improvement, and Authority: Toward a Framework for Understanding the Histories of the Southern Backcountry during the Era of the American Revolution," in *An Uncivil War,* 3–36.

11. Bernard Bailyn, *Voyagers to the West: A Passage in the Peopling of America on the Eve of the Revolution* (New York: Alfred A. Knopf, 1986), 499–544.

12. David Hackett Fischer, *Albion's Seed: Four British Folkways in America* (New York: Oxford University Press, 1989), 605–782.

13. Terry G. Jordan and Matti Kaups, *The American Backwoods Frontier: An Ethnic and Ecological Interpretation* (Baltimore: Johns Hopkins University Press, 1989), especially 29–37.

14. Gregory H. Nobles, "Breaking into the Backcountry: New Approaches to the Early American Frontier," *William and Mary Quarterly,* 3d ser., 46 (October 1989): 641–70; Albert H. Tillson Jr., "The Southern Backcountry: A Survey of Current Research," *Virginia Magazine of History and Biography* 90 (July 1990): 387–422; Warren R. Hofstra, "The Virginia Backcountry in the Eighteenth Century: The Question of Origins and the Issue of Outcomes," *Virginia Magazine of History and Biography* 101 (October 1993): 485–508.

15. Robert D. Mitchell, "Introduction: Revisionism and Regionalism," in *Appalachian Frontiers: Settlement, Society, and Development in the Preindustrial Era,* ed. Robert D. Mitchell (Lexington: University Press of Kentucky, 1991), 1–22.

16. Mitchell, *Commercialism and Frontier,* 22–24.

17. Robert D. Mitchell, Edward F. Connor, and Warren R. Hofstra, "European Settlement and Land-Cover Change: The Shenandoah Valley of Virginia During the Eighteenth Century," National Geographic Society, *Final Report* No. 4381-90, (Washington, D.C., 1993).

18. George Washington, March 11 to April 13, 1748, *Washington Diaries,* 1:6–23; George Washington's Professional Surveys, July 22, 1749–October 25, 1752, *The Papers of George Washington,* Colonial Series, ed. W. W. Abbot et al.,

10 vols. (Charlottesville: University Press of Virginia, 1983–1995), 1:8–37; Mitchell, Connor, and Hofstra, "European Settlement and Land-Cover Change."

19. Mitchell, Connor, and Hofstra, "European Settlement and Land-Cover Change."

20. Mitchell, *Commercialism and Frontier*, 25–31; Warren R. Hofstra, "Land Policy and Settlement in the Northern Shenandoah Valley," in *Appalachian Frontiers*, 105–26.

21. Hofstra, "Land Policy and Settlement," 109–11.

22. Mitchell, Connor, and Hofstra, "European Settlement and Land–Cover Change." These figures are derived from the Frederick County land records contained in Northern Neck Surveys, 1722–1781, Library of Virginia, Richmond, Va. and the Frederick County Deed Books for 1743–1781 (hereafter cited as FDB), Frederick County Courthouse, Winchester, Va.

23. Mitchell, Connor, and Hofstra, "European Settlement and Land-Cover Change."

24. William W. Hening, ed., *The Statutes at Large: Being a Collection of All the Laws of Virginia . . .* , 13 vols. (Richmond: 1809–1823), 5:78–80.

25. Frederick County Order Book 1 (1743–1745), Frederick County Courthouse, Winchester, Va.; Warren R. Hofstra and Robert D. Mitchell; "Town and Country in Backcountry Virginia: Winchester and the Shenandoah Valley, 1730–1800," *Journal of Southern History* 59 (November 1993): 619–46.

26. Richard L. Morton, *Colonial Virginia*, 2 vols. (Chapel Hill: University of North Carolina Press, 1960), 2:533–34.

27. The Capitulation of Fort Necessity, July 3, 1754, *Washington Papers*, Col. Ser., 1:157–73.

28. George Washington, *The Diaries of George Washington, 1748–1799*, ed. John C. Fitzpatrick, 4 vols. (Boston: Houghton Mifflin, 1925), 1:110; Fitzpatrick, ed., *The Writings of George Washington from the Original Manuscript Sources, 1745–1799*, 39 vols. (Washington, D.C.: Government Printing Office, 1931–1944), 2:251.

29. See especially Stuart E. Brown Jr., *Virginia Baron: The Story of Thomas, 6th Lord Fairfax* (Berryville, Va.: Chesapeake Book Co., 1965), 45–50, 97–98.

30. Brown, *Virginia Baron*, 72–79, 166–67.

31. Warren R. Hofstra, *A Separate Place: The Formation of Clarke County, Virginia* (White Post, Va.: Clarke County Sesquicentennial Committee, 1986).

32. Mitchell, *Commercialism and Frontier*, 9–13; Mitchell, "Content and Context: Tidewater Characteristics in the Early Shenandoah Valley," *Maryland Historian* 5 (Summer 1974): 75–92.

33. Hofstra and Mitchell, "Town and Country."

34. Hofstra and Mitchell, "Town and Country"; Lorena S. Walsh, "Com-

munity Networks in the Early Chesapeake," in *Colonial Chesapeake Society*, ed. Lois Green Carr, Philip D. Morgan, and Jean B. Russo (Chapel Hill: University of North Carolina Press, 1988), 200–41.

35. Hofstra and Mitchell, "Town and Country."

36. Mitchell, *Commercialism and Frontier*, 31–36.

37. Mitchell, *Commercialism and Frontier*, 133–49; Warren R. Hofstra, "The Opequon Inventories: Frederick County, Virginia, 1749–1796," *Ulster Folklife* 35 (1989): 42–71.

38. William J. Hinke and Charles E. Kemper, eds., "Moravian Diaries of Travels through Virginia," *Virginia Magazine of History and Biography* 11 (October, January, April 1903–1904): 113–31, 225–42, 370–93; 12 (July, October, January 1904–1905): 55–82, 134–53, 271–84.

39. Carville V. Earle and Ronald Hoffman, "Staple Crops and Urban Development in the Eighteenth-Century South," *Perspectives in American History* 10 (1976): 7–78.

40. Account Book, 1744–1752, James Wood Papers, Library of Virginia, Richmond, Va.

41. Hening, *Statutes*, 6:268–70.

42. Augusta County Deed Books 2:460, 25:291–93, Augusta County Courthouse, Staunton, Va.

43. Hening, *Statutes*, Supplement (1700–1750), 431–32; Mitchell, *Commercialism and Frontier*, 155–56.

44. Turk McCleskey, "Rich Land, Poor Prospects: Real Estate and the Formation of a Social Elite in Augusta County, Virginia, 1738–1770," *Virginia Magazine of History and Biography* 98 (July 1990): 449–86; Albert H. Tillson Jr., "The Militia and Popular Political Culture in the Upper Valley of Virginia, 1740–1775," *Virginia Magazine of History and Biography* 94 (July 1986): 285–306; Tillson, *Gentry and Common Folk: Political Culture on a Virginia Frontier, 1740–1789* (Lexington: University Press of Kentucky, 1991).

45. Robert Dinwiddie to George Washington, September 11, 1754, *Washington Papers*, Col. Ser., 1:206–7; Washington to John Robinson, November 9, 1756, *Washington Papers*, Col. Ser., 2:11–18.

46. Andrew Burnaby, *Travels through the Middle Settlements in North America in the Years 1759 and 1760*, 3d ed. (London: T. Payne, 1798), 73–74.

47. Washington to Dinwiddie, August 4, 1756, *Washington Papers*, Col. Ser., 3:318; Dinwiddie to Washington, August 19, 1756, *Washington Papers*, Col. Ser., 3:397.

48. The activities of Bruin and the Bush brothers have been reconstructed from FDBs 5–16.

49. Owen Jones Letterbook, 1759–1781, Owen Jones Papers, Historical Society of Pennsylvania, Philadelphia, Pa. See also Mitchell, *Commercialism and Frontier*, 157–60; Thomas M. Doerflinger, A *Vigorous Spirit of Enterprise:*

Merchants and Economic Development in Revolutionary Philadelphia (Chapel Hill: University of North Carolina Press, 1986), 96–97, 169, 215–16.

50. Mitchell, *Commercialism and Frontier*, 156–57.

51. Mitchell, *Commercialism and Frontier*, 93–97; Chester R. Young, "The Effects of the French and Indian War on Civilian Life in the Frontier Counties of Virginia, 1754–1763" (Ph.D. diss., Vanderbilt University, 1969).

52. FDBs 4–6.

53. FDB 6:76–85.

54. Hofstra and Mitchell, "Town and Country"; James E. Vance Jr., *The Merchant's World: The Geography of Wholesaling* (Englewood Cliffs, N.J.: Prentice-Hall, 1970), 68–79.

55. Hofstra and Mitchell, "Town and Country"; Doerflinger, V*igorous Spirit of Enterprise*, 112–14.

56. Dumfries Ledger, 1758–1759, John Glassford and Company Papers, Manuscript Division, Library of Congress, Washington, D.C.

57. Mitchell, *Commercialism and Frontier*, 100.

58. Mitchell, *Commercialism and Frontier*, 148–49.

59. Richard K. MacMaster, "The Cattle Trade in Western Virginia, 1760–1830," in *Appalachian Frontiers*, 130–34.

60. Mitchell, *Commercialism and Frontier*, 162–65.

61. Mitchell, *Commercialism and Frontier*, 144–46, 172–73.

62. Alexandria Ledger, 1765–1766, John Glassford and Company Papers; Thomas M. Preisser, "Alexandria and the Evolution of the Northern Virginia Economy, 1749–1776," *Virginia Magazine of History and Biography* 89 (July 1981): 282–93.

63. Thomas A. Lewis, *For King and Country: The Maturing of George Washington, 1748–1760* (New York: Harper Collins, 1993).

"A Parcel of Barbarian's and an Uncooth Set of People": Settlers and Settlements of the Shenandoah Valley

WARREN R. HOFSTRA

𝓘N 1748 AT THE YOUNG AGE OF SIX-teen George Washington crossed the Blue Ridge for the first time. Considering the distaste he expressed for the people he encountered and the hard life he was forced to share with them, he might have recrossed the ridge never to return. But during the next ten years he came back time and time again, first as a surveyor in Thomas, Lord Fairfax's, Northern Neck Proprietary and then as commander of Virginia forces during the Seven Years' War. For Washington the West meant promise and opportunity. To the young man the region beckoned wealth in abundant land and a chance to earn honor and reputation due to its strategic importance in the conflict with the French and the Indians. For the elder statesman the West became a key to national unity.

The people of the West, however, remained a problem. The settlers and their way of life represented a constant threat to the aspirations for wealth and recognition of the ambitious surveyor, landowner, and military commander. Washington, in short, saw his hopes imperiled by the very people who made them possible. His frustrations provide the key to explaining the character of the settlers of the Virginia backcountry and the nature of the settlements they created.

𝓦ASHINGTON'S FIRST ENCOUNTER with the Virginia backcountry came when Fairfax gave him the opportunity to accompany surveyor James Genn on an expedition to proprietary lands along the Shenandoah River and the Potomac's western branches. In his journal Washington complained continuously. If rain did not confine the party to tents, then wind or smoke drove them from the tents into the weather. Insects were a constant nuisance. The party suffered over "the Worst Road that ever was trod by Man or Beast." The inhabitants were puzzling and annoying. A local justice of the peace served them dinner with "neither a Cloth upon the Table nor a Knife to eat with." German settlers seemed "as Ignorant a Set of People as the Indians." The rest were simply "a parcel of Barbarian's and an uncooth set of People."[1]

Washington was, however, exuberant about the land. The young man passed the "best part" of his first full day in the Shenandoah Valley relishing the "most beautiful Groves of Sugar Trees" and admiring the "richness of the Land." Along the Shenandoah River he found "the Land exceeding Rich & Fertile all the way produc[ing an] abundance of Grain Hemp Tobacco &c." Even while Indians ravaged the region during the war, Washington could describe it as a "very valuable valley," a "fertile and populous valley," or the "finest part of Virginia."[2]

After his first trip to the backcountry, Washington returned as a surveyor five times in four years. He did well. With "a good Reward and Dubbleloon [as a] constant gain every Day that the Weather will permit . . . going out," he indulged his ambitions for land. By 1752 he owned three tracts near the Shenandoah River totaling more than fifteen hundred acres.[3]

Although he retired from surveying in 1752, Washington returned again to the backcountry, this time for preferment and reputation. Between 1753 and 1758 he served the colony of Virginia in a variety of diplomatic and military posts for which he was not only headquartered in Winchester but also responsible for the security of the entire Virginia frontier from the Potomac River to the North Carolina border. On the very day Virginia Governor Robert Dinwiddie commissioned him colonel of the Virginia Regiment, Washington described his appointment to Warner Lewis as the "chief part of my happiness, i.e. the esteem and notice the Country has been pleasd to honour me with." There were perils, however, that Washington recognized well. "I believe our Circumstances are brought to that unhappy Dilemma that no Man can gain any Honour by conductg our Forces at this time; but will rather loose in his reputation if he attempts it," he explained to Lewis. That dilemma had to do directly with the people of the backcountry. Washington knew that the disastrous defeat of Edward

Braddock's expedition to Fort Duquesne in July 1755 had profoundly disillusioned these people and created an "infallible mean's of preventg all from assistg that are not compelled." But without the crucial provisions and services these people could provide, Washington envisioned "insurmountable obstacles" that would cast him "in the light of an idle indolent body, have his conduct criticized, and meet perhaps with approbious abuse."[4]

Washington complained bitterly to Dinwiddie and other officials about the many ways the backcountry people subverted his authority and undermined the discipline of his troops. First, frontiersmen displayed little of that deference traditionally accorded a man of Washington's position—little of the respect for command Washington needed to inspire his troops. Within two months of his appointment and shortly after arriving in Winchester during an Indian attack in October 1755, Washington reported to Dinwiddie that

> in all things I meet with the greatest opposition no orders are obey'd but what a Party of Soldier's or my own drawn Sword Enforces; without this a single horse for the most urgent occasion cannot be had, to such a pitch has the insolence of these People arrivd by having every point hitherto submitted to them; however, I have given up none where his Majestys Service requires the Contrary, and where my proceedings are justified by my Instruction's, nor will I, unless they execute what they threaten i,e, "to blow out my brains."[5]

Composed of citizen-soldiers from local communities, the county militia represented a second serious problem for Washington. On April 14, 1756, a council of war convened in Winchester "to take such steps as shall be thought most expedient on the present Critical Conjuncture." The backcountry lay in the grips of another series of devastating Indian raids. Although the militia captains had been ordered "to get what vollenturs they could encourage to go in search of the Indian Enimy who are dayly ravaging our Frontiers and committing their accustomed cruelties," only fifteen men had reported. Washington had already observed that "you may, with almost equal success, attempt to raize the Dead to Life again, as the force of this County," but on this occasion he complained to John Robinson, Speaker of the House of Burgesses, that "the timidity of the Inhabitants of this County is to be equalled by nothing but their perverseness." To Dinwiddie he forsook the distant prospects, if any, that I can see, of gaining Honor and Reputation in the Service. [They] are motives which cause me to lament the hour that gave me a Commission: and would induce me at any other time than *this*, of imminent danger; to resign without one hesitating moment, a command, which I never expect to reap either Honor or Benefit from.[6]

The people in their hurried evacuation of the backcountry presented Washington with the third and perhaps most graphic illustration of his inability to secure the colony's frontiers and, at the same time, his own military reputation. In Winchester during the emergency of October 1755, Washington "found every thing in the greatest hurry and confusion by the back Inhabitants flocking in, and those of the Town removing out." Nothing could alleviate the "panick [that] prevails among the People." "I have done every Thing in my Power, to quiet the Minds of the Inhabitants, by detaching all the Men that I have any Command over, to the Places, which are most exposed," Washington explained to Dinwiddie the next spring, "yet nothing I fear will prevent them, from abandoning their Dwellings, and flying with the utmost Precipitation." Faced with the embarrassment of having no one to protect, Washington in a communication to British commander in chief John Campbell, earl of Loudoun, later admitted the "impossibility of continueing in this Service without loss of Honour."[7]

In other ways the back inhabitants acted even more directly to destroy the discipline and effectiveness of the Virginia Regiment. They refused to provision it, for instance. On his first military expedition to the Ohio, Washington blamed the slowness of his march on the people:

Hitherto the difficulty I have met with in Marching has been greater than I expect to encounter on Ohio where probably I may be surround'd by the Enemy; and this occasion'd by those who had they acted as becometh every good Subject, would have exerted their Utmost abilitys to forward our just designs Out of Twenty four Waggons that were impress'd at Winchester, we got but Ten after waiting a week, and some of those so illy provided with Teams that we could not travel with them without the Soldiers assisting them up the Hills. when it was known they had better Teams at home.

While his commissary officers struggled in 1756 to lay up supplies for the coming winter, Washington found that the people were selling cattle to Pennsylvania butchers. Dinwiddie advised that he "threaten them in a Military Manner," but Washington responded that even "military threats will not deter the pennsylvania Butchers from driving away the cattle."[8]

Desertion in the Virginia Regiment was a great problem. In one instance during the summer of 1757, twenty of ninety new recruits disappeared en route to Winchester. A brief taste of camp life then convinced a quarter of the remaining force to desert. The evening after receiving their first pay, twenty-four more men vanished. Washington blamed the county militia. "The spirit of Desertion was so remarkable in the Militia," he observed, "that it had a surprising effect upon the Regiment, and encouraged many of the Soldiers to desert."[9]

The refusal of Winchester tavern keepers to obey his orders against serving liquor to soldiers also bedeviled Washington. To the tavern keepers, however, the business with soldiers was a boon. Washington admitted that the town abounded with taverns. Between 1754 and 1763 the county court dispensed an average of fourteen ordinary licenses a year.[10] As early as October 1755 Washington issued orders for confining all soldiers found in taverns after the evening call to quarters. Meeting with little cooperation by the next summer, Washington threatened to prosecute recalcitrant tavern keepers and did haul some before the county court. Finding no support from the bench, Washington then secured another commission of the peace from Dinwiddie and commented in September 1756 that he hoped this might "have the intended effect: The number of Tippling Houses kept here, is a great grievance." The new court appeared cooperative at first, issuing only eight licenses that year. The next year, however, the number jumped to ten, and in 1758 it peaked at nineteen.[11]

Washington was soon calling on Dinwiddie for another new commission. His difficulties in the fall of 1757 were, however, more serious and could have destroyed his command. A court of inquiry held in September revealed not only the crime of embezzlement by the quartermaster but also large amounts of suspicious credit held by soldiers in Winchester ordinaries. Washington's men were apparently selling military supplies to the townspeople in return for drink. Search warrants eventually revealed a long list of contraband in thirteen homes, but the constable and practically every other authority in town had refused to cooperate with the search. A local merchant had to be specially deputized to serve the warrants. Moreover, the county court dismissed the accused in a procedure Washington described as not only "absurd and irregular, but expressly illegal."[12]

Washington was dumbfounded. He summed up his frustrations with the people, his command, and his career in a long letter to Dinwiddie:

> Were it not too tedious, I cou'd give your Honor such instances of the villainous Behaviour of those Tipling-house-keeper's, as wou'd astonish any person: but the little I have already said, will suffice to convince your Honor, that it is impossible to maintain that discipline and do that Service with a Garrison thus corrupted by a sett of people, whose conduct looks like the effect of a combination to obstruct the Service, and frustrate the methods pointed out for their own preservation: and when some of those [ ] practices were at length proved, the Laws made for the punishment of such gross offences, trifled with by the Magistrates, in the manner the above fact, and the enclosed will render conspicuous: I could [not] believe did I not see it, that these are the people of a country whose bowels are at this juncture torn by the most horrid devastations of the most cruel and barbarous enemy.[13]

Washington's anguish, however, does not mean that the behavior of the people of the Shenandoah Valley can be simply dismissed as villainy, treachery, or perversity. Many of their actions—and Washington's problems—can be explained by the nature of their settlements and the conditions under which these settlements took shape.

$\mathcal{M}$UCH OF THE DIFFICULTY WASHington experienced in defending the Virginia frontier stemmed from its vulnerability. By the 1750s Virginia settlement thrust across the Potomac watershed and deep into the Alleghenies toward the Ohio Valley. No area of English settlement in North America was as indefensible. "We are more contiguous to the French and their Indian Allies," Washington warned Loudoun in 1757, "and more expos'd to their frequent Incursions than any of the Neighbouring Colony's." The forces producing this dangerous situation, however, were beyond Washington's control and had begun to shape the history of the backcountry long before his appearance in the region.[14]

By 1730 the settlement of Virginia had been proceeding for more than a century. Fueled by speculative interests in land and an expansive, exhaustive tobacco economy, the populated area of the colony had pushed out from a core along the James and York rivers north to the Northern Neck and south to the edge of the Southside. But the Piedmont was still wilderness.

Between 1728 and 1732, however, Virginia Governor William Gooch and his Council issued ten land orders for more than 360,000 acres west of the Blue Ridge in the Shenandoah Valley. The move was not speculative: the land was to be settled—and fast. Each order gave its recipient only two years to fix one family on the land for every one thousand acres under order. Since most of the recipients were from Pennsylvania or New Jersey, these requirements touched off a migration to Virginia from the North, where rapid population growth, economic expansion, and the closing of the Pennsylvania land office had rendered land scarce and expensive. For a while in the eighteenth century, therefore, Virginia had two, distinct frontiers: one pushing west from the Tidewater and the other extending southwest from Maryland and Pennsylvania.[15]

Gooch had good reasons for acting precipitously. The first was strategic. Since a 1701 act by the House of Burgesses "for the better strengthening the frontiers," land policy in Virginia had been propelled by the need for a western buffer against encroachments by the French and the Indians. Governor Alexander Spotswood's much-celebrated Knights of the Golden Horseshoe expedition to the Shenandoah River in 1716, legislation passed in 1720 organizing the western frontier into Spotsylvania and Brunswick counties, and the 1722 Treaty of Albany dividing Indian territory from a European zone of settlement at the Blue Ridge, all reflected this imperative. The preamble to the county act had unequivocally warned that "the frontiers towards the high mountains are exposed to danger from the Indians, and the late settlements of the French." This was why Gooch was eager to rush people into the Shenandoah Valley under the impetus of large land orders and family settlement requirements.[16]

He had a second reason, however. All Northern Neck land west of the Blue Ridge was in dispute. Reading a long and confusing series of royal charters to their own advantage, the Virginia Council, the colony of Maryland, and Lord Fairfax each laid claim to the region. At the same time Gooch had acted, Robert Carter, Lord Fairfax's agent, granted nearly sixty thousand acres along the Shenandoah River to members of his own family in the name of the proprietary. Clearly Gooch hoped that patents issued to settlers under his Council's orders would affirm Virginia's claim to the disputed territory. He was wrong in one sense. In 1745 the Privy Council awarded Fairfax the entire region bounded by the Blue Ridge, the Potomac River, and the line connecting the headsprings of the Potomac and Rappahannock.[17]

In another sense Gooch was correct. His land policy effectively settled the area. The formation of Frederick and Augusta counties in 1738 represented one measure of the speed with which the region west of the Blue Ridge developed. Six of the eight counties that by the Revolution reached east from the Blue Ridge would not be created for another twenty years. In 1754, when the white tithable populations of Frederick and Augusta numbered 2,173 and 2,616 respectively, no Piedmont county exceeded 1,700 white tithables. Maryland and Pennsylvania would not establish western counties until the late 1740s and 1750s. The scene of Washington's operations during the Seven Years' War was therefore an island of settlement surrounded on all sides by a sparsely populated wilderness. No wonder he would attribute the "ruinous state of the frontiers, and the vast extent of land we have lost [as] . . . in great measure owing to maryland & Pennsylvania giving ground so much faster than we do: whereby we are left exposed in a very fine tract of land as low as monocasy, on the maryland side." Perhaps Gooch had succeeded all too well in his attempts to erect a buffer zone in western Virginia.[18]

In another crucial way Gooch's land policies had left the backcountry vulnerable. Its people were dangerously dispersed. They had taken up land in enclosed, often detached, family farms without establishing centralized locations for defense or trade. This tendency toward dispersal was already evident in Pennsylvania, where William Penn's plans for settlement in townships with town centers had been openly ignored. Nor were there any immediate, practical reasons to cluster settlement in the Virginia backcountry. Iroquois expansion in the seventeenth century and tribal policies of depopulating fringe areas to improve hunting and trapping had left few Indians in the Shenandoah Valley to alarm settlers and encourage settlement around fortified locations. The isolation of the region denied any immediate possibility for trade and obviated the need for commercial centers. All of these diffusing forces, however, could have been overcome by a land policy mandating clustered settlement, but Virginia land policy was notably silent on this score.[19]

Moreover, the procedures followed in taking up land under the Virginia Council's orders encouraged dispersal. The territories where orders empowered recipients to locate settlers were intentionally large and vague. In the area surrounding Winchester, the center of Washington's operations, two sets of orders, one to Alexander Ross and Morgan Bryan for up to a hundred thousand acres dated October 28, 1730, and the other to Jost Hite and his partners for another hundred thousand on October 21, 1731, were instrumental in fixing people on the land. Ross and Bryan's patents could come from anywhere in the huge area defined by North Mountain and the Opequon Creek from the Potomac to the Opequon's headwaters thirty-five miles south. Hite's were bounded only by the "Several Branches of the Sherundo River." Left to their own inclinations settlers, as Dinwiddie put it, "scattered for the Benefit of the best Lands." Statements in land suit depositions made it clear that neither Hite nor Ross attempted to interfere with this process by imposing any prior structure on their settlements. In 1754 one settler, Jonathan Langdon, testified that he had been "encouraged to come from Pennsylvania hearing of the cheapness of land in this colony—Searching for land found some he liked—Before he settled it, hearing of the orders to Hite and mackay, went to Mr Hite & told him of the affair."[20]

Defending these scattered settlements of independent, dispersed family farms created real problems for Washington. There was little he could do to protect an isolated farmstead from Indians who, as he said, "prowl about like Wolves; and like them, do their mischief by Stealth." The remedy Washington unsuccessfully proposed to Dinwiddie in April 1756 required just the kind of clustered settlement and cooperative farming the settlers had forsaken:

> I do not think it unworthy the notice of the Legislature to compel the Inhabitants (if a General War is likely to ensue, and things to continue in this unhappy situation for any time) to live in Townships, working at each others Farms by turn.[21]

A final consequence of the land policies that shaped Shenandoah Valley settlement and magnified Washington's troubles developed from the migration from Pennsylvania these policies encouraged. Philadelphia was fast becoming America's largest city and the port of entry for a rapidly growing immigration of non-English peoples. As large numbers of Scotch-Irish, Germans, and second-generation Pennsylvanians of varied backgrounds pushed south and west in search of land and opportunity, they created a pluralistic society in the Virginia backcountry in which settlers of English heritage were outnumbered two to one. Thus most of the people of the backcountry had only limited experience with Virginia institutions of society and government. Small farm, general agriculture based on grains, livestock, and free labor further distanced the backcountry from the lowcountry. The weakness of established institutions in the backcountry only magnified its vulnerability by decreasing the possibility of its people acting together in the common defense. Thirty years after the Seven Years' War one visitor to Winchester still found the inhabitants "much divided; made up, as they are, of different nations, and speaking different languages, they agree in scarcely anything."[22]

Thus the origins of many of the difficulties Washington experienced in defending the Virginia backcountry lay in the land policies of the Gooch administration. These policies were designed to protect colonial land claims and populate a frontier buffer zone. But maintaining the buffer proved nearly impossible in the face of attack. Extending deep into the Alleghenies it lay dangerously exposed to French and Indian strongholds. Dispersed settlement by culturally diverse peoples unaccustomed to Virginia's traditions of governance made the problems of organizing for the common defense immense. The backcountry was not without order, however. But the order backcountry peoples established in their own settlements both amplified Washington's problems and helps explain the very origins of those problems. A detailed examination of settlement communities, then, is necessary for a full understanding of why Washington so often found himself bitterly at odds with people he was sworn to protect.

THE OPEQUON SETTLEMENT TOOK shape throughout a broad area surrounding the homestead of German settler, Jost Hite. Hite and a band of at least sixteen families arrived in the Shenandoah Valley in the spring of 1732. Hite fixed himself at the strategic location where the Valley Indian trail—soon to become the Philadelphia wagon road—crossed the Opequon Creek ten miles south of the future site of Winchester. There he built what was called Hite's fort. Everyone else, however, scattered in a way that would have left the fort of little use in an emergency. Only one of Hite's six sons and daughters settled adjacent to the fort. Others could soon be found as far south as Cedar Creek, west as far as the South Branch of the Potomac, and north almost to the lower edge of the Shenandoah Valley. Other families, including many Scotch-Irish, dispersed as well in a search for good land that superseded needs for security.[23]

A prosopographical study of the families that took up sixty-four tracks of land covering thirty-five square miles in a region surrounding Hite's settlement and extending west from the Opequon to Little North Mountain reveals a great deal about the organization of backcountry communities. Seven patents or deeds for these tracts were issued in the 1730s, ten in the 1740s, thirty-four in the 1750s, and the remainder by the Revolution. The average tract covered 351 acres; the mean, 341. Twenty-five belonged to Scotch-Irish families, thirteen to Germans, and twenty-six to English, Virginia, or other settlers of undetermined origin. Opequon, then, was a small farm settlement of ethnically varied peoples.[24]

The settlement pattern these people generated in taking up the land revealed no evidence of residential clustering. No agricultural villages emerged. Farmsteads, located equal distances of about one-half mile apart, were sited on each tract independently according to local topography and access to fields or water, not according to collective social needs. Nor did ethnic groups congregate. As one of his first official acts in Virginia, Jost Hite patented a tract of 5,018 acres of prime limestone land encompassing the entire Opequon watershed to the west of his homestead. Between 1736 and 1750 he sold this land in fourteen lots. Here a very influential German could have structured the ethnic pattern of settlement. But seven tracts went to Scotch-Irish settlers, six to German, and one to an English family. Every purchaser shared a boundary with a family of a different ethnic group. Moreover, Hite's activities generated no central places for trade or commerce. Shortly after settling, Hite was operating a mill, an ordinary, and perhaps a store. But a town did not emerge around these functions, and the only person ever to build another house nearby was his own son. The pattern of settlement that emerged at Opequon, then, was one of dispersed family farms lacking ethnically distinct neighborhoods and demonstrating no centralizing tendencies for social, commercial, or defensive purposes.[25]

Dispersal, however, did not mean isolation—social, economic, or otherwise. Across the pattern of scattered farms and diffused ethnic groups a net of social relations bound individuals and families together. A detailed examination of the Scotch-Irish who took up the twenty-five tracts of land at Opequon reveals how these networks functioned as communities. Nineteen individuals representing eleven families acquired these tracts. All were immigrants from the north of Ireland; many had arrived with Hite. Like Hite's family they dispersed, taking up noncontiguous tracts in the search for good land. Twenty-two tracts bordered the Opequon; seventeen were on limestone land. But most significant, all these men and women were related; they composed a single kin group. Nonetheless, nearly everyone had a German neighbor.[26]

A crucial nexus between land and family acted as the primary bond of community for this Scotch-Irish kin group. Nineteen of twenty-five second-generation marriages in which surnames of both partners could be determined were made within the kin group or with other allied families. Only one marriage occurred with a German, and that ended in separation. Eighteen of the initial nineteen landowners passed 95 percent of their total acreage to sons, sons-in-law, or close connections within the community. Much of this land was conveyed by will only at the death of the parent, thus prolonging the economic dependence of the rising generation and employing patrimony as a means of perpetuating family lineage.[27]

Religious and educational institutions helped bind the community. Spiritual life centered about a Presbyterian meeting house constructed by Opequon settler William Hoge on his own land in the early 1730s. By 1735 the Donegal Presbytery of Pennsylvania was providing ministers on supply. Although early church records have been lost, a 1745 deed from Hoge to sixteen church leaders links thirteen directly to the Opequon community through ties of family or land ownership. One of the signers of this deed and an initial landowner at Opequon, John Wilson, kept a school for the community.[28]

Dispersal and ethnic intermixing, then, presented no insurmountable barrier to establishing and maintaining the social ties and institutions measurable as the warp and weft of community. Family, land, ethnicity, congregation, and school bound the Scotch-Irish at Opequon together in spite of the distances and separations characterizing the overall settlement pattern.

Not only were the social forms of community life decentralized, but economic activity was as well. A sample of probate inventories of Scotch-Irish settlers at Opequon helps reveal the nature of production and exchange there. All of the twelve sample estates, appraised between 1749 and 1768, belonged to members of the kin group and nine to leaders in the Opequon church. The picture of small farm agriculture these inventories portray is one of great diversity, emphasizing livestock, grains, and domestic industry. Notably lacking were references to tobacco and slaves.[29]

Farm animals appeared in every inventory; a full complement of cattle, horses, swine, and sheep were found in eight. The average estate contained ten cattle, ten sheep, nine swine, and five horses. Much of the beef and pork produced was probably consumed in subsistence, but a herd of ten cattle would have yielded at least one animal for sale a year in addition to small surpluses of butter and cheese.[30]

The presence of saddles in seven of twelve inventories suggests that horses provided transport for persons and small quantities of goods. Wheeled transport was rare, only one cart and one wagon appearing. That most farmers, however, could readily assemble a plow team of two or four horses testifies to the importance of grains in the agricultural economy at Opequon. Plowing and harrowing equipment was found in nine inventories, and sickles or scythes in eight. Wheat was the most common crop, but rye, barley, oats, and corn also appeared.

Sheep were found in large numbers at Opequon, more for the sake of wool than mutton. Nearly every Opequon family engaged in some phase of woolen or linen production. Ten of the sample twelve had spinning wheels, and three had looms. The inventories also yield evidence of other forms of domestic industry, including woodworking, coopering, shoemaking, brewing, distilling, and milling.

Available at the "dispersed general store" at Opequon would then have been a wide variety of products from field and workshop. Meat products included pork and beef; diary products, cheese, butter, and milk. Hides for shoes and harness could be had. Wheat, rye, and corn flours were available for bread. So were flour barrels for storage. Corn would also have been wanted for feed, rye for whiskey, and barley for beer. Wool and broken flax were obtainable for spinning; woolen or linen yarn, for weaving.[31]

That these goods and services were exchanged throughout the Opequon economy is further evidenced by the inventories. Steelyards and scales for weighing commodities prior to barter or sale were found in one-third of the inventories. Four estates had debts due. One physician, Robert White, was owed more than £130 in bonded debt when he died in 1755. Debts recorded in account books were indicative of ongoing exchange within the farming community. When James Vance died in 1751, he had debts of more than £12 on his books. The diversity of activities indicated in his inventory suggests that neighbors may have turned to him for a variety of goods including beef (he had the largest herd of cattle in the Opequon sample), pork (he had twelve pigs), or wool (thirteen sheep). His plowing and harrowing equipment, scythes and sickles, or barley, oats, wheat, rye, hay, corn, flax, hemp, and two spinning wheels imply numerous ways to trade goods and services.

Two significant features of this highly diversified economy should be emphasized. First, all exchange occurred without central places and organized markets, at least for the first twenty years of the Opequon settlement. Second, the exchange of goods and services permeated the ethnic barriers that defined social communities at Opequon. The career of German blacksmith Stephen Hotsinpiller probably best demonstrated the solvent properties of commerce. After immigrating from Germany and marrying the daughter of a Germanna, Virginia, settler, Hotsinpiller purchased land from Hite in his 5,018-acre tract and took up residence at Opequon. Inventory accounts clearly indicate that while several of the Scotch-Irish owed Hotsinpiller, probably for blacksmithing, Hotsinpiller owed his own neighbor, a Scotch-Irish distiller, £10.[32]

The process of community formation at Opequon was repeated throughout the Virginia backcountry. Initially, areas of select land, concentrated settlement, and dense community networks would have been separated by regions of sparse population and attenuated social ties. As intervening land was taken up, communities would resemble sets of overlapping circles. In the Shenandoah Valley this process was probably not complete until the Revolution. During George Washington's years in the region, communities would have possessed distinct geographical and social identities.

While one community was forming at Opequon, another was taking shape ten miles to the north around the settlement of Alexander

Ross. Ross was a Quaker who left Ireland as an indentured servant in the 1690s for Chester County, Pennsylvania, where he achieved a position of modest wealth and considerable prominence in Quaker affairs. When he and Morgan Bryan petitioned William Gooch for Virginia land rights in October 1730, they promised that "they & divers other Families of the Sd Province [Pennsylvania] amounting to one hundred are desirous to remove from thence & Settle them Selves" in Virginia. Ross soon patented a 2,373-acre tract for himself and located seventy families in the lower Shenandoah Valley. By 1734 Quakers were meeting regularly on his land.[33]

Dispersal was as much the rule at Hopewell as it was at Opequon in spite of centralizing tendencies in Ross's religious activities. Tracts patented under Ross's orders were located as far south as Opequon and north a day's journey to the Potomac. Numerous small meetings sprung up under the auspices of Hopewell, beginning in 1738 with the Tuscarora Meeting twenty miles to the north and Smith's Creek Meeting sixty miles south. The loss of the Hopewell Meeting records before 1759 prohibits the detailed study of Quaker community life, but the Friend's proscription of marriage outside the meeting would have maintained the same unity of kinship and congregation that developed at Opequon.[34]

During the 1740s scattered communities emerged to the west of Hopewell and Opequon along the broad bottom lands of Patterson Creek and the Potomac's South Branch. While surveying manor lands along these waters for Lord Fairfax in 1747, James Genn found numerous squatters where previous surveyors had found no one eleven years earlier. In 1754 this area was organized as Hampshire County with an initial count of 570 tithables. Settlements there displayed the same ethnic diversity, small farm economy, and community ties as Hopewell and Opequon. One such settlement developed about the activities of the Van Meter family of Salem County, New Jersey. The Van Meters had been connected with the Virginia backcountry since the 1720s when John Van Meter, an itinerant Dutch trader, first viewed the South Branch and his sons acquired an order for land in the Shenandoah Valley. One son, Isaac, eventually secured title to a tract on the South Branch, where his sons, Henry, Garret, and Jacob, their families, and other relatives including Abraham, son of Jost Hite, had settled by the mid-1740s. Moravians traveling along the valley in the 1750s encountered enough of these kinsmen to distinguish a discrete "district where Hollanders have settled." Other communities developed about the Scotch-Irish families of such men as William Cunningham and his sons, John, William, and Robert. From all this activity historian Richard K. MacMaster concludes that

> the picture that begins to emerge is one of former neighbors, cousins and in-laws, moving together and recreating in the South Branch country the ties of family and friendship that they had known in New Jersey. . . . Settlers of English, Scotch-Irish, Dutch, German, Welsh, or any other background necessarily had neighbors who came from different origins.[35]

In addition to the network of dispersed, rural communities, towns represented the only other settlement form in the Virginia backcountry by the 1750s. In Washington's experience Winchester, located halfway between Opequon and Hopewell, represented the most significant urban place. James Wood, surveyor for Frederick County and first clerk of the county court, founded Winchester in 1744 when he laid off twenty-six lots on a portion of his own land traversed by the Philadelphia wagon road. The town, whose site travelers described as "low & disagreeable," grew slowly at first. By 1748 it boasted at least one ordinary where George Washington was treated to "Lodgings . . . a good Dinner . . . Wine & Rum Punch in Plenty & a good Feather Bed with clean Sheets." But five years later Moravians could still find only "sixty houses rather badly built."[36]

During the next seven years, however, Winchester grew rapidly. By 1760 traveler Andrew Burnaby could record two hundred houses and perhaps a thousand people in the town. The demand for goods and services by the Virginia Regiment generated much of this growth. Designation as the seat of Frederick County in 1752 and the accompanying economic leaven of court days also contributed, as did trade with two thousand or more migrants a year traveling the wagon road to the upper Shenandoah Valley and the Carolinas.[37]

Significant in this pattern of growth, however, was the absence of traditional central-place functions such as retail markets for rural surpluses.[38] By the 1750s the dispersed economies of communities surrounding Winchester operated through the decentralized exchanges of independent producers and consumers, with little merchant specialization. Dependent on trade with soldiers, travelers, and the local populace primarily on court days, Winchester was poorly integrated into the surrounding rural economy. Only seven of sixty-nine court orders for new roads between 1743 and 1753 mentioned the town. Even by the 1780s the town still figured in only 5 percent of the road orders. Moreover, the townspeople created a community very different from Opequon or Hopewell. Only two of fifty-three lot owners in 1753 shared the same last name. Religious life was not organized on a congregational basis in the town until the 1760s. Winchester was a center for specialized commercial activities and not a self-sustaining, well-integrated kinship community.[39]

$\mathcal{W}$HAT IN THE CHARACTER OF THE settlements and settlement pattern of the Virginia backcountry helps explain the difficulties George Washington faced in mobilizing a people for their common defense and in maintaining discipline among his troops? Many of George Washington's misunderstandings with the people of the backcountry developed from his own tendency to view their recalcitrance as selfish individualism—as private interest placed before public service. He often appeared ignorant of or insensitive to the power of local attachments. In September 1756 he warned an officer at an isolated fort to "guard against the selfish views & discontents of the Augusta people; who prefer private to publick interest, by all accounts." But Washington failed to realize that most people in rural, backcountry neighborhoods had no reason to conceive a public interest beyond family and community. During the emergency of October 1755, when he and local officials tried in vain to raise the Frederick militia, it took Thomas Bryan Martin, Lord Fairfax's nephew and secretary, to explain to him why not more than twenty-five men had mustered, "they having absolutely refus'd to stir, choosing as they say to die with their Wives and Family's."[40]

Ordered "to repair with his Company forthwith to Winchester," a local militia captain put the argument more forcibly when he reminded a scornful Washington "that his Wife, Family, and Corn was at stake, so were those of his Soldrs therefore it was not possible for him to come." No conflict between private interests and public service troubled this man—his obligation, both public and private, was to the defense of home and community. That principal obligation also explains the widespread reluctance to supply the Virginia Regiment when sacrificing provisions endangered family subsistence and security. This was not perversity—this was a matter of priorities.[41]

Nor was this "timidity," the term Washington so often used for cowardice. Backcountry peoples customarily defended their own communities with vigor, organized aggressive military operations against the Indians, and effectively relieved the suffering of those attacked. The fortified houses to which the people of local communities repaired in time of emergency apparently made Washington's work more difficult. During the crisis of April 1756, Washington warned John Robinson that "should this panic and fear continue, not a soul will be left on this side the Ridge: and what now remain, are collected in small Forts (out of which there is no prevailing on them to stir)." These were not the forts built and manned by the Virginia Regiment but simple stone houses that "had small stockade forts about them; and whenever an alarm took place, the neighboring people took shelter in them, as places of security against their savage foes." At Opequon, Scotch-Irish landowner Robert Glass fortified his own single-room, twenty-foot-square stone cabin in such a fashion.[42]

Whereas Washington and local officers failed on numerous occasions to raise the militia for the common defense, the men of local communities readily banded together in informal military units to retaliate against Indian raiding parties and recover captives or stolen goods. One such instance took place after an Indian raid on the Young family in the Cedar Creek neighborhood about ten miles from Opequon. After brutally murdering several members of the family, including a baby, the Indians departed with two of Young's daughters, several guns, and other plunder. Samuel Fry then raised an impromptu force of thirty to forty men, pursued the Indians all the way to the Allegheny River, and recovered both captives and booty. This was at a time when Washington could barely get fifteen militiamen to turn out, and discipline problems would have made an expedition to the Allegheny tactically impossible.[43]

The people of local communities often cared for their own when left homeless in the wake of such terrible Indian raids. The Quakers were best organized for these relief efforts. During the fall of 1757 the Philadelphia Yearly Meeting sent £50 to eleven Hopewell families who were "Much Reduced Being driven from their Habitation and are unable to Labour for a Livelyhood."[44]

Even in flight many backcountry peoples apparently acted as communities. Washington estimated that "while one half of them sought shelter in paltry forts (of their own building) the other shou'd flee to the adjacent counties for refuge." In April 1756 he observed them "retreating to the securest parts in droves of fifties." These droves may or may not have been kin groups, but Washington's comments do indicate that evacuation was not the act of desperate individuals.[45]

Corresponding to the primary attachment of people to rural communities was the weakness of county political institutions. Popular endorsement of local authority was critical to stability in eighteenth-century Virginia government and society. The county court, the parish vestry, and the officer corps of the militia provided a unifying arena where the leadership class displayed superiority and power and the ordinary people expressed deference toward social betters and the dominion they represented.

For long-settled areas of Tidewater Virginia, these associations led to a close conjunction of county and community—the county literally became the unit of community. In Middlesex County, for instance, rapidly shifting family alliances caused by high rates of death and remarriage among the settlement generation of the 1650s soon generated kinship networks within local neighborhoods not dissimilar to the communities of the eighteenth-century backcountry. But as wealthy elites emerged with the development of a commercial, slave-based, tobacco economy and grew to dominate the court, vestry, and militia, the people of Middlesex increasingly looked beyond the neighborhood to the institutions of county government for political stability and order. As historians Darrett and Anita Rutman have observed:

> Living within a settled family, the individual looked out at the families immediately about in the neighborhood, a comfortable circle of friends and kin (and increasingly the latter). The precinct embraced a second, wider circle of families at least familiar from regular encounters at church and militia musters. Court day involved one with a still larger circle. . . . The court bounded the society as nothing else did. . . . What kept the county society one was the existence of the court as an administrative and judicial heart.[46]

In the backcountry of the 1750s, the process by which circles of social interdependence and political authority ascended from the neighborhood to the county stopped at the local level. Many communities had developed their own machinery of social order through the congregation. Presbyterians employed the church session as an instrument of discipline, and Quakers were especially adept at resolving disputes within the meeting. In 1748, for instance, two Hopewell Quakers, Evan Thomas and William Jolliff, stood before the meeting and admitted that "passion & anger" had led them to "fighting & quarreling with each other." Acknowledging this "breach of the known rules of our Discipline," they pledged themselves "to be more careful & circumspect in our lives." Without the mediation of the meeting, the case would have been heard by a justice of the peace or the county court.[47]

In other measurable ways the institutions of county government were weak. Although Frederick County was organized in 1738, the first court did not convene until late 1743. Thirteen local men had been appointed to the bench, but during the court's first half year an average of only five and never more than eight justices sat at monthly sessions. Turnover was high. Only three of the first justices still occupied the bench after ten years, and none appeared on the new commission of 1756. Numerous instances during this first decade indicated an absence of public deference toward the court. In June 1744 two attorneys, James Porteous and John Quinn, were fined for "indecently behaving and swearing before the court." On another occasion the court had to issue an order that "no person or persons presume to race or pace thru' the public street by the Ct. House" during public times.[48]

The Frederick Parish vestry was both disorganized and unsound. Charged with managing the established church's affairs and property, the vestry also held important civil powers to oversee poor relief and to tax for the purpose. Frederick Parish was created with the county in 1738, but not until April 1744 did the governor call for vestry elections. This first vestry was responsible for organizing the Anglican communion and constructing churches. It was, however, a disaster. By 1752 the vestry had collected £1,500, but built nothing. That year an act of the Virginia Assembly dissolved this vestry, by now suspected of misappropriating funds for private purposes. A new vestry began its work, but even by September 1753 a floor had to be laid hurriedly in the Winchester church to accommodate a party of Indians in town for treaty negotiations with Virginia. No record exists of early ministers, and the Frederick pulpit would not enjoy stability until the arrival of Charles Mynn Thruston in 1768.[49]

Whereas the leadership class of eighteenth-century Tidewater Virginia was synonymous with the social and economic elite, no comparable group of local leaders displaying both wealth and political prominence had emerged in Frederick County by the time of George Washington's arrival. It was a justice of the peace, after all, who had surprised Washington by serving dinner without a knife or table cloth. David Vance, an Opequon settler, sat on the first court, and Vance was a recent immigrant. At the time of his appointment he owned only one hundred acres. His holdings eventually became substantial, but they never lifted him conspicuously above his fellows. The same was true for another magistrate with roots at Opequon, George Hoge. Peripatetic son of community patriarch William Hoge, George eventually acquired some of his father's land but lived on the South Branch for awhile before departing for North Carolina in 1756. The situation of the court changed somewhat in the 1750s with the arrival of George William Fairfax, Lord Fairfax, and Thomas Bryan Martin on the bench, but even these men did not carry sufficient weight to prevent the collusion of the court with local tavern keepers in the attempt to defraud the Virginia Regiment.[50]

The militia, like the court and vestry, was an organ of local government. Many of Washington's problems with the institution can be explained within the familiar backcountry context of fragile authority structures and a society of individuals professing a primary attachment to local communities. Not surprisingly, the officer corps of the militia was closely integrated into the court. Three of the four primary officers and five of fifteen captains were justices of the peace. Nonetheless, the number of delinquencies at musters was immense. Between 1755 and 1762, 675 Frederick men were charged with 1,330 offenses. Even in neighboring Augusta County only 159 men skipped musters during the same period. Delinquency as well as the problem of harboring deserters signified a lack of deference, or as Washington put it, a "want of Order, regularity, and Obedience" that was directed not only at him but at most militia officers, including precinct captains. In the fall of 1754, for instance, James Lemon brought charges before the Frederick court against Edmond Cullen for "Cursing and Insulting him when on duty" and against three German settlers "for opposing and striking him when by virtue of the governor's warrant he came to impress a horse."[51]

Attachments to local communities that superseded commitments to county government cannot fully explain the events of September

1757, when Washington and his officers uncovered a ring in Winchester receiving embezzled supplies. Certainly the role that some magistrates played in the operation fits the pattern previously set by the vestry—a pattern in which public property was appropriated for private use. The collusion between local officials and town citizens is suggestive of the world historical geographer James T. Lemon has depicted as one in which people placed "material gain over that of public interest," where "communities, like governments, were necessary evils to support individual fulfillment." An absence of shared values does not necessarily imply criminal activity, but it does suggest that in this setting individuals would be least inclined to turn down any opportunity for material gain even at the expense of the general welfare in time of emergency. That this episode took place in the only town of the region is significant. Winchester was the scene of rapidly shifting entrepreneurial activity that would have attracted the most individualist-minded people and discouraged the formation of kinship networks. Winchester was probably not dissimilar to Germantown, Pennsylvania, where social historian Stephanie Wolf described a "pattern of individualism and pragmatism as opposed to one of communalism and tradition." To Washington the actions of townspeople might well appear "selfish," "infatuated," or "villainous," but these actions are also understandable in the context of liberal individualism and the great opportunity for personal gain implicit in the economic growth of the town.[52]

Thus the nature of backcountry settlement and the mentality of settlers as inferred from the structure of their settlements goes a long way in explaining the anxieties Washington felt as colonel of the Virginia Regiment. Fulfilling his responsibility to defend the backcountry was complicated by the vulnerability of dispersed settlements extending deep into enemy territory. But his job was made even more difficult by the localism these settlements engendered. Bonded by ties of kinship, ethnicity, land, and congregation, settlers felt a far stronger attachment to their own communities than to the institutions of county government about which community life and the common defense had traditionally been organized in Virginia. The growing force of individualism and opportunism, especially in the towns, would create the most perplexing problems for Washington. Together these difficulties imperiled Washington's highest ambitions for honor, esteem, and reputation from public service. These ambitions would, of course, be later fulfilled far beyond the wildest imaginings of youth, but Washington would never forget—nor would he entirely overcome—his experiences in the Virginia backcountry.

NOTES

1. George Washington, March 18, 21, 26, April 3, 4, 6, 1748, *The Diaries of George Washington*, ed. Donald Jackson and Dorothy Twohig, 6 vols. (Charlottesville: University Press of Virginia, 1976–1979), 1:12, 15, 18, 19; George Washington to Richard, 1749–1750, *The Papers of George Washington*, Colonial Series, ed. W. W. Abbot et al., 10 vols. (Charlottesville: University Press of Virginia, 1983–1995), 1:43–44.

2. Washington, March 13, 1748, *Washington Diaries*, 1:7; Washington to Robert Dinwiddie, October 5, 1757, *Washington Papers*, Col. Ser., 5:3; Washington to Dinwiddie, October 24, 1757, *Washington Papers*, Col. Ser., 5:25; Washington to Dinwiddie, April 27, 1756, *Washington Papers*, Col. Ser., 3:59.

3. Washington to Richard, 1749–1750, *Washington Papers*, Col. Ser., 1:44.

4. Washington to Warner Lewis, August 14, 1755, *Washington Papers*, Col. Ser., 1:362–63.

5. Washington to Dinwiddie, October 11, 1755, *Washington Papers*, Col. Ser., 2:102.

6. Frederick County Deed Book, 18:16–17. All Frederick County deed, will, and order books (hereafter cited as FDB, FWB, or FOB) are deposited in the Frederick County Courthouse, Winchester, Va. Public records for the area of Frederick County recorded between 1734 and 1743 are deposited in the Orange County Courthouse, Orange, Virginia (hereafter cited as ODB, OWB, or OOB). Washington to John Augustine Washington, May 28, 1755, *Washington Papers*, Col. Ser., 1:289; Washington to John Robinson, April 16, 1756, *Washington Papers*, Col. Ser., 3:6; Washington to Dinwiddie, April 22, 1756, *Washington Papers*, Col. Ser., 3:33.

7. Washington to Dinwiddie, October 11, 1755, *Washington Papers*, Col. Ser., 2:101, 104; Washington to Dinwiddie, April 16, 1756, *Washington Papers*, Col. Ser., 3:1; Washington to John Campbell, earl of Loudoun, January 10, 1757, *Washington Papers*, Col. Ser., 4:89.

8. Washington to Dinwiddie, April 25, 1754, *Washington Papers*, Col. Ser., 1:88–89; Washington to Dinwiddie, August 4, 1756, *Washington Papers*, Col. Ser., 3:318; Dinwiddie to Washington, August 19, 1756, *Washington Papers*, Col. Ser., 3:361; Washington to Dinwiddie, September 8, 1756, *Washington Papers*, Col. Ser., 3:397.

9. Douglas Southall Freeman, *George Washington: A Biography*, 8 vols. (New York: Charles Scribner's Sons, 1948–1957), 2:258–59; Washington to Dinwiddie, May 23, 1756, *Washington Papers*, Col. Ser., 3:171.

10. Chester R. Young, "The Effects of the French and Indian War on Civilian Life in the Frontier Counties of Virginia, 1754–1763" (Ph.D. diss., Vanderbilt University, 1969), 332, table 23.

11. For Washington's orders, see *Washington Papers*, Col. Ser., 2:124; 3:280–82, 338–40. Court actions are detailed in FOB, 7:97, 118. Washington's hopes for the new court are expressed in a letter to Dinwiddie, September 8, 1756, *Washington Papers*, Col. Ser., 3:397.

12. These proceedings are detailed in a series of letters and statements, see *Washington Papers*, Col. Ser., 4:423–26; 5:1–13.

13. Washington to Dinwiddie, October 9, 1757, *Washington Papers*, Col. Ser., 5:12.

14. Washington to Loudoun, January 10, 1757, *Washington Papers*, Col. Ser., 4:83.

15. John J. McCusker and Russell R. Menard, *The Economy of British America, 1607–1789* (Chapel Hill: University of North Carolina Press, 1985), 202–4; James T. Lemon, *The Best Poor Man's Country: A Geographical Study of Early Southeastern Pennsylvania* (Baltimore: The Johns Hopkins University Press, 1972; New York: W. W. Norton, 1976), 56–57. At the time the migration to the Shenandoah Valley began in the 1730s, settlement in Pennsylvania had just pushed west of the Susquehanna River. A variety of factors, including high quit rents, boundary disputes, speculation in land warrants, and rumors of poor soil, simultaneously discouraged the settlement of western Maryland. See Frank W. Porter III, "From Backcountry to Country: The Delayed Settlement of Western Maryland," *Maryland Historical Magazine* 70 (Winter 1975): 329–49.

16. William W. Hening, ed., *The Statutes at Large; Being a Collection of All the Laws of Virginia . . .*, 13 vols. (Richmond: 1809–1823), 3:204–9; 4:77–79. The Knights of the Golden Horseshoe expedition promoted interest in the West but not migration. The 1720 county act encouraged land speculation in the Piedmont by relieving speculators of the obligation to pay for treasury rights until settlers appeared to buy the land.

17. Northern Neck Land Grant Book C:77, 78, Library of Virginia, Richmond; Stuart E. Brown Jr., *Virginia Baron: The Story of Thomas 6th Lord Fairfax* (Berryville, Va.: Chesapeake Book Company, 1965), 39–100.

18. Hening, *Statutes*, 5:78–80; Young, "French and Indian War," 431–40, tables 28–37; Washington to Robinson, November 9, 1756, *Washington Papers*, Col. Ser., 4:16–17.

19. Some settlers complained that they were "so far distant from any Settlement (but especially from any such as could supply them with any Provisions

or Necessaries) that they could scarcely procure any one thing necessary nearer than from Pennsylvania or Fredericksburg." *Hite et al.* vs. *Fairfax* Papers, transcript by Hunter B. McKay, p. 1521, Handley Library Archives, Winchester, Va. See also, William M. Gardner, *Lost Arrowheads and Broken Pottery: Traces of Indians in the Shenandoah Valley* (Thunderbird Museum Publication, 1986), 89–90.

20. H. R. McIlwaine, Wilmer L. Hall, and Benjamin J. Hillman, eds., *Executive Journals of the Council of Colonial Virginia*, 6 vols. (Richmond: Virginia State Library, 1925–1966), 4:229, 253; Robert Dinwiddie to the Lords Commissioners for Trade and Plantations, January 1755, as quoted in Young, "French and Indian War," 12; deposition of Jonathan Langdon, March 1754, in *Hite et al.* vs. *Fairfax* Papers, transcript by McKay, p. 1713.

21. Washington to Dinwiddie, April 7, 1756, *Washington Papers*, Col. Ser., 2:333.

22. Robert D. Mitchell, *Commercialism and Frontier: Perspectives on the Early Shenandoah Valley* (Charlottesville: University Press of Virginia, 1977), 43, figure 12; Francis Asbury, June 21, 1783, *Journal of Rev. Francis Asbury*, 3 vols. (New York: Lane & Scott, 1852), 1:461.

23. Jost Hite was a native of Germany who with many other Palatines migrated to England in 1709 and to New York a year later to labor at a Royal Navy tarworks. After the collapse of that project he lived in Ulster County, New York, for a number of years before relocating in Pennsylvania and acquiring extensive landholdings along the Perkiomen Creek. See Klaus Wust, *The Virginia Germans* (Charlottesville: University Press of Virginia, 1969), 32–33; Henry Z. Jones, Ralph Conner, and Klaus Wust, *German Origins of Jost Hite: Virginia Pioneer, 1685–1761* (Edinburg, Va.: Shenandoah History, 1979).

24. The pace of land granting represents a poor measure of settlement because of the moratorium on land granting imposed during the dispute over Northern Neck lands. Most of the tracts had probably been settled by the 1740s and certainly by the time of Washington's appearance in the region. All information on Opequon landholdings was derived from Frederick and Orange county deeds and wills, and the Northern Neck Land Grant Books and Regal Government Land Books in the Library of Virginia, Richmond.

25. Information on farm and house siting was derived from archaeological and architectural field surveys; see Clarence R. Geier and Warren R. Hofstra, "An Archaeological Survey of and Management Plan for Cultural Resources in the Vicinity of the Upper Opequon Creek" (Richmond: Virginia Department of Historic Resources, 1991), 70–73, 95–100; Hofstra, "Adaptation or Survival? Folk Housing at Opequon Settlement, Virginia," *Ulster Folklife* 37 (1989): 42–71.

26. The structure of the Scotch-Irish settlement at Opequon has been more fully treated in Warren R. Hofstra, "Land, Ethnicity, and Community at

the Opequon Settlement, Virginia, 1730–1800," *Virginia Magazine of History and Biography* 98 (July 1990): 423–48.

27. Hofstra, "Land, Ethnicity, and Community," 434–38.

28. FDB, 1:275; FWB, 3:40.

29. The only slave appeared in the inventory of William Reid recorded in 1752. All inventories are found in the FWBs.

30. These averages are very close to those James T. Lemon found on Pennsylvania farms in his study of the historical geography of southeastern Pennsylvania. From an examination of 207 inventories in Chester and Lancaster counties he found an average of 8.3 cattle, 12.3 sheep, 6.7 swine, and 3.8 horses per farm in 1750. Lemon also discovered that the average family of five consumed 250 pounds of beef a year. With each animal dressing out at about 450 pounds, some surplus would have been available for market each year. See Lemon, *Best Poor Man's Country*, 150–69, tables 28, 29; Mitchell, *Commercialism and Frontier*, 140–44.

31. For use of the term "dispersed general store," see Joseph S. Wood, "Elaboration of a Settlement System: The New England Village in the Federal Period," *Journal of Historical Geography* 10 (October 1984): 331–56; Wood, "Village and Community in Early Colonial New England," *Journal of Historical Geography* 8 (October 1982): 333–46.

32. Elizabeth Chapman Denny Vann and Margaret Collins Denny Dixon, *Brumback-Hotsinpiller Genealogy . . .* (Englewood, N.J., 1961), 21–26.

33. McIlwaine, *Executive Journals*, 4:229; *Hopewell Friends History, 1734–1934, Frederick County, Virginia* (Strasburg, Va.: Shenandoah Publishing House, 1936), 12–95.

34. *Hopewell History*, 68–95.

35. Richard K. MacMaster, *The History of Hardy County, 1786–1986* (Salem, W. Va.: Walsworth Press, 1986), 1–34; Young, "French and Indian War," 438, table 35; William J. Hinke and Charles E. Kemper, eds., "Moravian Diaries of Travels through Virginia," *Virginia Magazine of History and Biography* 11 (January 1904): 237. See also Charles Morrison, "The Swan Ponds Manor of Thomas, Sixth Lord Fairfax," *West Virginia History* 35 (October 1973): 26–39; Morrison, "Early Fairfax Land Grants and Leases along the South Branch of the Potomac," *West Virginia History* 38 (October 1976): 1–22; Morrison, "Early Land Grants and Settlers Along Patterson Creek," *West Virginia History* 40 (Winter 1979): 164–99.

36. FOB, 1:264; Philip Vickers Fithian, *Journal, 1775–1776*, ed. R. G. Albion and L. Dodson (Princeton: Princeton University Press, 1934), 13; Washington, March 16, 1748, *Washington Diaries*, 1:11; Hinke and Kemper, "Moravian Diaries," 141. One town, Stephensburg, six miles to the south of Hite's settlement, was chartered in 1758, the year Washington took up permanent residence at Mount Vernon.

37. Andrew Burnaby, *Travels through the Middle Settlement in North America in the Years 1759 and 1760*, 3d ed. (London: T. Payne, 1798; New York: A. Wessels, 1904; New York: Augustus M. Kelley, 1970), 74; Mitchell, *Commercialism and Frontier*, 46.

38. Central-place theory and applications are treated by many authors. For introductory and summary statements, see Walter Christaller, *Central Places in Southern Germany*, trans. Carlisle W. Baskin (Jena: Gustav Fisher, 1933; Englewood Cliffs, N.J.: Prentice Hall, 1966); Brian J. L. Berry, *Geography of Market Centers and Retail Distribution*, Foundations of Economic Geography Series, ed. Norton Ginsburg (Englewood Cliffs, N.J.: Prentice Hall, 1967).

39. Thomas K. Cartmell, *Shenandoah Valley Pioneers and Their Descendants: A History of Frederick County, Virginia* (Winchester, Va.: Eddy Press, 1909; Bowie, Md.: Heritage Books, 1989), 50–51, 91–92, 132–33, 180–84, 189–90. No evidence exists for a Lutheran congregation in Winchester before 1762. The Anglican church did not receive a permanent rector until the late 1760s.

40. Washington to Peter Hogg, September 8, 1756, *Washington Papers*, Col. Ser., 3:402; Washington to Dinwiddie, October 11, 1755, *Washington Papers*, Col. Ser., 2:101.

41. Washington to Dinwiddie, October 11, 1755, *Washington Papers*, Col. Ser., 2:104.

42. Washington to Robinson, April 27, 1756, *Washington Papers*, Col. Ser., 3:64; Samuel Kercheval, *A History of the Valley of Virginia*, 5th ed. (Strasburg, Va.: Shenandoah Publishing House, 1973), 84; Cartmell, *Shenandoah Valley Pioneers*, 274–75.

43. Kercheval, *Valley of Virginia*, 85.

44. Letter from Hopewell Quakers to Meeting for Sufferings of the Philadelphia Yearly Meeting, September 9, 1757, as quoted in *Hopewell History*, 118.

45. Washington to Dinwiddie, September 17, 1757, *Washington Papers*, Col. Ser., 4:411; Washington to Robinson, April 24, 1756, *Washington Papers*, Col. Ser., 3:48.

46. Darrett B. Rutman and Anita H. Rutman, *A Place in Time: Middlesex County, Virginia, 1650–1750* (New York: W. W. Norton, 1984), 125, 126, 241.

47. Hopewell Minutes, 1748, *Hopewell History*, 52.

48. FOBs, 1:1, 5:294, 7:118; Cartmell, *Shenandoah Valley Pioneers*, 24; FOB, 2:311.

49. Cartmell, *Shenandoah Valley Pioneers*, 180–84; Young, "French and Indian War," 2.

50. Vance purchased his one hundred acres from Jost Hite in May 1742 and nine years later acquired a grant from Lord Fairfax for an additional 407 acres, see ODB, 6:174; Northern Neck Land Grant Book G:543. For Hoge's landownings, see FDBs, 2:58, 4:234.

51. Young, "French and Indian War," 57–58; Washington to Loudoun, January 10, 1757, *Washington Papers*, Col. Ser. 4:87; FOB, 6:85, 114.

52. Lemon, *Best Poor Man's Country*, xv; Stephanie Grauman Wolf, *Urban Village: Population, Community and Family Structure in Germantown, Pennsylvania, 1683–1800* (Princeton: Princeton University Press, 1976), 329.

"Engaged in Enterprises Pregnant with Terror": George Washington's Formative Years among the Indians

J. FREDERICK FAUSZ

On FEBRUARY 22, 1800, THE RIGHT Reverend John Carroll, archbishop of Baltimore, delivered a stirring eulogy at St. Peter's Church for the recently deceased George Washington. In this personal, patriotic tribute, Carroll paid less attention to Washington's famous deeds as general or president than he did to the formative, frontier exploits of the youthful surveyor and soldier in "that vast Western region . . . then known only by the . . . cruelties practiced by the savage Indians." What American, asked the archbishop, had not reflected on the future leader "clambering over lofty Western mountains, fording unfathomed and rapid rivers, exposing his invaluable life to innumerable accidents of treachery and hostility—without shuddering for his existence and admiring his cool, collected courage in conquering obstacles and surmounting danger?"[1]

As a fellow member of the Chesapeake gentry elite, the archbishop appreciated how rare and significant it was that young Washington had chosen to leave his comfortable roots as a Tidewater planter to pursue profitable employment and public service, immediate fame and lasting fortune, on the western frontier. Washington's active involvement in backcountry "enterprises pregnant with terror" brought him special appeal as a self-made man among successive generations of western pioneers, who identified with his efforts to "people the wilderness, beautify it by cultivation, and multiply the resources of his native province." Archbishop Carroll correctly perceived that Washington had no peer as an early western hero, symbolizing as he did both the past heritage and future potential of an expansive Chesapeake empire extending from the Atlantic to the Appalachians. Washington alone combined the personal experiences of semiliterate pathfinders in the West, such as Daniel Boone, with the direct, policy-making authority of powerful politicians of the East, such as Thomas Jefferson. According to the professional opinion of the prelate, Washington's harrowing adventures within the "inhospitable confines of the savage Indian" were particularly important for providing the "training and education by which Providence prepared . . . [him] for the fulfillment of his future destinies." Because no other frontiersman was in the unique position to translate early personal impressions into eventual national policies, it is important to analyze the reciprocal impact of Washington's youthful, formative relations with the Indian inhabitants who dominated the Ohio Country.[2]

GEORGE WASHINGTON WAS THE product of an area and an era especially conducive to profitable frontier enterprises. His homeland in the Northern Neck, that strategic peninsula bounded by the Rappahannock and Potomac rivers, was the last colonized and most opportunistic region in Tidewater Virginia. Possessing a special energy and a distinctive identity for a century before his birth, the Northern Neck was a land of new beginnings and limitless potential for aggressive, competitive dynasties rooted in fertile soils and mercantile profits.

Capt. John Smith and Sir Samuel Argall had explored the populous and bountiful Potomac shores in the first two decades of the seventeenth century, but it was only after the sudden, devastating 1622 Powhatan Uprising in the James River basin that the region to the north became popular for entrepreneurial speculation and white settlement. Finding Virginia "plentifull in nothing but want, and wanting nothing but plenty," the shocked survivors of the Indian attack pursued armed aggression against their Powhatan neighbors, while making profitable alliances with distant Potomac River Algonquians, whose vital food and valuable warriors helped save the colony.[3]

After 1622, the Virginia colonists quickly learned to differentiate between hostile and hospitable Indians, pursuing the "peace of warres" by raiding the former and the "wares of peace" by trading with the latter. Several urbane and university-educated Kentish gentlemen, including Gov. Sir Francis Wyatt, George Sandys, and William Claiborne, dominated the military, political, economic, and social affairs of the bloodied colony because they recognized and respected the central role that Indians played in their physical survival and financial success. Under Governor Wyatt, the Council of State at Jamestown developed into a cohesive, strong, and self-sufficient oligarchy of "chieftains"— hardened frontiersmen who used their private armies to monopolize English laborers, tobacco production, the exploration and exploitation of prime lands, and all Indian policies.[4]

These self-styled "sons of wrath," acculturated to local American realities, replaced the stockholders of the Virginia Company as the dominant policymakers in the Chesapeake and forged a new direction for Virginia. In so doing, they established the earliest model of the frontier elite—high-status gentlemen who combined military, political, social, and economic leadership, merged public service with profitable private interests, and integrated aristocratic formality with popular familiarity. Even genteel poets like Wyatt and Sandys commanded brutal campaigns against the Indians in order to earn acceptance and respect from ruthless, low-born veteran militiamen and prove that their practical ability to lead was consistent with their theoretical right to rule. Indian warfare in the forests of America diminished the importance of the ascribed status of European aristocrats and accentuated the achieved status of self-made frontiersmen.[5]

Throughout the 1620s, Virginia's militant oligarchs established lucrative entrepreneurial enterprises with native nations in the northern Chesapeake, and for a quarter-century after Maryland's founding in 1634, they fought fellow Englishmen for control of the Indian maize and fur trades. "Sons of wrath" like Colonel Claiborne, Capt. Henry Fleet, Samuel Mathews the Elder, and John Mottram were the first Englishmen to settle along the Northern Neck frontier because the south bank of the Potomac allowed them to continue their now-illegal fur trade with the Susquehannocks and to plot the downfall of Maryland without much official interference.[6]

The first Washington to reside in this rough-and-tumble Northern Neck was George's great-grandfather, John, the Immigrant, who, in 1657 brought his new Maryland bride to Westmoreland County. The eve of the Stuart Restoration was a critical time of transition for a region still scarred by the bloody Virginia-Maryland rivalries over the fur trade, Indian allegiances, conflicting charter rights, disputed territorial boundaries, and persistent religious prejudices. John Washington was one of the new breed of young, recent immigrants who challenged the dying dominance of fur traders in the Northern Neck and felt contempt for their dependent but still dangerous Indian business partners. Arriving the very year that Claiborne's Chesapeake beaver empire finally came to ruin, Washington witnessed the rapid disintegration and depopulation of once-trusted, but increasingly irrelevant, local tribes and longed to expand his agricultural profits on their prime riverine lands.[7]

In the summer of 1675, Washington and fellow planters from both sides of the Potomac River brought their so-called Indian problem to an opportunistic and fatal conclusion. Although the sudden mobilization of the local county militias was officially explained by recent raids of nearby Doeg Indians (who were avenging previous murders by white farmers), it was no coincidence that Washington's enthusiasm for public service was linked to private profits. Only the year before, he had patented five thousand acres between Virginia's Dogue and Little Hunting creeks—the traditional Doeg homeland—and risked forfeiture of the grant if he did not "plant and seat" that tract by 1676. Duty to country and a desire for reward thus compelled Colonel Washington of the Westmoreland County Militia into battle, along with Maryland troops under Maj. Thomas Truman and other Virginia units commanded by notable founders of Northern Neck dynasties, including Col. George Mason, Maj. Isaac Allerton, Maj. Richard Lee, and Capt. Giles Brent the Younger, who was himself half Indian.[8]

By late September 1675, this intercolonial force of some 750 militiamen had abandoned the pursuit of the Doeg and was besieging a large fortress occupied by friendly Susquehannock Indians along Maryland's Piscataway Creek. The Susquehannocks, who had warmly welcomed John Smith in 1608 and loyally served as Claiborne's indispensable trading partners for twenty-five years, were perplexed by the sudden aggression of their longstanding and still-current English allies. Five chiefs emerged from the fort under a flag of truce to parley with the colonists, but Washington, Truman, or both, had the unarmed envoys bound and brutally murdered. Maryland officials later impeached Truman for "barbarous cruelty" and "horrid Crimes" against the Indians (although they merely fined him), while Washington endured little more than a tongue-lashing from Gov. Sir William Berkeley. Soon after the gruesome bloodshed at Piscataway Creek, however, the Susquehannocks began calling John Washington "Caunotaucarius"—Iroquoian for "devourer of villages."[9]

The shocking, cold-blooded murders convinced the remaining Susquehannocks to shoot their way through the English lines in order to save their women and children. They did so and exacted a "fierce and frequent" revenge on vulnerable colonial homesteads during their trek throughout lower Virginia. Fearful of "where the Storme would light" next, "the dread of a[n] ... approaching calamity made the giddy-headed multitude madd" enough to support Nathaniel Bacon's rebellious vigilantism. Committing treason against an aging governor and nurturing the popular bloodlust in his ragtag army, Bacon specialized in the senseless slaughter of innocent Indians, "whether they be Friends or Foes," falsely claiming that "it was impossible to distinguish one nation from another"—"are not the Indians all ... [one] color?"[10]

Virginia's fourth and final Indian war of the seventeenth century ended in 1677. This last frontier conflict—and first true race war—with the indigenous Indians of the Tidewater Chesapeake brought significant changes to the Old Dominion. The colonists who slaughtered Indian allies or burned Jamestown to the ground during Bacon's civil war had, in a few rash moments of criminal conduct, ruined a generation of comparatively enlightened intercultural relations and discredited several decades of local self-government. The chaos in the colony prompted royal officials to expand and solidify their political authority and commercial control over the Virginians. With the death of Claiborne and Governor Berkeley in 1677, Virginia had no remaining leaders with meaningful memories of friendly Indians. The Chesapeake gentry would retain their increasingly honorific militia ranks for several more generations, but their ability to influence Indian policy was eclipsed by professional governors-general sent to colonial capitals by bureaucrats in London. The presence of raiding and trading Indians had provided Virginia's early frontier elite with significant military and political leverage for three quarters of a century. With the end of Indian dominance in the Tidewater, gentlemen-planters expanded onto Indian tribal lands and exploited African tribal labor and thereby discovered new sources of profits and power. No longer Indian-fighters, county militia colonels justified their existence by reawakening familiar patterns of prejudicial paranoia against a new, African source of ethnic diversity in the Chesapeake.[11]

𝒜LTHOUGH GEORGE WASHINGTON was born a half century after the climactic events of the late 1670s, his impressionable early years were influenced by the Northern Neck's mixed legacy of Indian relations. Familiar landscapes and local place-names would have reminded him of how the actions of ancestors had laid the foundations of the family fortune and reputation. His birthplace at Wakefield along Pope's Creek, as well as his father's Chotank property on the Potomac, were especially valuable parcels because they encompassed Indian "old fields"—fertile, waterside sites that had supported native farming for generations. One of Washington's earliest memories was of his boyhood home at Little Hunting Creek, or Epsewesson, where the Doegs had greeted John Smith in 1608. Mount Vernon would later be built there and provide a vantage point from which the descendants of John Washington, "devourer of villages," could look directly across the Potomac and clearly see where the burned, broken, and bloody Susquehannock fort once stood.[12]

Such constant reminders of chaos and conquest perhaps left an indelible impression about the inevitability of white "progress," but they also underscored the fact that the Northern Neck, like the young Washington, was still in its adolescence. Even seven decades after John Washington's death, the south shore of the Potomac lacked the regional maturity and creature comforts that were commonplace in the oldest, wealthiest, and most prominent sections of Tidewater Virginia. The absence of overdevelopment and complacency meant that the region retained much of its frontier flavor, provoking enthusiasm and ambition for expanded estates and entrepreneurial investment. As late as the 1730s, George Washington's father was able to purchase acreage that had never been cultivated, and he was the first colonist to experiment with the mining of iron ore along the Rappahannock River. In that same decade, new market towns like Fredericksburg appeared and prospered along the fall line, while scores of English, German, and Scotch-Irish immigrants began farming the fresh, fertile lands of the Shenandoah Valley. In the 1740s, investment-conscious planters in the Northern Neck considered the verdant valleys on both sides of the Appalachians as their virtual suburbs and aggressively promoted the Potomac River as the highway to a vast backcountry empire.[13]

George Washington was at precisely the right place at exactly the right time to take advantage of these new opportunities in the West. His dearest friends and most dedicated patrons were in the forefront of frontier expansionism—including Thomas, Lord Fairfax, and Col. William Fairfax, father-in-law of his brother, Lawrence Washington. By 1745 Lord Fairfax, whose Culpeper forebears had gained a foothold in the Chesapeake during the disruptive, opportunistic days of the Susquehannock war and Bacon's Rebellion, was the powerful proprietor of some five million acres in a "greater Northern Neck" extending across the Alleghenies. The enormous, exciting potential of this distant paradise was symbolized by Fairfax's decision to leave his exquisite estate at Leeds Castle in Kent for residence at Belvoir on the Potomac and a later seat at Greenway Court in the Shenandoah Valley, ten miles from Winchester. With the arrival in America of this incomparably wealthy and politically influential peer, the young, orphaned Washington had found a patron who would provide an outlet for his adolescent energy and satisfy his yearning for adventure and preferment.[14]

Washington was blessed by the fortuitous convergence of a family alliance with the Fairfaxes and Britain's emerging imperial interest in the trans-Appalachian region. It seemed as if profiteers throughout Britain, France, and North America suddenly and simultaneously awoke from a languid sleep to realize the vast potential of the Ohio Country. Political leaders and land speculators on both sides of the Atlantic scrambled to make the Chesapeake backcountry the next theater of operations in the century-long "Great War for Empire" between England and France. Virginians in the Northern Neck were especially anxious to exploit this rich region for patriotic and profitable motives—but which established planters and heirs of Tidewater dynasties were willing to risk their own lives in the forested frontier of the Ohio Country dominated by thousands of Indian warriors? Nearly three generations had elapsed in the Tidewater Chesapeake without significant contact with, or knowledge of, native nations in their natural setting. Before Virginia could play a leading part in the western territories, a new breed of well-born but acculturated frontiersman had to be recruited for "a Service precarious and uncertain." Illiterate hunters and mixed-blood interpreters already in the backcountry did not inspire confidence as leaders, while affluent English aristocrats, residing only for a short time in America, lacked the critical identification with local loyalties and colonial interests. What the times required were sturdy, brave, adventurous—and yet educated and socially prominent—young men, who could emulate the military victories and profitable enterprises of Virginia's first founders.[15]

GEORGE WASHINGTON WAS JUST such a man, made for the times. At seventeen, he was already an accomplished, practicing surveyor of western lands—a profession that epitomized the dynamic process of transforming "savage" tribal territories into "civilized" European real estate along dangerous, distant frontiers. But the skills learned in the Northern Neck only half prepared him for survival and success in transitional regions still controlled by Indian societies. There, in the backcountry, amid the complex cultural mosaic of numerous native nations, he would need to learn strange new lessons of warfare and diplomacy in order to win Indian allies to the English side.

In one critical decade between 1748 and 1758, Washington the frontiersman was influenced by a wide variety of encounters with Indians, and these formative relations helped determine his later decisions about their futures, as well as their opinions of him and the American nation he represented. The knowledge he gained in the West was always broader than it was deep, more superficial that substantive, and he never displayed a sympathetic understanding for native peoples with different beliefs and lifeways. His roles as surveyor, diplomat, and military officer changed too often and too quickly in that fleeting decade of firsthand experience, forcing him to concentrate on expedient, limited objectives for his political superiors. Washington never confused his specifically political and military missions with purely scientific research on native cultures. Because of the place and prejudices that he inherited within Virginia's planter hierarchy and given his youthful need to please powerful patrons in high positions, he never questioned his duty to his country, his class, and his culture—especially in gaining vital Indian support for British policies that ultimately doomed the Ohio Valley tribes.

Washington employed and exploited the native peoples of the West as functional, expedient necessities—not unlike the "Indian walking dress," buckskin leggings, and matchcoat he wore for efficiently traversing forested terrain. Preoccupied with immediate objectives and important destinations, he quickly passed through woodlands and passed by native villages without a keen sense of observation or appreciation. In March 1748, he was "agreeably surpris'd at the sight of thirty odd Indians coming from war," and although he observed them for hours, he failed to record any important details, including their tribal affiliation: "Nothing remarkable [happened] on thursday but only being with the Indians all day so shall slip it." Never a careful scholar, Washington saw no practical benefit in trying to comprehend the complex cultural diversity of the backcountry. In his opinion, both Indian assistance and Indian resistance would soon be rendered moot by inescapable, irrepressible colonial expansionism.[16]

Washington's opinions about Indians should be understood in the context of contemporary planter values, which had long condoned the permanent enslavement of Africans and blatantly discriminated against persons considered inferior by race, culture, or class. Washington's journals are filled with pejorative remarks about such inferiors. He complained about the "parcel of Barbarian's and an uncooth set of People" he encountered on his long journeys, describing some German settlers "as Ignorant a Set of People as the Indians." When the constant discomfort of sleeping outdoors or on dirty cabin floors overwhelmed him, he lamented that "I have never had my Cloths of[f] but lay and sleep in them like a Negro." Washington repeated his era's common prejudices about native savagery and treachery, ignorance and inferiority, and he truly respected Indian warriors, as he would wild and dangerous beasts, only to the extent that they represented a threat to his survival. He differentiated between Indians and "men" in his writings, with the latter term being reserved for white soldiers, and like other prominent contemporaries, he generally denigrated even friendly Indians—who "'come when we send for them, . . . go when they are bid, and . . . do whatever is desired of them.'"[17]

Given these attitudes, Washington faced a dilemma in performing his duties on the western frontier. He admitted that he was "not . . . so good a Woodsman" and needed to rely on the forest skills of Indians, and yet he "did not think their Company agreeable." Only gradually and grudgingly did Washington accept his dependence on, and inferiority to, Indians with regard to essential frontier knowledge; whenever possible, he relied on acculturated colonists to be his trusted tutors and intermediaries. Washington received an accelerated, advanced education in forest survival from the many backcountry traders, hunters, interpreters, and guides who lived on the fringes of European settlement, such as Christopher Gist (Indian name: "Annosanah"), renowned Ohio Company scout and interpreter; John Fraser, a blacksmith, trader, and interpreter living at Turtle Creek, Pennsylvania; John Davison, trader and interpreter from Logstown, Pennsylvania; George Croghan ("Brother Bucks"), Pennsylvania's chief Indian agent; Thomas Cresap, trader-surveyor from Shawnee Old Town,Maryland; and lesser-known "servitors" from the Alleghenies—Barnaby Currin, John McGuire, Henry Steward, and William Jenkins.[18]

Their predominant Celtic origins and their occasional ambivalence about the alleged superiority of English civilization helped make these frontiersmen as adept at crossing cultural boundaries as they were at traversing rushing streams. A few of them proved indispensable in guiding Washington, the surveyor, to the Ohio Company's half million acres and in assembling Indian chieftains for the important Logstown conference of June 1752. None of them, however, possessed the gentry status, family connections, or high military rank that Gov. Robert Dinwiddie deemed necessary in October 1753 for delivering his message of warning to the French. Virginia's governor preferred breeding over experience in his personal emissary, and while Major Washington was not a bad choice to negotiate with cultured French officers, he certainly had much to learn if he were to accomplish the second, and most critical, objective of the trip—gaining vital Indian allies to help thwart the French advance in the West.

O<small>N NOVEMBER 22, 1753, GEORGE</small> Washington entered a strange Old American World still dominated by Indians when he "call'd upon" the cabin of Shingas, "king" of the western Delawares, near the strategic Forks of the Ohio River. His familiar, genteel surroundings in the Tidewater Potomac were only a few weeks away and some two hundred miles distant, but they may as well have been on another planet. As an uninvited white intruder, Washington was virtually alone, overwhelmingly outnumbered, totally isolated, and completely dependent. He could only hope for good faith and fair treatment from the scarred and suspicious war sachems who had found refuge in the Alleghenies. The cruelty and duplicity of Europeans over many decades had forced thousands of those western Indians from their traditional homelands in the East, and now their mountain sanctuary was itself the new focus of exploitative expansionism and dynastic conflicts between England and France.[19]

Shingas accompanied Washington's party the forty miles or so to Logstown, where the Virginia major met Monacatoocha, or Scarouady, a battle-hardened Oneida war chief whom the Onondaga Council of the Iroquois Six Nations had appointed to lead the Ohio Valley

Benjamin West's contemporaneous view of Anglo-Indian diplomacy, "The Indians giving a Talk to Colonel [Henry] Bouquet . . . in Octr. 1764," captures the tension and drama that accompanied intercultural parleys over the fate of the Ohio Country in the mid-eighteenth century. From William Smith, *An Historical Account of the Expedition Against the Ohio Indians* (London, 1766). Reproduced with the permission of The Newberry Library, Chicago, Illinois.

Shawnees. Terrifying in appearance, with symbols of tomahawks and bows carved into his cheeks and chest, he outranked Shingas by tribal tradition and confederation responsibilities. Through interpreter John Davison, Washington told Monacatoocha that the Iroquois League should be informed of his mission to the French and that he wanted to address a gathering of local Indian leaders as soon as possible. As a goodwill gesture, he gave Monacatoocha a "String of Wampum and a Twist of Tobacco" and later entertained him and other Indian "great Men" in his tent for more than an hour. On the afternoon of November 25, Washington met the third, and most powerful, member of the local Indian triumvirate when Tanacharison (Tanaghrisson), the Half-King, arrived back in Logstown for the hastily scheduled parley. He was the senior Seneca chief of the Ohio Iroquois, or Mingos, and commanded much respect among the English as a dedicated Francophobe. He told Washington of a Frenchman's recent threat to "tread under my Feet all that stand in Opposition"—especially "Flies, or Musquitos, for Indians are such as those."[20]

Washington used such valuable information in the delicate diplomacy he conducted with several sachems the next day in the council longhouse at Logstown. He addressed the chiefs as "Brothers" (i.e., diplomatic equals) of Governor Dinwiddie in contrast to the French proclivity to address Indians as children, and he was deferential in requesting "Advice and Assistance" from "good Friends & Allies . . . [held] in great Esteem." Tanacharison agreed to accompany Washington in delivering Dinwiddie's warning to the French, along with guides and guards from the nearby Mingo, Shawnee, and Delaware villages— but not right away. When Washington balked at this unexpected delay, the Half-King became angry and issued a veiled threat about "Fear[ing] some Accident [that] should befal" the Virginian if he departed hastily without Indian bodyguards. "As I found it was impossible to get off without affronting them in the most egregious Manner," Washington wrote, "I consented to stay." And stay he did, another four days, because the Indians reputedly needed to retrieve France's "Speech-Belt" of wampum from another village so that the Half-King could properly return it to the French commander. Washington suspected cowardice or duplicity on the part of the chiefs, but he was finally assured by more knowledgeable frontiersmen that the "returning of Wampum" would officially signify the Indians' "abolishing of Agreements . . . and shaking of all Dependence upon the French." He was learning patience within the context of Indian ceremonial duties and symbolic obligations, and he wisely concluded that "an Offence offered at this Crisis, might be attended with greater ill Consequence, than another Day's Delay."[21]

Washington was at the mercy of strange customs and dependent upon the goodwill of Indian allies that Britain so desperately needed to counter the French in the Ohio Country. He was aware that the Chippewas, Ottawas, and other native nations to the north had already pledged their support to the French and that they were pressuring the Mingos, Shawnees, and Delawares to form an unprecedentedly strong alliance against the English. Unlike the outnumbered and outgunned Susquehannocks that John Washington had dealt with so cavalierly, the large and strategically placed Ohio tribes were in a perfect diplomatic and geographic position to manipulate the European powers.[22]

The leverage exercised by these Indians was evident when Washington and Tanacharison finally reached French officials at Venango and Fort Le Boeuf. Washington wrote that never in his life had he "suffer'd so much Anxiety" as in trying to keep Tanacharison out of the clutches of Capt. Philippe Thomas Joncaire. An adopted Seneca and skilled Iroquoian linguist of "very great Influence among the Indians," Joncaire used "all possible Means" to win over the Indians, including the generous dispensing of liquor. Washington realized that alcohol rendered the chiefs "incapable of the Business they came about," and he "strictly charg'd" interpreter Davison "not to be out of their Company," as long as Tanacharison and the other chiefs remained at the French garrison. Washington delivered Governor Dinwiddie's message of warning to the French commandant at Fort Le Boeuf on December 12, but that proved to be the easiest part of the expedition. For the following four days, the young Virginian watched and waited with great apprehension as the French tried every means to win back the Indians' loyalty. Washington was finally able to leave Fort Le Boeuf on December 16—with his Indian delegation intact—because he had cannily shamed the French into honoring their promise to provide muskets to Tanacharison's warriors and had embarrassed the Half-King into fulfilling his pledge to abstain from Joncaire's liquor.[23]

The tenuous friendship between Washington and the Logstown chiefs assumed greater significance with the commencing of Anglo-French warfare in spring 1754. The French had responded to Dinwiddie's warning with a large offensive into western Pennsylvania as soon as winter subsided, and by early April, Colonel Washington was already leading some 160 Virginia militiamen into the backcountry—a force that would eventually confront the enemy at Great Meadows. That same month he wrote Tanacharison "with Love and . . . Gratitude for your

constant Attachment to us" and implored him "to come in all Haste to
. . . [his] Assistance." Washington signed the note, "your Friend and
Brother, Conotocarious"—adopting the fearsome Iroquoian appella-
tion of his great-grandfather, which the Half-King had apparently begun calling him on their previous journey to Venango and Fort Le Boeuf.
In May Washington promised Tanacharison that additional troops
would soon arrive to "protect you against your treacherous Enemy the
French." At the same time, he dispatched to the chief a local warrior
who had recently returned from Tidewater Virginia, reporting that he
had been "well . . . received by . . . our Grandees [who] . . . had given
him all that his Heart could wish."[24]

Tanacharison finally responded by mounted messenger on the
evening of May 27, alerting Washington to a contingent of French troops
encamped near present-day Summit, Pennsylvania. After a forced night
march, Washington and forty militiamen met up at daybreak with
Tanacharison, Monacatoocha, and about a dozen warriors. They held
a hasty field parley and agreed "to go hand and hand and strike the
French," marching into battle "one after the other, in the Indian Manner." What followed on the morning of May 28, 1754, was a brief and
bloody skirmish that "set the world on fire"—plunging England and
France into a full-scale war for control of North America and earning
the rash young Washington equal amounts of praise and opprobrium.
When the smoke of battle cleared, ten dead Frenchmen, variously described as soldiers or diplomats, lay bullet-torn and scalped, and another twenty-one Frenchmen were Washington's prisoners. Some
accounts state that Tanacharison personally tomahawked to death the
prominent French commander of the expedition, Joseph Coulon de
Villiers, sieur de Jumonville.[25]

French officials were outraged by the killing of reputed envoys in
violation of "the most sacred laws of civilized nations." Like his great-
grandfather before him, Washington was considered by some to be a
bloodthristy assassin of innocent diplomats. Both Washington and
Governor Dinwiddie tried to appease critics at Whitehall by blaming
the Indians for the attack, even asserting that the English were acting
as auxiliaries to Tanacharison. Washington reported on the enormous
pressure exerted by his Indian companions: "It was the Opinion of the
Half-King . . . that . . . [French] Intentions were evil, and . . . if we had
been such Fools as to let them go, . . . [he] would never help us any
more to take other Frenchmen." Protestations of innocence aside, Wash-

ington had coolly and calculatingly ordered Tanacharison to send the fresh French scalps to Delaware, Wyandot, and Iroquois villages in a conscious effort to attract additional Indian allies to the English cause. While he was concerned about his standing with British officials, Washington may have found the reputation as a cold-blooded assassin to be an advantage in his subsequent dealings with seasoned warriors. This ruthless war-deed, when coupled with his imposing nickname of Town Destroyer, was perhaps what an Iroquois orator referred to when he told Washington that his people "expected every Day to be cut in Pieces by you."[26]

ONCE THE INDIANS AND THE Virginians had shed French blood together, their alliance grew stronger and friendlier, if only temporarily. Washington's victory, however minor and however tainted, had sufficiently deflated the French Canadian reputation for complete mastery of forest warfare, and his encampment at Great Meadows soon received an influx of Indian warriors and their families, including Tanacharison's one hundred Mingos. Many were impressed enough to want to serve under Washington's command, but others, including some twenty-five Shawnee families, sought protection because of the "eminent . . . Danger" from French retaliation. At a rather comical ceremony to welcome his new guests, Washington presented Tanacharison with a George II silver gorget and gave him the nickname of Dinwiddie (which he said meant "The Head of Everything"), and similarly honored the son of an influential Seneca matron, dubbing him Fairfax (which he said meant "First of the Council"). Washington's Anglo-Indian force was at its peak on June 12, 1754, when he mustered "One Hundred and Thirty Men, and about Thirty Indians" to repel a rumored French attack that never materialized.[27]

Thereafter, Washington's military situation at Fort Necessity quickly deteriorated. Allied Indian warriors grew bored with the inactivity of camp life and began to drift away, and Washington soon discovered that flattery was no substitute for military momentum and the distribution of gifts to his auxiliaries. Local chieftains refused to parley with Governor Dinwiddie at Winchester, the Delawares and Shawnees actually renounced their allegiance to the English, and a couple of Washington's "trusty" Indian messengers turned out to be French spies. When a frustrated Washington convened an important conference with representatives of the Six Nations and forty Ohio chiefs at Christopher Gist's plantation in 1754, he sadly discovered that the Iroquois, along with their Delaware "nephews" and Shawnee "grandsons," were predicting an imminent French victory. Above all, though, they were growing weary of the constant coaxing and coercion that both sides employed to gain their support. What it meant to be an Indian in a dangerous world of intruding European authority and white prejudice had been revealed the previous December when Washington encountered twenty frightened warriors, presumably Iroquois, who had discovered the bodies of seven scalped settlers along the Monongahela and immediately "turn'd about & ran back, for fear of the Inhabitants rising & takeing them as the Authors of the Murder."[28]

In the absence of sufficient presents and confidence-building British offensives, Washington was hard pressed to retain the loyalty and support of the Ohio Indians. The Gist conference demonstrated his desperation, as he resorted to exaggerated platitudes and disingenuous promises that almost surely alienated senior Indian leaders, whose wisdom was only exceeded by their cynicism. Did the chieftains truly believe, as Washington asserted, that "the English, your real friends, are too generous" to drive "you off from your Lands" or that "the Governors of Virginia and Pennsylvania . . . sent an Army to maintain your Rights; to put you in the Possession of your Lands, and to take Care of your Wives and Children"? Claiming that he had "drawn the Sword in your Cause, and in your Defence," Washington pleaded for "Warriors to sharpen their Hatchets . . . and unite with us vigorously in our Battles," so that he could "deliver your Country and make it sure to your Children." While he was feigning such sincere respect and friendship, however, Washington made a mockery of the parley process by trying to circumvent the traditional patterns of Iroquois authority over the Ohio tribes. In the midst of formal negotiations with the Six Nations, he conspired with Shingas to circulate "a great War-Belt, to invite all those Warriors who would receive it, to act independently from their King and Council." This deceptive means of obtaining favorable tribal decisions anticipated the intense factional rivalries that would soon divide the native nations of North America, but it did nothing to alleviate Washington's desperate military situation at Great Meadows.[29]

The Gist conference ended with the Iroquois refusing to get involved until either the "cowardly" French or the "foolish" English demonstrated an unequivocal dominance in the field. Words were cheap, but veteran warriors came dear. When a combined force of eight hundred French Canadians and Huron, Abenaki, Algonquin, Nipissing, and Ottawa auxiliaries finally attacked Washington's garrison at Fort Necessity on July 3, 1754, Tanacharison and the other Indians had already abandoned the Virginians. Unable to defend his position without Indian allies or colonial reinforcements, Washington surrendered after suffering severe losses. As his men marched out of the fort, they were attacked by their "own Indians, Shawnesses, Delawares, and Mingos . . . [whom] many of the English knew . . . and called to them by their name[s] to Spare their Goods." Washington recognized "sundry of them, [who] came up and spoke to us, and told us they were our brothers, and asked us how we did." Besides pelting the retreating troops and pillaging their abandoned supplies, some of the French Indians killed and scalped two wounded and three drunken militiamen with the encouragement of Capt. Louis Coulon de Villiers, the expedition's commander and avenging brother of the slain Jumonville.[30]

Following the debacle at Great Meadows, Washington again suffered harsh criticisms of his military abilities from many hostile quarters. Tanacharison observed that "the colonel was a good-natured man, but had no experience; he took upon him[self] to command the Indians as his slaves, . . . but would by no means take advice from the Indians." When Gen. Edward Braddock, newly arrived commander of British forces in North America, discovered in spring 1755 that many tribes were "entirely against us," he laid the blame on Dinwiddie, Washington, and other Virginia leaders, who had "behaved to the Indians with so little discretion, and so much unfair dealing, that we must at present be at great expense to regain their confidence."[31]

Of course, General Braddock would not live to "regain their confidence." The circumstance of his death, however, in the catastrophe that befell his abortive expedition to Fort Duquesne on July 9, 1755, certainly proved the inestimable value of Indian allies. While Braddock and his regulars moved blindly through the backcountry, without the keen eyes of native scouts or flank support from Indian auxiliaries, a mere 250 French regulars and Canadian militiamen, supported by six hundred veteran warriors, were able to cut the redcoated columns to ribbons. How was it possible, wondered Washington and the other survivors of Braddock's sobering debacle, that the French were able to summon hundreds of loyal Indians from a dozen tribes, including the Osage from the distant Missouri prairies, while the English had difficulty maintaining even the temporary, tenuous allegiance of a mere handful of nearby Indians? One reason, of course, was that the large, expansionistic population of land-hungry English colonists and their tradition of extensive slaveholding frightened and offended native nations more than the small numbers of acculturated French Canadian traders and self-sacrificing Jesuit priests ever could. To overcome their negative reputation in the desperate competition for vital native support, the English had "to regain ... [Indian] confidence" with exaggerated promises and expensive presents.[32]

THE DESTRUCTION OF GENERAL Braddock's army was, like the Powhatan Uprising of 1622, a watershed event so terrifying that it transcended simplistic ethnic prejudices and transformed Virginia's relations with Indians. In the aftermath of Braddock's defeat, frequent raids by French and Indian "Conquerors" ripped open the "bowels" of Virginia's once-productive backcountry, and Washington was helpless to prevent the slaughter of several settler families only twelve miles from his Winchester garrison. In April 1756, he reported to Governor Dinwiddie that "the Blue Ridge is now our Frontier, ... no men being left in this County." Impressed by the ability of enemy warriors to "Plunder, Kill, Scalp, and Escape" with virtual impunity, Washington became convinced that "the only Troops fit to Cope with Indians" were other Indians—"infinitly valueable" as allies because they were better than "the best white men ... in the Woods." "Scarce anything can be done" to protect frontier settlements, he wrote, without "a Body of Indians." Advocating mobile raiding parties of allied warriors and colonial rangers instead of defensive fortifications, Washington asserted that "Indians, to Us, are of the utmost importance"; not having them as allies would result in "the most fatal consequences to this part of the continent" and "to the British Affairs in America."[33]

Frontier warfare proved to be an intense acculturative experience, as Europeans and Indians came into close contact on a regular basis and adopted nearly identical clothing, weapons, and tactics. At least superficially, the once-obvious distinctions between "civilized" and "savage" behavior became more blurred as the war went on. When the inexperienced, status-conscious Colonel Washington first arrived in the backcountry fresh from the Northern Neck, he insisted on red regimental uniforms for his troops in the belief that Indians would be awed by the "Power and greatness" of the European clothing. Four years later, however, it was Washington who convinced Gen. John Forbes and Col. Henry Bouquet to permit the Virginia militiamen to dress "Indian-style" in buckskin shirts and even breechcloths. Colonel Bouquet observed that "it would be easier to make Indians of our White men," rather than the other way around, and Washington did not find it particularly ironic or immoral to entertain Indian warriors at Fort Loudoun "with great Civility & send them out on scalping Parties."[34]

Washington and his British superiors eventually succeeded in recruiting Indian allies, although they were more often Catawba, Cherokee, and Nottoway warriors from the South than members of key Ohio Valley tribes. Familiarity with and proximity to people of vastly different cultures, however, frequently bred more contempt than understanding, as Washington painfully discovered with his "many extraneous concerns" in trying to please and appease his native forces. Much of Washington's correspondence between 1756 and 1758 dealt with the problems of keeping the warriors fed, clothed, and contented. "Every service of theirs must be purchased," he wrote about the five hundred "mercenary" tribesmen at Fort Loudoun in April 1758, "and they are easily offended." While Washington's militiamen routinely suffered a cruel shortage of clothes, blankets, flour, rum, and timely pay, Virginia officials were usually most anxious to fund "a large quantity of proper indian goods to reward ... [the] Services" of native auxiliaries. In requisitioning crops from local farms, Washington was sensitive to the settlers' complaints that the "Indians ... eat and waste triple what" the white troops did, and he clearly resented it when a war chief, after observing the poor provisions at Fort Loudoun, asked "if we meant to starve them as well as ourselves."[35]

On a few occasions, Washington expressed sympathy for loyal Cherokee allies, who did endure the same sort of privation and empty promises as the colonial soldiers. In August 1758, he also lavished praise on the heroic Catawba war chiefs, Captain Bullen and Captain French, and buried them with military honors after they were killed in combat. At most other times, though, he was very critical of the Catawbas as being "of little use, but a great expense" and condemned the Cherokees as "the most insolent, most avaricious, and most dissatisfied wretches I have ever had to deal with." Washington was obligated to act with diplomatic "Sollicitude" toward Indian allies as a military commander, but as a Tidewater aristocrat who was "teased incessantly," he resented those "savages [who] look upon themselves in a more important light than ever." His shrill complaints over several years finally caused Governor Dinwiddie in May 1757 to order him to "no longer . . . have concern with, or the management of, Indian affairs."[36]

Despite Dinwiddie's prohibition, Washington continued to take an active, if perhaps more circumspect, interest in Indian affairs—with good reason. He had personally survived two hostile encounters with Indian enemies, and his Virginia militiamen suffered a hundred casualties in over twenty skirmishes between March 1756 and January 1757. Washington was clearly frustrated with garrison duty and the onerous burden of protecting vulnerable settlements along a 350-mile frontier with only seven hundred men. He would have resigned his post but for a sense of duty and the awful realization that "the murder of poor innocent Babes and helpless families may be laid to my account here!" He repeatedly urged an offensive against the "Hold of Barbarians" at Fort Duquesne in order to remove the source of enemy Indians who practiced "their Hellish Arts" throughout the backcountry. "The only method of effectually defending . . . [the Virginia and Pennsylvania] frontiers against such an enemy," he wrote in September 1757, "is by carrying the war into their country. . . . Unless an Expedition is carried on against the Ohio next spring, this country will not be another year in our possession."[37]

English officials did not disagree with the objective, but they realized that the strong and strategic Forks of the Ohio could neither be taken nor held without substantial support from Indian allies. When that infamous fortress finally fell to the Virginia militia on November 25, 1758, it was already a burned and abandoned citadel. The French had deserted and destroyed it when their Ohio Indian allies defected. The diplomatic actions of the League Iroquois, rather than the military threat posed by Britain's Western Expedition, doomed Fort Duquesne, as the Six Nations dramatically shifted the balance of power and the weight of manpower to the English side in the critical Easton Treaty conference of October 1758.[38]

IRONICALLY, WASHINGTON WAS PROBably less ecstatic about the new Iroquois alliance than other English commanders, not only because it cheated him out of personal revenge against the French (450 skulls were found in the Fort Duquesne area to remind him of the tragic Braddock campaign) but because his gentleman's code of honor could not condone the Indians' practice of shifting allegiances. At the beginning of his military career, Washington pronounced that "nothing is a greater stranger to my Breast, or a Sin that my Soul more abhors than that black and detestable one, Ingratitude." Dubious loyalties and alliances of convenience, however, were so commonplace in this great war for Indian support that many English officers, including Washington, sarcastically referred to "our Friendly Indians (as they call them)." In May 1758, Washington observed that it was "the nature of Indians, that nothing will prevent their going where they have any reason to expect presents, and their cravings are insatiable." That very month, Bedford County officials reported how seventy warriors, whom they identified as Cherokee allies, had gone on a bloody rampage in their area; when the colonists asked who they were, the Indians "cald them selves Sumtimes Cherokees & sumtimes Shonees [Shawnees, i.e., French allies]." At a critical moment in the English advance to Fort Duquesne, General Forbes was outraged by the sudden, "villainous desertion" of Chief Little Carpenter and a dozen warriors, who fled with much-needed guns, ammunition, and horses.[39]

The fall of Fort Duquesne and the rising of Fort Pitt on its ashes was symbolic of a significant turning point in European-Indian relations and of complex maneuvering by different native auxiliaries. George Mercer reported in September 1759 that "the Savages come in . . . great Numbers begging Remission of their Sins and Forgiveness for past Offences." Capt. Robert Stewart similarly wrote from Fort Pitt that "the Indians not only of this Voisinage, but of several remote Nations beyond the Lakes, are of the best Disposition towards us & sincerely inclin'd to . . . cultivate a strict & permanent Friendship with us[;] they have already brought us near Fifty of their Captives." In that same letter of September 1759, Stewart noted how "very desireable" it was that the Shawnees—past French but now English, allies—were warring with the Cherokees—past English friends but now English enemies. The frontier world of Indian allegiance had turned upside down, as the Miamis shifted sides one month after the English victory at Fort Duquesne and slaughtered two complete villages of French settlers near Fort Detroit. In 1759 and 1760, however, the formerly loyal Cherokees were attacking Englishmen—"leav[ing] . . . no room to doubt what part our old allies are determined to act." Captain Stewart, the veteran

Virginia militiaman, assessed the situation in a letter to Washington: "If it is true that the Creeks and Cherrokees have enter'd into a League against us, I tremble for our Southern Colonies! As from what the Ohio Indians have done, we may easily conceive, that the united Force of such Warlike & Formidable Nations can effect to our prejudice."[40]

THE SHIFTING INDIAN ALLEGIANCES that followed the fall of Fort Duquesne was one signal of the precarious fate that awaited the native nations east of the Mississippi. The great war for Indian support all too quickly became a great war for Indian survival in eastern America. As the French were rolled back from the Ohio Country and the British concentrated on capturing Quebec and Montreal, the backcountry tribes of all current and previous loyalties faced a future that would not include the leverage of playing off one European power against the other. All Indians would soon be considered irrelevant unless they were both powerful and hostile, and every tribe in every area would eventually be treated as impediments to western expansion. After 1758 the middle of America would be increasingly dominated by land-seeking English colonists, who had excessively long memories with regard to former Indian foes and exceedingly short ones toward former Indian friends.

John Washington's legacy of advancing frontiers by double-crossing Indian allies was magnified and expanded into national policy by his great-grandson. As commander in chief of the Continental army, George Washington finally achieved the broad powers and extensive forces necessary for his long-denied pursuit of Indian affairs. During the Revolutionary War, the Senecas and Mohawks—enraged that the Iroquois had never received the Ohio Country as promised by the 1758 Easton Treaty—supported the British against the colonists. In 1779 Washington ordered Maj. Gen. John Sullivan to attack the traditional Seneca homeland of his former comrade in arms, Tanacharison, and "lay waste all the settlements around . . . that the country may not be merely overrun but destroyed." "You will not by any means listen to any overture of peace before the total ruin of the settlements is effected," Washington instructed Sullivan. "Our future security will be in their inability to injure us . . . and in the terror with which the severity of the chastizement they receive will inspire them." The emotional wounds of that devastating, scorched-earth campaign lasted long after the land

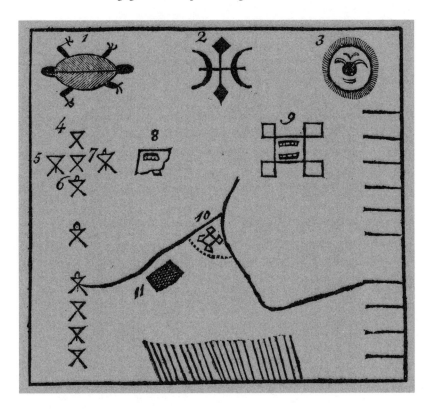

An Ohio Indian drew this view of the strategically placed Fort Pitt (labeled 10) and "Pittsboro" (11) on bark about 1762. It was reproduced in William Bray's "Observations on the Indian Method of Picture Writing," in *Archaeologia VI* (1782), 159–162. Courtesy of the Edward E. Ayer Collection, The Newberry Library, Chicago, Illinois.

had healed, as Chief Cornplanter personally explained to President Washington a decade later: "When your army entered the country of the Six Nations, we called you Town Destroyer; and to this day when that name is heard, our women look behind them and turn pale and our children cling close to the necks of their mothers." Washington's experiences in the backcountry had taught him that "no troops in the universe can guard against the cunning and wiles of Indians" as guerrilla fighters. But he also learned that by aggressively "carrying . . . war into their country," a large invading army could neutralize even the strongest tribe, provided it had "malice enough" to destroy crops, dev-

Engraved silver medal presented to the Seneca council orator, Red
Jacket (Segoyewatha), c. 1750–1830 by President Washington during
their 1792 parley in Philadelphia. When Washington assured Red
Jacket that he was not the reason the Ohio tribes were fighting the
United States, the Seneca challenged him "to point out ... what you
think is the real cause." (Quoted in Daniel Richter, "Red Jacket," in
Encyclopedia of North American Indians, ed. Frederick E. Hoxie [Bos-
ton: Houghton Mifflin, 1996], 532–533.) Reproduced with the
permissionof the Buffalo and Erie County Historical Society, Buffalo, New York.

astate villages, demoralize dependents, and deplete warrior populations
in an exhausting war of attrition.[41]

Just six years after his "chastizement" of the Senecas, General Washington was portrayed as the American Joshua, leading his people "to
found an empire, and to rule a world" in Timothy Dwight's epic poem,

The Conquest of Canaan. There was little doubt about where this new Canaan was located, which people the savage, beast-like Canaanites most resembled, or how the conflict over values and territories would be decided. With the West on their minds and the recent heroics of the Revolutionary War fresh in their memories, Americans gave George Washington, the Father of His Country—the Destroyer of Their Country—an unprecedented mandate of political popularity as the first president. In that ultimate office for managing Indian affairs, Washington pursued uncompromisingly aggressive policies against old Indian enemies and former Indian friends on behalf of his land-hungry constituents. The twice conquered Ohio Country represented the tangible fruits of victory, the young nation's first frontier of fresh lands and new beginnings—in Washington's words, a Canaan-like "Land of promise" ideally suited for settlement by "the poor, the needy and oppressed of the Earth," including Northern Neck tobacco planters with exhausted soils and crushing debts.[42]

"The God of battles, to whom he made his solemn appeal," wrote Archbishop Carroll, had allowed Washington to win the "freedom of an immense territory, destined to be the habitation of countless millions." Having "penetrated into the inhospitable confines of the savage Indian" as a young officer, Washington was ideally prepared to "render them the abodes of peace and introduce into their bosom the improvements of civilization" by "just and necessary warfare." The words of the gentry cleric, writing in 1800, accurately reflected President Washington's policy priorities as the new nation invaded and exploited western lands long occupied and still claimed by thousands of Indians. Soon after he took office, Washington consciously provoked the Ohio tribes into climactic combat by encouraging hordes of American farmers to "Increase and Multiply" in the backcountry. Washington well knew what the Indian response would be, having listened, almost forty years earlier, as his closest Indian associate, Tanacharison, chastised both the English and the French as "Disturbers in this Land." The "Country between" belonged to no European and could never be the home of white men, he had said, for "the Great Being above allow'd it to be a Place of Residence for us." "I desire you to withdraw," the Half-King had warned in 1754, "for I am not afraid to discharge you off this Land."[43]

When the Ohio tribes predictably retaliated against the provocation of settler invasion, Washington was well prepared. He organized a permanent, million-dollar-a-year American army of five thousand men to crush the native "aggressors." "The Indians," wrote Washington, "must be convinced that the Americans are all one people—that they shall never attack any part with impunity." The new frontier army, including mounted rangers that Washington had advocated since the 1750s, was sent into action in 1791, even as several western tribes were still negotiating treaties in good faith. The president's memories of old frontier horrors were perhaps still too vivid when he ordered his soldiers to slaughter those "animals of prey"—Indians who refused to leave their settled villages for fear of literally becoming as nomadic and scattered as wild beasts. Was this what Washington intended when he wrote that "every people should pursue the same path in 'the process of society from the barbarous ages to its present degree of perfection'"?[44]

Years before, immediately after the fall of Fort Duquesne, Washington had hoped that the Ohio Country, the new West, would be a frontier of fresh starts, rather than repeated mistakes. In an enlightened proposal of November 1758, he had advocated, very Claiborne-like, the establishment of a "free, open and . . . equitable" fur trade with the Ohio Valley Indians. The "reciprocal advantages" and "beneficial consequences" of such a well-regulated business partnership would be the most "effectual way of rivetting . . . [Indians] to our interest." This new beginning in Anglo-Indian relations would, according to Washington, circumvent the "sinister views of designing, selfish men" and "remove those bad impressions that the Indians received from the conduct of . . . rascally Fellows divested of all faith and honor." Many key tribes, however, already regarded Washington himself as the worst of those "rascally Fellows." He learned in 1759 that the influential Delawares and Shawnees were "greatly incens'd against you, who they call the Great Knife & look on you to be the author of their greatest misfortunes."[45]

The years of bitter, atrocity-ridden campaigning had taken their toll on all participants. Too many bloody deeds, too many bloody scenes in this war had produced a mutual brutalization and a reciprocal distrust across the cultures that time could not quickly erase. In September 1759, Captain Stewart questioned why there was so little interest in the fur trade idea, given Virginia's "many public Spirited Gent[leme]n . . . who must have an Inclination to advance the Interest of their Country by increasing their private Fortunes. What can be the reason that

none of them embraces so favourable an opportunity of accomplish-
ing so desireable an End?"[46]

The primary reasons were the desire for land and an accompanying distaste for the native people on it. Colonial entrepreneurs, most
particularly Washington, quickly soured on the fur trade idea because
it would have promoted and prolonged an Indian presence in the Ohio
Country and discouraged the profitable speculation in, and white expansion into, the new western territories. Less than a year after Washington made his fur trade proposal, he was himself deeply involved as
"a Partner in the Scheme" to secure a substantial portion of frontier
lands. As George Mercer, his business partner and Northern Neck neighbor, wrote: "We will leave no Stone unturned to secure to ourselves this
Land." Governor Dinwiddie had initiated this intense scramble for real
estate in 1754, when he authorized the distribution of 200,000 acres of
western land to Virginia's combat veterans—"in a Proportion due to
their respective Merit, as . . . represented to me by their Officers."[47]

Clearly, Colonel Washington had his sights set on a substantial
portion of that "Charming Country." By heritage and profession, he
knew the social, as well as the economic, value of extensive holdings
for Virginia gentlemen, and by the age of twenty, he had already patented some twenty-three hundred acres of prime Shenandoah Valley
land. As Washington explained to a prominent Virginia politician, his
persistent interference in frontier Indian policies during the war with
France was because he owned "property in the Country, and . . . [was]
unwilling to loose it." Two decades later, in the midst of the Revolutionary War, Washington observed that "a great and lasting War can
never be supported on this principle [of patriotism] alone. It must be
aided by a prospect of Interest or some reward." Washington was indeed rewarded for his military service and knowledgeable investments,
acquiring some fifty-eight thousand acres west of the Alleghenies, including over forty thousand acres in the Great Kanawha Valley and
extensive holdings in southwestern Pennsylvania, central Ohio, and
Kentucky. At his death, he still held title to some forty-five thousand
acres of western lands. How sadly ironic, but entirely predictable, that
Washington, who freely admitted that England's victory in the West
was mostly attributable to the actions of Indians, would see America's
vast new frontier in terms of real estate yet to be wrested from native
peoples.[48]

When Washington was confronted with the personal choice of investing in Indian furs or owning Indian lands, he decided as his great-grandfather had. Standing amid the burned fortress at the strategic Forks of the Ohio, he perhaps reflected upon the economic boost that another burned stockade some two hundred miles to the east and eighty-three years in the past had given his Northern Neck forebear. Along the equally beautiful, but similarly bloodied, banks of another notable river, Washington could clearly envision the confluence of the familiar eastern frontiers of the past and the unknown western frontiers of the future. At the Forks of the Ohio, which Indians had consistently prevented him from reaching until his final days of militia service, the destiny of America seemed truly manifest and purely white. From this dearly won vantage point, Washington grasped the vast economic potential of the Ohio River's thousand-mile length and its 200,000-square mile watershed. For the rest of his life, he strove to make his own Potomac, flowing between Mount Vernon and the site of the Susquehannock fort, "the Channel of conveyance of the extensive and valuable Trade of a rising Empire"—an empire of canals and cities, forts and farmsteads constructed on the Indian old fields of former native nations. Unlike the "American Cincinnatus" who returned to his beloved plantation, the Indian veterans of the Great War for Empire would not have the luxury of resigning commissions to return to the security of their fields. For them, the critical war for the West did not end in 1763, or 1783—or ever.[49]

The most famous Washington, as well as the first Washington, came to know the fruits of frontier warfare, the lucrative spoils that accompanied success, and the intimate connection between punitive town destruction and profitable town creation. How unremarkable it was, how typically American it would turn out to be, that John Washington's descendant became Great Knife—America's highest-ranking and most revered Indian fighter. Only through the assistance of Indians was Washington able to see the Ohio Country, to survive his experiences there, to build a reputation as a military commander, and to achieve what Archbishop Carroll called the "fulfillment of his future destinies" as a national icon of frontier heroism. But a few years of joint Anglo-Indian campaigning could not erase two centuries of cultural prejudice, and every cruelty of combat, even if committed on Britain's behalf, solidified the English fear of "Savage Fury."[50]

Washington was proud of his frontier experiences and wrote that "few Persons ... have had better oppertunity's to become acquainted" with the "Tempers ... Customs and dispositions" of Indians in the backcountry. But he also "acknowledge[d] my incompetency" in Indian affairs, admitting in 1757 that "we are strangers to the only proper method of managing ... them." If close contact in war did not promote mutual understanding between the English and the Indians, it did provide the former with the practical frontier adaptations in tactical expertise to eventually vanquish the latter. Washington spent his formative years "engaged in enterprises pregnant with terror" and became much admired by his common countrymen for surviving so many close calls in his western adventures. But his early exposure to the expansive landscapes of a potential new empire only strengthened his resolve to secure it for his race and culture from temporary Indian allies, whom policymakers and profit motives would never allow to become permanent friends. Washington would have remained a dime novel curiosity as a western traveler if he had not attained later military power and political prominence by engaging in terrible and terroristic "chastizements" against the Indians who threatened or at least inconvenienced his white constituents. "No man ever intended better," young Washington wrote in 1756, "nor studied the Interests of his Country with more affectionate zeal than I have done." How symbolically fitting it is, then, that Mount Rushmore features the larger-than-life image of this reviled town destroyer and revered nation builder, casting a long shadow over the sacred but conquered lands of Indians.[51]

$\mathcal{I}$N 1757, EXACTLY ONE HUNDRED years after John Washington arrived in the Northern Neck, his great-grandson brazenly asserted that "Virginia is a Country young in War ... [having] Lived in the most profound and Tranquil Peace, never studying War nor Warfare." George Washington's militia rank, his wealth as a gentleman-planter of Doeg lands, and his very presence as a military commander in the distant Alleghenies at that time, however, clearly demonstrated how long and successfully war had promoted the territorial expansion and comfortable prosperity of Virginia. In the same year, Washington also observed that "an Indian will never forget a promise made to him ... For which reason, nothing ought ever to be promised but what is performed."[52]

Reflecting upon Washington's long and significant career in the history of the Ohio Valley frontier, is it any wonder that the Indians who knew Great Knife first, best, and longest would quickly discover and always detest the awful truth behind his hypocritical pretense of "Sincerity and Esteem"? Can we be surprised that the keen sachems of the council fires accurately grasped the contradictions between Washington's words and his deeds, or that they reluctantly fought alongside him—and ultimately against him—in a desperate effort to achieve their unwavering goals of tribal sovereignty and territorial security?[53]

"Be of good Courage, my Brethren, deliver your Country, and make it sure to your Children," Washington had promised the Ohio Valley Indians in June 1754, when they were still powerful and dominant along the fertile frontier. "Our conduct alone will answer in our Behalf. Examine the Truth yourselves."[54]

NOTES

1. John Carroll, *Eulogy on George Washington, Delivered in St. Peter's Church, Baltimore, February 22, 1800* (New York: P. J. Kennedy & Sons, 1931), 9–10. The title quotation is from p. 8.

2. Carroll, *Eulogy*, 9–10. On Washington's frontier role, see Thomas A. Lewis, *For King and Country: George Washington—The Early Years* (New York: John Wiley & Sons, 1993); James Titus, *The Old Dominion at War: Society, Politics, and Warfare in Late Colonial Virginia* (Columbia: University of South Carolina Press, 1991); Charles H. Ambler, *George Washington and the West* (Chapel Hill: University of North Carolina Press, 1936); Richard Slotkin, *Regeneration through Violence: The Mythology of the American Frontier, 1600–1860* (Middletown, Conn.: Wesleyan University Press, 1973), 330–32, 344–45; James Thomas Flexner, *Washington: The Indispensable Man* (New York: New American Library, 1984), 1–2. On the images of Daniel Boone and Thomas Jefferson, see J. Gray Sweeney, *The Columbus of the Woods: Daniel Boone and the Typology of Manifest Destiny* (St. Louis: Washington University Gallery of Art, 1992); Donald Jackson, *Thomas Jefferson and the Stony Mountains: Exploring the West from Monticello* (Urbana: University of Illinois Press, 1981). Francis Jennings wrote that "Washington's most hagiographical biographers rarely report accurately his transactions with Indians or Indian lands"; see Jennings, ed., *The History and Culture of Iroquois Diplomacy: An Interdisciplinary Guide to the Treaties of the Six Nations and Their League* (Syracuse, N.Y.: Syracuse University Press, 1985), 254.

3. Susan Myra Kingsbury, ed., *Records of the Virginia Company of London*, 4 vols. (Washington, D.C.: U.S. Government Printing Office, 1906–1935), 4:73, 448, 450, 468, 508; Capt. John Smith, T*he Generall Historie of Virginia, New–England, and the Summer Isles* (London: Michael Sparkes, 1624), 153–54; J. Frederick Fausz, "Fighting 'Fire' with Firearms: The Anglo-Powhatan Arms Race in Early Virginia," *American Indian Culture and Research Journal* 3 (Winter 1980): 33–50.

4. Samuel Purchas, "Virginias Verger; or, A Discourse Shewing the Benefits Which May Grow to this Kingdome from American English Plantations" (1625), *Hakluytus Posthumus; or, Purchas His Pilgrimes*, 20 vols. (Glasgow: James Maclehose and Sons, 1905–7), 19:257; Smith, *Generall Historie of Virginia*, 155; J. Frederick Fausz, "Merging and Emerging Worlds: Anglo–Indian Interest Groups and the Development of the Seventeenth-Century Chesapeake," in *Colonial Chesapeake Society*, ed. Lois Green Carr, Philip D. Morgan, and Jean B. Russo (Chapel Hill: University of North Carolina Press, 1988), 51–59.

5. *Virginia Company Records*, 3:437; Fausz, "Merging Worlds," 54–55. Wyatt was the first Virginia governor without prior military experience, but he and his councilors were immortalized in a contemporary poem about their Indian raids, which was sung to the tune, "All those that be good fellowes;" see "Good News from Virginia, 1623," W*illiam and Mary Quarterly*, 3d ser., 5 (July 1948): 351–58.

6. Stephen R. Potter and Gregory A. Waselkov, "Indian Towns and English Plantations: An Archaeological Analysis of Algonquian and Anglo Settlement Patterns in Virginia's Northern Neck" (paper presented at the annual meeting of the Organization of American Historians, Washington, D.C., March 1990), 1, 6, 11; Fausz, "Merging Worlds," 60–86. See also Stephen R. Potter, *Commoners, Tribute, and Chiefs: The Development of Algonquian Culture in the Potomac Valley* (Charlottesville: University Press of Virginia, 1993).

7. Douglas Southall Freeman, *George Washington: A Biography*, 7 vols. (New York: Charles Scribner's Sons, 1948–1957), 1:15–21. Ironically, Capt. Nicholas Martiau, "progenitor of . . . George Washington," was heavily involved in the trading oligarchy of the 1620s and 1630s and died in 1657, the year that John Washington arrived in Virginia; see Virginia M. Meyer and John Frederick Dorman, eds., *Adventurers of Purse and Person: Virginia, 1607–1624/5*, 3d ed. (Richmond: Dietz Press, 1987), 417–30.

8. Wilcomb E. Washburn, *The Governor and The Rebel: A History of Bacon's Rebellion in Virginia* (Chapel Hill: University of North Carolina Press, 1957), chap. 2; Raphael Semmes, *Captains and Mariners of Early Maryland* (Baltimore: The Johns Hopkins University Press, 1937), 518–23; Freeman, *Washington*, 1: 21–22; *Mount Vernon: An Illustrated Handbook* (Mount Vernon: The Mount Vernon Ladies' Association of the Union, 1974), 15; L. E. Moore, "A

Little History of the Doeg" (Fairfax, Va.: Environmental and Heritage Resources Office, Fairfax County Government, n.d.).

9. Washburn, *Governor and Rebel*, 23–29; Freeman, *Washington*, 1:22–25; Barry C. Kent, *Susquehanna's Indians* (Harrisburg: Pennsylvania Historical and Museum Commission, 1984), 46–49; Alice L. Ferguson, "The Susquehannock Fort on Piscataway Creek," *Maryland Historical Magazine* 36 (March 1941): 1–9.

10. "A True Narrative of the Rise, Progresse, and Cessation of the Late Rebellion in Virginia . . . by his Majestyes Commissioners" (1677), in *Early American Indian Documents: Treaties and Laws, 1607–1789*, ed. Alden T. Vaughan, vol. 4, *Virginia Treaties, 1607–1722*, ed. W. Stitt Robinson (Frederick, Md.: University Publications of America, 1983), 74–78; *The Diaries of George Washington*, ed. Donald Jackson and Dorothy Twohig, 6 vols. (Charlottesville: University Press of Virginia, 1976–1979), 1:183n–84n.

11. Fausz, "Merging Worlds," 84–91; Washburn, *Governor and Rebel*, chaps. 7–9; Stephen Saunders Webb, *1676: The End of American Independence* (New York: Alfred A. Knopf, 1984), 124–63; William L. Shea, *The Virginia Militia in the Seventeenth Century* (Baton Rouge: Louisiana State University Press, 1983), 122–40.

12. Freeman, *Washington*, 1:36–37, 52. Two works that thematically link the Indian wars of the seventeenth and eighteenth centuries are: David Horowitz, *The First Frontier: The Indian Wars and America's Origins, 1607–1776* (New York: Simon and Schuster, 1978); and Ian K. Steele, *Warpaths: Invasions of North America* (New York: Oxford University Press, 1994).

13. Freeman, *Washington*, 1:48–74, 148–49, 160–61.

14. Freeman, *Washington*, 1:186–89, 447–513; Paul K. Longmore, *The Invention of George Washington* (Berkeley: University of California Press, 1988), chap. 1; Stuart E. Brown Jr., *Virginia Baron: The Story of Thomas, 6th Lord Fairfax* (Berryville, Va.: Chesapeake Book Company, 1965), chaps. 6–7, 9–11, 14.

15. The quote is from George Washington to Gov. Robert Dinwiddie, March 10, 1757, *The Papers of George Washington*, Colonial Series, ed. W. W. Abbot et al., 10 vols. (Charlottesville, Va.: University Press of Virginia, 1983–1995), 4:112. The 1,200–1,400 Indians reported living in western Pennsylvania by 1730 grew to some 3,000–4,000 twenty years later. About 2,400 Indians, mostly Iroquois, inhabited the Cuyahoga Valley by 1743 to be close to French traders; see Michael N. McConnell, *A Country Between: The Upper Ohio Valley and Its Peoples, 1724–1774* (Lincoln: University of Nebraska Press, 1992), 22–23, 210. By 1768, some 1,800 Shawnees, 3,500 Delawares and Munsees, 1,000 Wyandots, and 600 Mingos were reported in the Ohio Country—refugees from eastern conflicts who swelled the population there, even though their total numbers had been reduced elsewhere by war and epidemics. Another 1,000 Ottawas and 4,000 Miamis lived farther west, while the Six Nations to

the east maintained a population of 7,500. Using a ratio of one warrior for five "others," the Ohio Indians closest to English settlements alone could have mustered 1,400 warriors; see Helen Hornbeck Tanner, ed., *Atlas of Great Lakes Indian History* (Norman: University of Oklahoma Press, 1987), 44, 58–59, 66.

What made the frontier situation particularly perilous for the English was the ability of the French to recruit 800–1,000 Indian allies for key engagements from areas well beyond the limits of the Ohio Country—including the "Seven Nations of Canada" (Lac des Deux Montagnes Iroquois, Algonquins, and Nipissings; Caughnawaga Iroquois from Sault St. Louis, Abenakis of St. Francis, Hurons of Lorette, near Quebec City, Akwesasne Mohawks of St. Regis River); the "Lakes Indians" from the Detroit area (Hurons, Ottawas, Chippewas, Potawatomies); Ojibwas ("Sauteurs") from Lake Superior; Menominees from Green Bay; and Winnebagos, Mesquakies, Sauks, and Iowas.

There was, of course, nothing accidental about the simultaneous, multicultural interest shown in the Ohio country by British, French, and Americans. Colonial incursions had already pushed eastern tribes like the Delawares onto the distant territories of little-known peoples, when large-scale sponsored expansionism was given a boost by the British capture of Louisbourg in 1745. The French had to respond to tribal defections, British claims, and American incursions to protect their territory, and the governors of Canada gained greater autonomy to control military operations in the interior after 1750. The French attack on the Miamis in 1752, in which Chief Memeskia was killed and eaten at Pickawillany, reflected the desperation of the underpopulated Canadians to bring former Indian allies back into the fold as their most effective weapon against the British. On the eve of the Seven Years' War in America, both colonial powers sought the allegiance of the Six Nations, as well as that of the strategically located Allegheny Iroquois, Delawares, and Shawnees; see Steele, *Warpaths*, 175–183; Jennings, ed., *Iroquois Diplomacy*, 48–52.

16. Washington, March 23, 1748, *Washington Diaries*, 1:13; Washington, March 25, 1748, *Washington Diaries*, 1:15; George Washington, *The Journal of Major George Washington, Sent by the Hon. Robert Dinwiddie, Esq. . . . to the Commandant of the French Forces on [The] Ohio* (Williamsburg: William Hunter, 1754), 20–21.

17. Washington, April 4, 1748, *Washington Diaries*, 1:18; *Washington Diaries*, 1:182n. (quote attributed to Gov. James Glen of South Carolina); Washington to Richard, 1749–1750, *Washington Papers*, Col. Ser., 1:44.

18. Washington, March 15, 1748, *Washington Diaries*, 1:9; Washington, December 5, 1753, *Washington Diaries*, 1:146; Freeman, *Washington*, 1:283, 286, 290; for biographical information on individuals mentioned, see *Washington Diaries*, 1:12n, 130n, 154n, 183n, 192n, 208n. Additional information on cultural intermediaries may be found in Francis Jennings, *Empire of Fortune: Crowns,*

Colonies, and Tribes in the Seven Years War in America (New York: W. W. Norton, 1988). See also the excellent chapter on "The Traders" in Lewis, *King and Country*, 47–72.

19. Washington, *Journal of Major Washington*, 3–4. The spelling of often-variable Indian personal names conforms to the conventions of the *Washington Diaries* and *Washington Papers* series published by the University Press of Virginia. Indians were very suspicious of English surveyors, and some even refered to a compass as a "land stealer." Christopher Gist quoted in Lewis, *King and Country*, 53.

20. Washington, *Journal of Major Washington*, 5–8. See the excellent chronology of treaties, gazetteer, and biographical directory in Jennings, ed., *Iroquois Diplomacy*, which are indispensable for comprehending the complex events of this period.

21. Washington, *Journal of Major Washington*, 9–12. Lewis provides keen insights on the different cultural assumptions underlying European and Indian approaches to diplomacy; see *King and Country*, 59–60, 78–79.

22. See Jennings, *Empire of Fortune*, chaps. 4–5. Tanacharison referred to the Ohio frontier as "a Country between" the opposing forces of the French and English that belonged to neither of them; see Washington, *Journal of Major Washington*, 7. Gist reported that a Delaware messenger asked him, "Since 'the French claimed all the land on one side of the River Ohio and the English on the other side . . . where [did] the Indians' land lay?'" Quoted in Lewis, *King and Country*, 56.

23. Washington, *Journal of Major Washington*, 13–15, 19.

24. Washington, April 3, 1754, *Washington Diaries*, 1:183; Washington, May 19, 1754, *Washington Diaries*, 1:189–90. Washington first used the alias Caunotaucarious or Connotaucarious (his spellings) in correspondence to Governor Dinwiddie in April 1754; see Washington, April 3, 1754, *Washington Diaries*, 1:184N; Washington to Dinwiddie, April 25, 1754, *Washington Papers*, Col. Ser., 1:87–88.

25. Washington, May 27, 1754, *Washington Diaries*, 1:194–95; Washington to Dinwiddie, May 29, 1754, *Washington Papers*, Col. Ser., 1:110–12; Robert C. Alberts, *A Charming Field for an Encounter: The Story of George Washington's Fort Necessity* (Washington, D.C.: National Park Service, 1975), 16–20.

26. Washington, May 27, 1754, *Washington Diaries*, 1:198; Washington, June 18, 1754, *Washington Diaries*, 1:202; Alberts, *Charming Field*, 20.

27. Washington, June 1–12, 1754, *Washington Diaries*, 1: 199–201; Alberts, *Charming Field*, 21–25.

28. Washington, December 23, 1753, *Washington Diaries*, 1:156, 156n.; Washington, June 12, 1754, *Washington Diaries*, 1:201; Washington, June 18–21, 1754, *Washington Diaries*, 1:202–9; Alberts, *Charming Field*, 24, 27.

29. Washington, June 18–21, 1754, *Washington Diaries*, 1:203–8.

30. Alberts, *Charming Field*, 30, 38–39, 41–45; Lawerence Henry Gipson, *The British Empire before the American Revolution*, 15 vols. (New York: Alfred A. Knopf, 1958–1970), 6:31, 40–42.

31. Alberts, *Charming Field*, 45; Gipson, *British Empire*, 6:52–53, 77–78. Braddock himself was undiplomatic and offensive to Indians and colonists alike. Monacatoocha reported that "he looked upon us as dogs, and would never hear anything that was said to him," while Shingas recalled that Braddock rejected Indian assistance and "said that No Savage Should Inherit the Land"; see Jennings, *Empire of Fortune*, 152–55. Gen. John Forbes was not any more favorably inclined toward native allies, writing in 1758 that "our Indians I have at length brought to reason by treating them as they always ought to be, with the greatest signs of scorning indifference and disdain, that I could decently employ"; see *Washington Papers*, Col. Ser., 6:145–146n. Just before the surrender at Great Meadows, Scarouady burned Logstown and abandoned the English, while in the immediate aftermath of the defeat, Tanacharison relocated his handful of followers at Croghan's outpost on Aughwick Creek (near Mount Union, Pa.). After bitterly denouncing Washington, the Half-King died there on October 4; see McConnell, *Country Between*, 110. Lewis provides Tanacharison with an epitaph that is fittingly ironic: "The English called him a half-king, derided him as an unreliable savage, and marched on toward catastrophe"; see *King and Country*, 81.

32. Gipson, *British Empire*, 6:90–97; Alberts, *Charming Field*, 47–53; John Joseph Mathews, *The Osages: Children of the Middle Waters* (Norman: University of Oklahoma Press, 1961), 222–26; Willard H. Rollings, *The Osage: An Ethnohistorical Study of Hegemony on the Prairie-Plains* (Columbia: University of Missouri Press, 1992). See W. J. Eccles, *The Canadian Frontier, 1534–1760* (Albuquerque: University of New Mexico Press, 1974), 1–11, for a succinct overview of the differences between English and French relations with Indians.

33. Washington to Dinwiddie, April 27, 1756, *Washington Papers*, Col. Ser., 3:59; Washington to Dinwiddie, October 9, 1757, *Washington Papers*, Col. Ser., 5:12; Washington to Dinwiddie, April 24, 1756, *Washington Papers*, Col. Ser., 3:45; Washington to Dinwiddie, October 24, 1757, *Washington Papers*, Col. Ser., 5:25; Washington to John Campbell, earl of Loudoun, January 10, 1757, *Washington Papers*, Col. Ser., 4:87; Washington to Gen. John Forbes, June 19, 1758, *Washington Papers*, Col Ser., 5:224; Washington to Col. Henry Bouquet, July 16, 1758, *Washington Papers*, Col. Ser., 5:292; Washington, Memoranda, September 17–November 15, 1757, *Washington Papers*, Col. Ser., 4:404; Washington to John Robinson, October 25, 1757, *Washington Papers*, Col. Ser., 5:33.

34. Washington to Dinwiddie, March 7, 1754, *Washington Papers*, Col. Ser., 1:72; Washington to Bouquet, July 3, 1758, *Washington Papers*, Col. Ser., 5:257–58, 259n.; Washington to Adam Stephen, July 16, 1758, *Washington Papers*, Col.

Ser., 5:290; Bouquet to Washington, July 14, 1758, *Washington Papers*, Col Ser., 5:287; Dinwiddie to Washington, April 5, 1757, *Washington Papers*, Col. Ser., 4:129. Gen. John Forbes wrote to Col. Bouquet that he supported "equiping Numbers of our men like the savages," because "in this country wee must comply and learn the Art of Warr from Ennemy Indians"; see Forbes to Bouquet, June 27, 1758, *Washington Papers*, Col. Ser., 5:259n.

35. Washington to Dinwiddie, September 17, 1757, *Washington Papers*, Col. Ser., 4:407, 409; Washington to Gen. John Stanwix, April 10, 1758, *Washington Papers*, Col. Ser., 5:117; Washington to William Fairfax, August 11, 1754, *Washington Papers*, Col. Ser., 1:187; Washington to Dinwiddie, December 19, 1756, *Washington Papers*, Col. Ser., 4:62–66; Washington to Robinson, December 19, 1756, *Washington Papers*, Col. Ser., 4:67–69; Washington to George Mercer, December 20, 1756, *Washington Papers*, Col. Ser., 4:69–70; Washington to Loudoun, January 10, 1757, *Washington Papers*, Col. Ser., 4:80–82, 86. Excessive and redundant gift-giving by Virginia and Pennsylvania caused each to suspect the other of seeking leverage to gain Indian lands and led Washington to support the appointment of a special Indian superintendent for the southern tribes.

36. Washington to Dinwiddie, November 5, 1757, *Washington Papers*, Col. Ser., 5:44–45; Washington to Bouquet, August 24, 1758, *Washington Papers*, Col. Ser., 5:417; Washington to Dinwiddie, May 24, 1757, *Washington Papers*, Col. Ser., 4:163; Washington to Forbes, June 19, 1758, *Washington Papers*, Col. Ser., 5:224–26; Washington to Dinwiddie, May 29, 1757, *Washington Papers*, Col. Ser., 4:170; Washington to Dinwiddie, June 10, 1757, *Washington Papers*, Col. Ser., 4:192; Washington to Dinwiddie, April 16, 1757, *Washington Papers*, Col. Ser., 4:136; Dinwiddie to Washington, May 16, 1757, *Washington Papers*, Col. Ser., 4:154. After his rebuke by Dinwiddie, Washington complained that "I and my officers were involved in inconceivable trouble [with the Cherokees], as we had neither an interpreter nor a right to hold conferences with them; [and] nothing to satisfy their demands of things"; see Washington to Dinwiddie, October 5, 1757, *Washington Papers*, Col. Ser., 5:2–3. Colonel Bouquet confirmed Washington's negative opinion of the Catawbas, writing that "they have behav'd in the most shameful manner, and run away as a parcell of theives rather than Warriors without seeing me; they have never killd a deer, and there is the strongest suspicions that the Scalp they pretend to have taken, was an old one"; see Washington to Gov. Francis Fauquier, July 10, 1758, *Washington Papers*, Col. Ser., 5:275–76.

37. Washington to Loudoun, January 10, 1757, *Washington Papers*, Col. Ser., 4:83; Washington to Stanwix, October 8, 1757, *Washington Papers*, Col. Ser., 5:10; Washington to Dinwiddie, April 22, 1756, *Washington Papers*, Col. Ser., 3:33–34; Washington to Richard Washington, April 15, 1757, *Washington*

Papers, Col. Ser., 4:133; Washington to Dinwiddie, September 24, 1757, *Washington Papers*, Col. Ser., 4:420.

38. Jennings, *Empire of Fortune*, 396–404. Washington provided the first reports to Williamsburg about the fall of Fort Duquesne, writing that the "possession of this fort has been [a] matter of great surprise to the whole army—and we can not attribute it to more probable causes than those of [French] weakness, want of Provisions, and desertion of their Indians"; see Washington to Fauquier, November 28, 1758, W*ashington Papers*, Col. Ser., 6:158–160. Washington also reported on the immediate, salutory impact of the Treaty of Easton for the Western Expedition: "A number of the Indians who have come over to our Alliance by the late Treaty at Easton are now upon their March to Join us to go to War. The Troops are therefore to receive them as Friends, & they will be known by their Carryg red Handkerchief with white Spots at the end of a Pole", see Washington Orderly Book, November 3, 1758, *Washington Papers*, Col. Ser., 6:105. The primary reason that the Six Nations and their Ohio allies suddenly became supportive of the English was the (false) promise made at the Easton conference "to restore to the Iroquois all the land 'Westward of the Allegheny or Appalaccin Hills'"; see Jennings, *Empire of Fortune*, 402.

The contest for the interior proved divisive among all parties, as Virginia competed with Pennsylvania over land claims, as English traders, agents, and interpreters vied with each other for advantage, and as the Ohio tribes often defied the wishes of the Iroquois council at Onondaga. In only a decade and a half, the Ohio tribes quickly matured into a distinct military and diplomatic force to be reckoned with—from the Treaty of Lancaster (1744), in which the Six Nations renounced their claims to the Ohio Country and virtually invited British land companies onto the lands of the Ohio tribes, to the Treaty of Easton (1758), in which the British began the process, subsequently strengthened in the Proclamation Line of 1763 and the Quebec Act of 1774, of restricting colonial access to key western territories in deference to essential Indian allies. Ironically, by "winning" the war, the American colonists lost ground in pursuing their economic destinies, while seemingly "shattered" pro-French tribes relocated ever westward (the Delawares to Muskingum, the Shawnees to Chillicothe), where they united and reasserted their military and diplomatic leverage for another generation; see Jennings, ed., *Iroquois Diplomacy*, 48–59; McConnell, *Country Between*, 208–9.

39. Washington to Dinwiddie, May 29, 1754, *Washington Papers*, Col. Ser., 1:107; Capt. Robert Stewart to Washington, June 3, 1760, *Washington Papers*, Col. Ser., 6:431–32; Washington to Maj. Francis Halkett, May 11, 1758, *Washington Papers*, Col. Ser., 5:175; William Callaway to Washington, May 15, 1758, *Washington Papers*, Col. Ser., 5:183–84; Forbes to Washington, November 19–

20, 1758, *Washington Papers*, Col. Ser., 6:146n; Hugh Cleland, *George Washington in the Ohio Valley* (Pittsburgh: University of Pittsburgh Press, 1955), 225–26.

40. Mercer to Washington, September 16, 1759, *Washington Papers*, Col. Ser., 6:343; Stewart to Washington, September 28, 1759, *Washington Papers*, Col. Ser., 6:361–62; Stewart to Washington, December 31, 1758, *Washington Papers*, Col. Ser., 6:177; Stewart to Washington, April 14, 1760, *Washington Papers*, Col. Ser., 6:412. Governor Dinwiddie's diplomacy accounted for the English alliances with the Catawbas and Cherokees in 1756, but the latter were at war with the colonists in 1760–1761. In October 1759, a year after the Easton Treaty with the Six Nations, George Croghan and Gen. John Stanwix negotiated agreements with former French allies in the Ohio Country, including the Ottawas, Twightwees/Miamis, Wyandots, Shawnees, and Delawares; see Stewart to Washington, September 28, 1759, *Washington Papers*, Col. Ser., 6:364n.

41. Washington's orders to Sullivan are quoted in Richard Drinnon, *Facing West: The Metaphysics of Indian-Hating and Empire-Building* (Minneapolis: University of Minnesota Press, 1980), 331–32; Barbara Graymount, *The Iroquois in the American Revolution* (Syracuse: Syracuse University Press, 1972), 192, chap. 8, passim; Anthony F. C. Wallace, *The Death and Rebirth of the Seneca* (New York: Alfred A. Knopf, 1968), 141–45, 218; Washington to Robinson, October 25, 1757, *Washington Papers*, Col. Ser., 5:33; Washington to Dinwiddie, September 24, 1757, *Washington Papers*, Col. Ser., 4:420. Sullivan boasted that "the Indians shall see that there is malice enough in our hearts to destroy everything that contributes to their support"; see Drinnon, *Facing West*, 331–32. Sullivan's invading army consisted of four thousand veteran troops, including a contingent of Daniel Morgan's riflemen, plus artillery and some twelve hundred packhorses. After their successful campaign, the troops were disbanded, ironically, at Easton, on the twenty-first anniversary of the famous treaty with the Iroquois; see Jack M. Sosin, *The Revolutionary Frontier, 1763–1783* (New York: Holt, Rinehart and Winston, 1967), 121–22.

42. Drinnon, *Facing West*, 66; Burton Ira Kaufman, "Washington's Farewell Address: A Statement of Empire," in *Washington's Farewell Address: The View from the twentieth Century*, ed. Kaufman (Chicago: Quadrangle Books, 1969), 176. The desperate indebtedness of Northern Neck planters helped motivate western expansionism; according to historian T. H. Breen: "The West held special attraction for gentlemen who were down on their luck and yet eager to commence the 'new Era.' . . . No Virginian entertained this vision of renewal more enthusiastically than did George Washington." See Breen, *Tobacco Culture: The Mentality of the Great Tidewater Planters on the Eve of the Revolution* (Princeton: Princeton University Press, 1985), 183–84. We should not underestimate the liberating sense of power and prerogative that Washington enjoyed as the arbiter of Indian affairs in the 1790s. He had been a

truly frustrated subordinate when he wrote in 1756: "My strongest representations [to superiors] of matters relative to the peace of the Frontiers are disregarded as idle & frivolous; my propositions and measures, as partial & selfish;
and all my sincerest endeavours for the service of my Country, perverted to
the worst purposes." See Washington to Robinson, December 19, 1756, *Washington Papers*, Col. Ser., 4:68.

43. Carroll, *Eulogy*, 10–11, 15; Kaufman, "Statement of Empire," 176; Washington, *Journal of Major Washington*, 7; Wiley Sword, *President Washington's
Indian War: The Struggle for the Old Northwest, 1790–1795* (Norman: University of Oklahoma Press, 1985), 4–6, 26–30, chaps. 5–14.

44. Washington, January 25, 1790, *Washington Diaries*, 6:15; Sword,
Washington's Indian War, 131, 201–7, 231; Wallace, *Seneca*, 218.

45. Washington to Fauquier, November 28, 1758, *Washington Papers*, Col.
Ser., 6:159; Washington to Fauquier, December 2, 1758, *Washington Papers*, Col.
Ser., 6:161–62; Stewart to Washington, September 28, 1759, *Washington Papers*,
Col. Ser., 6:361.

46. Stewart to Washington, September 28, 1759, *Washington Papers*, Col.
Ser., 6:361.

47. Mercer to Washington, September 16, 1759, *Washington Papers*, Col.
Ser., 6:343, 345n–46n. As of 1774, Washington had registered some twenty-
three thousand acres of the 200,000-acre total in his name, since he frequently
purchased the land bounties of his former militiamen; see Longmore, *Invention of Washington*, 152–53.

48. Stewart to Washington, September 28, 1759, *Washington Papers*, Col.
Ser., 6:361; Washington to Robinson, October 25, 1757, *Washington Papers*, Col.
Ser., 5:34; Washington to John Bannister, April 21, 1778, quoted in Edmund S.
Morgan, *The Meaning of Independence: John Adams, George Washington, and
Thomas Jefferson* (New York: W. W. Norton, 1976), 53, n.31; Ambler, *Washington and the West*, 173–74, 204, chap. 8; Cleland, *Washington in Ohio Valley*,
chaps. 5–6. In 1770 and 1784, Washington made extensive tours of his western
lands, and in the former year, he purchased Great Meadows and the site of
Fort Necessity; see Alberts, *Charming Field*, 57.
    On June 3, 1763, only four months after the Treaty of Paris, Washington
joined other prominent Potomac planters in forming the Mississippi Company. Petitioning the Crown for 2,500,000 acres vacated by France but inhabited by thousands of Indians, the company represented the elite of frontier
land speculators (each member was to receive no less than fifty thousand acres).
The Proclamation Line of 1763, however, all but doomed this bold effort at
enjoying the spoils of war; see *Washington Diaries*, 1:311, 313–14. See Woody
Holton, "The Ohio Indians and the Coming of the American Revolution in
Virginia," *Journal of Southern History* 60 (August 1994): 453–78

49. Quoted in Kaufman, "Statement of Empire," 173; also see pp. 174–84;

Sword, *Washington's Indian War*, 2–6; Richard C. Wade, *The Urban Frontier: Pioneer Life in Early Pittsburgh, Cincinnati, Lexington, Louisville, and St. Louis* (Chicago: University of Chicago Press, 1959); Francis Jennings, "The Indians' Revolution," in *The American Revolution: Explorations in the History of American Radicalism*, ed. Alfred F. Young (DeKalb, Ill.: Northern Illinois University Press, 1976), 320–48. Washington wrote to a young Virginia planter in 1767, urging him to move to the Alleghenies, "where an enterprising Man with very little Money may lay the foundation of a Noble Estate in the New Settlements Upon Monongahela for himself and posterity. . . . [That is] how the greatest Estates we have in this Colony were made; was it not by taking up and purchasing at very low rates the rich back Lands which were thought nothing of in those days but are now the most valuable Lands we possess?" Quoted in Ambler, *Washington and the West*, 136.

50. Washington to Dinwiddie, April 22, 1756, *Washington Papers*, Col. Ser., 3:33. In that letter, a strained and frustrated Washington wrote: "If bleeding, dying! would glut their [the raiding Indians'] insatiable revenge—I would be a willing offering to Savage Fury and die by inches to save a people! I see their [the white settlers'] situation, know their danger, and participate [in] their Sufferings without having it in my power to give them further relief than uncertain promises." Two days later, he reported that "everyday we have accounts of such cruelties and Barbarities as are shocking to human nature"; see Washington to Dinwiddie, April 24, 1756, *Washington Papers*, Col. Ser., 3:45.

For developments among the Ohio Indians after 1760, see McConnell, *Country Between*, chaps. 8–11; Colin G. Calloway, *Crown and Calumet: British-Indian Relations, 1783-1815* (Norman: University of Oklahoma, Press, 1987).

51. Washington to James Cuninghame, January 28, 1757, *Washington Papers*, Col. Ser., 4:106; Washington to Dinwiddie, March 7, 1754, *Washington Papers*, Col. Ser., 1:72; Washington to Robinson, June 10, 1757, *Washington Papers*, Col. Ser., 4:198–99; Washington to Dinwiddie, December 19, 1756, *Washington Papers*, Col. Ser., 4:65. Perhaps the most important lesson that Washington learned in the backcountry was to look for lessons: "Knowledge in military matters," he wrote, "is to be acquired by practise and experience only"; see Washington to Dinwiddie, September 17, 1757, *Washington Papers*, Col. Ser., 4:412. When rampant indebtedness and insolvency in the 1760s threatened to undermine the political power and social status of the Tidewater grandees, Washington, the self-made commander of frontier fame, was in an enviable position to exploit his popular reputation as an Indian-fighter, even as the traditional patterns of community deference declined; see Breen, *Tobacco Culture*, 175, chap. 5. Lewis reminds us that Washington's record of military accomplishments prior to 1775 was dismal indeed, since his first four engagements included the murderous ambush of sleeping Frenchmen (May

28, 1754), a humiliating surrender of Fort Necessity (July 4, 1754), the massacre of General Braddock's army (July 9, 1755), and the accidental slaughter of fellow Virginia militiamen near Loyalhanna (fourteen killed and twenty-six wounded by "friendly fire" on the foggy night of November 12, 1758); see Lewis, *King and Country,* 268.

52. Washington to Loudoun, January 10, 1757, *Washington Papers,* Col. Ser., 4:90; Washington to Dinwiddie, May 30, 1757, *Washington Papers,* Col. Ser., 4:172. Although diplomatic duplicity was to be expected, even Washington's routine dealings with Indians were based on his presumption of their "unmeaning promises and capricious Humours"; see Washington to Dinwiddie, December 19, 1756, *Washington Papers,* Col. Ser., 4:63.

53. Washington, June 18, 1754, *Washington Diaries,* 1:204. "It is Works and not Words that People will Judge from," observed Washington, "and where one Man deceives another . . . his word being disregarded all confidence is lost"; see Breen, *Tobacco Culture,* 175.

54. Washington, June 21, 1754, *Washington Diaries,* 1:206. In the aftermath of the Peace of Paris (1783), Indian allies of the British responded angrily to the news that their territory had been signed away at treaty time, regarding it as "'an Act of Cruelty and injustice that Christians only were capable of doing.'" The Creeks and Cherokees, bloodied in the king's service, "were so incredulous that they simply dismissed reports of the peace settlement as a 'Virginia lie.'" See Calloway, *Crown and Calumet,* 10-11.

Part Three

A Stake in the West:
George Washington as Backcountry
Surveyor and Landholder

PHILANDER D. CHASE

$\mathcal{D}$URING THE LAST SUMMER OF THE
Revolutionary War, with peace at hand, General Washington took a
soldier's holiday from the tedium of his headquarters on the Hudson
River and spent a little more than two weeks touring the New York
frontier. He returned to his duties refreshed and eager to discuss the
abundant resources of the backcountry. "I . . . could not but be struck
with the immense diffusion & importance" of the inland navigation,
Washington wrote a French acquaintance, "& with the goodness of that
providence which has dealt her favors to us with so profuse a hand.
Would to God we may have wisdom enough to improve them. I shall
not rest contented 'till I have explored the Western Country, & traversed those lines . . . which have given bounds to a New Empire."[1]

That resolve was not the sudden enthusiasm of a bored middle-aged
man but an expression of a continuing interest in the West and a commitment to its development that began in Washington's youth when
the Blue Ridge marked the frontier and the western country was defined
for him principally by the waters of the Potomac and the Shenandoah,
not those of the Hudson, the Mohawk, the Mississippi, or even yet the
Ohio. The West was as much a part of Washington's adult life and
thought as was his native Tidewater society, for he had come of age in
two very different houses of the influential Fairfax family: Belvoir, the
handsome brick mansion on the Potomac Tidewater occupied by William Fairfax, agent for Lord Fairfax's Northern Neck Proprietary, and
Greenway Court, the modest stucco hunting lodge in the Shenandoah
Valley where the proprietor himself resided. During his teens and twenties Washington was an intimate at both houses, and he found much to

admire at each: social refinement and creature comforts at Belvoir and rich soil and good hunting at Greenway Court. If Washington early conceived an ambition to become a great Tidewater planter, he also was attracted irresistibly by Lord Fairfax's West. It was his good fortune to find that his opportunities on both sides of the Blue Ridge could be made to complement one another.

Washington knew Belvoir first, and it was there that his path to the West began. Deprived of his father at the age of eleven, George spent part of his adolescence at Mount Vernon with his half-brother Lawrence Washington, and he became well acquainted with Lawrence's in-laws and near neighbors at Belvoir. Amid the fine furnishings that the boy saw when he visited the Fairfaxes, he must have heard much talk about the vast lands awaiting development in the backcountry. In 1745, when George was thirteen, a mania for western land speculation was unloosed among Virginia's perennially land-hungry gentry by news of two recent events. A treaty signed with the Six Nations at Lancaster, Pennsylvania, the previous summer opened the Shenandoah Valley and part of the Ohio Valley to English settlement for the first time, and in London in April 1745 the Privy Council agreed after many years of dispute to extend the boundaries of Lord Fairfax's proprietary west to the head springs of the Potomac, giving him control of more than five million acres of land, roughly half of which lay in the largely unsettled region west of the Blue Ridge.[2] During the next ten years the proprietary land office at Belvoir became a busy place frequented by settlers, speculators, and surveyors hunting for choice western tracts.

Opportunities on the Virginia frontier fortuitously opened just as Washington was entering adulthood, offering an uncommon chance for an ambitious young man of relatively limited means to acquire the land, wealth, and even public honor necessary to rise in the competitive Tidewater society. Such opportunities were especially plentiful for men who engaged in land surveying. The surveyors that young Washington undoubtedly saw coming on business to Belvoir were no mere hirelings or minor governmental functionaries. They were respected professionals on a par with lawyers, doctors, clergymen, and military officers. "Their class-conscious contemporaries," historian Sarah S. Hughes says in her ground-breaking study of Virginia's colonial surveyors, recognized them "as gentlemen," and they "were numbered among the colony's practical-minded intellectual elite, the minority who collected books and subscribed to newspapers. . . . These men wore no crude frontiersman's buckskins when they sat on the county court or rode into Williamsburg. Their satin waistcoats, brocaded vests, patent slippers, and powdered wigs were of the latest English fashions."[3]

For all their finery, however, Virginia's eighteenth-century survey-ors felt more at home on a county court than in Williamsburg, where the seats of power were monopolized by an aristocratic clique that stood a step above them in the social hierarchy. "Not the most prominent politicians, soldiers, or speculators," Hughes says, "surveyors formed a corps of secondary leaders whose influence was most formidable in their counties." Their surveyorships, to which they were appointed by counties, made them important local figures by conferring on them the "potential power to control access to land" within their respective jurisdictions. In addition, surveyors commonly held a number of other key county offices, serving as vestrymen, magistrates, sheriffs, coro-ners, militia officers, and sometimes burgesses. Nor were their economic activities restricted to surveying. Most surveyors supplemented their incomes by working as planters, merchants, millers, or distillers. The affluence that they thus achieved, their plural offices, and their refined lifestyle all marked surveyors as members in good standing of the county gentry, a comfortable and honorable station in life.[4]

The benefits to be derived from surveying varied with the work habits of individual surveyors and the areas in which they worked. If a surveyor was energetic, ambitious, and willing to sacrifice some com-fort, he could find no better employment than in a frontier county. An expanse of unclaimed wilderness awaiting division into private hold-ings promised a high volume of work and a correspondingly large num-ber of surveying fees. Although the legally established fees were less in frontier counties than elsewhere in the colony, a diligent surveyor work-ing only a few months a year in the backcountry could earn an annual cash income that was exceeded only by the colony's finest trial lawyers. Frontier surveyors could further profit from the many opportunities they had to patent or purchase choice tracts of land in their own names. It was not unusual for surveyors to acquire estates of ten to twenty-five thousand acres, and they often acted, Hughes says, "as junior partners in the great land speculations of the day," becoming "men of influence and wealth in their own right, whose assistance was requisite to the success of any land venture."[5]

$\mathcal{S}$O LIKELY A CHOICE WAS SURVEYING
as a beginning profession for young George Washington that it is a bit
surprising to find his half-brother Lawrence urging George at the age
of fourteen to follow the Potomac, not upstream to the backcountry
but downstream to the Chesapeake Bay and on to the sea.
Lawrence Washington, who had served under Adm. Edward Vernon in
the Caribbean a few years earlier, could conceive of no better life for
George than one in the British navy or aboard a Virginia merchant
ship. So in early September 1746, he proposed such a career in separate
letters to the boy and his mother, Mary Ball Washington. George, who
was then home with his mother at Ferry Farm, the family's modest
plantation near Fredericksburg, gratefully accepted Lawrence's advice,
but Widow Washington was not so easily persuaded by her stepson.
"She seems to intimate a dislike to George's going to Sea, & says several
Persons have told her its a very bad Scheme," a family friend wrote
Lawrence on September 18. "I find that one word against his going has
more weight than ten for it."[6] If the widow did not immediately veto
Lawrence's plan, she certainly did so the following year when she received a letter dated May 19, 1747, from her own half-brother in England. The young man, Joseph Ball wrote her, "had better be put
apprentice to a Tinker" than be sent to sea, where "they will . . . Cut him
& Slash him and use him like a Negro, or rather, like a Dog."[7]

Sometime during the summer of 1747, probably soon after his
uncle's letter reached Ferry Farm, George, then age fifteen, began seriously preparing himself to be a professional surveyor. His previous
education had consisted of learning the rudiments of knowledge from
local tutors or on his own from standard texts. Washington's surviving
schoolbooks indicate that as a boy he studied a good deal of mathematics, including geometry and decimals and such useful applications
of the subject as computing interest, converting money, measuring
plank, and gauging solids and liquids. As part of that practical instruction, one of his schoolbooks, begun when he was thirteen, includes a
short section on land surveying reduced to its basic elements for lay-
men. With pen, drawing compass, and plotting scale, the boy performed
ten hypothetical exercises on paper to learn how to draw the boundaries of a tract to scale, how to determine its acreage, how to lay off a
given quantity of land in a few simple shapes, and how to divide a tract
into two sections. Although those exercises are preceded by a brief explanation of "The going round and Measuring a Piece of Wood Land"

on the ground, there is no evidence that Washington's initial exposure to the art of surveying included any training beyond the edges of his desk.[8]

During the summer and fall of his fifteenth year, Washington, under the direction of some experienced practitioner, worked his way through a much more comprehensive and specialized course on surveying, which he meticulously recorded in his youthful handwriting on the pages of another schoolbook.[9] Derived from more than one source, the course begins, as do many eighteenth-century surveying textbooks, with some mathematical instruction, consisting in this case of a number of geometrical definitions and problems followed by a few rules and exercises concerning square roots and plain trigonometry. Washington's instructor, who may have been a surveyor or assistant surveyor for one of the Northern Neck counties in the vicinity of Ferry Farm, took the material for the geometry lessons from the more numerous geometrical definitions and problems that appear in one of the popular surveying textbooks of the time, William Leybourn's *The Compleat Surveyor.*[10] Although the sources of the lessons on square roots and plain trigonometry have not been identified, they too undoubtedly are based on some printed work.

The mathematical skills that Washington learned in those introductory lessons were designed solely to prepare him to perform the surveying exercises that follow in a long section of the schoolbook entitled "The Art of Surveying and Measuring of Land."[11] Much of the material in that main body of the course was derived from John Love's similarly titled textbook, *Geodaesia; or, The Art of Surveying and Measuring of Land Made Easie.*[12] Washington's instructor did not simply plagiarize Love's well-known work, however. To teach surveying as it was practiced in mid-eighteenth-century Virginia, the instructor variously selected, abstracted, altered, and supplemented the lessons in *Geodaesia*, which had been written in England more than a half century earlier.

The instructor's modifications are evident in the first surveying lesson, which he begins: "Because the two Pole Chain is most in use among Surveyors Measuring Lines in Virginia & other American parts I shall chiefly insist on that Measure it being the best for Wood Land."[13] One of the indispensable tools of the trade for many years, a surveyor's chain, consisting of a series of interconnected wrought iron links each 7.92 inches long, was used to determine distances between points on the ground. The two-pole chain, which contains fifty such links, making it thirty-three feet long, was favored by Virginia surveyors because it was easier to handle in rough wooded terrain than was the one hundred link, four-pole chain commonly used in England. Because John Love based the lessons in *Geodaesia* on the four-pole chain, the initial surveying lessons in Washington's schoolbook, which taught him to convert chain lengths to feet or rods and to compute and lay off acreage with chain measure, are adjusted in most cases to allow for the use of the shorter chain.[14]

As in *Geodaesia*, those lessons are accompanied by several conversion tables that facilitate the making of the necessary mathematical computations. To aid him further in his work, Washington on September 20, 1747, purchased from his distant cousin Bailey Washington a two-foot Gunter scale, a rule made of brass, wood, or ivory, inscribed with variously marked and numbered lines, that simplified the trigonometric calculations involved in drawing the boundaries of a survey to scale on paper.[15]

In subsequent lessons Washington learned to make effective use of another indispensable surveying instrument, a circumferentor, or plain surveying compass. Composed of a magnetic compass housed in a brass case, with open brass sights and mounted on a staff or tripod, a circumferentor was used to determine the bearings of survey lines in degrees marked by the compass needle. Washington's first circumferentor, as also his first surveyor's chain, may have been part of the set of surveyor's instruments that his father left in a storehouse at Ferry Farm when he died in 1743.[16] Whether with those inherited instruments or similar ones from another source, Washington soon became adept in the art of traverse surveying, a technique that had first appeared in Virginia during the 1640s and had become the dominant method of surveying in the colony by the beginning of the eighteenth century. Well suited to laying off large tracts of uncultivated land where visibility is limited, traverse surveying requires its practitioner to follow the bounds of a tract, sighting lines from corner to corner with a circumferentor, determining the magnetic compass bearing of each line, and measuring its length with a chain.[17]

Many of the surveying exercises in Washington's schoolbook, however, concern special techniques for solving certain types of problems commonly encountered by Virginia surveyors: determining the length of a line across an inaccessible area such as a marsh or creek, plotting an entire field from one or two stations, locating a place on a map by triangulation, surveying an irregular shoreline with a series of offsets, and dividing tracts in various complex ways. Emphasis seems to have been put on the last category because more exercises deal with the division of land than with any other type of problem. One of those exercises requires a tract to be apportioned among three tenants according to the different sums that each contributed to the total annual rent of the property, and another problem demands the division of a piece of land into three equal parts so as to give each tenant "the benefit of a Pond about the Middle thereof."[18]

The last pages of the schoolbook include three handsome surveys of fields at Mount Vernon that Washington apparently made soon after finishing his course work to gain additional experience and perhaps to demonstrate his abilities to his half-brother. One of those surveys, which is undated, is a plan of a small piece of meadowland on Hell Hole Run a short distance east of the mansion house, and another

A surveying compass made for Washington by David Rittenhouse of Philadelphia (Smithsonian Institution).

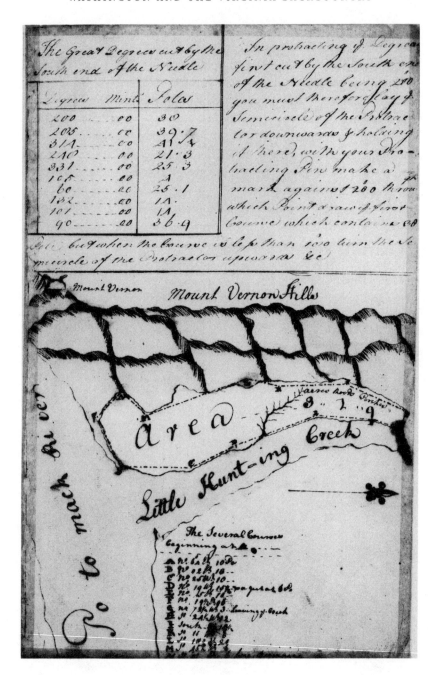

Washington's survey on Little Hunting Creek near the Mount Vernon
mansion, circa 1747 (Library of Congress).

one, also undated, depicts a similar tract on Little Hunting Creek to the west of the house. The third survey shows a "Plan of Major Law. Washington's Turnip Field" strikingly superimposed on a compass rose and neatly signed "Survey'd by me This 27 Day of February 1747/8 G.W." Made a little more than two weeks after Washington's sixteenth birthday, which occurred on February 11, it is ample evidence of the high level of surveying skill that he had attained at that age.[19]

Washington's training as a surveyor culminated during the spring of 1748 in a brief frontier apprenticeship under the surveyor for Prince William County, James Genn, an experienced professional who was charged with laying off large tracts of land along the South Branch of the Potomac River in the far western part of Lord Fairfax's proprietary. On March 11, 1748, Washington set off from Mount Vernon on his first journey to the Virginia backcountry in the company of George William Fairfax, the twenty-four-year-old son of William Fairfax. The next morning they met Genn at George Neville's ordinary in what is now Fauquier County and proceeded across the Blue Ridge to the Shenandoah Valley. The fully assembled surveying party also included two chain carriers, a marker to blaze trees at the corners of surveys, and a guide.[20]

Although all the surveys made during the expedition were drawn and submitted to the proprietor's office by Genn, Washington kept in a small notebook an unofficial record of the bearings and lengths of the lines for each survey with which he assisted. For the party's first survey—a 3,023-acre tract run on March 15 for George William Fairfax on Cates Marsh and Long Marsh runs in the Shenandoah Valley, a few miles northeast of present-day Berryville, Virginia—Washington made two copies in his notebook, on the second of which he wrote: "The Mannor how to Draw up a Return when Surveyd for His Lordship or any of the Family."[21] Washington clearly anticipated much future employment by the Fairfaxes.

After finishing that one survey in the Shenandoah Valley, Genn and his party proceeded to the South Branch of the Potomac, where their main task awaited them. Delayed by heavy rains, they did not begin surveying there until March 29, when they ran a five-hundred-acre tract for James Rutledge. During the next eight days the party surveyed twenty "lots" along the South Branch, varying in size from 238 acres to 680 acres. On his copy of the lines for the fourth lot Washington wrote: "This Lot Survey'd myself." On April 9 Washington and George William Fairfax left the others still working on the South Branch and headed home to Fairfax County.[22]

Washington's first trip west of the Blue Ridge, abbreviated as it was, gave him invaluable and otherwise unattainable experience in backcountry surveying. It also introduced him to the rigors of the wilderness life that he was to lead off and on during the next several years as both surveyor and soldier. That Washington found the latter experience as valuable as the former is indicated by the fact that he recorded his first impressions of the backcountry and his first lessons in living there in the same notebook in which he entered the technical data about Genn's surveys.

Washington's account of the night of March 15, which Genn's party spent at Isaac Pennington's house in the Shenandoah Valley, is a classic tale of a tenderfoot's initiation into the ways of the frontier. Not "so good a Woodsman" as his companions, Washington took off his clothes and attempted to go to sleep on a straw pallet provided by his host, only to jump up a few minutes later and redress rapidly, having found the bedding infested with lice and fleas. "I made a Promise," he wrote, "not to Sleep so from that time forward chusing rather to sleep in the open Air before a fire."[23] Such discomforts did not daunt Washington. He seemed to take pride in overcoming wilderness conditions of all kinds, and he saw many things that pleased him, particularly in the Shenandoah Valley. After a Sunday ride to Lord Fairfax's quarter near Greenway Court, Washington wrote: "We went through most beautiful Groves of Sugar Trees & spent the best part of the Day in admiring the Trees & richness of the Land."[24] Washington had found a region and an occupation well suited to his tastes and ambitions.

However promising, those prospects yielded no immediate results. More than a year and a half were to pass after Washington's return from the South Branch before he again crossed the Blue Ridge, and he apparently made only limited use of his newly acquired surveying skills during that time. Two undated maps of Alexandria drawn by Washington—a survey of the town site and a plan of the lots into which it was first divided—have often been cited as evidence that he assisted in laying out the town prior to the public sale of lots on July 13, 1749. There is no record of Washington's so doing, however, nor did he ever claim such a distinction. Alexandria was officially surveyed by the deputy surveyor of Fairfax County, John West Jr., and Washington prob-

Washington's survey of Lawrence Washington's turnip field, drawn when he was only sixteen years old, 27 February 1747/8 (Library of Congress).

ably copied West's surveys for the use of Lawrence Washington who, according to the list of purchasers inscribed beside the town plan, bought two lots in the new town.[25]

In the normal course of events, a novice surveyor such as Washington should have begun his career as an assistant to a county surveyor like James Genn. That Washington remained professionally inactive for many months after leaving Genn with much work still to be done on the South Branch suggests that Washington wanted and expected something better than an assistantship. If so, his patience, as well as his ambition, was eventually rewarded. On July 20, 1749, Washington appeared before the justices of the newly formed county of Culpeper, and presenting a commission that appointed him county surveyor, took the oaths of public office for the first time in his life.[26]

The appointment of a boy of seventeen to a position as prominent as that of county surveyor was unprecedented in colonial Virginia. Washington could not possibly have obtained the Culpeper surveyorship at that age without the strong support of the Fairfaxes, and he was suitably grateful for their help. "I shoud be glad," he wrote his younger brother Jack nearly six years later, "to hear you live in Harmony and good fellowship with the family at Belvoir, as it is in their power to be very serviceable upon many occasion's to us as young beginner's. . . . To that Family I am under many obligations."[27] "Young beginner's" did not become county surveyors just by achieving "Harmony and good fellowship" with the influential Fairfaxes, however. Washington's character was also a factor. In the teenage boy the Fairfaxes saw something that distinguished him from his contemporaries, and it had little to do with his surveying skills. As useful as his training as a professional surveyor was for him, nothing in it was exceptional by the standards of the time. What were exceptional in young George Washington were his ambition, self-discipline, and perseverance, his capacity for hard work, and his willingness to accept serious responsibilities. Those qualities clearly foreshadowed his future greatness. Washington's appointment as surveyor of Culpeper County was only the first of several occasions during his early years when he leapfrogged to important positions over older, more experienced men.

Because Washington's surveying commission was issued by the president and masters of the College of William and Mary, it has often been assumed that he studied at the college or stood an examination by its faculty. In truth, he did neither. The college had been empowered to appoint county surveyors by its 1693 charter principally to provide it with a source of revenue, for the school was authorized to collect one-sixth of all surveyor's fees in return for its commissions. In practice the college encountered great difficulties in obtaining its share of the fees, and in making appointments the school's authorities regularly deferred to the wishes of powerful men within the colony.[28] Their commission of Washington as Culpeper surveyor was issued undoubtedly at the behest of Lord Fairfax in whose proprietary the new county lay. William Fairfax, who sat on the governor's Council, probably exerted his influence also and made any necessary arrangements to secure the commission while attending Council sessions in Williamsburg during the spring of 1749. Both men had come to consider Washington as something of an adopted son and had few qualms about advancing his interests.

O<small>N</small> JULY 22, 1749, TWO DAYS AFTER being sworn in as Culpeper County surveyor, Washington made his first professional survey on Flat Run in the eastern part of the county near present-day Brandy Station. He embellished his scale drawing of the four-hundred-acre tract with a compass rose and a sketch of Mount Poney, a local landmark, and signed his name in full with his new title "Surv[e]y[or] of Culpeper Cty."[29] That survey is the only one that Washington is known to have made in Culpeper County, however. During the remaining three and a quarter years of his professional surveying career, he worked exclusively in Frederick County, which then encompassed all of the Northern Neck Proprietary west of the Blue Ridge. Washington's reasons for doing so are not hard to understand. Culpeper County, although newly created, was formed from Orange County, a relatively well-settled area in which much of the land had already been surveyed and granted, while in Frederick County unclaimed lands were still plentiful along the Shenandoah and Cacapon rivers in 1749, a important consideration for a young surveyor who was eager to work and earn money.[30]

Washington's appointment as Culpeper surveyor was a valuable asset, nevertheless, for in Virginia one could not legally make public surveys without a commission as a county surveyor, assistant county surveyor, or special surveyor. Until sometime in August 1750, Washington carefully included the initials "S.C.C." (Surveyor of Culpeper County) after his signature on his Frederick County surveys as a mark of their legitimacy. On November 3, 1750, however, Henry Lee became surveyor of Culpeper County.[31] Washington may have resigned the office because it was more trouble than it was worth, or he may have been replaced for neglecting the county. In either case, he needed another appointment to make his subsequent surveys legal. The absence of any title at all on Washington's surveys after he ceased using "S.C.C." suggests that he may have become a special private surveyor to Lord Fairfax or one of several assistants to Frederick County surveyor James Wood, since Frederick assistants usually signed their surveys without title; but there is no record of Washington receiving either of those appointments, however. It is certain only that he continued surveying on the Virginia frontier until the fall of 1753 and that his work was never challenged.[32]

In the notebook in which Washington recorded his trip with James Genn to the South Branch of the Potomac, he wrote an undated memorandum, probably in 1749 or 1750, "to Survey the Lands at the Mouth of Little Cacapehon & the Mouth of Fifteen Mile Creek for the Gentlemen of the Ohio Com[pany]."[33] If Washington made any surveys on those tributaries of the Potomac or elsewhere for the land company in which his half-brother Lawrence was so actively involved, they have not survived. All of Washington's known professional surveys were made for grants in Lord Fairfax's proprietary, and as in the case of his surveying commission, Washington relied heavily on his connections with the Fairfax family to obtain good surveying assignments.

Northern Neck surveyors normally received their assignments in packets of warrants from the proprietary land office at Belvoir, although it is possible that Lord Fairfax may have given warrants to Washington on some occasions at Greenway Court or Winchester. Each warrant authorized the surveyor to lay off an approximate acreage of land for a claimant at a specific location by a fixed date, usually five or six months after the date of the warrant. The surveyor was chosen not by the claimant but by Lord Fairfax, his agent William Fairfax, or George William Fairfax, who often acted in place of his father. The most desirable set of warrants gave the surveyor several simple, compact tracts to survey near one another, so that he could complete the maximum number of surveys and collect the maximum number of fees for his time in the field.[34]

Sometime in the fall of 1749, Washington went to Belvoir to obtain warrants from Lord Fairfax and found that the proprietor had left for the Shenandoah Valley earlier in the day. "As your Lordship was not at Home," Washington wrote him a few days later, "I was inform[ed] by Colo. G[eorge William] Fairfax that you had not any Directions in Particular more than were given to the other Surveyors. . . . [T]herefore [I] have made bold to Proceed on General Directions from him as the Missing this Oppertunity of Good Weather may be of considerable Hindrance[.] I shall Wait on your Lordship at Frederick Court in November to obey your further Pleasure."[35]

Washington's first set of warrants from the proprietary's office directed him to the upper portion of the Cacapon River known as the Lost River, where he began surveying on November 1, 1749, about two weeks later than was ideal to take best advantage of the weather. Like other surveyors of the time, Washington usually worked only in the late fall and early spring, when temperatures were mild and the thin foliage made it easier to sight long boundary lines through thickly wooded areas. Despite his late start on the Lost River, Washington was able in eleven days to run fifteen surveys, varying in size from 330 acres to a little more than 400 acres. His work was made easier by the fact that many of these surveys adjoined one another allowing a single boundary line to serve for two tracts.[36] The Fairfaxes clearly started their protégé on his career with a very favorable set of warrants.

Washington's head chainman on the Lost River was John Lonem, who acted in that capacity on about half of Washington's surveys. Most Virginia surveyors used local people as chainmen and markers often employing different crews on consecutive surveys. Washington also followed that practice except in the case of Lonem, whose accuracy and speed with a chain apparently justified taking him frequently from survey to survey.[37] On a typical survey two chainmen measured the boundary lines and a marker notched the corner trees, while Washington determined the bearings of the lines with his circumferentor and wrote the essential data concerning courses, distances, and corner marks in rough form on a page in one of his small field books. In so doing, Washington made no attempt to correct bearings for magnetic declination, a practice that did not become standard in Virginia until some twenty years later, and he normally omitted the bearing and length of the final, closing leg of a survey. Washington, like other surveyors, usually calculated the last line mathematically when he later drew the survey, a convenient procedure that not only saved time in the field, but also guaranteed that each tract would be perfectly closed at least on paper.[38]

Washington put his surveys in finished form after leaving the field for more comfortable quarters at Mount Vernon, Ferry Farm, Greenway Court, or possibly Winchester, where in 1748 he found lodgings that offered "a good Dinner . . . Wine & Rum Punch in Plenty & a good Feather Bed with clean Sheets."[39] Almost any convenient place would do since he required only a small desk or table and a few days time to complete his work. Using the information that he had entered in his field book and the skills that he had practiced so diligently in his schoolbook, Washington drew a small map, or plat, of each tract to scale and computed its acreage. Then, below or beside the plat, he wrote a full description of the boundaries in a stylized clerical handwriting unlike that on any of his other documents. Many of Washington's earliest plats, such as the one for the tract in Culpeper County, were fairly elaborate drawings including compass roses, scales, and sometimes terrain features. As surveying became more and more a repetitious routine for him, Washington's drawing style gradually became simpler. Decorative items and all but the most essential letters and numbers eventually ceased to appear on most of his plats, although the plats remained neat and accurate by the standards of the time. Completed surveys were signed and taken to the proprietary office at Belvoir for issuance of grants, the final step in the process of acquiring new lands in the Northern Neck.[40]

Washington was soon bringing large numbers of surveys to Belvoir. In the spring of 1750 he returned to the Cacapon Valley, and beginning on March 30 he made forty-nine surveys in a little more than four weeks. Most of the tracts lay on the Cacapon and its tributaries, the Lost and North rivers, and David's and Trout runs, but some of them were on the nearby Little Cacapon River or the Potomac near the mouths of the Cacapon and Little Cacapon. Washington worked at an especially rapid pace on this trip. On seven occasions he made three surveys in a day, and one day he ran four.[41]

During the last two weeks in August 1750 Washington broke with the normal pattern of spring and fall surveying to run twelve surveys in the Shenandoah Valley in the vicinity of present-day Charles Town, West Virginia. Seven of those surveys, variously located on or near Flowing Springs, Evitts, and Bullskin Runs, were made for Lawrence Washington, and one survey at the head of Flowing Springs Run was made for his other half-brother, Augustine Washington. The fact that all but one of Washington's late summer surveys were granted by Lord Fairfax between October 13 and November 1, 1750, an unusually short time after surveying, suggests that the claimants were in a hurry to make good their titles, perhaps to forestall rivals.[42]

Washington returned to the lower Shenandoah Valley in the fall of 1750 and surveyed for almost seven weeks. The thirty surveys that he made during that time were scattered between Craig Run near Berryville and Flowing Springs Run near Charles Town.[43] Two of those surveys are significant because Washington made them for himself. On November 24, 1750, Washington surveyed a 453-acre tract known as Dutch George's, purchased from Thomas Rutherford of Frederick County and located near the head of Evitts Run, about five miles west of Charles Town.[44] The second tract Washington surveyed for himself that fall lay on the South Fork of Bullskin Run, about five miles southwest of Charles Town near present-day Summit Point, West Virginia. There on November 30 and December 3 Washington surveyed 456 acres, which he bought from James McCraken of Frederick County on December 3–4. About the same time, Washington surveyed approximately ninety-three acres of unclaimed land adjoining that tract and obtained a comprehensive grant from Lord Fairfax for 550 acres that included both the land purchased from McCraken and the previously ungranted land.[45] By these varied means, Washington at the age of eighteen became the owner of 1,003 acres of Shenandoah Valley land.

Washington found another opportunity to add to his holdings when he resumed work in the Valley the following spring. On April 9, 1751, he surveyed for himself a 760-acre tract of unclaimed land near the head of the South Fork of Bullskin Run, a short distance south of the land that he had bought from McCraken the previous December. Lord Fairfax formally granted those 760 acres to Washington nearly two years later on March 17, 1752.[46] Besides his own surveying, Washington did much work for others over a wide area during the spring of 1751. In twenty-three days between March 18 and April 9, he ran twenty-seven surveys on Bullskin Run and several other Shenandoah tributaries in its vicinity. Then, from April 12 to 27 Washington surveyed along the Cacapon and Little Cacapon rivers, running twenty-eight surveys in sixteen days. He finished his spring surveying on April 30 and May 1 by returning to the Shenandoah Valley to lay off tracts on Long Marsh

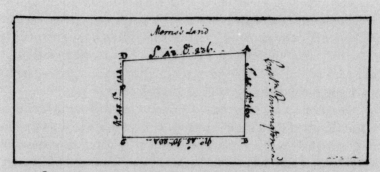

Washington's survey of a 225-acre tract near present-day Berryville, Va., for John Lindsey, 17 November 1750 (*George Washington Atlas*, plate 20).

and Cattail runs. In a little over six weeks Washington had made a total of fifty-seven surveys.[47]

There was no fall surveying for Washington that year. In September 1751, he went to Barbados in the West Indies with Lawrence, who was terminally ill, and he did not return to Virginia until the following January. On February 26, 1752, Washington surveyed a 861-acre tract adjoining the town of Fredericksburg for his brother-in-law, Fielding Lewis,[48] and in March he again took his surveying instruments across the Blue Ridge. Although Washington's field book for 1752 has not been found, surviving surveys for the period indicate that he worked in the Shenandoah Valley for several days in mid-March, and that later that month and in early April he surveyed in the Cacapon Valley.[49]

While working in the Shenandoah Valley, Washington acquired more land on the South Fork of Bullskin Run. On March 16–17, 1752, George Johnston of Frederick County sold Washington for £115 a 552-acre tract that Washington had surveyed for him on August 28, 1750. Adjoining both the land that Washington purchased from McCraken in 1750 and the 760 acres that he surveyed for a grant in 1751, the tract that Washington obtained from Johnston gave him a contiguous block of 1,862 acres on the South Fork of the Bullskin.[50] Including the 453-acre Dutch George's tract a few miles to the north on Evitts Run, Washington at the age of twenty owned 2,315 acres in the lower Shenandoah Valley. That holding matched Lawrence Washington's Mount Vernon plantation in acreage, if not in other respects.[51]

The cash to finance his land acquisitions came from surveying fees, which gave him a handsome income in return for his arduous backcountry labor. In a letter that he wrote to a friend sometime early in his surveying career, Washington said: "I have not sleep'd above three Nights or four in a bed but after Walking a good deal all the Day lay down before the fire upon a Little Hay Straw Fodder or bairskin . . . . there's nothing would make it pass of tolerably but a good Reward and Dubbleloon is my constant gain every Day that the Weather will permit my going out and sometime Six Pistoles."[52]

Washington's ledgers yield a more precise calculation of his surveying income. Although accounts have not been found for most of his clients, the few entries that exist show that he charged £2 3s. in Virginia money for a survey of less than one thousand acres, a sum that was due anytime after the survey was completed but in some cases was not actually paid until months or years later.[53] During the little more

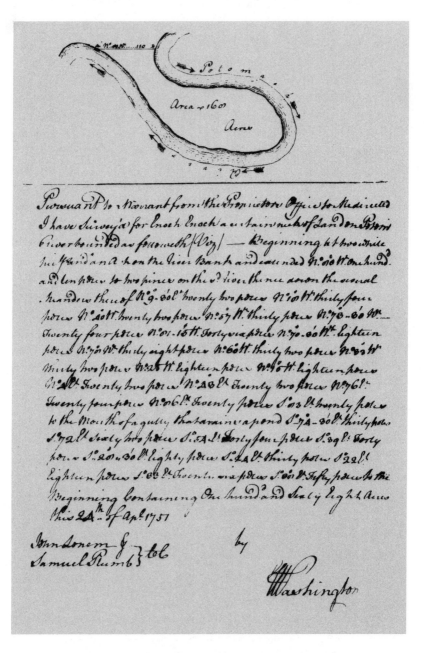

Washington's survey of a 168-acre tract near present-day Paw Paw, W. Va., for Enoch Enoch, 24 April 1751 (*George Washington Atlas*, plate 21).

than three years that Washington was a practicing professional surveyor, he made at least 190 surveys. At the rate of £2 3s. for each survey
(and a bit more for the few exceeding one thousand acres), Washington probably earned about four hundred pounds during his surveying
career. Even if all his fees were not paid promptly, Washington had
become by virtue of these earnings and his land acquisitions a young
man of considerable means and standing in Virginia by the spring of
1752. Only a very small percentage of the colony's inhabitants at that
time enjoyed an average cash income of more than one hundred pounds
a year, and only an equally small number owned as much as two thousand acres of land. To have both put one in a very exclusive class.

Washington's ambition extended far beyond being a successful frontier surveyor, however. After the fall of 1752, when he apparently laid
off only a single tract of 239 acres near his own lands on the South Fork
of the Bullskin, Washington stopped surveying for profit.[54] If his reasons for entering the profession were evident, so were his reasons for
leaving it. As lucrative as surveying on the Northern Neck frontier was
between 1749 and 1752, it offered only diminishing prospects for the
future. The supply of desirable new lands was already running low in
the proprietary by 1752, and Lord Fairfax's dominance of the
land-granting process prevented Northern Neck surveyors, whether
they held county appointments or not, from acquiring the political
and economic power that surveyors in other parts of Virginia were
often able to gain for themselves.[55] Unwilling to accept a role in life
that confined him to a pleasant but relatively obscure existence among
the county gentry, Washington sought greater distinction through military service. On November 6, 1752, after much solicitation on his own
behalf, he obtained a commission from Governor Dinwiddie appointing him adjutant of the militia in the colony's southern district with an
annual salary of one hundred pounds.[56] It was no coincidence that the
appointment, bringing with it a new source of income and the prestige
of military rank, came eleven days after Washington made what was to
be his last professional survey.

*W*ASHINGTON REACHED ANOTHER
turning point in his life in December 1754 when, two and a half years
after Lawrence's death, he gained control of Mount Vernon from his

half-brother's widow.[57] Prior to that time, Washington had begun planting tobacco on his Shenandoah lands, working the fields with slaves inherited from his father, and sending crops to market. He did not suspend operations there when he took over Mount Vernon, but his Shenandoah property, no matter how comparable in quantity or quality to Mount Vernon, could not match the Potomac plantation in location or prestige. Mount Vernon was henceforth to occupy the center of Washington's attention.

The close of Washington's professional surveying career did not end his surveying, however. As both a soldier and a planter, he found uses for some of the technical skills that he had acquired as a surveyor. During the Fort Necessity campaign in 1754, Washington lost, he later claimed, "a very valuable, and uncommon Circumferentor calculated not only for Superficial Measure, but for taking of Altitudes, and other useful purposes, which I carried out . . . imagining it necessary for laying of[f] Grounds for Forti[ficatio]ns &ca."[58] Military engineers in the eighteenth century routinely used surveying instruments to lay out defensive works, siege lines, and artillery positions according to precise mathematical formulas. If Washington's poorly conceived and executed works at Fort Necessity are any indication, his abilities in the military use of surveying instruments was inferior to his civilian employment of them, not a surprising conclusion since military engineering was a more exact science than was frontier surveying. Washington apparently never attained much proficiency in the science of military engineering, for during the Revolutionary War he relied on experienced American and foreign engineers. His familiarity with surveying, nevertheless, gave him an advantage over many other officers in planning fortifications and consulting with engineers.

Washington made much better and more extensive use of his surveying skills as a private planter. In 1771 he lamented rather awkwardly to his stepson's tutor that the boy was "totally ignorant of the mathematics, than which, so much of it at least as relates to surveying, nothing can be more essentially necessary to any person possessed of a large landed estate, the bounds of some part or other of which is always in controversy."[59] Washington certainly found that to be true of Mount Vernon's boundaries, which he repeatedly surveyed over the years in a variety of disputes. In addition, Washington frequently laid off fields and tenements and surveyed new acquisitions of land both near Mount Vernon and at more distant sites. As late as November 1799 he, in com-

pany with a fellow surveyor, spent three days on Difficult Run in northern Fairfax County running the lines of his land there and of a nearby
tract that had been offered to him in payment of a debt.[60] Only his
death five weeks later put an end to his surveying.

Washington's training and experience as a surveyor also had broader
implications for his life. Method and exactness may have come naturally to Washington, but his study of surveying, which was the apex of
his limited formal education, stamped those habits firmly on his mind.
"Every task," biographer Douglas Southall Freeman says of Washington, "was performed as if it were a land survey—step by step, with the
closest possible approach to absolute precision."[61] The laying of lines
across an uncharted wilderness nourished Washington's sense of order
and taught him well the lesson that system most often yields success.

Surveying channeled Washington's youthful ambition into productive activity and provided him the means to begin moving up in the
Tidewater society in which he so earnestly wished to rise. Just as important, surveying introduced him to the backcountry, giving him an
economic stake there and an enduring interest in its affairs.
Washington's preoccupation with Mount Vernon after 1754 did not
eclipse his vision of the West. He not only kept most of the Shenandoah
Valley lands that he acquired during his surveying career but added to
them. In the spring of 1753, Washington received grants from Lord
Fairfax for two lots in Winchester and for a 240-acre tract on the
Potomac River about twelve miles upstream from present-day Berke-
ley Springs, West Virginia. In April 1760 he patented 183 acres near his
Bullskin Run lands, and in December 1774 he bought 571 acres on Craig
Run, southeast of Berryville, from his friend George Mercer.[62]

These holdings seem small, however, when compared to the ones
that Washington eventually obtained in the greater West beyond the
Appalachian Mountains. Between 1768 and 1784, through various purchases and grants, he acquired 33,085 acres on the Ohio and Kanawha
rivers, 4,691 1/2 acres in southwestern Pennsylvania, and a half share in
a 6,071-acre tract on the Mohawk River in New York. In 1788 Washington bought five thousand acres on the Rough River in western Kentucky from Light-Horse Harry Lee, and two years later he used two
military land warrants that he had purchased from veterans to claim
3,051 acres on the Little Miami River near Cincinnati.[63] By the age of
fifty-eight Washington had increased his stake in the West to about
fifty-two thousand acres.

Washington sought to profit from his western lands through long-term leases to tenant farmers. As historian Paul Longmore writes in *The Invention of George Washington*, Washington foresaw in the West "not a Jeffersonian freeholder's empire, but the spread of the traditional system of land tenure, labor relations, and racial and class hierarchy."[64] The tenant system worked well for Washington in the Shenandoah Valley, perhaps because of the transfer of Tidewater social values to the region but more simply because a steady demand for land developed in the Valley after the French and Indian War and because Washington was able to find dependable agents to oversee his affairs there. In the mid-1760s Washington abandoned farming operations on his Bullskin Run plantation and began leasing it and his other Shenandoah holdings in tenements of varying sizes. During the Revolutionary War those lands, which fell mostly in newly created Berkeley County after 1772, were sadly neglected. Tenants changed without Washington's consent or knowledge, and most of the rents went unpaid. With the return of peace, Washington engaged Battaile Muse as land agent to correct matters. Muse did so promptly and collected annual rents totaling about £170 in Berkeley and Frederick counties until 1791, when Washington's nephew Robert Lewis assumed those duties.[65]

Although Washington had no desire to sell any of his Shenandoah lands during his lifetime, he found their rise in value a comforting confirmation of his business acumen and his status as a gentleman of great landed wealth. "Since I have been an Actor for myself," Washington wrote a young Fairfax County neighbor in 1797, "Frederick and Berkeley Counties were deemed much more remote—& in fact out of the inhabited World—than the Kanawha is now: and lands, which I then bought in the former at five pounds per hundred acres, and the highest (on account of small improvements) at twenty five pounds per hundd I could now sell, very readily at five pounds an *acre*."[66]

Washington derived little profit from his holdings west of the Appalachians, however. Despite his best efforts, his tracts in the Ohio and Kanawha valleys remained mostly unrented and brought him little income when on rare occasions they were leased. Part of the problem was the remoteness of those lands from Mount Vernon and Washington's inability to obtain competent managers for them. He had found "from long experience," Washington wrote a western Pennsylvania acquaintance in 1794, "that landed property at a distance from the Proprietor, is attended with more plague than profit."[67] A more fundamental reason for his western leasing difficulties, Washington realized, was that during the 1780s and early 1790s immigration into the trans-Appalachian region was impeded by Indian hostilities and the lack of convenient access to markets. "The land in [the] western country, . . . like all others," Washington wrote Richard Henderson of Bladensburg, Maryland, in 1788, "has its *advantages and disadvantages.* The neighbourhood of the Savages and the difficulty of transportation were the great objections."[68]

Those obstacles were largely removed during Washington's second term as president by the Indian defeat at Fallen Timbers, Jay's Treaty providing for British evacuation of western forts, and Pinckney's Treaty which opened navigation of the Mississippi. But the changes brought about by Washington's administration came too late to benefit his western land leasing ventures. Hard-pressed for cash and anxious to simplify his private affairs, Washington sold his Ohio and Kanawha lands to a French speculator in 1791, only to be bitterly disappointed when the deal collapsed two years later.[69]

In the spring of 1794, the aging president decided to sell all his western holdings except for his Shenandoah lands. He had not lost faith in the long-range value of the property, he wrote a prospective purchaser, financier Robert Morris, on May 26. "In my opinion," Washington assured Morris, it "promises the richest future harvest of any thing of the kind I have contemplated. . . . But, as the case is, I prefer present convenience to future advantages; and therefore, in my own days, which cannot be many, am disposed to turn my unproductive land into cash, that I may enjoy the comforts which may result from the interest thereof."[70]

A comfortable retirement was not Washington's only motive for attempting to cash in his western lands. It was also a matter of conscience. In a private part of a letter that Washington wrote to his personal secretary, Tobias Lear, on May 6, 1794, he gave another reason, one "more powerful than all the rest—namely to liberate a certain species of property which I possess, very repugnantly to my own feelings." Washington was referring to his numerous slaves, on whose labor he would be ever dependent unless he could find a substantial source of income outside the agricultural operations of his Mount Vernon plantation.[71]

Washington's efforts to fund his retirement and the freeing of his slaves by selling his western lands were not much more successful than were his earlier efforts to settle dependable rent payers on them. High sale prices and sales of large undivided tracts, if not the whole of his western holdings, were absolutely essential, Washington thought, for acquiring an investment sum sufficiently large for the purposes he had in mind. But that strategy greatly limited the number of potential purchasers for his offerings. Contrary to Washington's expectations, no "full handed" European investors, fleeing the effects of the French Revolution, came forth to accept his stiff terms.[72] During his life Washington sold only two Pennsylvania tracts and part of his Mohawk Valley land.[73] When he died in 1799, Washington still owned about forty-five thousand acres in the West, including his Shenandoah properties. In his will he directed his executors to sell all of that acreage and divide the proceeds among twenty-three heirs. The executors also were instructed to do what Washington had not done in life: His slaves were to be freed upon the death of Martha Washington.[74]

The ultimate dissolution of Washington's western lands does not belie their importance to him. On a personal level they represented a considerable investment of labor and money, a speculation that, for all of his care and system, involved some risk. Not only was Washington's social and economic well-being at stake but so was his sense of self-worth in the business in which as a youth he had first proved himself proficient. If he was often discomfited by defects in his formal education, Washington took pride in his ability to read a tract of land with his practiced surveyor's eye as expertly as a Latin scholar perusing a page of Cicero or Tacitus. His invariable description of his western lands as being of the first quality was not just a salesman's ploy. It was a point of personal honor. He had taken great pains to ensure that his tracts were, indeed, of first quality, and public recognition of that fact was as important to him as any financial return.[75]

Washington's western investments also were connected closely with his evolving nationalism in public life. As a young man he saw the Virginia backcountry stretching from the Shenandoah to the Ohio as a fine field for pursuing personal wealth and distinction through aggressive land speculation. By the end of the Revolutionary War, Washington's vision of the West had widened to encompass all the area between the Appalachians and the Mississippi, and he had concluded that neither private speculators nor individual states ought to control that "New Empire" because it was an invaluable resource indispensable to the future prosperity of the United States, a national asset that could best be developed under a strong central government. Washington's new ideas about the West were not incompatible in his mind with his unchanged expectation of profiting from his backcountry lands, for he viewed his efforts to lease them as a participation in the orderly development of the nation's frontiers. Only by restricting western inhabitants to compact, traditionally structured settlements such as he planned for his holdings, Washington thought, could national control of the trans-Appalachian region be assured.[76]

Washington likewise considered improvements to inland navigation to be vital to American interests in the West. Several major rivers from the Mohawk south to the James, Washington believed, might become serviceable routes into the backcountry if proper locks and canals were built to circumvent their falls and rapids, but he quite naturally focused his attention on improving the Potomac. In the early 1770s Washington played a leading role in forming a private company to open the navigation of the Potomac from its falls to Fort Cumberland, a distance of about 150 miles. Although the company accomplished little before the Revolutionary War ended its operations, Washington continued to be interested in western navigation, and soon after returning home from the war, he used his personal prestige and knowledge of the West to persuade the Virginia and Maryland assemblies to authorize a new Potomac Company.[77] Washington served as president of that company from 1785 to 1789 and was one of its most enthusiastic supporters until his death in 1799. "This is no Utopean Scheme," he assured a South Carolina correspondent in the fall of 1784.[78] Washington and his fellow investors in the Potomac Company were convinced that the Potomac could easily be linked to the Ohio by navigable tributaries and short portage roads and that the Potomac would soon become the main "Channel of Commerce" between east and west.[79]

Washington stood to benefit greatly from the successful completion of the Potomac navigation project. His lands in both the Tidewater region and the backcountry would be much enhanced in value, and as an investor in the Potomac Company, he would realize a handsome return on his money by sharing in the tolls that were to be levied on vessels using the company's locks and canals.[80] Washington's unequivocal support for the second Potomac Company, nevertheless, was spurred by more than personal considerations. "The consequences to the Union" of the contemplated navigation improvements, Washington wrote James Warren in October 1785, "are immense—& more so in a political, than in a Commercial point; for unless we can connect the New

States, which are rising to our view in the Regions back of us, with those on the Atlantic by interest, the only cement that will bind, . . . they will be quite a distinct People, and ultimately may be very troublesome neighbours to us."[81] The western settlers, Washington argued, must be provided cheap and easy means of transporting their products across the Appalachians to eastern seaports before they established close commercial ties with the Spanish at New Orleans or the British in Canada, for such connections, he feared, once established would not be easily severed and might eventually lead to political alliances with one of those powers and to western secession from the United States. "Happily for us," Washington wrote another correspondent, "the way is plain—and our *immediate* Interests, as well as remote political advantages, points to it. . . . Extend the inland navigation of the Eastern waters—communicate them as near as possible (by excellent Roads) with those which run to the Westward. Open these to the Ohio . . . and we shall not only draw the produce of the Western Settlers, but the Fur & peltry trade of the lakes also, to our Ports . . . to the amazing encrease of our Exports, while we bind those people to us by a chain which never can be broken."[82]

Washington's optimistic expectations for the Potomac Company, like those that he had for his western lands, were never fulfilled. The engineering and financial problems involved in opening the upper Potomac to navigation proved to be far more difficult to overcome than Washington and his partners envisioned. Although several canals eventually were completed between Georgetown and points above Harpers Ferry, the company lost money and went out of business in 1828 without achieving its ultimate goal of creating a water route to the Ohio Valley.[83] While it existed, however, the Potomac Company effectively embodied Washington's ideas on western development and national unity.

Among the Founders only Washington had extensive personal experience in the West. If his rather conservative views on land tenancy and the pace of western settlement did not coincide with those of his more democratically minded countrymen, it remains true that Washington possessed an intimate knowledge of the backcountry and a fondness for wilderness life that was unique among the major political leaders of his generation.[84] Because the West was such an integral part of his adult years, Washington could not abide the prospect of a sharp line of demarcation being drawn along the Appalachians.[85] As both a private citizen and president, he labored as energetically as he ever did when surveying to incorporate the western country into the political and economic life of the new nation, and he regarded his success in so doing to be one of the major achievements of his presidency.

NOTES

1. George Washington to Chevalier de Chastellux, October 12, 1783, Washington Papers, Library of Congress, Washington, D.C.
2. Douglas Southall Freeman, *George Washington: A Biography*, 7 vols. (New York: Charles Scribner's Sons, 1948–1957), 1:186–88.
3. Sarah S. Hughes, *Surveyors and Statesmen: Land Measuring in Colonial Virginia* (Richmond: The Virginia Surveyors Foundation, and the Virginia Association of Surveyors, 1979), 156.
4. Hughes, *Surveyors and Statesmen*, 156, 160, 163–64.
5. Hughes, *Surveyors and Statesmen*, 85, 156–61. See also Margaret Brown Klapthor and Howard Alexander Morrison, *G. Washington: A Figure upon the Stage* (Washington, D.C.: The Smithsonian Institution Press, 1982), 120.
6. Robert Jackson to Lawrence Washington, September 18, 1746, Washington Headquarters Library, Morristown, N.J. Lawrence Washington's letters to George and Mary Ball Washington have not been found, but William Fairfax, who carried them to Fredericksburg, wrote Lawrence Washington on September 10, 1746, that "George has been with us, and says He will be steady and thankfully follow your Advice as his best Friend. I gave him his Mother's letter to deliver with Caution not to shew his. I have spoke to Dr. Spencer who I find is often at the Widow's and has some influence, to persuade Her to think better of your advice in putting Him to Sea with good Recommendation." See Moncure D. Conway, *Barons of the Potomack and the Rappahannock* (New York: The Grolier Club, 1892), 236–38. See also Freeman, *Washington*, 1:190, 193–95.
7. Joseph Ball to Mary Ball Washington, May 19, 1747, Joseph Ball Papers, Library of Congress.
8. See volume 2 of the schoolbooks, entitled "Washington's School Copy-Book 1745," in the Washington Papers, series 1A, Library of Congress. The first page of this schoolbook, which begins with nineteen pages of geometry lessons, is dated "August 13th 1745" in Washington's handwriting. The surveying exercises immediately follow the geometry lessons. The upper parts of the second and third pages of the surveying section, which include the third step in drawing the boundaries of a tract and a sketch of a surveyor's chain, draw-

ing compass, and plotting scale, are at Cornell University, Ithaca, N.Y. See also, "School Exercises, 1744–1748," *The Papers of George Washington*, Colonial Series, ed. W. W. Abbot et al., 10 vols. (Charlottesville: University Press of Virginia, 1983–1995), 1:1–4.

9. This course appears in the latter part of volume 3 of Washington's schoolbooks at the Library of Congress. It contains thirteen pages of geometrical definitions and problems, six pages on square roots, ten pages on plain trigonometry, and thirty-eight pages of surveying lessons and exercises, a few of which bear dates in August and October 1747. Several pages are missing from the surveying section. Two of them, showing exercises dated September 29 and 30, 1747, are in the Gratz Collection at the Historical Society of Pennsylvania, Philadelphia. The names of persons mentioned in some exercises suggest that part or even all of the instruction may have occurred in the Chotank area of Stafford County or the Pope's Creek area of Westmoreland County, both of which were within a day's ride of Ferry Farm and were home to a number of Washington's relatives. See note 18 below and Lawrence Martin, ed., *The George Washington Atlas* (Washington, D.C.: United States George Washington Bicentennial Commission, 1932), pl. 8.

10. A copy of William Leybourn's *The Compleat Surveyor* (London: Printed by E. Flesher for George Sawbridge, 1679) was in Washington's library at Mount Vernon when he died in 1799. Although that copy bears William Fairfax's signature, there is no evidence that Fairfax was involved in Washington's surveying education or that Washington owned or used the book during his training. See Appleton P. C. Griffin, A *Catalogue of the Washington Collection in the Boston Athenaeum* (Boston: Boston Athenaeum, 1897), 550.

11. Washington's schoolbooks, vol. 3, Washington Papers, Library of Congress.

12. John Love, *Geodaesia; or, The Art of Surveying and Measuring of Land Made Easie* (London: Printed for J. Taylor, 1688). Although thirteen editions of *Geodaesia* were published between 1688 and 1796, no record of Washington's owning a copy of this work has been found.

13. Washington's schoolbooks, vol. 3, Washington Papers, Library of Congress.

14. The instructor errs in the lesson about converting chain links to feet, however, by treating each link as one-hundredth of a chain, which is true of a four-pole chain, but not of a two-pole chain, in which each link is one-fiftieth of the chain's total length. Thus, an example in the schoolbook shows that 36 chains and 7 links equals 36.07 times 33 feet, or 1,190.31 feet, but the correct answer is 36.14 times 33 feet, or 1,192.62 feet. See Washington's schoolbooks, vol. 3, Washington Papers, Library of Congress.

15. Washington paid 1s. 3d. for the Gunter scale. See Washington's private account book, 1747–1765, p. 2, Washington's Headquarters Library, Morristown,

N.J. Bailey Washington, who lived in the Chotank area, about twenty miles east of Ferry Farm, was five months older than Washington.

16. The set of surveyor's instruments was valued at £1 10s. in the inventory of Augustine Washington's estate that was recorded at the King George County court on July 1, 1743. See King George County Inventory Book, 1721–1744, 285–91, King George County courthouse, King George, Va.

17. For the development of traverse surveying in Virginia, see Hughes, *Surveyors and Statesmen*, 38–55.

18. Washington's schoolbooks, vol. 3, Washington Papers, Library of Congress. Although most of the problems in the schoolbook are hypothetical ones, several exercises involve undated surveys that include names of contemporary persons living on the lower Northern Neck and references to specific corner trees and other local landmarks. Those surveys cannot be located or otherwise identified, but their detailed descriptions suggest that Washington's instructor may have taken them as examples from actual surveys which he had made previously in a professional capacity. The persons for whom the surveys are said to have been made are Francis Jett (died 1766) of King George County; John Monroe (d. 1767) and John Watts, both of the Mattox Creek area in Westmoreland County; and Elizabeth Lund Washington and Henry Washington (1694–1748) both of the Chotank area in Stafford County. Elizabeth Lund Washington was the widow of Townshend Washington (d. 1743) and the mother of George Washington's distant cousin Lund Washington, who later served as manager of Mount Vernon for many years. Two of her other sons, Robert and Lawrence Washington, are mentioned in George Washington's will of July 9, 1799 as "the acquaintances and friends of my Juvenile years" (Fairfax County Courthouse, Fairfax, Va.). Henry Washington was the father of Bailey Washington, who sold George Washington a Gunter scale in September 1747.

19. Washington's schoolbooks, vol. 3, Washington Papers, Library of Congress. Washington was born on February 11, 1732, according to the Julian calendar that was used in Great Britain and its colonies until 1752, when the Gregorian calendar was adopted. Because the change in calendars required the addition of eleven days, Washington's birthday eventually was observed on February 22.

20. *The Diaries of George Washington*, ed. Donald Jackson and Dorothy Twohig, 6 vols. (Charlottesville: University Press of Virginia, 1976–1979), 1:5–6.

21. Washington's diary, 1748, Washington Papers, series 1B, Library of Congress. See also, Washington, March 13–15, 1748, *Washington Diaries*, 1:7–10. A third copy of the courses of George William Fairfax's tract and a plat of it, both in Washington's writing, are with the 1748 surveys of Mount Vernon fields in the last pages of Washington's schoolbook, vol. 3, Washington Papers, Library of Congress.

22. Washington's diary, 1748, Washington Papers, Library of Congress; Washington, March 16 to April 13, 1748, *Washington Diaries*, 1:10–23.

23. Washington, March 15, 1748, *Washington Diaries*, 1:9–10. Pennington lived on Buck Marsh Run near present-day Berryville, Va.

24. Washington, March 13, 1748, *Washington Diaries*, 1:7.

25. James D. Munson, "A New Look at the Founding of Alexandria," *Alexandria History* 7 (1987): 12. Washington's maps of Alexandria are in the map division of the Library of Congress.

26. Henry Howe, *Historical Collections of Virginia* (Charleston, S.C.: Babcock, 1845; Baltimore: Regional Publishing Co., 1969), 237. Washington's surveying commission was destroyed when the College of William and Mary's library burned in 1859. For the form, see Hughes, *Surveyors and Statesmen*, pl. 14, p. 96.

27. Washington to John Augustine Washington, May 28, 1755, *Washington Papers*, Col. Ser., 1:289–93.

28. Gov. Robert Dinwiddie wrote Lord Fairfax on May 6, 1752: "When yr Lordship shall think proper to apoint a private Surveyr that you will please lay your Commands on them to Acct with the Coledge for one Sixth of their receipts, which [I] shall be glad if this proves agreeable to yr own Opinion. The Comissary [college president William Dawson] says he will always have a due regard to any person recommended to the Coledge for their Commission." See Dinwiddie Papers, Virginia Historical Society, Richmond Va. See also Hughes, *Surveyors and Statesmen*, 23–27, 93–94, 96–99, 158.

29. *Washington Papers*, Col. Ser., 1:20–21, 33–34 n.6.

30. Hughes, *Surveyors and Statesmen*, 93.

31. "List of County Surveyors–1757," *Virginia Magazine of History and Biography* 50 (October 1942): 368–69.

32. Hughes, *Surveyors and Statesmen*, 92–93, 166–69, 171. See also note 28.

33. Washington, Memorandum, 1749–1750, *Washington Papers*, Col. Ser., 1:45.

34. An example of one of the warrants issued to Washington can be found in *Washington Papers*, Col. Ser., 1:11.

35. Washington to Thomas Lord Fairfax, October–November 1749, *Washington Papers*, Col. Ser., 1:39–40.

36. *Washington Papers*, Col. Ser., 1:20; Hughes, *Surveyors and Statesmen*, 113–14.

37. Washington paid Lonem 5s. on March 21, 1752, for "Carrying the Chain round 2 Tracts of Land." See Ledger A, p. 6, Washington Papers, Library of Congress.

38. Two of Washington's field books, covering the period 1749 to 1752, are in the Washington Papers, series 1c, Library of Congress. A page from one of those books is reproduced in *Washington Papers*, Col. Ser., 1:13. For a discussion of field procedures used by Virginia surveyors, see Hughes, *Surveyors and Statesmen*, 116–17, 124, 127–28.

39. Washington, March 16, 1748, *Washington Diaries*, 1:10–11.
40. Washington's finished surveys are scattered among a variety of repositories and private collections. For some examples, see *Washington Papers*, Col. Ser., 1:15, 21, 24, 32; Martin, *Washington Atlas*, pl. 20–21.
41. *Washington Papers*, Col. Ser., 1:20–25.
42. *Washington Papers*, Col. Ser., 1:25. Washington's field book for 1749–1750 indicates that for several of the August 1750 surveys he laid off large tracts on the ground which he later divided on paper among two or more persons. See Washington Papers, Library of Congress. Washington's youngest brother, Charles Washington, later inherited some of this land, including the site of Charles Town, from Lawrence Washington and settled on it during the Revolution.
43. *Washington Papers*, Col. Ser., 1:26–27.
44. Field book for 1750–1751, Washington Papers, Library of Congress; Northern Neck Land Grant Book G:465, Library of Virginia, Richmond, Va.
45. Field book for 1750–1751 and Ledger A, p. 5, both in Washington Papers, Library of Congress; Northern Neck Land Grant Book G:466; Frederick County Deed Book, 2:209–12, microfilm, Library of Virginia .
46. Field book for 1750–1751, Washington Papers, Library of Congress; Northern Neck Land Grant Book H:136.
47. *Washington Papers*, Col. Ser., 1:27–30.
48. Spotsylvania County Deed Book, E:46–49, microfilm, Library of Virginia.
49. *Washington Papers*, Col. Ser., 1:31.
50. Field book for 1750–1751 and Ledger A, p. 5, both in Washington Papers, Library of Congress; survey for George Johnston, August 28, 1750, deCoppett Collection, Princeton University, Princeton, N.J.; Northern Neck Grant Book H:458; Frederick County Deed Book, 2:476–81.
51. In 1752 Lawrence Washington owned 2,298 acres at Mount Vernon including a mill tract on Dogue Creek. See *Washington Diaries*, 1:240–41.
52. Washington to Richard, 1749–1750, *Washington Papers*, Col. Ser., 1:43–44. The doubloon, a Spanish gold coin, was worth 33s. to 36s. in sterling money at that time.
53. Accounts for Richard Barnes, John Welton, William Miller, and Darby McKeever in Washington's Private Accounts, September 10, 1747–1765, Washington Headquarters Library, Morristown, N.J.; Ledger A, pp. 1, 3–6, 234, Washington Papers, Library of Congress. Surveying fees were set by the General Assembly and varied from region to region within the colony. For some unknown reason Washington charged the £2 3s. fee authorized for counties along the fall line rather than the £1 11s. 3d. fee that was supposed to be collected in the Shenandoah Valley, see Hughes, *Surveyors and Statesmen*, 157–58, 190 n.7.
54. *Washington Papers*, Col. Ser., 1:31–32.
55. Hughes, *Surveyors and Statesmen*, 93.
56. *Washington Papers*, Col. Ser., 1:53.

57. Lease of Mount Vernon, December 17, 1754, *Washington Papers*, Col. Ser., 1:232-35.

58. Washington to Carter Burwell, April 20, 1755, *Washington Papers*, Col. Ser., 1:252-54.

59. Washington to Jonathan Boucher, July 9, 1771, *Washington Papers*, Col. Ser., 8:494–98.

60. Washington, November 6–8, 1799, *Washington Diaries*, 6:374–75.

61. Freeman, *Washington*, 2:385.

62. Northern Neck Land Grant Book H:287, 394, K:98; Ledger B, p. 129, Washington Papers, Library of Congress. Washington's property in Winchester consisted of a one-half-acre town lot and a five-acre lot in the commons. No buildings were erected on them during Washington's lifetime. See Battaile Muse to Washington, September 6, 14, 1785, *Washington Papers*, Confederation Series, ed. W. W. Abbot et al., 5 vols. to date (Charlottesville: University Press of Virginia, 1992–), 3:233–35, 248–49; Robert Lewis to Washington, August 19, 1794, Washington Papers, Library of Congress; and George Washington's will, July 9, 1799, Fairfax County Courthouse. John Baylis, one of the assistant surveyors for Frederick County, surveyed the 240–acre tract on the Potomac River for Washington. A survey for the 183-acre tract near Bullskin Run in Washington's writing, dated April 7, 1760, is at the Henry E. Huntington Library, San Marino, Calif. Washington paid £418 to George Mercer for the 571 acres on Craig Run.

63. Washington's acquisition of these lands constitutes another whole chapter in his life. For listings of them, see Washington's memorandum of lands offered to Robert Morris, May 25, 1794, Washington Papers, Library of Congress; broadside advertising Washington's lands for lease and sale, February 1, 1796, Marieta College, Marieta, Ohio; and Washington's will, July 9, 1799, Fairfax County Courthouse. See also, Roy Bird Cook, *Washington's Western Lands* (Strasburg, Va.: Shenandoah, 1930); Willard Rouse Jillson, *The Land Adventures of George Washington* (Louisville: Standard Printing, 1934).

64. Paul K. Longmore, *The Invention of George Washington* (Berkeley: University of California Press, 1988), 108.

65. Ledger A, pp. 248, 305–6, Washington Papers, Library of Congress; Lund Washington, "A List of General Washington's Rents Due," December 25, 1775, and rental accounts for Frederick, Berkeley, Fauquier, and Loudoun counties, 1788–1790, December 1791, December 25, 1792, December 1794, September 1, 1795, and December 1795, all owned by the Mount Vernon Ladies' Association of the Union.

66. Washington to Daniel McCarty, November 3, 1797, Washington Papers, New York Public Library, New York, N.Y.

67. Washington to James Ross, June 16, 1794, U.S. Presidents Collection, New York Public Library.

68. Washington to Richard Henderson, June 19, 1788, *Washington Papers,* Conf. Ser., 6:339–42.

69. The speculator was John Joseph de Barth. See Barth's bond to Washington for twelve thousand French crowns, March 21, 1791, Huntington Library; Washington to George Clendinen, March 31, 1791, Washington Papers, Library of Congress; Washington to Tobias Lear, April 3, 1791, in *The Writings of George Washington from the Original Manuscript Sources, 1745–1799,* ed. John C. Fitzpatrick, 39 vols. (Washington, D.C.: United States Government Printing Office, 1931–1944), 31:266–67; Lear to Barth, April 1 and May 2, 1793, Washington Papers, Library of Congress; Washington to Lear, April 5 and 8, 1793, Huntington Library; Washington to Barth, April 30, 1793, Pierpont Morgan Library, New York, N.Y.

70. Washington to Robert Morris, May 26, 1794, Chicago Historical Society.

71. Washington to Tobias Lear, May 6, 1794, Huntington Library.

72. Washington to Charles Morgan, January 17, 1795, Pittsburgh Historical Society. See also Washington to John Savary, March 25, 1795, Washington to Edmund Randolph, April 12, 1795, both in the Washington Papers, Library of Congress.

73. Washington sold his 2,813-acre tract at Washington's Bottom to Israel Shrive in 1795, and his 1,644-acre tract on Miller's Run to Matthew Ritchie in 1796, see Washington's agreement with Shreve, July 31, 1795, Historical Society of Western Pennsylvania, Pittsburgh, Pa.; typescript of George and Martha Washington's deed to Ritchie, Washington Papers, ser. 9, Library of Congress. For the sale of some of Washington's Mohawk Valley lands, see Eugene E. Prussing, *The Estate of George Washington, Deceased* (Boston: Little, Brown, and Company, 1927), 305–11.

74. George Washington's will, July 9, 1799, Fairfax County Courthouse. The executors failed to make good Washington's claim to the lands on the Little Miami River. Washington's Shenandoah Valley lands, his tract on the Potomac River near Berkeley Springs, and his Pennsylvania and New York lands were sold in accordance with the will. By agreement of the heirs, Washington's lands on the Ohio and Kanawha rivers were divided among them rather than being sold. The records concerning the sale of Washington's Kentucky lands are incomplete. See Prussing, *Washington Estate,* 292–95, 301–48; Jillson, *Land Adventures,* 41. Martha Washington freed her husband's slaves about a year after his death, but she could not free the slaves that she possessed by dower right.

75. For a discussion of Washington's ambition to grow crops of the best quality, see Longmore, *George Washington,* 70, 77–78, 84. See also, Klapthor and Morrison, *A Figure upon the Stage,* 130.

76. Washington objected to widely scattered settlements and to "Land Jobbers, Speculators, and Monopolisers," who, he thought, were attempting

to control all of the best western lands by making unprecedented claims of 50,000 to 500,000 acres. See Washington to James Duane, September 7, 1783, Washington Papers, Library of Congress; Washington to Jacob Read, November 3, 1784, *Washington Papers*, Conf. Ser., 2:118–23.

77. For the establishment of the two Potomac companies, see William W. Hening, ed., *The Statutes at Large: Being a Collection of All the Laws of Virginia* . . . , 13 vols. (Richmond: 1809–1823), 8:570–79, 11:510–16; Corra Bacon-Foster, *Early Chapters in the Development of the Patomac Route to the West* (Washington, D.C.: Columbia Historical Society, 1912). See also Washington to Thomas Johnson, July 20, 1770, *Washington Papers*, Conf. Ser., 8:357–60; Washington to Thomas Jefferson, March 29, 1784, *Washington Papers*, Conf. Ser., 1:237–41; Washington to James Madison, November 28, December 28, 1784, *Washington Papers*, Conf. Ser., 2:155–57, 231–35.

78. Washington to Jacob Read, November 3, 1784, *Washington Papers*, Conf. Ser., 2:118–23.

79. Washington to Thomas Johnson, July 20, 1770, *Washington Papers*, Col. Ser., 8:357–60. See also Washington to Henry Riddell, February 22, 1774, *Washington Papers*, Col. Ser., 9:493–96; Washington, October 4, 1784, *Washington Diaries*, 4:57–63.

80. See Washington to Henry Riddell, February 22, 1774, *Washington Papers*, Col. Ser., 9:493–96; Washington to Thomas Jefferson, March 29, 1784, *Washington Papers*, Conf. Ser., 1:237–41; Washington to Robert Morris, February 1, 1785, *Washington Papers*, Conf. Ser., 2:309–15; Washington to John Craig, March 29, 1785, *Washington Papers*, Conf. Ser., 2:469.

81. Washington to James Warren, October 7, 1785, *Washington Papers*, Conf. Ser., 3:298–301. See also Washington to Lafayette, July 25, 1785, *Washington Papers*, Conf. Ser., 3:151–55.

82. Washington to Jacob Read, November 3, 1784, *Washington Papers*, Conf. Ser., 2:118–23. See also Washington to Benjamin Harrison, October 10, 1784, *Washington Papers*, Conf. Ser., 2:86–98; Washington to George Plater, October 25, 1784, *Washington Papers*, Conf. Ser., 2:106–10; Washington, October 4, 1784, *Washington Diaries*, 4:65–68.

83. Bacon-Foster, *Patomac Route*.

84. On his final trip to the backcountry in 1784, Washington, who was then fifty-two years old, wrote in his diary entry for September 25: "I lodged this night, with no other shelter or cover than my cloak; & was unlucky enough to have a heavy shower of Rain," see Washington, September 25, 1784, *Washington Diaries*, 4:44.

85. See Washington to Jacob Read, November 3, 1784, *Washington Papers*, Conf. Ser., 2:118–23.

School for Command: Young George Washington and the Virginia Regiment

JOHN E. FERLING

$\mathcal{A}$s a congressman during the War of Independence and later as vice president of the United States, John Adams often lauded George Washington's abilities. He extolled Washington's facility for self-control and his ability to know himself. Adams also applauded Washington's courage, resourcefulness, and flair for making difficult decisions. Adams praised Washington's disinterested service; he spoke of the "purity of [Washington's] character," once calling him a "wise, virtuous, and good" man. But above all else, Adams paid tribute to Washington's uncanny capability to understand others. Washington had perfected this aptitude to a "Science," Adams declared. Washington, Adams went on, possessed "Talents of a very Superior kind. I wish I had as good."[1]

The endowments that Adams observed in Washington were also perceived by those who served with him during the War of Independence. Several who were close to General Washington remarked on his ability to make decisions. He knew his limitations, they often said, and as a result he had learned to elicit advice, to sift and sort and weigh the counsel until, with great deliberation, he made up his mind. He was "slow but sure in conclusion," Thomas Jefferson once remarked. Adams lauded the same quality in identical language. "He was slow, but sure," he said.[2]

Others who observed Washington praised his honesty and incorruptibility. Many men spoke of his "virtue," his selfless, sacrificial bent, his courage and dedication, his willingness to serve the nation in its hour of need, and to serve for the public good, not for private interest. Washington's Spartan lifestyle while he was commander of the Continental army impressed still other observers. So virtuous was Washington in the eyes of most of those about him that they probably would have agreed with the young Revolutionary War officer who saw in the general the "last stage of perfection to which human nature is capable of attaining."[3]

Few historians have used such language to describe the young George Washington who commanded the Virginia Regiment during the French and Indian War. As a callow provincial colonel, he sometimes acted rashly, throwing his men into battle when retreat would have been more advisable. He was absent from his army for long stretches. He bickered with his superior, the governor of Virginia, and he even furtively circumvented the chief executive to secure his ends. Some thought he tolerated an air of revelry, even licentiousness, among his officers. His behavior was not always disinterested; sometimes, in fact, he appeared to act more as the speculator than the soldier.

Indeed, there is much about Washington's performance during the French and Indian War that is disturbing. Throughout his life, however, Washington exhibited a capacity to learn from his mistakes. This ability makes the early period of Washington's career extremely important, for the man that the Revolutionary generation observed was not the same green, young colonel who led the Virginia Regiment in the 1750s. By 1775 he was an experienced officer who understood his earlier indiscretions and who was bent on avoiding the pitfalls that once caused him such difficulty.

*A*T MIDCENTURY BOTH FRANCE AND Great Britain claimed the American West to the Mississippi River. Three wars waged since 1689 had resolved nothing in this region. But immediately following the conclusion of King George's War in 1748, France took steps to secure its hold on the Ohio Country. By early in 1753 fifteen hundred French troops were stationed below Lake Erie. The French had erected garrisons throughout the backcountry; in addition, they had begun to fortify the route they had opened between Canada and the Ohio River.

If France controlled the Ohio Country, Britain's fur trade would immediately suffer crippling losses and British speculators would be denied access to the rich, flat lands that sprawled west of the mountains. Of greater importance, however, was the realization in London that if Britain lost its claim to the West, its colonies would be pinioned to the Atlantic coast. Much of the reason for the existence of the colonies would then be lost, for provinces that were overpopulated and unable to expand would be unlikely to remain in an economic state subservient to a faraway parent.

To forestall such an eventuality, the British government in 1753 directed Robert Dinwiddie, governor of Virginia, to notify the commander of the French army in the transmontane West that the Ohio Country belonged to Great Britain. Dinwiddie needed no urging. Five years earlier several Virginia planters had formed the Ohio Company and secured a royal grant to thousands of acres along the Ohio River. Lawrence Washington, George Washington's older half-brother, was one of the organizers of the company; George himself subsequently invested in the endeavor.[4]

Washington was twenty-one years old, a surveyor, and the master of a spent farm on the Rappahannock when Dinwiddie opened his search to find the right person to deliver his message to the French. Restive in his isolation at Ferry Farm and anxious to be recognized, young Washington hurried to the capital to volunteer for the dangerous mission.

Dinwiddie was impressed with his petitioner and asked him to carry the message to the French. The reasons for the governor's action are not difficult to fathom. Young Washington was a major in the Virginia militia, having been appointed to that rank during the previous year by Dinwiddie himself. In 1752 Dinwiddie had named Washington to be the military adjutant—commander of all militia forces—in the southwestern quadrant of the province. In 1753 he transferred Washington's command to the Northern Neck district. Not only had Washington sought the adjutancy, a sinecure that was with a modicum of prestige worth one hundred pounds annually, but he had been supported for the post by powerful benefactors, including the Fairfax family, the most influential clan in northern Virginia. In addition, Dinwiddie found much that he liked in young Washington. At six feet, two inches tall, Washington towered above his contemporaries. He was broad-shouldered, with long muscular arms; his waist was small and flat. He moved in a fluid, agile manner and he was an excellent, graceful horseman. He was cordial but quiet and disciplined, and there was a steely toughness in his features. Moreover, Dinwiddie knew that Washington had worked as a surveyor on the Virginia frontier since 1747; the young man should be used to the harsh demands of the mountain wilderness.[5]

Governor Dinwiddie's judgment was unerring. Traveling in the dead of winter, Major Washington survived his journey of several hundred miles through the wilderness, through the Indian country, to the very cusp of Lake Erie, where he encountered a French general at Fort Le Boeuf. By mid-January, two months after he had set out, Washington was back in Williamsburg with word that made hostilities inevitable: the French had rejected Britain's claim to the Ohio Country.

Thereafter Dinwiddie moved quickly. He urged the House of Burgesses to create an army of four hundred men, the Virginia Regiment, and he summoned two hundred frontier militiamen to serve as a supplemental force. Although young Washington was without military experience, the governor elevated him to the rank of lieutenant colonel, second in command beneath Col. Joshua Fry, like Washington a land speculator and frontier surveyor, although Fry had been formally educated in England. The initial assignment of the Virginia Regiment was to construct and maintain a fort at the Forks of the Ohio River.

With only 134 ill-trained, poorly equipped men under his command, Washington set out for the Ohio Country in the spring of 1754. He picked up additional men at Winchester, bringing his total to 159. He had not proceeded far before he received disturbing news. The French had at least four hundred men in western Pennsylvania; in addition, he discovered that the French had already constructed a fortress, Fort Duquesne, at the Forks of the Ohio. On the other hand, he understood that Colonel Fry was awaiting a rendezvous in Winchester with more than one hundred men. He also was told that he might be joined by as many as five hundred troops from North Carolina and Maryland. Weighing the evidence, Washington decided to push forward.

Advancing slowly through the hilly, dense wilderness and across rain-swollen streams, Washington's little army had moved to within twenty miles of the Ohio when word reached the commander that a detachment of perhaps fifty French troops were recruiting Indians along the Monongahela. When the party of Frenchmen was located, Washington elected to ambush them. It was a brazen decision. His act would invite a counterattack, one that might come before the arrival of reinforcements. Moreover, no civilian authority had yet declared war. Officially, Great Britain was still at peace with France.

Washington's surprise attack came early on the morning of May 28, 1754. Ten French soldiers were killed; twenty-two were taken prisoners. One of the dead was the sieur de Jumonville, the commander of this modest French force. His party had been on a diplomatic mission, much like Washington's embassy of the previous year. While Washington's brash move likely only hastened the inevitable, it was to have far-reaching consequences. The blow that he ordered against the French that cool spring morning resulted in the first bloodshed in what would come to be known as the French and Indian War, the fourth intercolonial war between France and Great Britain. This conflict would have global implications, for clashes would occur in Europe and Asia, on the high seas, and in the Caribbean. In North America hardly a person from Canada to the Carolinas would remain untouched by the conflagration, including those who inhabited the Virginia backcountry.[6]

In the weeks that followed his assault on Jumonville's party, Washington received few of the additional men that he had expected. In light of the overwhelming superiority of his adversary, a more experienced commander might have chosen to retreat. Young Washington, however, obstinately remained in Pennsylvania, waiting for reinforcements as well as the inevitable French counterattack. Indeed, as he waited he grew impertinent. Based upon what he had thus far seen of his adversary, he told the governor: "I flatter myself we shall have no g[rea]t trouble in driving them to Montreal." He was wrong. The blow from the French army came early in July 1754 at Great Meadows, where Washington had hastily constructed a circular stockade that he styled Fort Necessity. The showdown was a debacle for the young commander. He lost one-third of his men and surrendered the remainder, striking a bargain that enabled the vanquished to withdraw to Virginia.[7]

Although he remarked that his "inclinations are strongly bent to arms," Washington left Virginia's army soon after the Fort Necessity engagement. He returned to civilian life because Dinwiddie reorganized the Virginia Regiment, breaking it into companies; Washington would have been reduced in rank. He returned to Mount Vernon, an estate of approximately twenty-three hundred acres overlooking the Potomac River, which he had recently leased (together with eighteen slaves) from his former sister-in-law for an annual rental fee of fifteen thousand pounds of tobacco. He did not remain a civilian for very long, however. When Gen. Edward Braddock arrived in Virginia early in 1755 at the head of two British infantry regiments and a train of artillery, Washington agreed to join his "family" as a volunteer without pay. Washington found the sixty-year-old Braddock an imposing but friendly man, and if the young Virginian is to be believed, he spent considerable time in the company of this veteran officer, listening, watching, learning. His duties also brought him into contact with other British officers, men like Lt. Col. Thomas Gage, who were impressed by the sober young provincial with whom they obligingly shared their military manuals, the first such tracts that Washington had ever read. As the British army and a few hundred colonial auxiliaries pushed toward Fort Duquesne along the same wilderness road that the Virginia Regiment had cut the year before, Washington ran errands, kept the headquarters orderly book, and carefully observed life in a professional army.[8]

Accompanying Braddock was an experience that Washington was fortunate to survive. After only a few weeks, he fell prey to a camp disease, the sort of ailment that wiped out far more men in eighteenth-century armies than ever perished in combat. He was desperately ill for a time and not yet fully recovered when he rejoined Braddock on July 8. His timing could not have been worse. The next afternoon the advance units of Braddock's army stumbled into the forward elements of a large French and Indian force. Both were surprised, but the French and Indians recovered more quickly. Soon men "dropped like Leaves in Autumn," as one of the lucky British survivors later remarked. By the time the engagement ended, Braddock and more than five hundred redcoats were dead; another four hundred British and colonial soldiers had been wounded. Miraculously, Washington emerged unscathed. Two of his mounts went down with wounds and his coat was riddled with bullet holes, yet he was uninjured. Washington acted with great valor on that afternoon, impressing even hardened British veterans with his courage under fire. For instance, Braddock's aide, Robert Orme, publicly and privately lauded Washington's "Disposition Conduct and Gallantry." For the next few weeks, according to Washington's cousin, little else was discussed in Williamsburg, the capital of Virginia, save for the young colonel's heroic conduct next to Braddock.[9]

With his reputation enhanced and with Colonel Fry dead as the result of an accident, it was "unanimously agreed," according to his observant cousin in the capital, that Washington must again lead the Virginia Regiment. In 1755 he was indeed commissioned a colonel and given command of the provincial army. Washington was twenty-three years old, and he would spend slightly more than the next three years in this undertaking until December 1758, when an Anglo-American army of which he was a part at last took control of the Forks of the Ohio River.[10]

*W*HY HAD WASHINGTON REENTERED the military service? The only honorable course, he told his mother, was to answer his government's call. He was more candid with his brother. He sought command of the Virginia Regiment, he explained, in order to "gain by it." A career in the military was one means by which a young man of middling status in the eighteenth century might attain economic and social mobility. Horatio Gates, born to an English family of low rank, seized upon the British army as his vehicle to a better way of life and, like Washington, ultimately concluded his career in the high echelons of America's Continental army. In Massachusetts about the same time young John Adams, impatient for renown, confessed that he "longed more ardently to be a Soldier than a Lawyer," but he could never make himself enlist. A decade later, during the protracted period of peace between the French and Indian War and the American Revolutionary War, youthful Alexander Hamilton would have given anything for the opportunity that Adams had let slip through his fingers. "I contemn the grov'ling and condition of a Clerk or the like, to which my Fortune, &c., contemns me," he railed. "I wish there was a War."[11]

Washington was more fortunate. He had a war, and he seized his opportunity. When he had volunteered to carry Governor Dinwiddie's message to the French in 1753, Washington could, at best, anticipate a future as a modest and obscure Virginia planter, living comfortably but not majestically off the income he derived from his well-worn farm on the Rappahannock and his earnings as a surveyor. His prospects improved a year later when he gained Mount Vernon. With luck, in fifteen or twenty years he might live more prosperously; yet without a great fortune upon which to build, and denied a formal education, he was likely to be just another planter, powerful within his own little neighborhood, unknown outside that diminutive corner of Virginia. He wanted something else. He yearned for recognition. Military service could facilitate his dreams, and if he could secure a royal commission with at least the rank of major, he would outrank every other colonial soldier. When he spoke to his brother about gaining from his service, this is what he had in mind.

Colonel Washington faced a formidable challenge when he resumed command in 1755. Virginia's long frontier was ablaze, besieged by bands of Indians who pursued a strategy of guerrilla warfare. Pacification of the West would have been difficult under the best of circumstances, but Washington had to contend with an army that was perpetually understaffed, a force raised in a province without a long military tradition. A year after he took command, the military situation had actually deteriorated. The frontier had been pushed back. The Shenandoah Valley was lost, he had to report to Dinwiddie. Nor were matters any better by the end of 1756. In fact, by then Washington knew that one man in three who had served under him had perished in the course of his service.[12]

Stories about the army and its commander crept through Virginia that year. It was said that the soldiery lived in a bacchanalian atmosphere, its officers tolerating "the greatest Immoralities & Drunkenness." Despite repeated military catastrophes, it was suggested that Washington lived in a regal manner in a rented house in Winchester. The colonel was absent too much, others said. There were whispers that he neglected his duties, squandering his time on personal indulgences such as fencing lessons. His behavior, it was said, had destroyed morale within the army. One anonymous critic put his feelings in print. Writing as "The Virginia Centinel," this essayist blasted Washington as inexperienced and unsuited for command. The colonel and his officers, Centinel charged, were "rank novices, rakes, spendthrifts, and bankrupts" who abused their men and lived in "all manner of debauchery, vice, and idleness" while the Virginia countryside was being "ravaged in their very neighborhood."[13] To some, Colonel Washington appeared to be an immature, petulant, pompous martinet—and an unsuccessful one, at that.

Washington survived these allegations of malfeasance, although the military situation not only remained unimproved, but Governor Dinwiddie finally lost patience with his young commander. Washington retained his position because he was supported by well-placed, powerful proponents such as the influential Fairfax family and John Robinson, the Speaker of the House of Burgesses. His officers remained

Washington was forty-one years old when he posed for Charles Willson Peale (1772). He expected this to be his first and last portrait, and chose to be remembered as a soldier, not a planter. Courtesy of Washington and Lee University.

in his corner, too, menacingly holding out the prospect of a mass resignation should Washington be removed from command.[14]

How much longer Washington might have survived had the military situation not drastically improved can never be known. However, in 1758 a British army led by Gen. John Forbes arrived in America. When linked with provincial units, including the Virginia Regiment, it drove west across Pennsylvania to the Ohio. In late November the French scuttled Fort Duquesne. The land that Virginians had craved was at last in the possession of Englishmen. The frontier was not yet entirely quiet—the army of Virginia would continue to fight a series of Indian wars for three additional years under Washington's successor—but without the assistance of the French, the Indians were rendered a far less formidable foe.

Within thirty days of reaching the Ohio, Washington resigned his military post and returned to civilian life at Mount Vernon. Suddenly the carping about his performance ceased. Just as suddenly, Washington was looked upon as a successful military commander. Under his military leadership, Virginia had accomplished its primary objective. Moreover, upon his departure from the army each officer in the Virginia Regiment signed an address to Colonel Washington which lauded his achievements, in particular his "Patriotism, Courage and Conduct," including his "uncommon Perseverance." Washington, these officers wrote, had demonstrated a "Frankness, sincerity, and a certain Openness of Soul" that had rendered him an exemplary leader.[15] Their view reflected the prevailing judgment of Washington within the province. At the age of twenty-six, George Washington had become one of the most respected men in Virginia.

TWO DECADES LATER WHEN HE WAS selected by the Continental Congress to lead America's resistance to Great Britain, Washington continued to be seen as a proven leader. Congress found many reasons for appointing Washington. He was modest, discreet, polite, sober, patient, composed, and generous, it was said. John Hancock remarked simply that he was "a fine man." Eliphalet Dyer of Connecticut thought it important that he was not from New England, for the selection of a commander from another region could more "strongly Cement the Southern with the Northern Colonies." Many congressmen, however, were impressed with his martial background. Some had heard that he was courageous, others had been told of his reputation as an efficient and resolute administrator. But it was John Adams—the congressman who nominated Washington to command the Continental army—who best reflected the thinking of his colleagues. Colonel Washington, he said, had "great experience and abilities in military matters."[16]

In fact, Adams and his fellow congressmen knew next to nothing about Washington. They had little knowledge of any colonist who hailed from a section other than their own. Most had heard of Benjamin Franklin, famous for his scientific experiments. John Dickinson of Pennsylvania was known, too, mostly for his popular tract, *Letters from a Farmer in Pennsylvania.* Samuel Adams's name was familiar to activists everywhere. And most had heard of George Washington, although they knew little save that he had commanded the Virginia Regiment for several years during a war that had ended more than a decade and a half earlier. Congress believed that Washington could be trusted with the power he was being given. He had been observed closely by his colleagues during the three months that he had been with them in Congress. Otherwise, the congressmen who voted for Washington that warm June day in 1775 could only hope that the colonel's experience in the French and Indian War would be beneficial in the fiery trial that lay ahead.[17]

John Adams and his colleagues were fortunate. Washington's experience on the Virginia frontier twenty years earlier was crucial in his development as a leader. His conduct from 1775 onward suggests that he had learned much from his earlier mistakes, the blunders that had aroused the ire of "Centinel" and his governor.

Young Colonel Washington had committed three egregious errors while in command of the Virginia Regiment. His initial mistake was so calamitous that he almost did not survive to make the others. That, of course, was his decision to make his stand at Fort Necessity against a vastly superior adversary.

Washington never liked to be inactive. He feared losing the "esteem of mankind," as he put it, if he failed to fight and especially if he retreated. Always he longed to execute a brilliant stroke, always he thought in terms of the grand and audacious gesture. His folly at Great Meadows was a painful lesson, one that he did not learn immediately. During the first months of his Revolutionary War command, he wished to send his inexperienced army against the British regulars entrenched in Boston, but his general officers dissuaded him from such a course. Later, the French blocked his dream of assaulting the British in New York. Unfortunately, no one persuaded him of the folly of defending Fort Washington in the autumn of 1776, and when the British fell upon that installation, he suffered an even worse debacle than at Fort Necessity. Ultimately, Washington learned that what he termed a "war of posts" could serve his interests. Wisdom dictated, he finally acknowledged, that "we should on all occasions avoid a general action, or put anything to the risque, unless compelled by a necessity into which we ought never to be drawn." It was best to maneuver; at times, retreat was the wisest course. "Tis our business," Gen. Nathanael Greene told Washington, and Washington accepted the counsel, "to study to avoid any considerable misfortune, and to take post where the Enemy will be obliged to fight us and not we them." Washington continued to fear "reproach" when he pursued Fabian tactics, but he came to understand that it sometimes was prudent not to fight. It was a lesson that he fully grasped only with painful experience and only when, at last, he felt secure in his position. Even then, it was a course with which he was never entirely comfortable.[18]

Washington's second great mistake during the French and Indian War stemmed from his relations with the civil authorities. His actions and his captious manner eventually alienated Governor Dinwiddie, a powerful benefactor who had given the young man his opportunity to succeed as a soldier. Dinwiddie, who was more directly critical of Washington than any other man ever dared to be, ultimately charged his colonel not only with ingratitude, but with behaving in an "unmannerly" fashion. If anything, the governor appears to have been extraordinarily patient with Washington. Time after time the young commander accosted the chief executive: the pay was inadequate or late, the Indian scouts sent out from the capital were inferior sorts, there were not enough chaplains, there were too few troops, he had insufficient artillery, the militiamen were worthless, he should have been permitted to negotiate with the Indians, some of his subordinates—Dinwiddie's appointees—were useless, the governor was wrong to have cut the number of batmen allotted to each company, Williamsburg sent out confusing, inadequate instructions.[19]

But the crux of young Washington's complaints could be reduced to three charges. The war was being lost, he alleged, because he had an inadequate number of Indian allies, the Virginia Regiment was perpetually undermanned, and he was compelled to adhere to a misguided strategy. When Washington hammered away at these shortcomings, there could be no doubt that he was suggesting that unwise choices made in the governor's palace were to blame for his tribulations. The strategy imposed upon him by Governor Dinwiddie, the so-called string-of-forts strategy, particularly rankled young Washington. Restrained by the legislature from fielding a large force, Dinwiddie wished

John Hancock paid Charles Willson Peale's fee for rendering this portrait. It was painted while Washington consulted Congress in Philadelphia, just a few weeks after the liberation of Boston in March 1776. Courtesy of the Brooklyn Museum, Dick S. Ramsay Fund.

to erect small garrisons up and down the frontier. Operating from these installations, he reasoned, the Virginia army would at least be able to keep the frontier brushfire in check, though Washington might not be able to extinguish it altogether. Eventually, Dinwiddie hoped, the British army would destroy the opposition. Colonel Washington looked upon these tactics as madness. Impatient for action, he urged another expedition to the Ohio and the destruction of Fort Duquesne. Should Virginia continue "to pursue a defensive plan," he said repeatedly, "the country must be inevitably lost."[20]

When Washington did not have his way with the governor, he resorted to other tactics. He made it clear to the settlers on the frontier that the policy he was pursuing was not his own but Dinwiddie's. He also sought to undermine Dinwiddie by appealing to Speaker Robinson, a political foe of the chief executive. Dinwiddie's actions had placed him in an "unaccountable dilemma," Washington moaned. "I must beg your assistance," he beseeched. Once, he even hinted that if he did not receive greater assistance in securing new recruits, he would not lift a finger to help increase the army. "If I am to suffer, I can only say, that is but poor encouragement for the exertion of my zeal," he warned.[21]

Washington did not limit his carping to the policies of Dinwiddie. After the army of Virginia was brought under the command of the British general John Forbes in 1758, Washington's counsel was sought regarding the most advisable route for the force to take to the Ohio. When his advice was not followed, Washington cried piteously, repeatedly imploring his superiors to reconsider. Ultimately, General Forbes privately questioned Washington's suitability to lead an army, even remarking that his "Behaviour was no ways like a Soldier."[22]

Washington's relationship with the Continental Congress during the War of Independence was free of the acrimony that had characterized his dealings with Dinwiddie and Forbes. He was not reticent about approaching Congress, and, in fact, during the war hardly a month passed that he did not plead for something: additional supplies, a larger army, higher pay for his officers and soldiers, postwar pensions for those in the officer corps, a more draconian disciplinary code, or more aides to assist with his work. Washington, however, had learned from experience when to push the legislators and when it was expedient to let matters lie. He wisely refrained from siding with one faction in Congress, and he understood that it would be foolhardy to appeal over Congress to the general public. Above all, he knew better than to revert to the whining, plaintive manner that had so tarnished his relationship with Dinwiddie. Consequently, Washington generally refused to be drawn into the ubiquitous disputes that followed congressional decisions on the promotion of various officers, against his better judgment he bowed to political pressure to post his army in winter quarters at Valley Forge late in 1777, and he deferred—usually silently, if not serenely—to Congress's decisions concerning the size of the army.

The frequently whimsical nature of Washington's actions was his third great mistake during the French and Indian War. It was his lifestyle

Peale completed this portrait following the War of Independence. The artist rendered Washington as confident and triumphant, as he was both in 1784 and immediately after his earlier successes at Trenton and Princeton in the winter of 1776–77. Courtesy of The Art Museum, Princeton University, commissioned by the Trustees.

as much as anything that had provoked The Virginia Centinel in 1756, and, indeed, during the early period of his command his behavior often was irresponsible. The gravest charge levied by Centinel was that Washington seldom was with his army on Virginia's troubled frontier. It was not an ill-considered criticism. Washington was so busy pursuing rank in the British army that at times it did seem that he had little time for his command responsibilities. For instance, during the first six months after he resumed command in 1755, he was with his troops only about one-quarter of the time. Some of his time was consumed by a trip to Boston to beseech the assistance of Massachusetts governor William Shirley, the acting commander of all British forces in America, in securing a commission. When Colonel Washington returned to the Virginia frontier after an absence of several weeks, he discovered that the Indians had been quite active. Lt. Col. Adam Stephen, the commander of the Virginia Regiment during Washington's absence, reported to his commander that "we have been much harassed by the Indians" and employed in considerable "Bushfighting." During one of the months when Washington was away, one company of thirty-nine men suffered the loss of more than one-quarter of its personnel. Even Speaker Robinson, Washington's friend, was moved to advise that "things would be conducted much better if you was present" with the army.[23]

Robinson's judicious suggestion, however, did not prevent Washington from journeying to Philadelphia in 1757 to seek a commission from John Campbell, earl of Loudoun, the new British commander in chief. When Washington was not chasing after his own advancement, he often was on trips to look into his real estate investments or to visit with the Fairfaxes at Belvoir, their luxurious mansion near Mount Vernon. Eventually, his conduct was too much for both Dinwiddie and Loudoun. "Surely the Commanding officer should not be absent when daily Alarm'd with the Enemy's Intent's to invade our frontiers," the governor advised. Loudoun bluntly told his young supplicant that headquarters "with't doubt [is] the proper Place for the Com'd Officer" of an army.[24]

Washington learned from this criticism. During the War of Independence, he hardly lived in a grand or sumptuous manner. "General Washington setts a fine Example," John Adams reported to his wife during the anxious summer days in 1777 before the British campaign for Philadelphia. "He has banished Wine from his table. This is much to the Honour of his Wisdom," he added, for Adams was convinced that America could win its war with Britain only through a life of republican simplicity. Washington also usually selected a modest abode for his headquarters—a tavern at Morristown, a farmhouse at Valley Forge, for instance. He worked long hours, normally from about 5:00 a.m. until past 7:00 o'clock in the evening, interrupted only by a hurried breakfast, up to an hour's horseback ride for relaxation and exercise, and a midafternoon dinner. He also eschewed the pleasures that he had enjoyed in civilian life. He shunned billiards and cards, and he participated in a fox hunt, his favorite recreation at Mount Vernon, on only one occasion during this long war. Nor did Washington leave his men, save to appear before Congress, and that occurred only when the legislators requested that he come for consultation. Not until the fall of 1781, more than six years after he took command of the Continental army, did Washington return to Mount Vernon, and then only because it was near his route to Yorktown.[25]

INEXPERIENCED IN MILITARY MATTERS when the French and Indian War began, Colonel Washington not only learned from his mistakes, he gradually developed a feel for command through his day-to-day activities. Only twenty-two years old when he first assumed command, Washington had little time to secure the loyalty of his officers; some were tough, older men, and at least two had soldiered previously in Europe. His imposing size provided one asset. Not only was Washington considerably taller than most men in his day, but he was in excellent physical condition. As one observer noted, his "frame is padded with well developed muscles, indicating great strength." Washington's courage under fire at Fort Necessity and alongside Braddock, as well as on hundreds of lonely trails deep in hostile territory, also must have impressed the men who served under him. He had "a commanding countenance," in the words of one of his officers. What he undoubtedly meant was that Washington could be bold and tough with those beneath him. He did not shrink from criticizing inattention to detail among subordinate officers or their reluctance to take a hard, unbending line with the men. "You are afraid to do your duty," he abruptly accused one officer. Sometimes he was the educator, instructing his officers to read and improve themselves, especially to peruse military manuals. He told them that "unerring bravery" was certain

Washington was fifty-five years old and attending the Constitutional Convention when he sat for this portrait (1787). Both Washington's stepgrandson and the artist's son criticized some of Peale's paintings of Washington. In this instance, Peale likely failed to capture the steely toughness in Washington's eyes which many beheld. Courtesy of the Pennsylvania Academy of the Fine Arts, Philadelphia. Bequest of Mrs. Sarah Harrison (The Joseph Harrison Jr. Collection).

to win the respect of the men they commanded. And he charmed his subalterns, gaining their confidence through what one of his officers later remembered as his "easy, polite behavior." Another officer was struck that during "conversation he looks you full in the face, is deliberate, deferential, and engaging. His voice is agreeable rather than strong.

His demeanor at all times composed and dignified." Washington, in fact, often displayed the talents of a consummate performer, playing out one role when necessity dictated, shifting countenance when expediency suggested such a change. It was not without cause that John Adams, who perhaps understood Washington better than any other contemporary, called the Virginian "the best actor" he had ever known.[26]

In addition, Washington likely won over his seasoned officers with his unflinching attitude toward discipline within the regiment. Faced with the necessity of quickly making soldiers out of civilians, Washington imposed an iron regimen upon his men. He instituted brutal floggings—up to fifteen hundred lashes—for a variety of indiscretions. He frequently explained to Dinwiddie the necessity for making "several severe examples" of those who violated the army's code. Men were punished for embezzlement, running away, dereliction of duty, gambling, insolent behavior toward officers, cowardice, fighting with and even shooting at comrades, and for surrendering to the "all-aluring temptations of liquor," as Washington put it. He erected a gallows as a warning to the men, and ultimately executed two habitual deserters.[27]

As John Adams discovered many years later, Washington possessed a finely tuned ability to understand both himself and others. Early in life he learned how to play on his forceful traits, how to hide and overcome his weaknesses. In the course of the French and Indian War, he ascertained how best to relate to his officers. Washington was serious, resolute, cool, and aloof. He was one of them yet apart from them. He established few, if any, warm, companionable relationships within his circle of officers. He did not permit his officers to break through the barrier that he erected about himself; none were permitted to consider themselves his equal. He looked upon other men in terms of his superiors and his subordinates; the evidence suggests that his subordinates reciprocated in kind. The demeanor that he manifested proved successful. When he left the army at the end of 1758, his officers pledged their affection for him and their happiness at having the opportunity to serve under him. He taught them and the men they commanded to be "good Troops," they wrote.[28]

Later, during the War of Independence, Washington taught another generation of officers, most of them now younger than he was and with little command experience. He exhorted them to be diligent, to comport themselves in a dignified manner, and above all to "show an example of bravery and courage." At Harlem Heights and Princeton, where the general led the patriot advance to within only thirty yards of the British line, and at Trenton and Kip's Bay—where Washington, with enemy infantrymen nearby, galloped among his men desperately seeking to stay their pell-mell retreat—the American commander courageously put himself in harm's way. His actions often inspired his officers. After the engagement at Germantown, a young French volunteer declared that "Washington was intended for a great position—his appearance alone gave confidence to the timid and imposed respect on the bold." Partly because of Washington's conduct at Germantown, where he once again was in the midst of combat, another Continental officer concluded that "our men are now convinced they can drive the chosen troops of the enemy . . . whenever they attack them with ardor."[29]

Washington also believed that while it was wise to be pleasant toward one's subordinates, the circumspect officer would be somewhat aloof, keeping a barrier between himself and those beneath him. The military manuals that Washington had first begun to read in the 1750s almost uniformly cautioned officers of the imprudence of becoming overly familiar with their men. He never forgot that admonition. During the War of Independence, he observed that many qualities "independent of personal Courage, are requisite to form the good Officer," yet nothing was more important than the establishment of the proper relationship between a superior officer and his subordinate. Washington advised his senior officers to be "easy and condescending in your deportment to your officers, but not too familiar, lest you subject yourself to a want of that respect, which is necessary to support a proper command." Washington comported himself in that manner with his officers. While he often relaxed informally with members of his military "family," his young, loyal aides, he was reserved and virtually unapproachable toward higher ranking officers. He exhibited a "courteous demeanour," according to one observer, but what struck most who were in his presence was his august, distant manner.[30]

Washington derived other lessons from his days with the Virginia Regiment. When he had first taken command, he almost indiscriminately ordered the seizure of civilian property for the sustenance of his army. Purchase their wagons, horses, flour, and stocks of food, he directed, adding that these commodities simply were to be taken, if necessary. Later, he learned that such a course often was counterproductive;

confiscate enough possessions from the civilians, he discovered, and you would be seen as no less a plunderer than the Indian foe you were attempting to subdue.[31]

During the War of Independence there were times when Washington's unwillingness to seize civilian property caused problems. His lack of aggressiveness in this quarter likely contributed—though minimally—to the shortages in the army's pantry during the first days at Valley Forge late in 1777. For the most part, however, Washington's aversion to appropriating the property of civilians during the Revolutionary War was sagacious policy. "How disgraceful to the army is it," he asked his officers on more than one occasion, "that the peaceable inhabitants, our countrymen and fellow citizens, dread our halting among them, even for a night and are happy when they are rid of us?" Washington knew the answer to his query, and he sought endlessly to convince his officers of the need to prevent plunder and destruction.[32]

From his service with Braddock, as well as from military manuals, Washington learned how to organize an army. He rejected the advice of those who believed America's army should pursue guerrilla tactics. Instead, General Washington modeled the Continental army after a conventional eighteenth-century European army. He enforced a harsh disciplinary code, sought long-term enlistments, endeavored to foster an élan within the officer corps, and stationed his army in "advantageously situated" defensive posts so as to "effectually hinder the Enemy from extending themselves."[33]

But that was not all that Washington had learned from serving under Braddock. The catastrophe that befell Braddock taught him to be flexible; Braddock, he deduced, had sought to fight a European war in the American wilderness. A commander, Washington came to believe, had to adapt to circumstances, adjusting to adversity, to the environment, and to the foe. After suffering his own military disasters between August and November 1776, Washington demonstrated a refreshing—at times, even brilliant—versatility that frequently startled his enemies. He surprised his adversaries by his attacks at Trenton and Princeton and by striking at Germantown and Stony Point. First the British could not make Washington fight. "As we go forward into the country the rebels fly before us, and when we come back they always follow us," a thoroughly exasperated British officer noted. Yet when it suited his purposes, when Washington discovered that his foe had let

Clay bust of George Washington, by Jean Antoine Houdon (1785).
Courtesy of the Mount Vernon Ladies' Association.

down its guard, he might send his army into action. "We seem to be playing at bo peep," that same chagrined redcoat exclaimed.[34]

Finally, Washington learned how to respond to criticism. When he read the accusations of The Virginia Centinel, he instinctively composed a written response that included a threat to resign. Fortunately, he asked his brother, Austin, to edit his rejoiner. Austin destroyed the document, and soon enough the tempest died down.[35] Thereafter, Washington refused to allow himself to be drawn into such quarrels, whether in the Revolution or his presidency that followed. During the terrible winter at Valley Forge, for instance, Washington was aware that some officers, as well as some congressmen, had begun to question his abilities. He wisely refrained, however, from making a public issue of their criticisms. Much later, when he was president, Washington similarly understood that little gain could be had from responding openly to published attacks on his actions by two disgruntled Virginians, Edmund Randolph and James Monroe. In each instance, Washington permitted others to answer publicly for him. If and when Washington responded to his assailants, he did so covertly, leaving the public to conclude that base and contentious deportment was alien to his character.[36]

*T*HAT MORNING IN JUNE 1775 WHEN he proposed that Washington be selected to lead the Continental army, John Adams applauded the Virginian's bravery, praised him as a man committed to republicanism and liberty, and paid tribute to his "excellent universal character." Principally, however, Adams urged that Washington's "skill and experience as an Officer" would "command the Approbation of all America."[37] Around this veteran soldier, Adams said, the disunited colonies might unite, and united the colonies could win their war against Great Britain. Adams never had reason to regret his remarks, in part, at least, because of the lessons that Washington had learned many years earlier on a remote Virginia frontier.

NOTES

1. John Adams to Abigail Adams, December 27, 1796, Adams Family Papers, Microfilm Reel 382, Massachusetts Historical Society, Boston, Mass.; Adams to Abigail Adams, October 26, 1777, *Adams Family Correspondence*, ed. L. H. Butterfield et al., 8 vols. to date (Cambridge, Mass.: Harvard University Press, 1963–), 2:361; Adams to Robert Livingston, June 16, 1783, *The Works of John Adams, Second President of the United States: With a Life of the Author*, ed. Charles Francis Adams, 10 vols. (Boston: Little, Brown, 1850–1856), 8:73; Page Smith, *John Adams*, 2 vols. (New York: Doubleday, 1962), 2:1021.

2. Jefferson to William Jones, January 2, 1814, *The Writings of Thomas Jefferson*, ed. Andrew Lipscomb and Albert E. Bergh, 20 vols. (Washington, D.C.: Thomas Jefferson Memorial Association, 1903), 14:48; Adams to Abigail Adams, June 18, 1777, *Adams Family Correspondence*, 2:268.

3. Douglas Southall Freeman, *George Washington: A Biography*, 7 vols. (New York: Charles Scribner's Sons, 1948–1957), 5:436. On the character of Washington, see John E. Ferling, *The First of Men: A Life of George Washington* (Knoxville: University of Tennessee Press, 1988), 249–60.

4. Charles Ambler, *George Washington and the West* (Chapel Hill: University of North Carolina Press, 1936), 32–36; John Alden, *Robert Dinwiddie: Servant of the Crown* (Charlottesville: University Press of Virginia, 1973), 43–44.

5. John C. Fitzpatrick, *George Washington Himself: A Common Sense Biography Written from his Manuscript* (Indianapolis: Bobbs-Merrill, 1933), 147; Bernhard Knollenberg, *George Washington: The Virginia Period, 1732–1775* (Durham, N. C.: Duke University Press, 1964), 87; Rupert Hughes, *George Washington*, 3 vols. (New York: William Morrow, 1926–1930), 1:37–38; William S. Baker, *Early Sketches of George Washington* (Philadelphia: J. B. Lippincott, 1893), 13–14; Tobias Lear, *Letters and Recollections of Washington: With a Diary of Washington's Last Days, Kept by Mr. Lear* (New York: Charles Scribner, 1906), 137.

6. For extensive treatments of Virginia's war preparations and of Washington's first weeks in command of the Virginia Regiment, see Freeman, *Washington*, 1:272–376; James T. Flexner, *George Washington: The Forge of Experience* (Boston: Little, Brown, 1965), 53–92. See also George Washington to Dinwiddie, April 25, May 9, 18, 27 and 29, 1754, *The Papers of George Washington*, Colonial Series, ed. W. W. Abbot et al., 10 vols. (Charlottesville: University Press of Virginia, 1983–1995), 1:117–18; Washington to John Augustine Washington, May 31, 1754, *Washington Papers*, Col. Ser., 1:118; Robert Dinwiddie to Washington, March 15 and May 4, 1754, *Washington Papers*, Col. Ser., 1:75–76, 91–92. Dinwiddie had been instructed by London to avoid an attack upon French

personnel, if possible, but to force the removal of the French from the Ohio Country should they attempt to construct a fort on the Ohio River. See Alden, *Dinwiddie*, 44.

7. Washington to Dinwiddie, June 3, 1754, *Washington Papers*, Col. Ser., 1:124. For Washington's various accounts of his capitulation, see *Washington Papers*, Col. Ser., 1:157–73.

8. Washington to William Fitzhugh, November 14, 1754, *Washington Papers*, Col. Ser., 1:226; Robert Orme to Washington, March 2, 1755, *Washington Papers*, Col. Ser., 1:241; Washington to John A. Washington, May 6, 1755, *Washington Papers*, Col. Ser., 1:266–67; Washington to William Fairfax, June 7, 1755, *Washington Papers*, Col. Ser., 1:298–300; Washington, "Biographical Memorandum," *The Writings of George Washington from the Original Manuscript Sources, 1745-1799*, ed. John C. Fitzpatrick, 39 vols. (Washington, D.C.: Government Printing Office, 1931–1944), 29:41–42; Oliver L. Spaulding, "The Military Studies of George Washington," *American Historical Review* 29 (July 1924): 675–80.

9. Stanley Pargellis, "Braddock's Defeat," *American Historical Review* 41 (January 1936): 253–69; Paul E. Kopperman, *Braddock at the Monongahela* (Pittsburgh: University of Pittsburgh Press, 1977), 50–76, 164, 176; Douglas Edward Leach, *Arms for Empire: A Military History of the British Colonies in North America, 1607-1763* (New York: Macmillan, 1973), 365–66; Orme to Washington, November 10, 1755, *Washington Papers*, Col. Ser., 2:165.

10. Charles Lewis to Washington, August 9, 1755, *Washington Papers*, Col. Ser., 1:357–58.

11. Paul David Nelson, *General Horatio Gates: A Biography* (Baton Rouge: Louisiana State University Press, 1976), 6–9; John E. Ferling, "'Oh That I was a Soldier': John Adams and the Anguish of War," *American Quarterly* 36 (Summer 1984): 258–75; Alexander Hamilton to Edward Stevens, November 11, 1769, *The Papers of Alexander Hamilton*, ed. Harold C. Syrett and Jacob E. Cooke, 27 vols. (New York: Columbia University Press, 1961–1979), 1:4.

12. Washington to Dinwiddie, February 2, April 2, May 3, August 4, 1756, *Washington Papers*, Col. Ser., 2:314–15, 332–35, 3:85–86, 312–18; Washington to Robinson, April 16, November 9, 1756, *Washington Papers*, Col. Ser., 3–6, 8, 4:14, 16.

13. Dinwiddie to Washington, April 8, 1756, *Washington Papers*, Col. Ser., 2:343; "The Centinel No. X," *Virginia Gazette* (Williamsburg), September 3, 1756.

14. William Fairfax to Washington, April 26–27, May 20, 1756, *Washington Papers*, Col. Ser., 3:56–57, 167–68; Augustine Washington to Washington, October 16, 1756, *Washington Papers*, Col. Ser., 3:435–37.

15. "Address from the Officers of the Virginia Regiment," December 31, 1758, *Washington Papers*, Col. Ser., 6:178–80.

16. Eliphalet Dyer to Joseph Trumbull, June 16, 17, 1775, *Letters of Delegates to Congress, 1774–1789*, ed. Paul H. Smith et al., 24 vols. to date (Washington, D.C.: Library of Congress, 1976–), 1:495–96, 499; Silas Deane to Elizabeth Deane, June 16, 1775, *Letters to Delegates*, 1:494; Deane to John Trumbull, June 18, 1775, *Letters to Delegates*, 1:506; John Hancock to Elbridge Gerry, June 18, 1775, *Letters to Delegates*, 1:507; Robert Treat Paine to Artemas Ward, June 18, 1775, *Letters to Delegates*, 1:509; Adams to Abigail Adams, May 29, 1775, *Adams Family Correspondence*, 1:347.

17. Freeman, *Washington*, 3:444–47.

18. Washington to Reed, February 10, 26, 1776, *The Papers of George Washington*, Revolutionary War Series, ed. W. W. Abbot et al., 7 vols. to date (Charlottesville: University Press of Virginia, 1985–), 3:287–88, 370–73; Washington to President of Congress, September 8, 1776, *Writings of Washington*, 6:28–29, 32; Washington to Lund Washington, September 30, 1776, *Writings of Washington*, 6:138; Washington to John A. Washington, March 31, 1776, *Washington Papers*, Rev. Ser., 3:566–69; Washington to John A. Washington, November 19, 1776, *Writings of Washington*, 6:246; Nathanael Greene to Washington, September 5, 1776, *The Papers of Nathanael Greene*, ed. Richard K. Showman et al., 9 vols. to date (Chapel Hill: University of North Carolina Press, 1976–), 1:294–95. For succinct assessments of Washington's performance as commander of the Continental army during the American Revolution, see Freeman, *Washington*, 5:469–501; James T. Flexner, *George Washington in the American Revolution* (Boston: Little, Brown, 1968), 531–52; Ferling, *First of Men*, 249–66, 317–20; John Shy, "George Washington Reconsidered," in *The John Briggs Cincinnati Lectures in Military Leadership and Command, 1986*, ed. Henry S. Bausum (Lexington, Va.: Virginia Military Institute Foundation, 1986), 39–52; Marcus Cunliffe, "George Washington's Generalship," in *George Washington's Generals*, ed. George A. Billias (New York: William Morrow, 1964), 3–21; and Don Higginbotham, *George Washington and the American Military Tradition* (Athens: University of Georgia Press, 1985), 39–105.

19. Dinwiddie to Washington, November 16, 1756, September 24, 1757, *Washington Papers*, Col. Ser., 4:25, 422; Washington to Dinwiddie, March 9, May 18, 29, 1754, *Washington Papers*, Col. Ser., 1:73–74, 99–100, 116–17; Washington to Francis Halkett, May 11, 1758, *Washington Papers*, Col. Ser., 5:175; Washington to John Blair, May 28, 1758, *Washington Papers*, Col. Ser., 5:200.

20. Washington to Dinwiddie, November 9, 1756, October 9, 1757, *Washington Papers*, Col. Ser., 4:1–6; 5:10; Washington to Robinson, October 25, 1757, *Washington Papers*, Col. Ser., 5:34; Robinson to Washington, November 3, 1757, *Washington Papers*, Col. Ser., 5:43.

21. Paul K. Longmore, *The Invention of George Washington* (Berkeley: University of California Press, 1988), 42; Washington to Robinson, December 19, 1756, October 25, 1757, May 10, 1758, *Washington Papers*, Col. Ser., 4:67–68; 5:33, 172.

22. Washington to Col. Henry Bouquet, July 25, August 2, 1758, *Washington Papers*, Col. Ser., 5:324–25, 353–60; Washington to Gov. Francis Fauquier, August 5, 1758, *Washington Papers*, Col. Ser., 5:369–70; Washington to Robinson, September 1, 1758, *Washington Papers*, Col. Ser., 5:432–33; Gen. John Forbes to Bouquet, September 2, 1758, *Washington Papers*, Col. Ser., 6:3n.

23. "The Centinel No. X," *Virginia Gazette*, September 3, 1756; Stephen to Washington, March 29, 1756, *Washington Papers*, Col. Ser., 2:325; Peter Hog to Washington, April 3, 1756, *Washington Papers*, Col. Ser., 2:330n; Robinson to Washington, March 31–April 2, 1756, *Washington Papers*, Col. Ser., 2:329.

24. Dinwiddie to Washington, November 16, 1756, October 19, 1757, *Washington Papers*, Col. Ser., 4:25; 5:21. Washington alluded to Loudoun's criticism of his conduct in letters to Dinwiddie and Speaker Robinson written on December 19, 1756, see *Washington Papers*, Col. Ser., 4:64–68. The Loudoun quotation appears in Flexner, *Washington: The Forge of Experience*, 167.

25. Adams to Abigail Adams, September 1, 1777, *Adams Family Correspondence*, 2:335–36. For a profile of Washington's lifestyle during the war, see Ferling, *First of Men*, 257–60.

26. Flexner, *Washington in the American Revolution*, 138, 158–59; Freeman, *Washington*, 3:6; Adams to Benjamin Rush, June 21, 1811, *The Spur of Fame: Dialogues of John Adams and Benjamin Rush, 1805–1813*, ed. John A. Schutz and Douglass Adair (San Marino, Calif.: Huntington Library, 1966), 181. On the height of men at that time, see: Kenneth L. Sokoloff and George C. Villaflor, "The Early Achievement of Modern Stature in America," *Social Science History* 6 (September 1982): 435–81. On the size of men in the Virginia Regiment, see John Ferling, "Soldiers for Virginia: Who Served in the French and Indian War?" *Virginia Magazine of History and Biography* 94 (July 1986): 312.

27. Washington to Dinwiddie, October 11, 1755, April 16, 18, 19, 24, May 3, 23, June 25, August 4, September 8, October 10, November 9, 1756, October 9, 1757, *Washington Papers*, Col. Ser., 2:102, 3:1–3, 13–15, 20, 44–46, 81–84, 171–73, 222–25, 312–18, 396–400, 430–34, 4:1–6; 5:11; Washington to Robinson, April 24, August 5, November 9, 1756, *Washington Papers*, Col. Ser., 3:48–51, 323–31, 4:11–18; Washington to Loudoun, January 10, 1757, *Washington Papers*, Col. Ser., 4:81–84, 86–87; Washington, General Orders, October 18, 1755, May 1, July 6–8, August 30–31, September 1, 1756, *Washington Papers*, Col. Ser., 2:124, 3:70, 238–39, 382–83; Washington to Peter Hog, September 24, 1755, *Washington Papers*, Col. Ser., 2:60; Washington to Adam Stephen, November 18, 1755, *Washington Papers*, Col. Ser., 2:172; Washington to John David Wilper, June 30, 1758, *Washington Papers*, Col. Ser., 5:251; Washington, "Address to his Command," August 1756, *Writings of Washington*, 1:447.

28. "Address from the Officers of the Virginia Regiment," December 1758, *Washington Papers*, Col. Ser., 6:178–80.

29. Freeman, *Washington*, 4:518–19.

30. Washington, General Orders, July 7, 14, 15, 24, September 6, 1775, *Washington Papers*, Rev. Ser., 1:71–74, 114–15, 118–19, 163–64, 418–19; Washington to Col. William Woodford, November 10, 1775, *Washington Papers*, Rev. Ser., 2:347; Washington to Gov. William Livingston, February 11, 1777, *Writings of Washington*, 7:134. On the contents of the military manuals of the age, see Leach, *Arms for Empire*, 25–27.

31. Washington, General Orders, September 5, 10, 19, October 23, 1755, *Washington Papers*, Col. Ser., 2:51–52, 75, 94, 135; Washington to Robinson, October 25, 1757, *Washington Papers*, Col. Ser., 5:33–34.

32. Washington, General Orders, July 25, 1777, *Writings of Washington*, 8:465–66.

33. Washington to Robert Morris, George Clymer, and George Walton, April 12, 1777, *Writings of Washington*, 7:401. On the notion of fighting a guerrilla war, see John Shy, "Charles Lee: The Soldier as Radical," in *George Washington's Generals*, 22–53.

34. Dave Richard Palmer, *The Way of the Fox: American Strategy in the War for America, 1775–1783* (Westport, Conn.: Greenwood Press, 1975), 126.

35. Augustine Washington to Washington, October 16, 1756, *Washington Papers*, Col. Ser., 3:435–37.

36. On President Washington's handling of Randolph and Monroe, see Ferling, *The First of Men*, 458–65, 495.

37. *The Diary and Autobiography of John Adams*, ed. L. H. Butterfield et al., 4 vols. (Cambridge: Harvard University Press, 1961), 3:322–23; Adams to Abigail Adams, June 17, 1775, *Adams Family Correspondence*, 1:215; Adams to James Warren, June 20, 1775, *Papers of John Adams*, ed. Robert J. Taylor et al., 8 vols. to date (Cambridge: Harvard University Press, 1977–), 3:34.

George Washington and Revolutionary Asceticism: The Localist as Nationalist

DON HIGGINBOTHAM

*T*O SAY THAT GEORGE WASHINGTON'S pre-Revolutionary life in Virginia explains much about his character as a revolutionary figure is perhaps only to state the obvious. Even so, it seems that the subject is worth further exploration from the perspective of the study of comparative revolution. The Virginian was not an exile prior to the armed rebellion of 1775, as were the Kossuths, Lenins, Ho Chi Minhs, and Khoumanis of later revolutionary movements. Nor was his revolutionary persona in any way shaped by events in distant lands or by the reading of some seminal book or essay. He hardly planned or initiated a revolution against British rule. He was never a professional revolutionary, the kind one encounters in the nineteenth century, beginning with Blanqui, Buonarroti, Bakunin, Marx, and others. It is highly debatable whether Washington fits any of the definitions of a charismatic leader, a term loosely employed but usually emphasizing the revolutionary's dominating personality and ability to create political legitimacy in the absence of established governing institutions by his popularity and behavior.

Washington was, however, a hero of sorts long before the American Revolution. He had gained intercolonial recognition as Gov. Robert Dinwiddie's emissary to the French "intruders" in the Ohio Valley, as a military volunteer in the Braddock campaign, and afterward as commanding officer on the Virginia frontier during the Seven Years' War, fighting for his colony and for the British empire. But it was there, beyond the Blue Ridge, that his military accomplishments brought him his first tangible dividends. In 1758 the freeholders of Frederick County, that portion of the Northern Neck which extended into the Valley of

Virginia, had assembled at the courthouse in Winchester and elected him to the House of Burgesses. That same year Winchester's town fathers named a street after him. It was the first of such myriad honors and evidently the only one prior to the Revolution.[1]

These observations alone are enough to demonstrate that every revolution is unique, and therefore comparisons can be exaggerated or distorted, as the critics of such comparative historians as Crane Brinton and Robert R. Palmer have pointed out.[2] Even when these excursions result in discovering more contrasts than similarities, the undertakings can be beneficial for developing a broad interpretive framework in which to place Washington and the American Revolution. To Jefferson, writing soon after the treaty of peace that recognized American independence, the ultimate comparative question was what "prevented this revolution from being closed as most others have been by a subversion of that liberty it was intended to establish." His own answer was found in considerable part in "the moderation and virtue of a single character": Washington.[3]

Which of at least several different comparative approaches is most valid? Jefferson, with his rich classical knowledge, might well have been thinking of upheavals in the ancient world. Possibly he also had in mind Oliver Cromwell and the Puritan Revolution. For all their differences, Washington and Cromwell were both forty-three-year-old country squires when they turned to the most serious kind of soldiering. Still another leader from the early modern era could legitimately invite comparison with Washington, William the Silent. If the young Washington of Virginia adored Britain, the young William of Nassau-Dillenburg became a confidant of Charles V at Europe's foremost court. Both Washington and William went into opposition, renounced their royal ties, and became nation-makers; they were men of action rather than theory, talented at handling people.[4]

In any case, an examination of Washington's Virginia years within the context of themes developed by Bruce Mazlish in *The Revolutionary Ascetic* seems especially worth pursuing in a volume of essays that focuses on the Old Dominion.[5] According to Mazlish, a substantial number of revolutionaries in modern history have been ascetics. Drawing upon the studies of Max Weber and Sigmund Freud and their followers, Mazlish portrays many, but by no means all, revolutionaries as characterized by feelings of alienation from the dominant culture and by traits of self-denial, people principally unmindful of worldly, material pleasures associated with the comforts of home, family, and friends. Not only is this kind of revolutionary capable of cutting loose from past moorings—from kin, class, and province or region—but eschewing them enables the revolutionary more readily to oust from command and eliminate altogether old comrades in the cause and to risk the possibility of imprisonment or death.

Skeptics may assuredly argue that Mazlish casts his net too widely when he pulls in Robespierre, Lenin, Castro, and Mao together with Gandhi, and Arafat, even if they all share at least some forms of asceticism. Yet there have been revolutionaries who forsook the good life, and Mazlish demonstrates that total obsession with the revolution, sometimes including libidinal sublimation, has shown particular revolutionary leaders to be narcissists. They take themselves too seriously and, ultimately, see themselves as the revolution, without whom its values will erode and its cause will fail.

Does Washington fit the broad contours of Mazlish's revolutionary ascetics? Though the answer is clearly no, be it cultural alienation, or self-denial of familial and material wants, or narcissism, he certainly possessed the iron will and personal bravery that Mazlish discerns in his own revolutionary characters, to say nothing of his resolve to see his Potomac mansion go up in flames rather than have his plantation manager bargain with the British to save it.[6] In any event, a closer examination of Washington in relation to Mazlish's three categories may be helpful in understanding both his incorruptibility and the nature of his loyalties during the American Revolution. Though Washington has properly been hailed as the foremost nationalist of his age, both symbolically and as a relentless advocate of a strong American union, in critical respects he also remained throughout his life a committed localist, devoted to his roots—to people and place, which meant Virginia. For Washington, unlike some localists and nationalists—localists such as Patrick Henry of Virginia and Samuel Adams of Massachusetts, and nationalists such as Alexander Hamilton of New York—it was possible to be both.

*R*ATHER THAN EXPRESSING ALIENation from British culture, Washington, like other Tidewater planters, admired English ways. There were, of course, some differences between the country elites of England and Virginia—the English generally had greater wealth, which was not based on slavery or tobacco—but the similarities were more important to the Virginians, who felt they conformed closely to the Old World mold.[7] According to Edmund Randolph, whose own family was split by the Revolution, "almost every political sentiment, every fashion in Virginia, appeared to be imperfect unless it have a resemblance to some precedent in England." This "almost idolatrous deference" to things English, explained Randolph, was why Virginians before the Revolution had been more tolerant than other colonials when the mother country made mistakes.[8] Randolph might have added that cultural replication owed something to trans-Atlantic trade. Virginia, of all the mainland colonies, was "by far the most valuable to British interests. . . . The combined volume of colonial exports to, and imports from, Britain had grown to something more than a third of all British trade."[9]

That commerce had soared in volume and attendant riches for Virginians between Washington's youth and his manhood was abundantly evident to the planter John Wayles, Thomas Jefferson's father-in-law. He wrote in 1766 that "Luxury & expensive living have gone hand in hand with the increase of Wealth. In 1740 I don't remember to have seen such a thing as a turkey Carpet in the Country except a small thing in a bed chamber. Now nothing are so common as Turkey or Wilton Carpetts, the whole Furniture of the Roomes Elegant & every Appearance of Opulence."[10] William Eddis, in his *Letters from America,* also noted the change in colonial consumer patterns (even if he exaggerated somewhat) in claiming "that a new fashion is adopted earlier by the polished and affluent" Chesapeake planters "than by many opulent persons in the great metropolis."[11]

If Washington himself sought to become as English as his station and circumstances permitted, he sometimes encountered frustrations in his quest. First, there was the matter of his inadequate formal education. Over the generations his male clansmen had returned to England for schooling, and so had many other Virginians, such as the Blairs, Carters, Randolphs, Lees, George Wythe, and Thomas Nelson, their names on the rolls of a score or more institutions for the eighteenth century alone.[12] To do so was exceedingly expensive, and particularly for the first three generations of Washingtons, none of whom ever amassed the financial means to enter the upper ranks of the provincial notables. But their successful determination to send their sons abroad provides evidence for Louis B. Wright's contention that the rising gentry in Virginia was almost as concerned with passing on to its progeny the English cultural legacy as it was with the accumulation of wealth.[13]

Here, of course, Washington was an exception, explained by a shortage of family resources after the death of his father, when the boy was only eleven. Even out of the question for him was that more accessible institution, the College of William and Mary in Williamsburg, the colony's capital, where Robert Carter Nicholas, Thomas Jefferson, and the Harrisons broadened their horizons. But Washington particularly lamented his lost educational opportunity in the mother country and in his twenties spoke of "the longing desire, which for many years I have had of visiting . . . that Kingdom."[14]

Washington did, however, learn much about the glittering Georgian age from other family members. His Uncle Joseph Ball, son of a Lancaster County planter, had gone to England and eventually made it his home, having studied at Gray's Inn and been called to the bar; but he was back in Virginia for some years during Washington's childhood. Later, from Stratford by Bow, near London, Ball advised George's mother, Mary Ball Washington, against permitting her son to take to the sea for a career. Free with instructions and eager to know of doings in the Old Dominion, Ball also entertained family and friends with stories about his life across the ocean. Other, more immediate sources of information for Washington were his British-educated older half-brothers, Lawrence and Augustine Jr. (Austin), especially the former, who was clearly his idol and in every way a polished Englishman.[15]

When Washington spoke of that "longing desire" of "many years" duration, he told us a good deal. Imagine, then, what a heady feeling it must have been for the young man to be in the company of English gentlemen in Virginia. His educational deficiencies in general and his inability to immerse himself personally in metropolitan life were partly overcome by those opportunities, which came as a result of spending much of his teenage life in the home of Lawrence Washington. Lawrence, in addition to his British schooling, had held a commission in the king's army and had afterward named his estate Mount Vernon, after his commander in the Cartagena campaign of 1740–1741. It is reasonable to assume that Washington absorbed much from his cultivated brother, who supervised his entry into provincial high society. As a thirteen-year-old, the fatherless George was diligently copying maxims of manners and deportment from a popular English courtesy book. Lawrence had married into the powerful Fairfax family, which had come over to the colony as major players in the land game. It is common knowledge that George visited frequently at nearby Belvoir, where Col. William Fairfax lived with his son George William and the latter's wife, the former Sally Cary.

Just as those years helped Washington wear off his rough edges and attain a measure of sophistication through mixing and mingling with his Belvoir neighbors and their influential friends and visitors—in their two elegant sitting rooms—so he also expanded his intellectual world by dipping into the books in their library. Washington would eventually have his own library with well over nine hundred volumes on a broad variety of subjects. While there has been disagreement about the extent of his reading and the range of his intellectual interests, Paul Longmore has recently argued convincingly that Washington's self-education was more extensive than has been acknowledged.[16] Assuredly Washington believed that any man possessed of a sizable estate needed to read works on mathematics and agricultural practices. He likewise considered "Philosophy, Moral, Natural, &ca . . . very desirable knowledge for a Gentleman," as was "Classical knowledge."[17] If, as a new survey of the Old Dominion's preindependence years avers, "the British Enlightenment reached its height in the eighteenth century," surely "Virginia shared tangentially in its triumphs."[18]

It is small wonder, then, that Washington's years on the frontier gave him a degree of cultural shock, eliciting from him unflattering comments about the lack of table manners, cleanliness, and creature comforts of the settlers beyond the Blue Ridge. Not infrequently disdainful of frontiersmen at various stages of his life, he talked of extending the values of his own Tidewater region to the West. The uncivilized life, with its crudities and dearth of amenities, was not for him. His Britishness made it difficult if not impossible for him to comprehend the values of the squatters on his transmontane lands or the backcountry militiamen who rejected his calls to arms because of their concerns about leaving their own families exposed. It is unlikely that he ever possessed the gift of understanding fully those who were very different from himself and his Tidewater circle. Actually, Washington's ambitious activities in the West as a surveyor, land speculator, soldier, and legislator were all designed to enhance his standing in the East, not in any sense to make him a westerner. Unlike Lord Fairfax, he never moved to the Shenandoah Valley or gave serious thought to doing so.

In sum, his desire to enhance his Britishness drew him to the West, and his experiences there made him more of an Anglo-Virginian than ever.

Another dimension to Washington's Britishness, and a source of some further frustration as well, concerns his relationship with the British army. Both Lawrence Washington and Col. William Fairfax were British veterans with battlefield experience, and it takes little imagination to see Washington at Belvoir listening intently to their talk of campaigning in an age that still viewed war glamorously. He, too, wanted a British commission, and to that end between 1755 and 1757 he appealed to Generals Braddock, Shirley, and Loudoun, all to no avail, even though he was definitely worthy, given his combat record with Braddock and his impressive performance as colonel of the Virginia Regiment and commander of Virginia's frontier defenses during the most arduous period of the Seven Years' War.

It was European-style warfare that fascinated Washington, not backcountry tactics, which were already known as *guerrilla,* or *partisan,* methods and which were described in fascinating detail by contemporary chroniclers, especially Joseph Doddridge in his *Notes on the Settlement and Indian Wars of the Western Parts of Virginia and Pennsylvania* and Samuel Kercheval in his *History of the Valley of Virginia.* Those frontier techniques were used effectively in the War of Independence by Gen. Daniel Morgan, from Frederick County in the Shenandoah Valley. If Morgan's experience as a teamster with Braddock and later as a Virginia ranger led him to dress in Indian garb, to employ the thin skirmish line, and to favor the backwoodsman's long rifle, Washington's service beyond the Blue Ridge only reinforced his learning at the feet of Lawrence Washington and Colonel Fairfax.[19] As a young Virginia officer, Washington read British army manuals, observed the practices of his crimson-clad superiors, and trained and disciplined his own provincial troops in such a manner that he could find some professional officers agreeing with his claim that his regiment was the equal of any British unit in America. His ideas remained fundamentally the same in 1775 when, as commander in chief of the Continental army, he drew upon British precedents to organize and train his own troops. Unlike many later revolutionaries, he was militarily conservative.

Washington was, in the decade and a half between his military commands, much like an English country gentleman, possessed as he was of the manners and deportment of his British counterparts, with their customary military title to boot; he was henceforth known to one and all as Colonel Washington. He ransacked the *Country Magazine* and other metropolitan periodicals and gazettes to determine the latest styles and fashions before ordering clothing, furniture, silver plate, and other interior adornments from London, not to mention his 1758 acquisition of "A Neat Landscape after Claude Lorrain," quite likely the first of a number of paintings of rural scenes he would eventually own.[20] He also wrote for seeds, cuttings, and bulbs to grow gardens and hedge rows in conformity with those of the English squirearchy. A year or so after placing such orders, Washington would watch eagerly at his plantation wharf as crates containing his shopping-list items were removed from a British vessel and unpacked.

If he had no ancient plantation house that served as a wellspring of family lineage, few Virginians did before the 1720s, from which time forward, with the tobacco wealth now available to them, they brought over skilled artisans from Britain to build such stately Georgian brick edifices as Stratford Hall, Westover, and Berkeley. Although Mount Vernon, which Washington acquired in the 1750s, was a modest frame structure, he added to it several times over the years, and he rusticated its siding so as to give the appearance of being constructed of stone.

In establishing his country seat, Washington accepted the responsibilities that Virginia planters, imitative of the English gentry, had long assumed. He and other landed magnates of the Old Dominion were familiar with the themes, if not always the specific passages, found in Richard Brathwait's *English Gentlemen,* which proclaimed that the greater one's station in life the greater one's obligation to society.[21] He became a justice of the peace, vestryman, and member of the House of Burgesses, the equivalent—in Virginians' eyes—of the British House of Commons.

Local elites in the rural realms of England and Virginia also had a responsibility to be patrons to lesser neighbors and to help the needy. In Washington's case, were these sincere concerns, or were they more a matter of acting a part required of his social station? Initially, it may well have been more the latter reason. His occasional high-flown expressions about the sufferings of frontier folk from Indian wartime depredations in the 1750s—"I could offer myself a willing Sacrifice ... provided that would contribute to the peoples ease"—were inconsistent with his general attitude toward civilians incapable of making great sacrifices in areas where Washington's Virginia Regiment could hardly afford them protection.[22]

Quite likely Washington grew in his sense of real feeling and obligation for others. As a planter he came to realize that at times the patron's role could be a difficult one. His own father, Augustine, a justice of the peace, had discovered as much when farmer Job Shadrick sought his aid in obtaining redress after suffering abuse from Capt. John Bayes of the militia. When Augustine Washington demanded in writing an explanation from Bayes, the latter "flung the Letter in the fire and said that Col. Washington might kiss his backside."[23] As for Washington himself, in a quiet, unassuming way, he lent sizable sums to those in financial distress, even at the risk of his own solvency, as he explained to Capt. Thomas Posey, a small planter and old military companion, who repeatedly prevailed on Washington's liberality, notwithstanding his notoriously poor management of his own affairs.[24] And Washington accepted the burden of serving as executor or advisor for so many friends that he pictured himself in January 1775 as having had in the last year or two "scarce a Moment that I can properly call my own."[25] Whatever the demands on his physical and material resources, he reserved something for philanthropy. "Let the Hospitality of the House, with respect to the Poor, be kept up," Washington instructed Lund Washington. "Let no one go hungry away," and let some "money in Charity to the Amount of Forty or Fifty Pounds a Year" also be given to assist the indigent and afflicted.[26] It was easier to meet those public obligations because he had in 1764 employed Lund, his third cousin, as his business manager, a position similar to that of a steward on a spacious British estate.[27]

Washington nevertheless shared with his British gentry counterparts a desire to be a hands-on planter. Serious-minded agrarians in England and Virginia often preferred to call themselves farmers and boasted of their attention to the details of cultivating crops, raising livestock, and erecting storehouses and other dependencies. By birth and by habit, Washington was a true countryman, early to bed and early to rise but not without spare hours for the centuries-old English pastimes, particularly horse racing, riding, and fox hunts. In the mother country, only the great nobles such as the Bedfords, the Shelburnes, and the Rockinghams, like the West Indian sugar lords, could be habitual absentees and avoid the minutia of husbandry. Still, Washington and other Virginia gentlemen found opportunities to mix business with enjoyment on occasional trips to Williamsburg, Alexandria, and Annapolis, tiny urban enclaves where "long-tailed families" attended dinners, balls, and plays, to say nothing of indulging their "pleasures of the turf."[28]

Withal, Washington was not blinded by his Britishness. There is hardly a sense of deep regret, of wistfulness on his part, when the empire disintegrated in the War of Independence, as one finds in such Virginians as William Byrd III and Robert Carter Nicholas. This is not to say, however, that he was already deeply alienated from Britain by the mid-1760s, that his slights from the British army and his difficulties at getting an adequate return on his tobacco in London had made him bitter, suspicious of all that England did.[29] In fact, Washington never lost his affinity for the English country gentry, which, like its Virginia counterpart, was sometimes critical of the corruption of Hanoverian court life and the rapaciousness of London mercantile houses. His sympathies for the landed elite of the mother country were still much in evidence at the time of the French Revolution, for he saw in that segment of society the finest representations of British life.

Washington's recent biographer John E. Ferling maintains that the pre-Revolutionary "Washington who began his amazing ascent by carefully identifying with the habits and styles of the elite—and generally British—role models never abandoned the practice." Corresponding regularly after 1783 with prominent Englishmen, Washington sought their advice on a variety of subjects as "he made Mount Vernon into a grand English country manor house, carefully fashioned and furnished after its counterparts across the ocean, and had he had his way it would have been worked by English farmers not by American yeomen."[30]

Indeed, Washington's quarrel with Britain in the American Revolutionary crisis was principally with its political leadership and decidedly less with its cultural and institutional configurations. His criticisms of British imperial practices and policies evolved over a decade or so. The same pattern of disenchantment was probably also true of most of the Revolution's leaders. Doubtless there were some, however, whose alienation was cultural and was manifested relatively early, although they were not the Revolution's most influential helmsmen after 1776.[31]

$\mathcal{A}$s for self-denial, washington certainly struck some contemporaries as distant and aloof. There was a reserve to the man, especially when in groups and in the presence of strangers and those he did not know well. Were he devoid of natural human feelings, he might have appeared indifferent to women. He did not take a wife as early as some men, and his marriage is often portrayed as one of convenience—he needed a mistress for Mount Vernon, while Martha Custis sought a father and manager for her son and daughter and their properties.

If the above notions were wholly correct, a search for the causes of the impersonal Washington might go back to a preoccupation of some of his biographers—that of parental influences. One might theorize that the Washington who lost his father as a boy, who—in the opinion of some writers—was denied warmth and affection by his strong-willed mother, had turned cold, fearing that hurt might come to him in any intimate relationship.

Douglas Southall Freeman and other Washington scholars have turned to the same familial sources to account for what were admittedly aggressive qualities in the young man's makeup. But before his mother, in particular, is convicted for all his failings, a note of caution is in order. There is no learned consensus as to the roots of aggressive behavior. If domineering mothers—if that is what Mary Ball Washington was—may generate visible aggressions in their sons or daughters, they are just as likely to leave their offspring timid and straitlaced. Conceivably, too, Washington, were he severely damaged by his mother's influence, might have become effeminate, when in truth we know that he was strongly attached to the opposite sex and manly in all other respects as well. There are, one should add, multiple varieties of character, and to explain the grown man simply in terms of putative childhood determinants appears to leave small room for personal development.

In short, one may not weave together so easily the strands of Washington's personal life. Distant though he was at times, he had a healthy enjoyment of worldly pleasures. Whatever his reserve around some men, he was ever a gallant with women, once he passed his awkward teens. Did Washington speak from personal experience when in 1783 he observed to a female friend that "once the Woman has tempted us and we have tasted the forbidden fruit, there is no such thing as checking our appetites, whatever the consequences may be"?[32]

In any event, Washington could unbend in his letters in ways that would have surprised some of his contemporaries, let alone later generations. The Virginian expressed worry concerning certain performance responsibilities of elderly Col. Joseph Ward, a former army comrade who had lately taken a young bride. If the colonel had failed to "review his *strength,* his arms, and ammunition before he got involved in an action," then Washington would "advise him to make the *first* onset upon his fair del Tobaso, with vigor, that the impression may be deep, if it cannot be lasting, or frequently renewed."[33]

Despite the unceasing, titillating speculations about Washington's feelings for George William Fairfax's wife, Sally, with whom he carried on a flirtatious correspondence almost up to the time of his own nuptials, Washington's marriage to Martha Dandridge Custis seems to have been highly gratifying in every respect. To be sure, he and Martha had hardly the time to fall madly, deeply in love before their wedding, owing to his military duties—they seem to have become engaged during his second visit to White House, the Custis estate on the Pamunkey River in New Kent County. Doubtless he had not in his "contemplation of the married state," as he cautioned a relative in after years, "look[ed] for perfect felicity before consent[ing] to wed."[34]

Yet there is no reason to doubt that Washington considered Martha to be quite physically attractive at the time of their courtship. She was thought to be very handsome by the family of her first husband, Daniel Parke Custis.[35] Even if she may have been slightly plump when she gave her hand to Washington, that condition hardly resulted in the stigma that it would become for some people in a more recent period. Multiple pregnancies (she had had four), high-calorie diets, and negative attitudes about vigorous female exercise combine to explain why many upper-class women were somewhat heavy by today's standards. Her portrait by John Wollaston, completed a year or so before her engagement to Washington, shows a remarkably pretty face and an overall appearance consistent with what Lois Banner has described as the eighteenth-century ideal of femininity: "buxom, yet small and delicate," with "sensuality coy and indirect."[36]

Since Washington possessed healthy attitudes about romantic love and marriage, he was far different from the kind of revolutionary type portrayed by Erik Erikson: one who displays "special powers of sublimation" because of "passionate devotion and minute service to public causes."[37] Time and again Washington declared that he prized domes-

Martha Washington by Charles Willson Peale. Courtesy of The Mount Vernon Ladies' Association.

tic felicity above all other pleasures and rewards. Just before the wedding of his nephew George Augustine to Martha's niece Fanny Bassett, Washington wrote that he had "always considered marriage as the most interesting event of one's life, the foundation of happiness or misery."[38] Unfortunately, only three of George and Martha's letters to each other are known to have survived,[39] but they bespeak a tenderness and sensitivity for his "dear Patcy" often lacking in an age when communications between husband and wife were not uncommonly formal. All three letters, two from him and one from her, begin with "My Dearest," what must have been their customary salutation. As commander in chief of the Revolutionary army, Washington urged Martha to join him in camp and stay as long as possible, and this she loyally and willingly did, although she confessed to a dislike of distant travel, unfamiliar places, and warlike activity. Though torn by a yearning to minister to a grieving Burwell Bassett over the loss of his wife and her own sister, Anna Maria (Nancy) Bassett, Martha in December 1777 explained to her brother-in-law that her greater obligation was to her husband, who was likely to call her north at any moment: "If he does, I must goe." Each year she usually set out from Mount Vernon in the autumn and returned—much to her husband's visible distress—in the spring with the opening of the next military campaign. "I was," she recalled, "a kind of perambulator during eight or nine years of War." The prospect of ever undergoing such "fatiegue" again would be "too much for me to bear."[40]

The good life that Washington pursued to the fullest at Mount Vernon provides ample additional evidence that he manifested no zeal for self-denial. Martha Washington always presided over an abundant table, whether at camp or at home. Dinner, reported a French visitor, "was in the English fashion, consisting of eight or ten large dishes of meat and poultry, with vegetables of all sorts, followed by a second course . . . of 'pies and puddings.'"[41] Although Washington lacked a facile tongue—he listened more than he talked—both he and Martha enjoyed leisurely dinner conversations with old friends, new guests, and various family members that sometimes stretched on for several hours into the late afternoon, concluding with apples, nuts, and with more wines.

There were swarms of Washington relatives who came to Mount Vernon, further indication that family was indeed meaningful to George Washington. (He would have derived little sense from the ongoing debate as to whether the American family, at various times and places, was nuclear or extended in its structure.) Relatives paraded in and out of his home throughout his entire married life or in other ways engaged his attention: Custises, Lewises, Dandridges, Bassetts, Washingtons, and more—perhaps as many as eighty-six of these kinfolk had some interaction with him. They often stayed for weeks, months, and longer—and sometimes remained in his employment as an overseer or secretary. One could say of his family (and many other planter clans then and later) that "its borders were permeable and its structure was elastic."[42]

Washington displayed a particular fondness for young people. He could scarcely have been more giving to his Custis stepchildren, John Parke (Jack) and Martha Parke (Patcy). Washington sought for Jack all the educational opportunities that had eluded him, composing detailed missives to tutors and teachers on his aspirations for Jack and traveling with him to enroll at King's College in New York City. The young man, no scholar and in love with a Maryland belle, soon dropped out of school in favor of marriage, much to Washington's distress. That pain could hardly be compared to his feelings when sixteen-year-old Patcy died of epilepsy. For three weeks thereafter Washington eschewed all business activity, and for three months—except for one occasion—he did not spend a night away from Martha. Several years later a more mature Jack Custis could better appreciate what Washington had meant to his mother and to him as well. "I am extremely desirious," he assured Washington, "to return you Thanks for your parental Care[,] which on all Occasions you have shewn for Me. . . . Few have experience'd such Care and Attention from real Parents as I have done."[43]

Washington was endlessly doing favors for his brothers, cousins, nephews, and nieces. He wrote long, avuncular letters to his younger relations on making their mark in the world, doubtless filled with the same maxims and principles that his own deceased older brother Lawrence had imparted to him years earlier and thoroughly typical of the concerns of Lord Chesterfield in his famous epistles to his son, published in the 1760s and constituting yet another popular form of courtesy literature. In his family letters, Washington frequently expressed "love" and "affection" for both male and female relatives, words hardly consistent with the marble image of the man and, for that matter, not even comfortable terms for many twentieth-century men to employ toward those of their own sex.

Although Washington gave more than he received, his kinfolk at times reciprocated. In his 1761 effort at reelection to the House of Burgesses, his brothers John and Samuel were the first two voters at the polls, followed shortly thereafter by his brother Charles, who joined them in voting for George. His cousin Lund faithfully managed his estates during his long eight and one-half year absence in the Revolu-

WASHINGTON AND THE VIRGINIA BACKCOUNTRY

tionary War. During his presidency his five nephews served in the federalized militia force that suppressed the Whiskey Rebellion. Before taking his leave of that army at Fort Cumberland, Maryland, Washington instructed his oldest nephew to set an example for his two brothers and two cousins. Washington later willed his swords to these same nephews, charging that they never "unsheath them for the purpose of shedding blood, except it be for self defence, or in the defence of their Country and its rights."[44]

Washington had a much healthier family relationship than some Virginia planters, such as William Byrd II and Landon Carter. Byrd fought with his wife over countless matters, including his marital infidelity and his cheating at cards. Carter considered his children unappreciative and disrespectful of their father and scarcely endeavored to avoid unpleasant domestic scenes. Even so, Washington's own deep commitment to kindred was hardly unique. Those ties seem generally to have been growing stronger within his social orbit in the second half of the eighteenth century; families appear to have become less patriarchal, authoritarian, and emotionally restrained. Assuredly those bonds were almost wholly unknown to Mazlish's revolutionary ascetics.[45]

Thus, it should not surprise us to learn that Washington was one of the few revolutionary helmsmen in modern history to be praised for his family life. The link between statecraft and domesticity was of the highest importance to Americans of the third quarter of the eighteenth century. Nothing could be more revealing in this respect than New York's advice in 1775 to its delegates in the Continental Congress on the appointment of a commander in chief. "On a General" for America, they declared, such a man should have "in his property, his kindred, and connexions . . . sure pledges that he will faithfully perform the duties of his high office, and readily lay down his power when the general weal shall require it."[46] It was widely perceived in the Continental Congress that Washington, a family man and large-scale cultivator, would make burdensome sacrifices in drawing his sword and would be eager to return to his former station in life at the earliest moment. John Adams, making the point graphically, spoke of this "gentleman of one of the first fortunes upon the continent, leaving his delicious retirement, his family and friends, sacrificing his ease, and hazarding all in the cause of his country!"[47]

Kenneth Silverman rightly says that Americans praised the non-military dimensions of Washington more than his martial side, and

John Parke Custis by Charles Willson Peale. Courtesy of The Mount Vernon Ladies' Association.

they did not neglect his immediate family, during the war or afterward. Poets rhapsodized over his loving relationship with his wife, who prayed that

> Heav'n give the angels charge, to protect my Hero George
> And return him safe back to my arms!

Washington's Family by Edward Savage, National Gallery of Art. Courtesy of The Mount Vernon Ladies' Association.

Artists picked up the same themes. Congress early in the war expressed an interest in portraits of both George and Martha Washington. Charles Willson Peale, who had limned miniatures of the Washingtons, converted them into mezzotints entitled *His Excellency George Washington Esq.* and *Lady Washington.* At a later time Edward Savage's *Washington's Family* was quite popular in engraved form; it portrays George, Martha, and Martha's two grandchildren, whom the Washington's adopted. Undoubtedly, Washington's countrymen saw him as a father figure not only because he was a nation-maker (and another George to replace George III?) but also because of his well-known domestic sensibilities.[48] That was definitely the opinion of Brissot de Warville, a French traveler in 1788, who, like other observers, declared that "Americans speak of him as they would of a father"; but not one who was austere or authoritarian, completely dehumanized, as would be the fate of Washington at the hands of nineteenth-century biographers.[49]

The Revolutionary generation's appreciation of close familial bonds may be hard for Americans in the late twentieth century to comprehend. David Potter, describing post-1960 American society, found it increasingly characterized by indirect and fragmented relationships compared with earlier periods when direct and integral relationships were more the rule than the exception. "Today," stated Potter, countless young people do not even "know their cousins and have no idea of clan."[50]

Washington's domestic orientation quite properly elicited the praise of his Northern Neck neighbor and fellow soldier Henry Lee of Stratford Hall. If Lee began the most quoted sentence of his famous Washington eulogy by saying that the soldier-statesman was "first in war, first in peace, and first in the hearts of his countrymen," he concluded it by asserting that "he was second to none in the humble and endearing scenes of private life."[51] Washington, himself, as Revolutionary chieftain, had said on countless occasions that his greatest desire was to spend the rest of his days back in Virginia, sitting "under my own vine and fig tree."

Yet not all in the Old Dominion felt that way after the onset of the Revolution, which there and elsewhere left some men restless and eager for new experiences on distant horizons. Generals Nathanael Greene of Rhode Island and Anthony Wayne of Pennsylvania both became planters in Georgia. In terms of Virginia's first families, those possessed of wanderlust were undoubtedly exceptions, but they included Henry Lee himself, the dashing ex-cavalryman who dissipated his energies and resources in one postwar speculative enterprise after another, dying far from his native acres. Lee's relative Richard Henry Lee also displayed little sign of missing home during his long departures in public service and came to visualize New England society as the prototypical ideal for a republican America.[52]

$\mathcal{W}$ASHINGTON'S BEHAVIOR REGARDing alienation and self-denial implicitly casts light on Mazlish's third category: that of the revolutionary's possible narcissism. There is simply no evidence that during Washington's generalship or later his mind turned to narcissistic thoughts, the kind that have been the undoing not only of certain revolutionary ascetics but also of a whole panoply of revolutionary types ranging from Latin American caudillos to Third World nation-makers such as the Nkrumahs and Sukarnos. And yet one might ask if Washington had earlier shown signs of narcissism in his intemperate carping to Dinwiddie and in his near-rebellious behavior toward Gen. James Forbes in the Fort Duquesne campaign? It is more probable that Washington, only in his early-to-middle twenties at the time, revealed marks of immaturity as he grappled with his own sense of worth and identity during a period in which he had far more responsibility than most men his age ever have.[53]

In his later public life, when there were moments for dreaming about his future, the mature Washington's attention turned to private concerns, to his Virginia world. He not only corresponded frequently with Martha but he wrote often to clansmen, friends, and business associates. He was saddened by the death of two brothers and a brother-in-law, and he worried about the orphans of his brother Samuel (several of whom became his responsibility). He carried on a voluminous epistolary exchange with Lund Washington, his manager.[54] Washington, at the time he assumed his military role in the Revolution, was already embarked on a course of economic diversification and a program of enlarging his house and gardens. They were activities that he watched as closely as possible from afar as they went forward under Lund's capable supervision. Indeed, throughout his adult lifetime Mount Vernon was growing and changing. Eventually, his estate, part of which had belonged to his great-grandfather, the immigrant John, numbered seventy-six hundred acres: his "Mansion House Farm" and four outlying farms. Displaying great creativity as a farmer, landscape designer, and architect, Washington in his minutely detailed directives to Lund and his subsequent managers (both during the Revolution and during his presidency) offers abundant evidence that he could hardly wait to return to take over the personal direction of what seemed to be a hundred and one enterprises.

Mount Vernon and all it meant to Washington ever remained the centerpiece of his life. Lionized by men of affairs, sought out by visiting dignitaries, all but deified by hosts of his countrymen, he kept his prewar values and priorities in place, something no narcissist could do. Still, he recognized that he had symbolic significance for the Revolution, both during the war itself and in the post-1783 years as well. As W. W. Abbot says: "We have only to look at the record of his willingness to sit for any artist who wished to paint his portrait, to correspond with any French, German, English, Dutch, Irish, Italian, Swedish, or American man or woman who wrote him a letter, and to open the doors of his house to any stranger, foreign or domestic, who came to pay homage or only to have a look." What he did and said mattered to people and to himself, for he was a proud man, conscious of his honor and reputation for his own lifetime and for posterity. Although some historians have a different view, I believe that Washington was deeply reluctant to attend the Constitutional Convention in 1787 and to accept the presidency two years later.[56] He did so, of course, but only out of a sense of obligation and responsibility when confronted with the insistence of leaders throughout the country. Rather than seeking new opportunities to return to the limelight and reinforce his fame, he recognized that he could lose his hard-earned reputation along with the peace and tranquility of Mount Vernon if he returned to the national arena.

He was content for history to be the final judge of his record as it stood in 1787. He never, then or after his final retirement, wished to contribute to that judgment by penning a memoir or autobiography, but he did desire to do so in another way: by organizing and copying his papers for the benefit of future chroniclers, an undertaking he launched during the Revolutionary War, continued during the Confederation years, and returned to after his presidency. In fact, he considered erecting at Mount Vernon a building for their storage and preservation. On his deathbed he implored his secretary Tobias Lear to be sure his manuscripts were properly secured.[57]

If Washington's paramount concern was with documents bearing on his contributions to Virginia and the United States, this essay has endeavored to show that the public and private lives of statesmen are not easily separated. Washington's intention was to maintain some measure of his privacy, at least, at the expense of history. That explains why, for example, he singularly ignored the request of his former aide and secretary and would-be biographer, David Humphreys, for information about his family and early years.[58] Surely his attitude did not stem from a fear that he had more to hide which would reflect negatively upon his character than do most human beings. For other luminaries that has not always been the case. Even for leaders who maintain their public ideals in the face of acclaim, there has always been the temptation to compromise their family life. It has been true of some famous twentieth-century Americans, and it was also a temptation that men succumbed to in the Founders' generation.

How different in this respect was Washington from Benjamin Franklin, whose wife was probably no more educated and cultivated than Martha, and who seemed to consider his loyal, devoted Deborah

Franklin to be an embarrassment, remaining apart from her for five- and ten-year stretches, even though, in the last case, he knew she was troubled by his broken promises to return and was gravely ill and longed to see him a final time.[59] It may tell us a good deal about Washington to say that Martha Washington hardly came across as a repressed or neglected spouse but rather as a happy, healthy, well-adjusted woman. Contemporary portrayals of her personality and character are notably consistent over a period of twenty years, beginning with the first known assessment by Mercy Otis Warren in April 1776. If Warren recorded Martha's openness and amiable disposition at that time, so did Abigail Adams—"her great ease and politeness" and "modest and unassuming" ways—in 1789, and so did the young English architect Benjamin Latrobe—her "good humoured free manner . . . was extremely pleasant and flattering"—in 1796.[60]

Had it been written then, Washington might well have called to mind the title of a song, although it would have involved changing the state. He would have called it "Virginia on My Mind." The Old Dominion does contain the key to why Washington was a safe man to lead a Revolution. We find it not only in his experiences as a Virginia officer in the Seven Years' War and in his seventeen-year career as a legislator in the House of Burgesses, subjects that have been addressed elsewhere.[61] But, even more important, we locate it in his domestic values and family life. This safe leader, a general and president who willingly, even eagerly, relinquished power, knew that in Virginia he found far more gratification than in any post or laurel ever bestowed upon him. It was, to recapitulate, the Virginia of deference and patriarchy, of well-born, well-connected friends and family, of Mount Vernon, and not the Virginia of the West, with its social fluidity and native cultures.

Washington said as much publicly and in his correspondence with quotable men of affairs. It was also what his countrymen wanted to hear—however much they pressed him to overcome his reluctance to serve. Theirs was a neoclassical age in which men took as warm and moving gospel the stories of Cato, who extolled the joys of rural retirement in the Sabine hills away from the pomp and corruption of Rome (Washington's friend Landon Carter named his home Sabine Hall), and of Cincinnatus, who relinquished his sword in favor of the plough. Washington was equally eloquent innumerable times to friends and family. And never more so than in his letter to Martha informing her that he had accepted the command of the Continental army in 1775: "I should enjoy more real happiness and felicity in one month with you, at home, than I have the most distant prospect of reaping abroad, if my stay was to be Seven times Seven years."[62] Sixteen years later, after accepting the highest civil office in the land, the pull of home had not diminished. To Dr. David Stuart, a family member, he wrote: "I can truly say I had rather be at Mount Vernon ... than to be attended at the Seat of Government by the Officers of State and the Representatives of every Power in Europe."[63] Therefore, is it any wonder that he returned to his great house on the Potomac fifteen times during his presidency?

Paradoxical as it may seem, Washington was both a localist and a nationalist. His love of Virginia had led him to revolt and that same love kept his nationalism—powerful though it became owing to his service in the Continental Congress and his performance as commander in chief—within appropriate bounds.

NOTES

1. Lucille Griffith, *The Virginia House of Bugresses, 1750–1774* (University, Ala.: University of Alabama Press, 1970), 94–96; Garland R. Quarles, *George Washington and Winchester*, Winchester–Frederick County Historical Society Papers, Vol. 7 (Winchester, Va.: Winchester-Frederick County Historical Society, 1974), 38.

2. Even so, both scholars still provide us with a starting point for comparative studies of the American Revolution. Crane Brinton, *The Anatomy of Revolution* (New York: Vintage Books, 1956); R. R. Palmer, *The Age of Democratic Revolution: A Political History of Europe and America, 1760–1800*, 2 vols. (Princeton: Princeton University Press, 1959–1964). An illuminating dissection of earlier western European revolutions is Perez Zagorin, *Rebels and Rulers, 1500–1660*, 2 vols. (Cambridge: Cambridge University Press, 1982).

3. *The Papers of Thomas Jefferson*, ed. Julian P. Boyd et al., 26 vols. to date (Princeton: Princeton University Press, 1950–), 7:106.

4. Michael Walser, *The Revolution of the Saints: A Study in the Origins of Radical Politics* (Cambridge: Harvard University Press, 1965); C. V. Wedgwood, *William the Silent: Prince of Orange, 1533–1584* (New Haven: Yale University Press, 1944).

5. Bruce Mazlish, *The Revolutionary Ascetic: Evolution of a Political Type* (New York: Basic Books, 1976). Mazlish calls for more psychological studies of the American Revolution in his "Leadership in the American Revolution:

The Psychological Dimension," in *Leadership in the American Revolution*, Library of Congress Symposia on the American Revolution, vol. 3 (Washington, D.C.: Library of Congress, 1974), 113–33.

6. E. M. C. (Ellen M. Clark), "A Wartime Incident," Mount Vernon Ladies' Association of the Union, *Annual Report* (1986): 23–25; Fritz Hirschfeld, "The British Raid on Mount Vernon," *Naval History* 4 (Fall 1990): 7–9; idem, "'Burnt All Their Houses': The Log of HMS *Savage* during a Raid up the Potomac River, Spring 1781," *Virginia Magazine of History and Biography* 99 (October 1991): 513–30.

7. In addition to the better-known studies of the Virginia elite, the following works have been helpful in seeing the similarities between the gentries: G. E. Mingay, *English Landed Society in the Eighteenth Century* (London: Routledge and Kegan Paul, 1963); Mark Girouard, *Life in the English Country House: A Social and Architectural History* (New Haven: Yale University Press, 1978); Daniel D. Reiff, *Small Georgian Houses in England and Virginia: Origins and Development through the 1750s* (London: Associated University Presses, 1986).

8. Edmund Randolph, *History of Virginia*, ed. Arthur H. Shaffer (Charlottesville: University Press of Virginia for the Virginia Historical Society, 1970), 166, 176.

9. Warren M. Billings, John E. Selby, and Thad W. Tate, *Colonial Virginia: A History* (White Plains, N.Y.: KTO Press, 1986), 253.

10. John M. Hemphill, "John Wayles Rates His Neighbors," *Virginia Magazine of History and Biography* 66 (July 1958): 305.

11. William Eddis, *Letters from America*, ed. Aubrey C. Land (Cambridge: Harvard University Press, 1969), 57.

12. T. Pape, "Appleby Grammar School and Its Washington Pupils," *William and Mary Quarterly*, 2d ser., 20 (October 1940): 498–501; Richard Beale Davis, *Intellectual Life in the Colonial South, 1585–1763*, 3 vols. (Knoxville: University of Tennessee Press, 1978), 1:356–58.

13. Louis B. Wright, *First Gentlemen of Virginia: Intellectual Qualities of the Early Colonial Ruling Class* (San Marino, Calif.: Huntington Library, 1940).

14. George Washington to Richard Washington, September 20, 1759, *The Papers of George Washington*, Colonial Series, ed. W. W. Abbot et al., 10 vols. (Charlottesville: University Press of Virginia, 1983–1995), 6:358.

15. Douglas Southall Freeman, *George Washington: A Biography*, 8 vols. (New York: Charles Scribner's Sons, 1948–1957), 2:190–99. Volume 7, appearing after Freeman's death, was written by John Alexander Carroll and Mary Wells Ashworth. Joseph Ball's informative letterbook for the years 1743–1760 is in the Library of Congress.

16. Paul K. Longmore, *The Invention of George Washington* (Berkeley: University of California Press, 1988), especially 213–26.

17. Washington to Jonathan Boucher, January 21, 1771, *Washington Pa-*

pers, Col. Ser., 8:426; Washington to Boucher, May 13, 1770, *Washington Papers*, Col. Ser., 8:335.

18. Billings, Selby, and Tate, *Colonial Virginia*, 216.

19. Don Higginbotham, *Daniel Morgan: Revolutionary Rifleman* (Chapel Hill: University of North Carolina Press, 1961).

20. Davis, *Intellectual Life*, 3:1244.

21. Brathwaite's *The English Gentlemen* was an essential volume in the libraries of the rising Virginia gentry in the late seventeenth and early eighteenth centuries. See Wright, *First Gentlemen of Virginia*, 15, 16, 32, 131, 185, 189, 231.

22. Washington to Robert Dinwiddie, April 22, 1756, *Washington Papers*, Col. Ser., 3:34.

23. A. G. Roeber, *Faithful Magistrates and Republican Lawyers: Creators of Virginia Legal Culture, 1680–1810* (Chapel Hill: University of North Carolina Press, 1981), 92.

24. For a discussion of the Washington-Posey relationship as "a particularly good example of the way that the etiquette of debt operated between men of unequal social standing," see T. H. Breen, *Tobacco Culture: The Mentality of the Great Tidewater Planters on the Eve of the Revolution* (Princeton: Princeton University Press, 1985), 97–101.

25. *The Writings of George Washington from the Original Manuscript Sources, 1745–1799*, ed. John C. Fitzpatrick, 39 vols. (Washington, D.C.: Government Printing Office, 1931–1944), 3:262.

26. *The Papers of George Washington*, Revolutionary War Series, ed. W. W. Abbot et al., 7 vols. to date (Charlottesville: University Press of Virginia, 1985–), 1:431.

27. Since planter hegemony was somewhat more fragile in Virginia than used to be recognized, it was critical to the continued dominance of planters that they perform their customary role in a responsible manner. As one historian notes: "Popular acceptance of gentry authority was never axiomatic. It depended upon their success in fulfilling these complex multiple tasks as well as on the continued apathy of men outside the governing elite toward public affairs." Keith Mason, "Localism, Evangelicalism, and Loyalism: The Sources of Oppression in the Revolutionary Chesapeake," *Journal of Southern History* 56 (February 1990): 26, 27, and authorities cited therein. This problem of dominance did not exist for the English rural elite.

28. Washington's social activities in these regional centers are meticulously recorded in his diaries, see *The Diaries of George Washington*, ed. Donald Jackson and Dorothy Twohig, 6 vols. (Charlottesville: University Press of Virginia, 1976–1979).

29. Washington's difficulties with tobacco are treated in Curtis P. Nettels, *George Washington and American Independence* (Boston: Little, Brown, 1951), 64–72; Bruce A. Ragsdale, "George Washington, the British Tobacco Trade,

and Economic Opportunity in Prerevolutionary Virginia," *Virginia Magazine of History and Biography* 97 (April 1989): 133–62.

30. John E. Ferling, *The First of Men: A Life of George Washington* (Knoxville: University of Tennessee Press, 1988), 481, 482.

31. See Pauline Maier, *The Old Revolutionaries: Political Lives in the Age of Samuel Adams* (New York: Alfred A. Knopf, 1980).

32. *Writings of Washington*, 27:128.

33. Ibid., 28:15.

34. Ibid., 33:500–501.

35. Jo Zuppan, ed., "Father to Son: Letters from John Custis IV to Daniel Parke Custis," *Virginia Magazine of History and Biography* 98 (January 1990): 86; Freeman, *Washington*, 2:292–94.

36. Lois W. Banner, *American Beauty* (New York: Alfred A. Knopf, 1983), 46.

37. Erik H. Erikson, *Dimensions of a New Identity* (New York: W. W. Norton, 1974), 57–58.

38. *Writings of Washington*, 18:152.

39. The possibility of the existence of yet another surviving letter from George to Martha is examined in Freeman, *Washington*, 2:405–6.

40. Martha Washington to Burwell Bassett, December 27, 1777, Martha Washington to Sally Fairfax, May 17, 1798, Martha Washington to Annis Stockton Boudinot, January 15, 1784, Mount Vernon Ladies' Association of the Union, Mount Vernon, Virginia (hereafter cited as ViMtvL). The library at Mount Vernon has the originals or typescripts of all known Martha Washington letters. See also *"Worthy Partner": The Papers of Marth Washington*, ed. Joseph E. Fields, with and introduction by Ellen McCallister Clark (Westport, Conn. and London: Greenwood, 1994). For Martha's wartime travels, see also James Thomas Flexner, *George Washington*, 4 vols. (Boston: Little, Brown, 1965–1972), 2:282, 517.

41. Francois Jean Marquis de Chastellux, *Travels in North America in the Years 1780, 1781, and 1782*, 2 vols., trans. Howard C. Rice Jr. (Paris: Prault, 1786; Chapel Hill: University of North Carolina Press for the Institute of Early American History and Culture, 1963), 1:109.

42. Miriam Anne Bourne, *First Family: George Washington and His Intimate Relations* (New York: W. W. Norton, 1982), 207–9; Joan E. Cashin, "The Structure of Antebellum Planter Families: 'The Ties that Bound Us Was Strong,'" *Journal of Southern History* 56 (February 1990): 56.

43. Jack Custis to Washington, June 10, 1776, *Washington Papers*, Rev. Ser., 4:485.

44. *Writings of Washington*, 37:287–88.

45. Michael Zuckerman, "William Byrd's Family," *Perspectives in American History* 12 (1979): 255–311; Jack P. Greene, ed., *The Diary of Colonel Landon*

Carter of Sabine Hall, 1752–1778, 2 vols. (Richmond: Virginia Historical Society, 1965), esp. Greene's introductory essay, 1:3–61; Daniel Blake Smith, *Inside the Great House: Family Life in Eighteenth-Century Chesapeake Society* (Ithaca: Cornell University Press, 1980); Rhys Isaac, *The Transformation of Virginia, 1740–1790* (Chapel Hill: University of North Carolina Press, 1982); Jan Lewis, *The Pursuit of Happiness: Family and Values in Jefferson's Virginia* (New York: Cambridge University Press, 1983).

46. *American Archives . . .*, 4th series, ed. Peter Force, 6 vols. (Washington, D.C.: Clarke & Force, 1837–1846), 2:1281.

47. John Adams to Elbridge Gerry, June 18, 1775, *Letters of Delegates to Congress*, ed. Paul H. Smith et al., 24 vols. to date (Washington, D.C.: Library of Congress, 1976–), 1:504.

48. Kenneth Silverman, *A Cultural History of the American Revolution* (New York: Columbia University Press, 1976), 317, 361, 429–34, quotation on 602. Silverman is particularly good on contemporary images of Washington. Several recent accounts contribute substantially to the subject of Washington's location in the American mind. See my review of these and other new Washington studies, "The Washington Theme in Recent Historical Literature," *Pennsylvania Magazine of History and Biography* 114 (July 1990): 423–37.

49. J. P. Brissot de Warville, *New Travels in the United States of America, 1788*, ed. Durand Echeverria (Paris: Buisson, 1791; Cambridge: Harvard University Press, 1964), 104, 344–45.

50. David M. Potter, *History and American Society*, ed. Don E. Fehrenbacher (New York: Oxford University Press, 1973), 313–15.

51. Albert Bushnell Hart, ed., *Tributes to Washington* (Washington, D.C.: George Washington Bicentennial Commission, 1931), 16–17.

52. Charles Royster, *Light-Horse Harry Lee and the Legacy of the American Revolution* (New York: Alfred A. Knopf, 1981); Maier, *Old Revolutionaries*, chap. 4.

53. For a cautionary note on the complexities of early manhood, see Lucian W. Pye, "Personal Identity and Political Ideology," in *Psychoanalysis and History*, ed. Bruce Mazlish (Englewood Cliffs, N.J.: Prentice-Hall, 1963), 150–73.

54. A sizable collection of Lund Washington's letters to George Washington is in ViMtvL along with a useful sketch of Lund. The editors of the *Papers of George Washington* note the bulk and diversity of Washington's private wartime correspondence; see *Washington Papers*, Rev. Ser., 2:xvii.

55. W. W. Abbot, "An Uncommon Awareness of Self: The Papers of George Washington," *Prologue* 21 (Spring 1989): 10.

56. See, for example, Flexner, *Washington*, 3:chap. 13; Barry Schwartz, *George Washington: The Making of an American Symbol* (New York: Free Press, 1987), 144–45; Ferling, *First of Men*, chaps. 13–14.

57. Abbot, "Uncommon Awareness of Self," 10, 12, 14–15, 17.

58. Washington, however, provided Humphreys considerable assistance concerning his public service. See Rosemarie Zagarri, *David Humphreys' "Life of General Washington"* (Athens: University of Georgia Press, 1991). It has been pointed out that after the War of Independence, Washington for the first time showed a concern to preserve his personal letters as well as his business and public correspondence. But "the reticence of the great man tends to make these letters less revealing than the unguarded texts of the rare survivals from earlier years." See Abbot, "Uncommon Awareness of Self," 17.

59. Claude-Anne Lopez and Eugenia W. Herbert, *The Private Franklin: The Man and His Family* (New York: W. W. Norton, 1975), chap. 14.

60. Bernard Knollenberg, *George Washington: The Virginia Period, 1732–1775* (Durham: Duke University Press, 1964), 72; Freeman, *Washington*, 4:77; *New Letters of Abigail Adams, 1788–1801*, ed. Stewart Mitchell (Boston: Houghton Mifflin, 1947), 13, 15, 30, 57–58, quotation on 13; *The Virginia Journals of Benjamin Henry Latrobe, 1795–1798*, ed. Edward C. Carter II (New Haven: Yale University Press, 1977), 168. Martha shared with her husband a stoical attitude about making the most out of life's vicissitudes, including the need for personal sacrifices when duty called. See Martha Washington to Mercy Otis Warren, December 26, 1789, June 12, 1790, ViMtvL.

61. I, along with other historians, have examined Washington's pre-Revolutionary public career, see my *George Washington and the American Military Tradition* (Athens: University of Georgia Press, 1985).

62. Washington to Martha Washington, June 18, 1775, *Washington Papers*, Rev. Ser., 1:3–4.

63. *Writings of Washington*, 31:54.

Contributors

PHILANDER D. CHASE is senior associate editor of the *Papers of George Washington* at the University of Virginia and series editor of its *Revolutionary War Series.* He received a B.A. in history from North Carolina State University in 1965, an M.A. in history from Duke University in 1968, and a Ph.D. in history from Duke in 1973. His dissertation is entitled "Baron Von Steuben in the War of Independence." Dr. Chase joined the Washington Papers project in 1973 as a National Historical Publications and Records Commission fellow and has remained with the project to date. In 1978 he received the Philip H. Hamer award for documentary editing from the Society of American Archivists for his work as an assistant editor on *The Diaries of George Washington,* 6 vols. (Charlottesville: University Press of Virginia, 1976–1979). He subsequently worked on the project's *Colonial Series,* 10 vols. (Charlottesville: University Press of Virginia, 1985–1995). Dr. Chase has written numerous reviews and has contributed to several historical reference works, including most recently George Washington entries for Richard L. Blanco, ed., *The American Revolution, 1775–1783: An Encyclopedia,* 2 vols. (Hamden, Conn.: Garland Publishing, 1992), and Robert A. Rutland, ed., *James Madison and the American Nation, 1751–1836: An Encyclopedia* (New York: Simon & Schuster, 1994). He served as chair of the Southern Historical Association's membership committee in 1992 and three years as treasurer of the Association for Documentary Editing.

J. FREDERICK FAUSZ is an ethnohistorian of Anglo-Indian relations in the seventeenth-century Chesapeake and of fur trading in colonial North America. He received his Ph.D. in early American history from the College of William and Mary and served as assistant editor of *The*

Complete Works of Captain John Smith while at the Institute of Early American History and Culture in Williamsburg. As a history professor at St. Mary's College of Maryland between 1978 and 1991, Dr. Fausz published several important essays on multicultural relations in the colonial Chesapeake, one of which received the 1990 Rachal "Best Article" Prize from the Virginia Historical Society. In 1991 he became dean of The Pierre Laclede Honors College and associate professor of history at the University of Missouri-St. Louis.

JOHN E. FERLING, professor of history at the State University of West Georgia, is a widely acclaimed biographer of George Washington and John Adams and scholar of colonial and Revolutionary America. His books include *The Loyalist Mind: Joseph Galloway and the American Revolution* (University Park: Pennsylvania State University Press, 1977), *A Wilderness of Miseries: War and Warriors in Early America* (Westport, Conn.: Greenwood Press, 1981), *The First of Men: A Life of George Washington* (Knoxville: University of Tennessee Press, 1988), *Struggle for a Continent: The Wars of Early America* (Arlington Heights, Ill.: Harlan Davidson, 1992), and *John Adams: A Biography* (Knoxville: University of Tennessee Press, 1992). He is the editor of *The World Turned Upside Down: The American Victory in the War of Independence* (New York: Greenwood Press, 1988) and *The American Revolution: The Home Front* (Carrollton: West Georgia College, 1976). Professor Ferling is the author of nearly two dozen articles in historical magazines and journals and in collections of essays. "John Adams, Diplomat" appeared in the April 1994 *William and Mary Quarterly*. A work in progress is *Ride the Whirlwind: Washington, Adams, and Jefferson in the American Revolution*.

DON HIGGINBOTHAM holds the Dowd Professorship at the University of North Carolina at Chapel Hill. He has served as president of the Southern Historical Association and of the Society for Historians of the Early Republic. He has been a member of the Board of Editors of the *American Historical Review* and the *William and Mary Quarterly*. He has written or edited seven books dealing with early America and military history, two of which have been History Book Club selections.

WARREN R. HOFSTRA is professor of history at Shenandoah University in Winchester, Virginia. He holds M.A. and Ph.D. degrees from

Boston University and the University of Virginia, respectively. In addition to teaching in the fields of American social and cultural history, he directs the Community History Project of Shenandoah University. This endeavor provides him with an opportunity to focus his own research and writing on community studies and the history of the Shenandoah Valley in its various regional settings. In conjunction with this effort he organized and chaired a conference at Shenandoah University in 1989 entitled "George Washington and the Virginia Backcountry," from which the papers in this volume have been drawn. He has published in the fields of social history, vernacular architecture, material culture, geography, archaeology, and economic history. He is interested in how all aspects of material and nonmaterial culture contribute to the historical development of communities and is currently engaged in an extended research project on settlement, social evolution, and landscape in the early Shenandoah Valley.

ROBERT D. MITCHELL is professor of geography at the University of Maryland, College Park. His research interests lie in historical and cultural geography, particularly in European colonization of colonial America, frontier environments, and urban development. He is author of *Commercialism and Frontier: Perspectives on the Early Shenandoah Valley* (Charlottesville, Va.:University Press of Virginia, 1977) and co-editor of *North America: The Historical Geography of a Changing Continent* (Totowa, N.J.: Rowman & Littlefield, 1987), and *Appalachian Frontiers: Settlement, Society and Development in the Preindustrial Era* (Lexington, Ky.: University Press of Kentucky, 1991).

BRUCE A. RAGSDALE is chief historian of the Federal Judicial History Office at the Federal Judicial Center in Washington, D.C. He formerly served as associate historian of the U.S. House of Representatives and is the author of *A Planters' Republic: The Search for Economic Independence in Revolutionary Virginia* (Madison, Wis.: Madison House, 1996).

DOROTHY TWOHIG is editor in chief of the *Papers of George Washington*. She completed graduate work at Columbia University and has served on the staff of *The Dictionary of American Biography*, 1957–1959, Columbia University; as assistant and associate editor of the *Papers of*

Alexander Hamilton at Columbia, 1959–1969; and as associate professor at the University of Virginia. In addition to the published volumes of the Hamilton and Washington papers, she edited *The Journal of the Proceedings of the President, 1793–1797* (Charlottesville: University Press of Virginia, 1981).

Index

Abbot, W. W., 242
Abernethy, Thomas P., 64, 65
Adams, Abigail, 244
Adams, John, 10, 11, 23, 29, 195, 201,
    204, 210–11, 213, 217, 238
Adams, Samuel, 225
Addison, Joseph, 11, 19
Alexandria, Va., 52, 78, 81, 168
Allerton, Isaac, 118
Ambler, Charles H., 64
Anglican Church, 41, 106
Augusta County, Va., 70, 94
    settlement patterns in, 73–74,
        75, 76
    militia service in, 76, 107
    hemp and cattle production, 80

Bacon, Nathaniel, 119
Ball, Joseph (uncle of GW), 162, 227
Baltimore, 52, 78, 79
Banner, Lois W., 234
Barbados, 177
Barth, John Joseph de, 193
Bassett, Burwell, 236
Bayes, John, 231
Baylis, John, 192
Beeman, Richard R., 66
Berkeley, Governor William, 118, 119
Beverley, William, 73, 75

Blue Ridge Mountains, 64
    See also Shenandoah Valley;
        Virginia backcountry
Bouquet, Henry, 125, 133, 150
Borden, Benjamin, Sr., 73
Boyd, Alexander, 78
Braddock, General Edward, 70, 88–
    89, 131, 132, 135, 149, 155, 200,
    211, 215, 223, 229
Breen, Timothy H., 20
Brent, Giles, 118
Bridenbaugh, Carl, 65–66
Brinton, Crane, 224
Brissot de Warville, J. P., 240
Bruin, Bryan, 77, 79
Bryan, Morgan, 95, 101
Burnaby, Andrew, 102
Bush, Daniel, 77, 79
Bush, Philip, 77, 79
Byrd, William II, 16, 238
Byrd, William III, 232

Campbell, John (earl of Loudoun),
    90, 92, 210, 229
Canals, 185, 186
Captain Bullen (Catawba war
    chief), 133
Captain French (Catawba war
    chief), 133

George Washington and the Virginia Backcountry
is typeset in Adobe Minion, a face designed by Robert Slimbach.
It is printed on archival-quality recycled paper.

DESIGNED BY GREGORY M. BRITTON

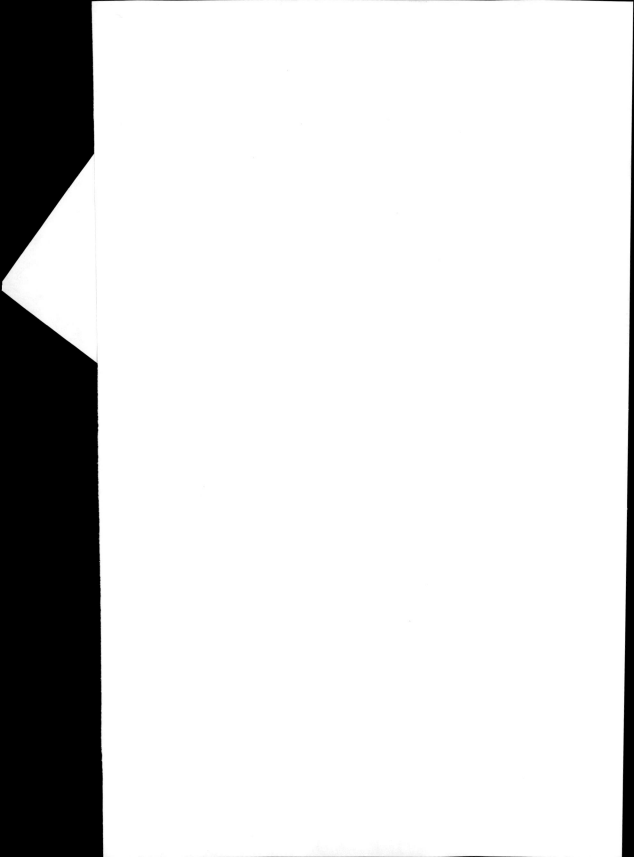

Science Concepts SECOND SERIES

Forces and Motion

Alvin Silverstein, Virginia Silverstein, and Laura Silverstein Nunn

Twenty-First Century Books
Minneapolis

Twenty-First Century Books
A division of Lerner Publishing Group, Inc.
241 First Avenue North
Minneapolis, MN 55401 U.S.A.

Website address: www.lernerbooks.com

Library of Congress Cataloging-in-Publication Data

Forces and motion / by Alvin & Virginia Silverstein & Laura Silverstein Nunn.
        p.   cm. — (Science concepts, second series)
    Includes bibliographical references and index.
    ISBN 978-0-8225-7514-6 (lib. bdg. : alk. paper)
    1. Force and energy—Juvenile literature. 2. Motion—Juvenile literature.
I. Silverstein, Alvin. II. Silverstein, Virginia B. III. Nunn, Laura Silverstein.
IV. Title.
QC73.4.S55 2009
531'.6—dc22   2007048826

Manufactured in the United States of America
1 2 3 4 5 6 – DP – 14 13 12 11 10 09

Contents

chapter one

Is the Force with You?

Are you ready to kick the game-winning field goal? the football player asks himself. He swings his leg back and kicks the ball with tremendous force, sending it flying way up in the air. The ball twists and turns until finally the referee throws his arms up and yells: "It's good!" Without that hard, forceful kick made by the football player, the ball might not have reached its target. Forces at work keep the action going in a football game.

From the first kickoff, the ball and the players are constantly in motion. Usually combinations of forces are working at the same time. Muscle force allows a football player to keep a strong grip on the football. Different muscles produce the forces that launch the ball into the air to be caught by a teammate, who also uses force to jump up into the air and then again to grab hold of the football. The force of gravity then pulls the player down to the ground, which exerts its own force as the player hits the ground.

It is easy to see forces at work in a football game, but forces and motion happen in your daily life all the time. You probably don't even realize it. What are the forces you face every day?

What Is a Force?

A force is a push or a pull. If the force is strong enough, it can make things move. You exert a force when you pull a door open or push it closed. Depending on how much force you use, you can close the door slowly and quietly or slam it shut.

When objects are already moving, forces can make them go faster or slower, or change the direction of their motion. When riding a skateboard, for example, you can make it go faster or slower, depending on how hard you push your foot against the pavement. When you

Many different forces are at work when a football player jumps to catch a pass.

hit a baseball with a bat, the force of your swing is transferred from the bat to the ball when they come in contact. Then the moving ball changes its direction and flies through the air away from your bat.

Forces often work in pairs. If you pull on a rubber band, you can stretch it out. But while you are pulling, the rubber band is also pulling against you. If you let go, the force of the elastic rubber band snaps it back to its original length. And if you pull too hard, with a force greater than the forces holding the rubber band together, it will break.

Forces can vary greatly. You would use much more force, for example, to grip a bowling ball than you would to pick up an egg. (If you used too much force on an egg, you would crack its shell.) The amount of force that is needed depends on the amount of matter an object contains (its mass). The bowling ball is much larger and heavier than an egg, so it would take a much greater force to lift it.

Forces may also be exerted in different directions. When you throw a baseball, you exert a force in the direction you want the ball to go. If you catch the baseball, you exert a force opposite to the direction the ball is traveling and in that way are able to stop its motion.

Forces Add Up

Usually more than one force is exerted on an object at one time. The combination of all the forces that act on an object is called the net force. The net force determines how much the object will move and in what direction. When two forces are exerted in the same direction, they can be added together like an equation. This will produce a net force that is greater than either of the original forces. For example, a bike rider pushes on the pedals to make the bike move. But if the bike starts going downhill, the force of gravity adds to the force of pedaling and the biker reaches the bottom of the hill much faster than if the ground were flat.

When two forces are exerted in opposite directions, the lesser force is subtracted from the greater one. The net force shows that the object will move in the direction of the greater force. For example, when two people engage in an arm wrestling match, they may both exert strong forces for a while as their joined hands sway in one direction and then the other. But eventually, the person who exerts the stronger force will win.

If two forces exerted in opposite directions are equal, they cancel each other and the net force is zero. The object does not move. Thus the net force shows whether an object will move at all and, if so, in what direction. For example, if you sit on a chair, the weight of your body is a force acting downward on the seat of the chair. The chair is exerting an exactly equal and opposite force holding you up. But how can an object like a chair exert a force? The strength of the wood or metal from which the chair was made provides the force to withstand your weight. A chair made of paper would not be strong enough to hold you up.

Units of Force

Forces are measured in units called newtons, named after the English scientist, Sir Isaac Newton (1642-1727), who made many discoveries about forces and the movements they produce. When scientists draw diagrams of forces, they use arrows to indicate the direction in which each force is acting. The longer the arrow, the stronger the force.

Net Force

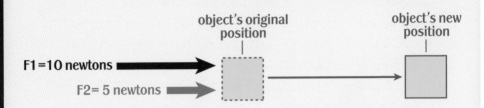

object's original position   object's new position

F1 = 10 newtons
F2 = 5 newtons

F1 (10 newtons) + **F2 (5 newtons)** = **15 newtons total force**

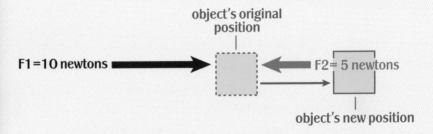

object's original position

F1 = 10 newtons   F2 = 5 newtons

object's new position

F1 (10 newtons) - **F2 (5 newtons)** = **5 newtons total force**

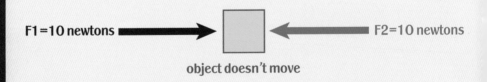

F1 = 10 newtons   F2 = 10 newtons

object doesn't move

F1 (10 newtons) - **F2 (10 newtons)** = **0 newtons total force**

These diagrams show how net force is determined. The force (F), measured in newtons, is added or subtracted depending on which direction the force is acting. The net force tells how far the object would move.

When two opposing forces are exactly equal, there is a balance, or equilibrium. Increasing one of the forces can throw off the balance. If a very heavy person sat down on the chair, for example, it might not be strong enough to hold the person up. It might break, dumping both the sitter and the pieces of the chair onto the floor. There, a new equilibrium will be reached, with the floor holding everything up.

chapter two

Contact Forces

In a game of pool, forces are constantly acting on the balls to send them smacking into other balls on the pool table. The force of your muscles holds the cue stick in place as you tap it against the cue ball. Depending on how you apply your muscle force through the cue stick, your ball may hit other balls and set them rolling. Some balls move in the opposite direction, while others go off at an angle. If you don't apply enough force, the balls may slow down and stop rolling. But if you are lucky, you will knock one or more balls into a pocket. Then the pocket applies its own force to stop the balls' motion.

The forces that move and stop the pool balls are examples of contact forces. They act directly between two objects that are physically touching each other. Almost everything you do involves contact forces. For example, you exert contact forces every time you kick a ball, open a door, or sit on a chair.

This photograph shows the results of contact forces between pool balls. After the player hits the cue ball and the cue ball knocks into the other balls, all the balls scatter in different directions.

Collisions

When a moving car collides with something, such as a tree or another vehicle, it can cause a lot of damage. The damage happens because the car and the object it hits suddenly come in contact. Each exerts a force on the other. The amount of force depends on the speed and the direction in which each object was moving before the crash. When a slowly moving car hits something that is not moving, such as a street sign, the car's fender might be a little dented. Hitting another moving car, however—especially one coming in the opposite direction at high speed—can demolish both vehicles.

Car crashes and the (physical) contact in sports such as pool and football are common examples of collisions. They all involve a sudden, forceful contact between two objects. Typically collisions produce motion or a change in the motion of the objects involved. Collisions may also damage one object or both objects. Boxers, for example, could damage their hands when they throw a punch if they did not wear padded gloves for protection. Padded helmets and other protective gear worn in many sports also help to prevent injury.

Blowing winds are another common example of collision forces. A gentle breeze lifting your hair may feel pleasant on a hot summer day. But storm winds can be much stronger and more violent. Air, blown at high speeds, collides with objects in its path. Hurricane winds can rip trees out of the ground and toss cars and people up into the air. A tornado can lift a whole house off its foundation or smash it to pieces.

Not all contact forces are so sudden and violent. Your fingers exert a gentle, controlled force when you pick up an egg and carry it. When you tap the shell of a hard-boiled egg with a spoon,

Did You Know?

Tropical storms officially become hurricanes when their winds reach 74 miles (119 kilometers) per hour. Hurricane Camille, which hit the coasts of Mississippi and Alabama in 1969, holds the record for highest recorded hurricane wind speed— 190 miles (305 km) per hour. The winds in a tornado blow even faster, reaching more than 200 miles (322 km) per hour.

you apply more force. But it is still a controlled force—just enough to crack the eggshell, not enough to smash the egg. You also use smoothly controlled contact forces to hold a pencil and write on paper or to turn the handlebars to steer your bike. A sailboat relies on wind force to move across the water. Experienced sailors know how to turn the sails to just the right angle to catch the breezes. They can even sail safely through a storm with winds strong enough to overturn the boat.

Sailors use the force of the wind to power their sailboats across the water. Turning the sails lets sailors move in different directions. The more they move with the wind, the faster they go.

Friction

What makes a rolling ball slow down and stop? How does stepping on the brake slow down your bike when you want to stop? In both cases, it is a contact force called friction. This force is produced when the surfaces of two objects rub against each other. The amount of friction depends on how hard the two objects press against each other and on the type of surface. A rough surface will produce more friction than a smooth surface. The less friction there is, the more easily objects can move. But with more friction, more work is required to move the same distance.

Friction slows down or even stops movement. When you kick a ball through the grass, for

What Happens When Your Shoes Are Too Tight?

Your feet are probably growing fast. You'll know it when you need new shoes, because you will start to feel the old ones pressing against your toes. When tight shoes exert a force against your feet, they press on the soft flesh covering your bones—and you feel pain.

While you are sitting, the force of your shoes against your feet and that of your feet against your shoes may be at equilibrium, so you don't notice the

example, friction makes the ball slow down and eventually stop. But on the smooth surface of a school gym, the ball may keep rolling until it hits a wall because the force of friction is weaker. Greasing car engines and other machine parts—coating them with a smooth, oily substance such as machine oil or

Friction causes this soccer ball to slow down when it rolls on the grass. The longer the grass, the more friction. The more friction, the sooner the ball comes to a stop.

tightness. But when you walk, your toes push harder against the shoes, and the shoes push back—ouch!

When you get new shoes, the forces that act as you walk in them may stretch parts of the shoe leather, which eventually molds itself to a comfortable shape. Until that happens, another force may be at work—friction, a rubbing between the shoe and your foot. The constant rubbing may make the outer layers of skin on your heels or toes separate, producing a blister.

graphite—smooths out any rough spots and reduces friction. Without this lubrication, the parts would act like sandpaper, rubbing against one another and wearing down their surfaces. In addition, friction produces heat, so lubrication keeps working parts from overheating.

Friction can sometimes be very helpful. For example, a rough road surface helps your bike tires grip the road. The tread on a bike or car tire makes its own surface uneven and adds to its gripping power. The constant friction between tire and road surface gradually wears down the surface of the tire, however. Eventually, the tire is worn bald—you can no longer see any tread. A bald tire has lost most of its gripping power and is unsafe. It should be replaced.

Creaky Joints

The human skeleton is made up of more than two hundred bones that fit together in joints. Each joint allows the bones to move, so that we can change the positions of our arms, legs, body, and head to walk, pick things up, and do many other things. A slippery, rubberlike material called cartilage coats the ends of the bones. Many joints also contain a watery liquid that helps the bones to slide smoothly over one another.

Without the force of friction, your bike would slide all over the place. You can see this happen when the roads are icy during cold weather. A frozen patch of ice is smooth and produces very little friction. The road becomes slippery for cars that drive over it. Sometimes little friction is good, especially if you like to ski. A skier can slide easily and quickly down a snowy trail because snow creates little friction.

Friction can also happen in the air. This kind of friction is known as air resistance, or drag. You may not be able to see or feel air, but it is filled with many tiny gas particles that are constantly moving. When you ride a bike, for example, these air particles create friction. If you are moving against a wind, you can feel the extra resistance on your face. You also have to pedal harder because the air resistance, like friction on the ground, slows down moving objects. Air resistance is most noticeable when you are moving really fast.

After years of living, humans may have less cartilage and fluid in the joints, so the bones rub against one another and produce friction. This friction makes the bones stick together rather than moving smoothly past one another. People with this condition, called arthritis, have stiff joints. Bending and other movements may be painful. Friction may also wear down the cartilage and even change the shape of the bones. Researchers are trying to find replacements for the cartilage or to develop ways to help the body repair arthritic joints.

Other Contact Forces

A game of tug-of-war is an example of another type of contact force, called tensional force. As two teams on opposite ends of a rope exert forces, they stretch and tighten the rope, transmitting tension through it. At the same time, the tension pulls equally on the people on either end of the rope.

If you jump on your bed, you are creating a spring force. This contact force happens when a spring that is compressed (squeezed together) or stretched exerts a force on an object that is in contact with it.

A game of tug-of-war determines which team can create more tensional force.

When you jump on your bed, the contact with your mattress compresses the springs inside it. As you rise in the air, the compressed springs then return to their original shape and exert a force that bounces you upward.

Experiment: Lifting Weights

Try this: Close your eyes and hold out your hands, palms up. Have a friend put a 1-pound (0.5 kilogram) weight in one hand and a 5-pound (2.3 kg) weight in the other. Can you tell which hand is holding the heavier weight? How do you know?

Next, have the friend take the weights and put the 1-pound (0.5 kg) weight in one of your hands and a 2-pound (0.9 kg) weight in the other. Can you tell which is the heavier one? Switch the weights to the opposite hand and try it again.

Your body has many tiny sensors in your skin, muscles, and joints. They respond to changes in pressure when a force acts on you. Nerves carry messages from these sensors to your brain, with information about the strength of the force. So you can easily tell the difference, for example, between the weights of a Ping-Pong ball, a golf ball, and a bowling ball. Your brain also figures out how much force your muscles must exert to hold an object or lift it.

chapter three

Forces at a Distance

You have probably heard that the English physicist and mathematician Sir Isaac Newton discovered gravity when an apple fell from a tree and hit him on the head. That's not exactly true, though. The idea of gravity as a force that holds things close to Earth had already been known for more than a century before Newton was born. Yet, Newton made further observations about the force of gravity at work.

While sitting by a window one day and gazing out at the garden, Newton watched an apple fall from a tree. He began to wonder why apples always fall straight down and never sideways or up. He also wondered whether gravity might work farther from Earth—even as far as the Moon. If so, it must be gravity that was holding the Moon in an orbit around Earth.

Newton figured that the strength of gravity would grow weaker as an object's distance from Earth increased. He worked out an equation to describe the relationship between distance and gravity. Then he used his equation to calculate the Moon's orbit—and it agreed with what astronomers (scientists who study objects outside of Earth's atmosphere) had observed. Newton thought that gravity was also responsible for the movements of the other planets in the solar system. His new law of "universal gravitation" was the first to describe, in mathematical terms, this force and its effects.

Although gravity is a force, it is not actually a contact force. It acts on objects at a distance—it does not touch them. Other forces that act at a distance include magnetism and electric force.

Sir Isaac Newton did not actually discover gravity as many people believe, but he did form the laws of gravity.

Gravity

Gravity is a force that pulls objects together. When you drop a rock, it falls to the ground. It is the pull of gravity that makes the rock fall when you let it go. Gravity also holds the planets of the solar system in orbit around the Sun. It even operates (although *very* weakly) between the Sun and distant stars.

Everything on Earth is affected by gravity. Any objects that have mass will produce a gravitational force. Some objects have a stronger gravitational pull than others. The more mass an object has, the stronger its gravitational force. When a bee sits on a flower, the pull of gravity between them is weak.

The same is true for two friends chatting together. But the gravitational pull of Earth is very strong. That's because Earth has such a large mass—about 6.5 sextillion tons (5.9 sextillion metric tons)! That's really heavy. Without Earth's gravity, you would float off into space.

You can feel the pull of gravity every time you walk on the ground, or when you pick up a ball or some other object. The pull of Earth's gravity on an object is a force called weight. In common speech, people often use *mass* and *weight* as synonyms. Actually, though, they are not the same thing. Mass, as mentioned earlier, is the amount of matter in an object. But the pull of gravity on that object is what gives it weight. In addition, your mass will always stay the same, but your weight can change, depending on where you are (in space). If, for example, you go to the Moon or another

How Much Do You Weigh?

The Sun's large mass—330,000 times larger than Earth's—gives it a much greater gravitational pull than that of any of the planets. So a person who weighs 100 pounds (45 kg) on Earth would weigh 2,800 pounds (1,270 kg) on the Sun. Mercury has the smallest mass of all the planets in our solar system and, therefore, the least gravitational pull. A 100-pound (45 kg) earthling would weigh only 38 pounds (17 kg) on Mercury.

Forces and Motion

planet, the gravitational pull is different from that on Earth, so your weight will be different there than it is on Earth even though your mass is the same in both places.

Mass is not the only thing determining how great the pull of gravity will be. The distance between two objects is also important. Gravity is very strong when the objects are close together. But as they get farther and farther apart, the gravitational pull is weaker. So you can walk on the surface of Earth without any fear of falling off because you and the planet are so close together.

A spaceship heading for the Moon, however, has rocket-powered engines that can overcome Earth's pull. As the ship gets close to its destination, the Moon's gravity begins to pull on it. Astronauts walking on the Moon will not fall off, but they can jump much higher than they can on Earth because the Moon's mass is much smaller than that of our planet. You would have to travel far out into space before the pull of Earth's gravity completely stopped acting on you.

Black Holes: A Space Vacuum Cleaner

Out in space, the pull of gravity is very weak. A black hole, however, is a dark region in space that exerts a tremendous force of gravity. It is like a gigantic vacuum cleaner, sucking in anything that gets too close—a star, a planet, a cloud of gas, or even light. Any matter that enters a black hole is crushed by powerful gravity until it disappears into "nothingness." Not even light can escape a black hole, so it remains dark and invisible.

Magnetism

Magnetism is another force that works at a distance. If you take a bar magnet and move it over a pile of metal paper clips, a strong attraction (force) will draw the paper clips to the magnet. The paper clips will cluster mostly around the ends of the magnet, called poles, where the force is very strong. The end that points toward the north is called the north pole, and the end that points toward the south is called the south pole.

This person is using a bar magnet to pick up paper clips. The different colors of the magnet mark the north and south poles.

Experiment: Try This!

You can make a paper clip chain using a magnet. If you take a magnet and move it over a pile of paper clips, the magnetic force will pull the paper clips to it. You will notice that the paper clips will start to hang off one another, dangling from the magnet. How do the lower paper clips hang on if they aren't touching the magnet? The magnetic force of the magnet travels through the paper clips, magnetizing them. Each paper clip is now acting as a magnet too. Even if you take the original magnet away, the paper clips will still cling together and attract small metal objects for a little while. They will gradually lose their weak magnetism, though, and the chain will fall apart.

Magnetism has very specific rules. It will work only with objects made of certain metals, such as iron and steel, but not for things made of plastic, rubber, or paper. Magnetism, like other forces at a distance, is strongest when two magnets are fairly close together. As the distance between them increases, the attraction (or repulsion) quickly drops.

If you experiment with two bar magnets, you will notice another interesting thing. When you move the north pole of one magnet close to the north pole of another magnet, you can feel the magnets repelling each other (pushing apart). The same thing happens if you put two south poles near one another. When the north pole of a magnet is brought near the south pole of another magnet, however, the two magnets will attract each other (pull together) and stick together tightly. You have to exert a lot of force to move them apart. Here is a simple way to remember this basic rule of magnetism—like poles repel, unlike poles attract.

You can also do a little magic trick using magnetism. Put a pile of paper clips on a table surface. You can move the paper clips around the table without ever touching them. Just move a strong magnet underneath the table and you will see the paper clips move around, following the pull of the magnet's force. This shows that magnetic force can work through materials, such as a wooden table. It can also exert a force through your hand and even through water.

Electricity

Magnetism is closely related to electricity, another force that works at a distance. In fact, scientists sometimes consider the two forces as a single force, called electromagnetism.

Every time you switch on a light, turn on the TV, or play video games, you are using electricity. But how are forces involved in electricity? Atoms— the tiny particles that make up our bodies and all the other matter on Earth—contain even smaller particles, some of which carry electric charges. These are protons, which carry a positive electric charge, and electrons, which carry a negative electric charge.

Normally, the number of protons in an atom is exactly the same as the number of electrons. Their charges cancel each other out, and the atom as a whole remains electrically neutral. But an atom can gain or lose electrons in a chemical reaction or if it bumps into an electron of another atom. If an atom gains some electrons, it becomes negatively charged. If an atom loses some electrons, it becomes positively charged. Inside the power cords that help run electrical appliances are thin wires of copper, a metal that can give up electrons. Electric current is carried by electrons moving along the copper wire.

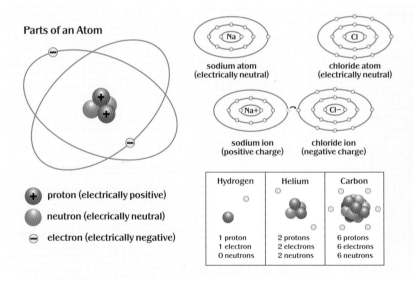

Atoms have three parts: protons, neutrons, and electrons. Protons and neutrons are at the center of the atom, and electrons circle around them. When an atom loses or gains an electron, it becomes electrically charged and is called an ion. The diagram on the top right shows an ion forming. The box in the lower corner shows the atoms of some common elements.

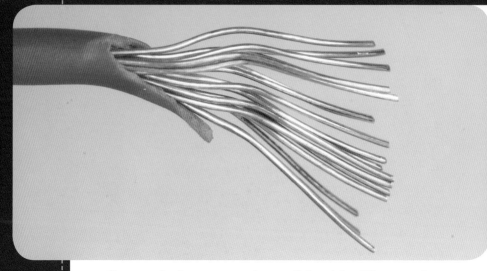

Copper wire is a great conductor of electricity. The atoms in the copper quickly move one electron to the next.

Every charged particle is surrounded by an electric field—a space in which the electrical charge exerts a force. In such a field, charged particles can exert an electrical force on one another, even when they are not physically touching. Just like a magnet, atoms with unlike charges are attracted to one another, and like charges repel one another.

Have you ever rubbed a balloon against your head? If you then hold the balloon 2 inches (5 centimeters) from your head, some of your hairs will stick straight out in the direction of the balloon. Why does this happen? When you rub a balloon against your hair, the balloon takes some of the electrons from your hair. The balloon becomes negatively charged and your hair positively charged. So when you bring the balloon close to your hair again, strands of hair are attracted to the balloon. (This is known as static electricity.)

If you put the balloon against a wall, it may even stick there. The wall is electrically neutral, but the electrons on the balloon repel the electrons in the outer layer of the wall, leaving many of the wall's atoms positively charged. Therefore, an electrical force can be exerted between a charged object and a neutral one. Electrical forces can also work between two negatively charged objects. For example, if you rub two balloons against your hair and then try to hang them close together, they will repel each other.

Every one of your hairs has millions of electrons. Rubbing the balloon against your hair transfers some of these electrons to the balloon.

chapter four

Forces at Work

Many people do not like working. But work is more than having a job, doing your chores, or getting your homework done. In science, *work* has a very specific meaning. Work is what happens when a force makes an object move. Work is done when you sit down, lift weights, dance, or kick a soccer ball.

The amount of work done depends on the strength of the force and how far the object is moved in the direction of the force. For example, it takes more work to kick a soccer ball than it does for you to sit down in a chair.

Work uses energy. When work is performed, energy is needed to overcome resistance to movement. When you try to lift a heavy book bag, for example, the bag's weight (created by gravity) goes against (resists) your efforts. You must use energy to do the work of lifting the book bag. The more work you do, the more energy you use.

Kinds of Energy

There are two main types of energy—potential and kinetic. Potential energy is stored energy that has the potential to perform work. For example, a big rock that sits on top of a hill has potential energy. The rock is not actively doing work but could do so because of its position. When gravity causes the rock to roll down the hill, the potential energy turns into kinetic energy.

Kinetic energy, or the energy of motion, is a form of energy that is actively performing work. (*Kinetic* comes from a Greek word meaning "motion.") Potential energy can be converted (changed) to kinetic energy and vice versa. Pushing the big rock back up the hill involves kinetic energy, which is turned into potential energy once the rock is resting on top of the hill.

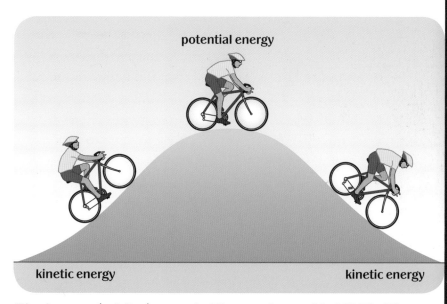

Kinetic energy (pedaling) moves the bike up to the top of the hill. The biker can coast down the other side as potential energy is converted to the kinetic energy that turns the wheels.

Kinetic and potential energy can exist in many different forms. Kinetic energy may include light energy, heat energy, mechanical energy, electrical energy, magnetism, and gravitational energy.

Potential energy can also include all these kinds of energy and some others, as well. Chemical energy, for example, is a kind of energy that is stored in the bonds that hold atoms together in molecules. The stored energy, or potential energy, is turned into kinetic energy when these bonds are broken and a chemical reaction occurs. The digestion of food and the explosion of a stick of dynamite are both examples of this kind of energy conversion.

Nuclear energy is a form of energy that is stored within atoms. Normally the inner structure of an atom remains unchanged. But under certain

Scientists working for the U.S. government detonated the world's first atomic bomb on July 16, 1945, in New Mexico.

conditions, a nuclear reaction may occur, changing the structure of the atom. In a nuclear reaction, some of the matter in the atoms is actually converted to energy. This is what happened in the atomic bombs that were used in 1945 at the end of World War II (1939–1945).

The various forms of energy can be converted into other forms of energy. For example, electrical energy can change into heat, sound, and light energy to operate a toaster, a telephone, and a lightbulb. Heat energy is turned into mechanical energy to make a car's engine perform. Your body stores the energy from foods in chemical forms—sugars, starches, and fats. When you lift your hand to turn the pages of a book, your muscles change chemical energy to electrical energy. (Your nerves and muscles use the chemical energy stored in sugar to power the electrical signals that travel from your brain to your hand to make it move.) Some of your stored energy is also changed into mechanical energy as your muscles move your hand against the resistance of gravity.

Taking Shape

Forces can have different effects on objects. We have seen how forces often cause movement, or they may cancel one another out, and the object doesn't move at all. Forces can also do a different kind of work—changing the shape or form of matter. The digestion of food, for example, changes large, complicated food chemicals into smaller chemicals so they can pass into the body's cells. The cells may make further changes, building the simple chemicals into proteins and other complex materials and working parts of your body.

Some substances, such as rubber, can change their shape when forces act on them. Rubber is elastic. That is, it has an ability to stretch into a new form—as long as a force is acting on it. When the force is taken away, however, the elastic substance springs back to its original shape. You can stretch a rubber band to two or three times its length. But when you let go, it snaps back to its original size.

Some substances, such as clay, are not elastic. They keep their new form. You can exert force on clay, molding it to whatever shape you want. After you are done molding it, the clay will stay in its new form, unless forces act on it again. Heating the clay in an oven can make the clay's form more permanent. (It can break, but you can't reshape it.)

How Much Work?

What do you think would take more work: carrying a 20-pound (9 kg) bag of cement to a garage 30 feet (9 meters) away or carrying a 5-pound (2.3 kg) bag of cement to the same place? It makes sense to say that it takes more work to move a heavier object than a lighter one. That is true.

Would it take more work to move the 5-pound (2.3 kg) bag of cement to the garage or to a shed 100 feet (30 m) away? The shed, of course. When you move an object a greater distance, you are doing more work than if you moved the same object a shorter distance. The amount of work you do depends on the amount of force you exert, as well as the distance the object is moved.

Scientists call the unit of work (the amount of force multiplied by the distance) a joule, named after James Prescott Joule, a British physicist who researched the scientific principle of work in the mid-1800s. You would have to exert 45 joules of work to carry the 5-pound (2.3 kg) bag of cement 30 feet (9 m) and 180 joules to carry the 20-pound (9 kg) bag the same distance.

James Prescott Joule studied heat and energy in the mid-1800s. The unit of work, a joule, was named after him.

chapter five

Simple Machines

When you think about machines, you probably picture a car, a tractor, or a bulldozer. But a machine is actually any device that performs work. It can also be a pair of scissors, a screwdriver, or even a broom. These are simple machines. There are six main types of simple machines—the lever, the wheel and axle, the pulley, the inclined plane, the wedge, and the screw. Complex machines, such as drills, cranes, and tractors, are combinations of simple machines that work together. Machines do not change the amount of work that has to be done. They just make work easier to do.

A machine needs energy to work, but it cannot create energy. The more work that has to be done, the more energy is needed. Most machines are not very efficient. Some of the energy supplied to the machine is lost due to the friction of the parts. Much of the energy in the fuel that runs a car engine, for example, is lost as heat that is carried off into the air by the

Backhoes and bulldozers are complex machines. Builders use them to move dirt when preparing land for construction.

car's exhaust. The efficiency of a typical car engine is only 25 percent! (That means that only 25 percent of the energy the engine uses actually does useful work.) Oiling the engine parts can reduce friction and cut down the heat loss, but friction cannot be eliminated completely.

A simple lever, on the other hand, is a machine with high efficiency. Using a lever involves very little friction, so it performs almost as much work as the amount of energy put in. You use simple machines to help you do things every single day. Let's find out more about how they work.

Levers

Have you ever used a screwdriver to pry open the lid of a paint can? Or swung at a ball with a baseball bat? Maybe you have been on a seesaw, riding on one end while a friend rode on the

A seesaw is an example of a first-class lever.

other. If so, then you already know about a simple machine called a lever. A screwdriver (when used as a pry bar), a baseball bat, and a seesaw are all levers.

A lever is a long rigid bar that pivots, or turns around a fixed point, called a fulcrum. The fulcrum is needed to support the lever. Otherwise, the lever will not work. Think of a hammer, for example, as a basic type of lever. If you try pulling a nail out of a wall with your bare hands, it is not going to come out very easily. The claw end of a hammer is a lever that rests against a fixed point on the wall (its fulcrum) as you exert force on the handle. As you move the hammer, the claw pulls the nail out of the wall. The lever makes the job a lot easier.

A lever is made up of three parts—the fulcrum, effort force, and resistance force (or load). The fulcrum is the pivoting point on a surface that supports the lever. The effort force is the work being done on the lever. The resistance is the object that you are trying to move or lift, such as the nail (lifted by the hammer).

Levers can be separated into three different classes—first-class levers, second-class levers, and third-class levers. Each class differs, depending on the position of the fulcrum, the amount of effort, and the amount of resistance.

First-class levers: A seesaw is an example of a first-class lever. If you sit on one end of a seesaw and a friend sits on the other end, you take turns going up and down. As you push yourself up, the force pushes your friend down. In a first-class lever, the fulcrum (the pivoting point at the center of the seesaw) is located between the effort force (you) and the resistance force (your friend). The effort and the resistance

Body Levers

When you watch a baseball game, it's an awesome sight when the pitcher winds up and then throws a fast ball right into the catcher's mitt with great speed. A baseball pitcher's arm works like a lever. The muscles in the forearm provide the force, the ball provides the resistance, and the fulcrum is the elbow joint. Actually, other levers are also operating as the pitcher throws the ball, with fulcrums in the wrist, shoulder, ankles, knees, and hips. These levers all help to increase the force that makes the ball move. You use these body levers, too—every time you walk, run, throw a ball, or kick a ball.

move in opposite directions. The effort moves down in order to lift the resistance up. If you move closer to the fulcrum, however, you will have a harder time lifting your friend into the air. For this reason, longer levers usually work better (i.e., with less effort) than shorter ones. Other examples of first-class levers are scissors (a double first-class lever), a crowbar, and a claw hammer.

Second-class levers: A wheelbarrow allows you to move a load that would be too heavy to carry. It combines two simple machines. One of them is a second-class lever. Unlike the first-class lever, the resistance (load) is located between the effort and the fulcrum. In this case, the fulcrum is located at one end of the lever—the wheel. Usually the fulcrum of a second-class lever is close to the load—the dirt or objects you are carrying in the wheelbarrow. At the other end of the lever (the effort), you exert force as you lift the handles to move the wheelbarrow. Other examples of second-class levers include a bottle opener, a nutcracker, and a paper cutter.

Third-class levers: A broom is an example of a third-class lever. The effort is located between the resistance and the fulcrum. When you use a broom to sweep up dust on the floor, the fulcrum is the hand holding the upper part of the broom, the effort is the hand that is pushing the broom, and the load (or resistance) is the dust that you are sweeping along the floor. Other kinds of third-class levers are a shovel, a fishing pole, a baseball bat, and tweezers.

The class of a lever is determined by where the fulcrum, load, and effort are in relationship to one another. This diagram shows the three classes of levers.

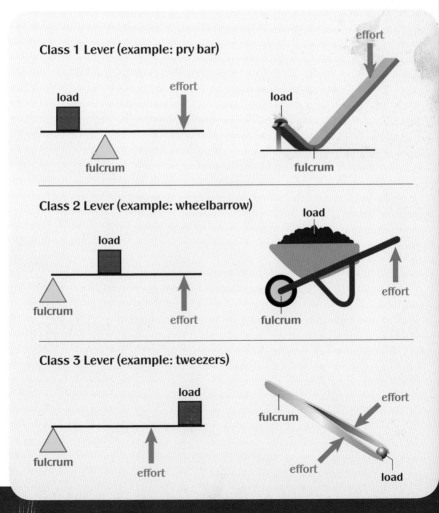

Class 1 Lever (example: pry bar)

load

effort

fulcrum

effort

load

fulcrum

Class 2 Lever (example: wheelbarrow)

load

fulcrum

effort

load

fulcrum

effort

Class 3 Lever (example: tweezers)

load

fulcrum

effort

fulcrum

effort

effort

load

The Wheel and Axle

Wheels are actually circular levers. They turn on an axle, a bar or rod that goes through the center of the wheel. Just as all levers need a fulcrum to work, all wheels need an axle. Even though the wheel moves, turning through a full circle, the axle does not move at all.

When you ride a bike, you exert force by pushing down on the pedals. The pedals are attached to the wheel by a chain. The chain carries the force to the wheel and makes it turn. As the

This bicycle uses a wheel and axle to make it easier for you to get from place to place.

Forces and Motion

wheel turns, its tire pushes against the road surface and moves the bike. Friction helps it grip the road without slipping backward. Thus, friction makes the bike move forward and also makes the front wheel turn. The faster you pedal your bike, the faster the wheels move.

Another example of a wheel and axle is the wheel on a wheelbarrow. This wheel works together with a second-class lever to move loads. The wheels on roller skates, bikes, and cars help get us from one place to another, sometimes across very big distances. A doorknob is also a kind of wheel. We turn doorknobs to open doors that allow us to get from one room into another. Airplane propellers and helicopter blades are also examples of a wheel and axle at work. The power produced by these machines allows the aircraft to move through the air. A screwdriver in its normal use (turning screws) is a wheel and axle too. A small effort turning the handle of the screwdriver produces a much larger turn of the screw. (A screw is a different kind of machine, however, which is discussed later.)

The Pulley

When the chain on a bike goes around the gears—the two small, grooved wheels toward the back of the bike—it is acting as a pulley, another simple machine. A pulley is a grooved wheel that turns on an axle and uses a rope, a belt, or a chain to lift loads or change the direction of force. When you ride a bike, the force you exert on the pedals makes the chain move. The chain is wrapped around the pulley, which turns it and causes the bike's wheel to rotate on its axle.

What Is a Gear?

Gears are wheels with teeth, or pegs, on their edges. Gears work in pairs. The teeth of two gears mesh together and turn in opposite directions. Gears at work can change both force and motion. Gears are not always the same size. For example, if one gear is larger than the other, the larger gear will turn more slowly but exert a greater force. The gears on a bike work as both pulleys and gears.

Raising a flag on a flagpole uses a pulley system. A rope tied to a flag is threaded through the groove around the pulley at the top of the flagpole and runs down the pole. You pull the end of the rope downward against the resistance (load), and the flag is lifted up toward the top of the flagpole. Pulleys are also used to raise the sails on a boat, open and close curtains or miniblinds, raise and lower an elevator, and lift hay into a hayloft.

The bicycle and flagpole are examples of a fixed pulley. This type of pulley does not move. It is attached to something. A fixed pulley does only one thing. It changes the direction of the force. It does not change the strength of a force, the distance over which it acts, or the speed of the movement produced.

Another type of pulley is called a movable pulley. A movable pulley moves both the load and the pulley.

The movable pulley moves along a rope or wire. The rope is wrapped around a wheel attached to a surface. The wheel supports the load, and the load moves in the same direction as the force applied to the rope. The movable pulley uses half the effort to lift or move a load, but the distance you can move it is limited. To move a load 1 foot (30 centimeters), you would have to pull the rope 2 feet (61 cm). Movable pulleys (often combined with a fixed pulley) are commonly used to handle heavy loads on construction sites and in auto repair shops.

A compound pulley combines a fixed pulley with a movable pulley. This type of pulley gives the best of both pulley effects. You use less effort to lift a load, and you lift the load by pulling downward. This is much easier than pulling up, since gravity helps in downward motions.

A fixed pulley helps raise a flag to the top of a flagpole.

Did You Know?
Stunts you may have seen on TV, where a person slides down a long rope while holding onto a pulley, use the ability of this simple machine to reduce effort and increase speed.

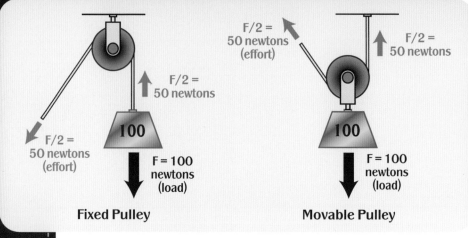

Pulleys make lifting heavy loads easier. The type of pulley depends on whether or not the pulley moves with the load.

Combinations of pulleys can be used to lift very heavy loads. A construction crane, for example, uses multiple pulleys to lift and carry heavy equipment. That way, the crane uses less force because the effort is applied over a longer distance.

The Inclined Plane

Would you rather climb straight up a mountain or walk up a road that winds slowly around the mountain to the top? You would probably choose the winding road because it is not so steep and it takes less effort to walk rather than climb. The winding road is actually an example of a simple machine called the inclined plane. An inclined plane is a sloping surface with one raised end.

Like other simple machines, an inclined plane is used to do work with less effort. But the amount

The winding road up this mesa (a flat-topped piece of land with steep sides) in Utah is an example of an inclined plane. Although it will take longer, it will be less work to follow the road than to climb the mesa straight up the side.

of work depends on the angle of the plane. For example, the smaller the angle, the less effort is needed. That explains why following the road up the mountain is easier than climbing the mountain directly. However, you have to travel a greater distance if you take the winding road. The extra distance may take more time. In this way, the inclined plane trades distance (and time) for effort.

A ramp is another example of an inclined plane. Using a ramp makes it easier to lift heavy things. For example, lifting a barrel that weighs 75 pounds (34 kg) onto a platform 6 feet (1.8 m) off the ground can be challenging, even for a strong person. But the work can be a lot easier to do if the person rolls the

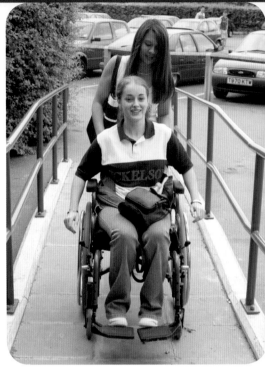

Ramps are another example of an inclined plane. They help people with wheelchairs get from one height to another.

barrel up a ramp and onto the platform. It may take a little extra time, but it takes a lot less effort.

The Wedge

When you bite into an apple, your teeth act like a wedge, a simple machine that can be used to split an object into two pieces. You cannot eat an apple whole, so your teeth exert force, cutting the larger piece of food into smaller pieces to make the food easier to eat. A wedge is thick at one end and gradually thins out toward the other end. It is actually a kind of inclined plane. Sometimes a wedge is made from two inclined planes back-to-back (a double inclined plane). Unlike a simple inclined plane, the back-to-back version is movable.

A wedge is used to exert force between two objects. This force can be applied in different ways—a wedge can split an object or hold objects together. Just as your teeth work like a wedge to slice through an apple, an ax is also a wedge that splits a log into two pieces. A nail is an example of a

A wedge such as this ax works as a double inclined plane to force two objects apart. In this case, the ax forces the two halves of the log apart. Wedges can also be used to hold things together, such as a doorstop between a door and the floor.

wedge being used to hold two objects together. You use a hammer to force the nail into place through two objects. The nail acts as a wedge, connecting one thing to another, such as one piece of wood to another. A doorstop is a wedge that is placed in the space between the door and the floor to hold them together and keep the door from moving.

We use wedges in everyday life. For example, zippers are wedges that help open and close clothes. Other kinds of everyday wedges include a pencil sharpener, a cheese grater, a knife, and a shovel. Wedges work better when the edge is very thin. For example, sharpening the blade of a steel knife will make the knife cut better than one that has a dull blade.

The Screw

In most cases, no matter how hard you try, you would not be able to pull a screw straight out of a piece of wood, even if you used the claw of a hammer. Like the wedge, the screw is a simple machine that is a form of inclined plane. The inclined plane of a screw is not straight, though. It is wrapped around a cylinder, forming a spiral. The ridges of the spiraled plane are called the threads of the screw.

Usually a screw has a pointed wedge at its tip. Like a nail, when force is applied, this wedge bites into wood or other solid materials. Turning the screw with a screwdriver inserted into the head of the screw drives it in farther. A screw holds more tightly than a nail. To take it out, you would have to unscrew it by turning the screwdriver in the opposite direction.

A bolt is a screw with a flat tip. It is used to fasten together hard metal parts, one of which has a threaded hole into which the bolt is screwed. If the angles of the threads on the bolt and hole are different, the bolt jams and cannot be screwed in. Examples of bolts are lightbulbs, jar lids, the blades of a fan, airplane propellers, and helicopter blades.

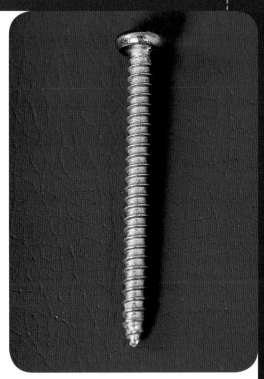

Screws are inclined planes wrapped around a cylinder. The inclined plane, called the thread, is visible on this screw.

chapter six

Forces in Fluids

Most of our planet—more than 70 percent—is covered with water. If you have ever gone swimming, you know that the forces that work in water are different from those on dry land. The water helps hold up the weight of your body. With very little effort, you can float. However, it takes more effort to push your way through water than it does to move through air. The resistance, or drag, is greater in water than in air.

The animals and plants that live in the water or spend a lot of time there have adapted in various ways to the conditions of their watery homes. The fins of a fish, for example, help it move efficiently through the water. Fins are lightweight and provide a lot of surface area to push against the water. Like birds, fish and other water animals usually have a streamlined body, with smooth curves that reduce drag.

Like other liquids, water flows. It moves easily from one place to another without external force being applied. (Solids require the application of an outside force to move.) Scientists use the term *fluid* for substances that flow. Fluids include liquids as well as gases, such as air and carbon dioxide. In fact, we live in an "ocean" of air.

Just like everything on Earth, air is filled with molecules—tiny particles too small to see without a powerful microscope. Far fewer molecules are in a gas like air than in a liquid like water. In fact, so few molecules exist in air that we usually don't feel them. (We do feel air molecules when the wind is blowing—they bounce off our skin with greater force than usual.) Some animals

When we feel wind, we are actually feeling air molecules bounce off our skin more forcefully than usual.

can fly, moving through air in much the same way as fish move through water.

Floating through the Air

Up in the sky, as it soars with its wings spread out wide, a bird appears as though it were floating on a sea of air. Birds have special adaptations for flight. Air can flow smoothly over their sleek, streamlined bodies without much resistance. Their wings can lift them off the ground and keep them airborne. Powerful chest muscles allow the bird to spread its wings and flap them up and down for movement through air.

Birds are much lighter than other animals of the same size. Their bones are partly hollow with a honeycomb structure inside. The framework provides strength, while the air pockets keep the bones light. Feathers provide a warm outer covering without adding much weight. The main flight feathers, called primaries, are located at the tips of the wings and can spread out like fingers. They help the bird rise into the air, steer, and soar across the sky.

Condors, like other birds, have bodies that are ideal for moving through air.

Catching a Ride

A condor is an enormous bird that uses warm rising air currents, called thermals, to lift it through the air. These air pockets heat up near the sun-warmed ground and rise to great heights. A condor normally flies at altitudes of 3,000 to 6,000 feet (about 900 to 1,800 m). But by using thermals, this bird is capable of soaring up to more than 15,000 feet (more than 4,500 m)—about the same altitude as small airplanes fly. Catching a ride on the thermals, a condor can soar for hours without flapping its wings.

Forces and Motion

Airplanes are designed to have some of the same qualities that birds have. An airplane's body is streamlined so that it can move smoothly through the air. The wings are curved, as well, so that the air above them moves faster than the air below them. The fast-moving air above the wings exerts pressure downward, while the slower-moving air underneath exerts pressure upward. The faster-moving air creates less pressure than the slower air. The difference in the pressures creates a force called lift, which lifts the plane into the air. In fact, the earliest airplanes were gliders, which used the natural lift of air currents to carry the planes hundreds of feet.

The force that moves an airplane is produced by engines that burn fuel for energy. In the early planes, this energy was used to turn propellers at the front of the plane. The pinwheel-like propellers had slanted blades that turned around an axle.

Some airplanes use propellers to create a force that moves the plane forward. Helicopters also use propellers to move through the air.

The movement of the propeller produced a pressure difference between the front and back of the blades, which pushed the plane forward. This forward-pushing force is called thrust. Some modern airplanes still use propellers, and so do helicopters.

Many planes, including jumbo airliners, are powered by jet engines. Air flowing into the front opening of a jet engine is compressed (tightly packed) and sent into a combustion area where a stream of fuel is burned. The energy produced when the compressed air and burning fuel explode sends a powerful jet of exhaust gases out the back of the engine. This backward flow of gas pushes the plane forward. Jet engines also provide the thrust needed to lift rockets and spaceships off the ground and into space.

Jet engines and rockets use the force of exhaust moving out of the engine to propel them forward or upward.

A hot air balloon doesn't need an engine to move through the air. It works on the basic scientific concept that hot air rises, while colder air falls. A hot air balloon is made up of three important parts—the burner (to heat the air), the balloon envelope (to hold the air), and the basket (to carry the passengers). To get the balloon to rise, fuel released from an onboard propane tank is ignited by burners, which then heat the air in the balloon envelope above. As the air molecules heat up, they start to move very fast.

Hot air balloons rise because the molecules in hot air are moving faster and spread out more than cold air molecules. The expanding molecules of hot air rise above the denser molecules of cold air.

The moving molecules bang into one another, forcing them to expand (spread out). The expanding air molecules push the balloon up into the air. As the air in the balloon cools down, the balloon starts to fall. By controlling the temperature of the balloon's air, passengers in the hot air balloon can control the movement of the craft.

Under Pressure

You probably don't feel it, but air is constantly pressing down on you with tremendous force. This pushing force is called air pressure, or atmospheric pressure. Air pressure exerts a force because billions of air molecules are banging into one another as they zoom back and forth. The total force of our planet's atmosphere—which is measured by weight—is about 5.75 quadrillion tons (5.2 quadrillion metric tons)! That comes to about 14.7 pounds for every square inch (1 kg per sq. cm), or about 1 ton (0.9 metric ton) of weight on your entire body. Then why don't you feel it? The fluids in your body exert their own pressure outward. For example, your lungs contain air and your cells and blood vessels contain liquids. At Earth's surface, the outward pressure exactly balances the air pressure acting on your body.

Why Do Your Ears Pop?

Have you ever been in an airplane and noticed that your ears start to pop as the plane climbs into the sky? That's because of a change in air pressure. The same thing may happen when you ride up in an elevator. At sea level, the air pressure outside your body is the same as the pressure of the fluids inside your body. As altitude increases, though, the atmosphere contains fewer gas molecules, so the air

Air pressure decreases the higher up you are from Earth's surface. That is because the force of gravity drops very quickly as the distance between two objects (you and Earth's surface in this case) increases. Earth's gravitational pull on the air molecules that form the atmosphere gets weaker as the altitude (height as a measure of distance) increases. With less gravity to hold them in place, fewer and fewer air molecules make up Earth's atmosphere at greater distances from its surface. So the atmosphere is much thicker close to the surface than it is on mountaintops.

Higher still, where airplanes fly and where spaceships go, the atmosphere gets thinner and thinner, with fewer molecules in the same size volume of air. The air pressure of the thinner atmosphere is lower. Still higher—out in space—no molecules exist at all. Scientists call a volume of space with no air molecules a vacuum. A vacuum can be created artificially here on Earth by pumping all the air molecules out of a container.

pressure is lower. When you are on a plane, the air trapped inside the tubes leading from your ears to your throat is at a higher pressure than the air outside your body. This difference in pressure makes your eardrums bulge outward, so your ears may pop as the tubes inside adjust. Swallowing can help release the pressure. Chewing gum during takeoff can help too. Chewing makes more saliva flow into your mouth, so you swallow more often.

Outer space is a vacuum. That means that outer space has no gas molecules and, therefore, no friction. Without friction to slow movement, objects in space just keep moving.

Everyday examples of a vacuum include vacuum-packed food packages and the vacuum tubes at drive-in banks. (Actually, not all the air molecules are pumped out of the vacuum tubes or the vacuum cleaners that suck up dust and dirt. They work on a partial vacuum.)

Pressure works not only in gases such as our atmosphere but also in liquids and solids. Water, for example, is heavier than air. That is, a volume of water weighs more than the same volume of air. The deeper you go underwater, the more water is above you. And you are experiencing not only the weight of the water above you, but also the weight of the air pressure that is pressing down on the water. This means that the pressure at the ocean bottom is much greater than the pressure at the surface.

Deep-sea divers breathe from tanks containing pressurized air. They wear special suits that contain air to balance the water pressure of the ocean. But even the best diving suits cannot handle the pressure in some of the deepest parts of the ocean where the seafloor is 6 miles (10 km) below the surface. There the pressure is one thousand times the pressure at the surface!

The nature of pressure includes not only its pushing force but also the area on which it is pressing. When you are standing still, for example, the weight of your body is pressing down on an area the size of the soles of your feet. But when you walk, the same body weight pushes on a much smaller area—first under the heel of one foot, then the sole, and finally the front part of your foot. You are therefore putting more pressure on a smaller area than when you were standing. In fact, the spike heels of some women's shoes place the whole weight of the body on such a small area of the floor that walking can actually make dents in a wood or linoleum floor!

This atmospheric diving suit allows a diver to reach depths of up to 2,000 feet (609 m) by keeping the pressure inside the suit constant.

On Their Toes

A ballerina wears special toe shoes for dance moves that place her entire body weight on the tips of her big toes. The shoes have special supports and padding to help her toes hold up all that weight. Even so, ballerinas sometimes break a toe bone when they land the wrong way after a leap.

If you try to walk on light, fluffy snow when you are wearing ordinary boots, you will sink in and leave deep footprints. But you can walk on the surface of the same light snow without sinking if you wear snowshoes or skis. The snowshoes and skis spread your weight out over a larger area on the snow surface so you don't sink. Some animals, such as snowshoe rabbits, have broad, furry feet that act as natural snowshoes in their winter home.

Snowshoes and the feet of showshoe rabbits work on the same principle. By spreading out the weight over a larger surface, the snowshoes and a rabbit's feet put less pressure on the snow. Then it doesn't collapse as much under the weight.

Floating and Sinking

If you throw a beach ball into a pool, it will make a little splash but then sit right on the surface of the water. It floats! The same thing will happen if you throw an apple into the pool, although it may go a little deeper in the water than the beach ball. What about a pebble or a penny? These things will sink right to the bottom. Why? It seems as though these objects, which are much smaller than a beach ball or an apple, would float, not sink. It's not the size that counts, however. Whether an object floats or sinks depends on buoyancy.

Buoyancy is the tendency of an object to float or rise when it is placed underwater. Buoyancy is caused by an upward force, called upthrust, that water exerts on floating objects. When an apple falls into a pool, some of the water is displaced, or pushed aside. The apple takes up the space where the water once was, and the level of the water rises slightly. The water pushes against the apple with a large enough force to keep it from sinking below the surface. An object will float if the

Eureka!

More than two thousand years ago, Greek mathematician Archimedes came up with a theory, now known as Archimedes' principle: The upward force of an object in a fluid is equal to the weight of the displaced fluid. According to legend, Archimedes made this discovery after noticing the water level rise as he got into his bath. Supposedly, he was so excited that he ran through the streets naked, yelling "Eureka! Eureka!" (Eureka is a Greek word meaning "I have found it.")

upthrust is the same as or greater than the weight of the object. You can feel this upthrust if you try to hold the apple underwater.

Why does one object float, while another object of the same surface size sinks? The reason is that one object may have a different density than the other. Density is the amount of matter in an object (its mass) divided by the volume it takes up. A beach ball is mostly filled with air, so its overall density is much

Water striders use surface tension to walk on water.

lighter than that of water. An apple also floats, even though it is solid all the way through. That's because its insides are made mostly of water. So the apple's density is close to that of the water in the pool. But if an object weighs more than the water it displaces, the object will sink. A rock is dense—it has more mass than a beach ball or an apple. The rock will sink because the upward force of the water is not strong enough to keep it at the surface.

How is it that a ship so enormous in size—and made of dense iron and steel—can float on water? Iron and steel are denser than water. A solid piece of iron would sink in a pool of water. But if that piece of iron were hollowed out in the shape of a bowl, it would have air inside it—and air is less dense than water. So a ship can be made of dense iron and steel, but on the inside, there is plenty of air to keep the ship afloat in deep water. The overall density of the ship (the hollow iron and steel shell plus the air inside it) is lower than that of the water. The large amount of water displaced by the ship is the same as the ship's weight—basically, the weight of the iron and steel in it. For this reason, ships require deep water to float.

Just like ships, submarines are iron-and-steel machines that can float in the water. But unlike ships, subs can also travel underneath the water's surface. Large tanks in a submarine are filled partly with water and partly with air. When a sub is traveling on the surface, the amount of air in the tanks is controlled to keep the sub afloat. For the craft to dive, air is released from the tanks and water is pumped in to take its place. With water in the tanks, the sub becomes denser and therefore heavier, causing it to sink below the surface. To get back up to the surface, compressed air (air under high pressure,

Scientists use this submarine to explore deep-sea environments. Submarines use tanks that can hold air or water to move from the surface to the depths of the ocean.

greater than the air pressure in the atmosphere at sea level) is pumped into the tank. The compressed air forces some of the water out, making the sub less dense—so it rises to the surface.

Fluid Power

What happens if you shake up a can of carbonated soft drink and then open it? A spray of foam shoots out. The can contains both liquid and a gas, carbon dioxide, which manufacturers forced into it under pressure. Applying a force to a gas such as air or carbon dioxide compresses it—that is, the pressure squeezes the same number of gas molecules into a smaller space. Shaking the can makes the molecules move faster, raising the pressure further and colliding with the liquid molecules. The constant collisions stir up the mixture of gas and liquid into a bubble-filled foam. Opening the can relieves the pressure and lets the foam gush out.

Gas under pressure can be used in machines to do work. A fire extinguisher, for example, is filled with compressed carbon dioxide. Pressing the handle releases the gas, which mixes internally (inside the container) with water and detergent and shoots out in a forceful jet of foam. The rubber tires of bicycles, cars, and trucks are filled with air under pressure. Filled with air, they are much lighter than they would be if they were filled with solid rubber, so less power is needed to make the vehicle move.

Fire extinguishers use fluid power to shoot out foam that puts out fires.

A pneumatic drill (used in construction) uses air that has been compressed to a very high pressure—ten times the usual pressure of the atmosphere. An air compressor driven by a diesel engine supplies high-pressure air to the pneumatic drill through a heavy-duty hose. The operator pushes down on the drill handle to let air in. High-pressure air sends the drill pounding down into the ground with enormous force. As the high-pressure air flows through the tubes inside the drill, a valve inside the tool flips over and makes the air flow the opposite way. Then the drill moves upward. The drill pounds up and down fifteen hundred times a minute. It can quickly break up pavement or roadway and even crack large rocks.

Unlike gases, liquids generally cannot be compressed. Applying pressure to liquids can change the direction in which they flow, but they

Pneumatic drills use compressed air for tough jobs like removing a cement sidewalk.

still take up the same amount of space. If you apply pressure to a liquid in a tube, the force will pass through the liquid and move it from one end to the other. This is how a tube of toothpaste works, for example. Depending on the sizes of the openings in the tube, the liquid can increase the force of the pressure you exert and do some useful work. A number of modern machines use hydraulic systems—that is, systems that rely on liquids to do work.

A water pistol is a hydraulic system. When you press the trigger, you apply force (pressure) to the water inside the pistol. This pressure pushes the water out through the nozzle, a very narrow opening. Because you are forcing a fairly large amount of water through a very small hole, it squirts out at a much higher speed than the rate at which you squeezed the trigger. (Liquid, pushed by the same amount of force, flows faster through a small opening than through a larger one.) A squeeze bottle with dishwashing fluid works the same way. Squeezing the bottle makes the liquid squirt out of the nozzle. If you took the nozzle top off and then squeezed, the liquid would flow out much more slowly.

The brake system of a car or truck is also a hydraulic

Did You Know?

The word *hydraulic* comes from the Greek word for water. But modern hydraulic machines usually use oil or other fluids rather than water. That is because water leaks easily, soaks into seals and gaskets, and causes metals to rust.

system. It is more complicated than a squeeze bottle, though. Pressing down on the brake pedal inside the car applies force to the narrow opening of the hydraulic brake system. The pressure forces fluid inside to flow through tubes to the brake pads and presses them against discs in the car's wheels. The contact between the brake pads and the discs produces friction, which slows down the spinning

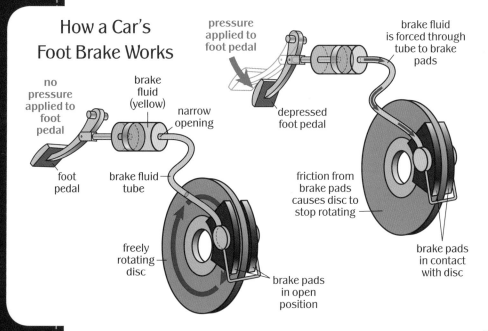

How a Car's Foot Brake Works

pressure applied to foot pedal

brake fluid is forced through tube to brake pads

no pressure applied to foot pedal

brake fluid (yellow)

narrow opening

depressed foot pedal

foot pedal

brake fluid tube

friction from brake pads causes disc to stop rotating

freely rotating disc

brake pads in open position

brake pads in contact with disc

Applying pressure to a car's brake pedal forces the hydraulic fluid through a tube to the brake pads, which press on the discs in the car's wheels. Friction slows down the spinning wheels. The hydraulic brake system multiplies the amount of force applied by the driver's foot, making it great enough to stop the car.

wheel and stops the car. The opening in the hydraulic system where the brake's force is applied is much smaller than the area of the brake pads. But the pressure remains constant all through the hydraulic fluid in the system. That means that the total force exerted on the brake pads is much greater than the force placed on the brake pedal. Just like the simple machines described in Chapter 5, this hydraulic system is a way to increase force and to do more work.

chapter seven

What's in Motion?

When you are sitting in a chair, are you in motion?

Are you in motion if you get up from the chair and

walk across the room? Are you in motion while you

are reading this book? An object is in motion when it

changes position from one place to another. So if you

are sitting still in a chair, you are not changing your

position, and therefore, you are not in motion. If you

are reading a book while sitting down, you are still not

in motion. Parts of you may be in motion, however.

Your eyes are moving as they follow the words in the

book, and your hand and fingers move when they flip

the pages. And you are definitely in motion when you

get up from your seat and walk across the room.

The Nature of Motion

How fast can you run? Not as fast as a car or a train.
You are probably used to thinking of "how fast" in

Looks Can Be Deceiving

We can usually tell if something is moving or not. If you fly a paper airplane through the air, you can see that it is moving. When we look at cars or buses, we can see that they are moving. But sometimes, objects look as if they are moving when they are really motionless. For example, when you sit in the back seat of a moving car and look outside, what do you see? The trees, houses, and parked cars are all whizzing by your window. They look as if they are moving, but in reality, they are not. You are moving in relation to these objects. So it appears they are too.

terms of speed—for example, in miles or kilometers per hour. (A champion runner who can run a "four-minute mile" is moving 15 miles [24 km] per hour. Race cars may go up to 200 miles [322 km] per hour or more.) Scientists who study the motion of objects are also interested in the speed of their motion, but they usually talk about velocity instead of speed. Velocity includes not only an object's speed but also the direction in which it is moving. A car may speed up or slow down as it moves through traffic. But even if its speed stays the same, its velocity will change if it goes around a curve or turns a corner.

Observing changes in velocity helps us understand how objects interact with one another and with the world around them. A change in velocity—whether it is an increase or decrease in speed or a change in direction—is called acceleration. The cars in a roller-coaster ride, for instance, are constantly accelerating: speeding up as they zoom downward, slowing down as they go up the next rise, and changing direction as they swing around turns. Usually, slowing down is called negative acceleration, or deceleration.

Although gravity makes objects fall, it is not the only force that determines how fast they fall. As an object falls, air molecules exert an upward force against it, providing resistance to its fall. At first it speeds up (accelerates) rapidly under the force of gravity. But as the object's speed increases, so does the air resistance. So although the object is still accelerating,

A roller-coaster car is constantly changing speed and direction. This is called acceleration.

it is doing so at a slower rate. Eventually, the resistance may be great enough to equal the weight of the object. Then the object stops accelerating. (Although it is still falling fast, it is not speeding up or slowing down.) It has reached what is called its terminal velocity. If you drop a ball off a table, it would not travel far enough to reach its terminal velocity.

When skydivers jump out of a plane, however, they are high enough to reach their terminal velocity. This speed varies, depending on the skydiver's weight and position. On average, it is about 120 miles (193 km) per hour, which is much too fast for a safe landing. However, the terminal velocity also depends on the surface area of the falling object. Skydivers stretch out their arms and legs to make their body surface larger. Air resistance over

A skydiver's terminal velocity changes depending on his or her position.

the larger surface slows down the fall, allowing the diver to enjoy the free fall longer. Divers ensure a safe landing by using a parachute, which spreads out and greatly increases the surface area.

The Laws of Motion

For thousands of years, scientists have been trying to figure out how and why objects move. It was not until the mid-1600s, however, that the causes of motion were accurately described by Sir Isaac Newton. In his now-famous three laws of motion, Newton describes various aspects of how forces and motion work.

Newton's First Law: *An object will stay at rest or continue to move in a straight line at a constant speed unless a force acts on it.* If you are in the back seat of

Falling Down

If you dropped a bowling ball and a golf ball off a tall building at the same time, both would hit the ground at the same time. You might think the bowling ball would get there first because it is heavier and, therefore, the force working against air resistance would be greater. However, gravity accelerates all objects at the same rate. The bowling ball would make a bigger dent in the ground, though, because its mass is so much greater and it hits with greater force.

a moving car and the driver suddenly slams on the brakes, the force exerted by the brakes to stop the car produces an immediate decrease in the car's velocity. Does your body stop suddenly too? That depends on whether you were wearing a seatbelt. While the car is moving, your body is moving at the same speed as the car. But when the car stops, your body continues moving forward if you are not wearing a seatbelt. You might not stop until you hit the windshield. If you are wearing a seatbelt, though, the seatbelt transmits the braking force through the frame of the car to you. This force stops your motion.

Newton's first law of motion is often called the law of inertia. Inertia is the tendency of a moving object to stay in motion unless an outside force acts on it. Inertia is also what keeps an object motionless unless a force acts on it to put it in motion. Usually objects resist being moved or changing their speed or direction. Only a force can move them. That brings us to Newton's second law.

If you dropped a golf ball and a feather off a tall building at the same time, the golf ball would hit the ground sooner. The feather is so light and its surface area is so large in comparison to its weight that the air resistance is enough to slow its fall. In a vacuum, however, a feather, a golf ball, and a bowling ball would all fall at the same rate. There are no air molecules in a vacuum to produce friction, which slows down moving objects.

Newton's Second Law: *The acceleration of an object is equal to the force acting on it divided by the object's mass.* The amount of force needed to move an object depends on how much inertia it has. Heavy objects have more mass—and more inertia—than light objects. So it takes more force to move a heavy object than it does to move a light object. Hitting a golf ball with a golf club, for example, sends it flying out from the tee. If you used the same amount of force to hit a bowling ball with a golf club, however, the result would be quite different. The impact might accelerate the much heavier bowling ball barely enough to roll it off the tee. (You'd probably break the golf club too.) Similarly, it takes much more force to throw a bowling ball than to throw a baseball because the mass and inertia of the bowling ball are much greater.

Newton's Third Law: *When one object exerts a force on another, the second object exerts an equal and opposite force on the first.* You may have heard this law stated in a different way: for every action, there is an equal but opposite reaction. Like any force, the reaction can change the direction and speed of an object's motion. A squid uses jet propulsion when it wants to make a fast getaway. Normally it uses its fins to swim, just as fish do. Meanwhile, it stores some of the water it "breathes" inside its elastic body. If it spots a predator or prey, it turns on the speed by contracting its body and shooting out a jet of water through a funnel-shaped opening. The squid points its funnel backward to move forward to pounce on prey. To escape a

Like a squid, an octopus moves through the water using jet propulsion. This octopus is also releasing ink to protect itself.

predator, it turns the funnel forward and jets backward. Using Newton's Third Law, a squid can move through the water at more than 25 miles (40 km) per hour.

Keep Moving

How much of a change in motion do a force and its reaction produce? That depends on the momentum. Momentum is a measure of an object's inertia, its tendency to keep moving at the same velocity. An object's momentum can be calculated by multiplying its mass by its velocity. Large objects usually have a greater momentum than smaller ones. Fast-moving objects usually have a greater momentum than slower ones. The greater an object's momentum, the more force would be needed to stop its motion. For example, you could easily stop a shopping cart that was rolling toward you, but you would not be strong enough to stop a car moving toward you at the same velocity.

Whenever a force produces a change in velocity, the momentum of the whole system remains unchanged. For example, when a batter swings a bat and hits a ball, the velocities of both bat and ball change suddenly. The ball, which was speeding toward home plate, is stopped by the bat (decelerated)

The impact of the ball and the bat causes the velocities of both to change suddenly, but the momentum of the whole system remains the same.

and then given a new velocity in a different direction. The momentum of the bat is transferred to the ball. Depending on how the ball was hit and how much force the batter put into the swing, the ball may pop up into the air, bounce down to the ground, or go flying out into the outfield or even over the wall for a home run. Its momentum changes dramatically.

But the ball exerted a force on the bat when it was hit. Part of its momentum was transferred to the bat, changing its motion in turn. The force was also transmitted through the bat to the batter's arms and body. And so, although the momentum of the bat, ball, and batter all changed individually, the overall momentum of the system (in this case, the bat + ball + batter) stayed the same.

If the force from the bat is great enough to send the ball flying out into center field, then why doesn't the force of the ball on the bat send the batter flying back toward the catcher's mitt? The reason is that the ball's mass is much smaller than that of the bat and batter. So it produces a much smaller change in the batter's momentum. Velocity is important too. A batter has to exert a lot of force to hit a home run off a slow curveball. A speeding fast ball has a much greater momentum, which is transferred to the bat and then back to the ball when it is hit.

A turning wheel has its own momentum, which means it tends to keep turning in a circle. This is called angular momentum. If you switch off an electric fan, for example, its blades will keep on rotating for a while. But without the force of the electric motor to drive the blades, friction will gradually slow their motion. Eventually the blades will stop moving until the fan is switched on again.

Moving in a Circle

Moving objects tend to keep moving in a straight line because of inertia. But when you swing a ball on a string around in a circle, the string exerts a force on the ball that pulls in toward the center of the circle. This force is called centripetal force. Meanwhile, the moving ball exerts an opposite force on the string, pulling outward. This force is called centrifugal force. If the string breaks, where will the ball go? Because of inertia, the ball will continue on a straight line in the direction it was moving when the string broke.

centripetal force

centrifugal force

Centripetal force and centrifugal force work in opposite directions. Centripetal force pulls inward and centrifugal force pulls outward.

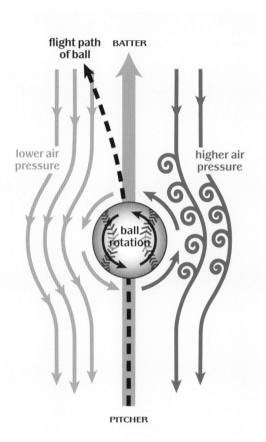

flight path
of ball BATTER

lower air
pressure

higher air
pressure

ball
rotation

PITCHER

When pitchers throw a curveball or slider, they add spin to the ball. This spin causes different pressures on different sides of the ball and then causes the flight path of the ball to curve.

Good bowlers use angular momentum to hook the ball. Careful placing of the fingers and a twist of the wrist make the ball spin as it rolls. Instead of going straight down the lane, it travels a path that suddenly curves just before it smacks into the pins. The curving path of the ball hits the pins at an angle and scatters them. The falling pins may then knock other pins down. Baseball players also use angular momentum when they throw curveballs and sliders. The curving motion of the ball makes it harder for the batter to predict its path.

Motion and Gravity

chapter eight

In ancient times, it seemed obvious to everyone that the Sun, the Moon, and the stars all move around our planet Earth. People could see it with their own eyes. The Sun rose in the east every morning, traveled across the sky over the course of the day, and set in the west in the evening. At night the Moon and stars also moved across the sky, each in their own paths. But as we have already learned, seeing can be deceiving when moving objects are involved. We see things from our own position in space, and their apparent movements are relative to where we are.

In the early 1500s, a Polish astronomer named Nicolaus Copernicus (1473–1543) proposed a revolutionary idea. Earth is not the center of the universe, he said. It is just one of the planets that revolve (move in a curving path, or orbit) around the Sun. Copernicus did not convince many people during his lifetime.

A century later, however, Italian astronomer Galileo Galilei (1564–1642) looked at the sky for the first time with a telescope, a device that gave a greatly magnified view. He was able to see planets and moons close-up and record their movements night after night. From his measurements and calculations, Galileo decided that Copernicus was right. Earth and the other planets do move in orbits around the Sun.

Galileo was able to plot the orbits of the planets and

> **Did You Know?**
> Many scientists believe that the force that started stars and planets moving in the first place is what remained of a great explosion that formed the universe. They call that explosion the big bang.

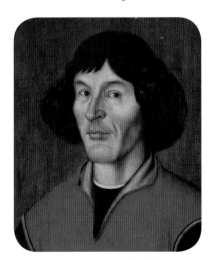

Nicolaus Copernicus (left) *and Galileo Galilei* (right) *both believed that the Sun, not Earth, was the center of the universe before the idea was universally accepted.*

even calculate the orbits of four smaller bodies—
moons—around the planet Jupiter. He published
his findings in 1632. Since then scientists have built
more powerful telescopes and made new discoveries.
They have even found planets revolving around
distant stars.

A Matter of Gravity

As we have seen, gravity is the force that makes
planets move in orbits around their stars. Without
gravity, the planets would travel in straight lines. But
stars are much larger than planets, so the gravitational
force they exert is greater. The Sun, for example,
constantly pulls on Earth and changes the direction
of its motion from a straight line to a curve. As the
motion continues, the curve closes into a nearly
circular orbit.

Actually, the orbits of Earth and the other
planets are not true circles but rather ellipses—sort
of squashed circles. This was first noted in the
seventeenth century by German astronomer Johannes
Kepler (1571–1630). Because its orbit is not perfectly
circular, Earth is farther from the Sun at certain times
of the year than at other times. Kepler also observed
that planets move faster when they are closer to the
Sun than when they are farther away.

The size of a planet's orbit depends on its
distance from the star around which it revolves. In
our solar system, Mercury is the closest planet to

Moving Light

How can we see stars that are so very far away? The same way we see everything else: light rays from the stars travel through space to our eyes and brain, where they are sorted into images. Stars produce these light rays by nuclear reactions that change some of their matter into energy. We see other objects, including planets and moons, by way of light rays that are reflected (bounced) off these objects. In these cases, too, the light rays must move to reach our eyes.

How fast does light move? About 186,000 miles (300,000 km) per second—that is, about 700 million miles (1,127 million km) per hour—when it is traveling through the vacuum of space. The distance between stars is measured in light-years—the distance traveled by light in a year. The closest star to our Sun is Proxima Centauri, located about 4.2 light-years away.

the Sun and therefore has the smallest orbit. Neptune is the farthest and has the largest orbit. (Earth is the third planet from the Sun.) A complete trip around an orbit makes up a planet's year.

In addition to their movements around the Sun, Earth and the other planets also rotate (turn) around an axis (an imaginary line from the North Pole to the South Pole). One complete turn around its axis makes up a planet's day. Earth's rotation is the reason for the Sun's apparent movement through the sky. The half of the planet facing the Sun has daylight, while it is nighttime on the other half. As for the movements of the Moon— the ancients got that one right. The Moon does revolve around Earth.

The Sun and other stars also move through space. The stars in our Milky Way Galaxy, for example, form a spiral that turns like a pinwheel. Gravitational attraction between stars influences their movements.

Modern Astronomy

Modern astronomers are still using Newton's law of universal gravitation to learn more about the universe. For example, some stars seem to wobble as they move through the sky, instead of traveling in a straight line. This effect may be caused by planets orbiting around the stars, as Earth revolves around the Sun. As the planets move in their orbits, their gravitational force pulls their star first in one direction and then in the other. From these small changes in the motions of the stars, astronomers can calculate where to look for the planets that caused them.

Planet	Average Distance from the Sun	Rotation (day)	Revolution (year)
Mercury	 36 million miles (58 million km)	59 Earth days	88 Earth days
Venus	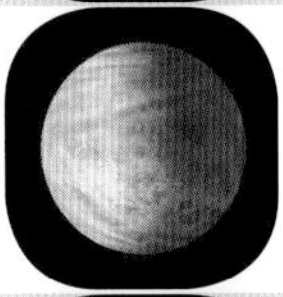 67 million miles (108 million km)	243 Earth days	225 Earth days
Earth	 93 million miles (150 million km)	23 hours 56 minutes	365.24 days
Mars	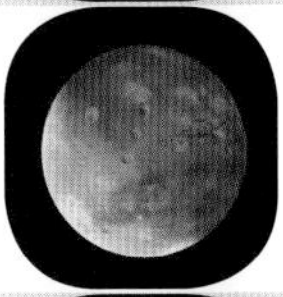 142 million miles (228 million km)	24 hours 37 minutes	687 Earth days
Jupiter	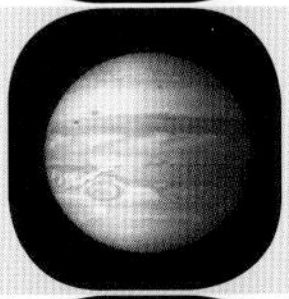 484 million miles (779 million km)	10 hours	12 Earth years
Saturn	 886 million miles (1.43 billion km)	10 hours 39 minutes	29 Earth years
Uranus	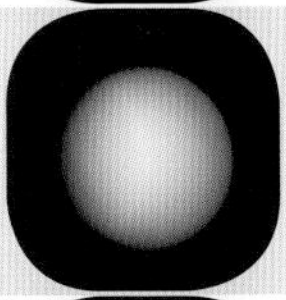 1.78 billion miles (2.86 billion km)	17 hours	84 Earth years
Neptune	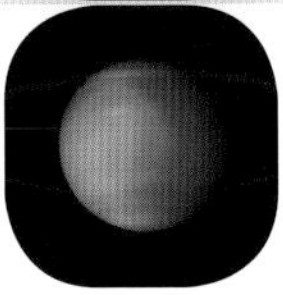 2.79 billion miles (4.49 billion km)	16 hours	164 Earth years

Pluto is not shown here because the International Astronomical Union demoted it in 2006 from planet to dwarf planet.

Gravity on Earth

Why is it so tiring when you have to stand still in one place for a long time? Your body is not in motion, so it might seem as if you are not doing any work. Actually, though, your muscles are constantly taking turns the whole time, contracting to hold you up against the pull of gravity and to keep you from tipping over.

If you lean forward or to the side, it gets really hard to keep from falling. The reason for that is that gravity is pulling on every part of your body and pulling harder on the heavier parts and those closest to the ground. When you lean forward, some heavy parts—your head and chest—get lower and are pulled down harder. Like any irregularly shaped object, your body acts as though its weight were centered at one point. This point is called the center of gravity. The force of gravity pulling on this point is equal to the average of the forces pulling on all of your body parts. When you are standing straight, your center of gravity is located somewhere around your waist, directly above the place where your legs separate. (Men usually have a somewhat higher center of gravity than women because, on the average, their shoulders and chests are broader and heavier, and their hips are narrower than those of women.) But when you are leaning forward or to the side, the center of gravity shifts toward parts of the body that are not as well supported. This shift makes it hard to avoid falling.

Body Senses

In addition to your five senses, you have a special set of sense organs that tell you where all your body parts are and whether you are in danger of falling over. Some of these sense organs are in your muscles and joints. Balance organs inside your ears let you know if you are right side up. Your brain also uses information on what your eyes are seeing to figure out where everything is. If you are moving and changing direction rapidly, the messages from the sense organs in your ears may not agree with those from your muscles and joints. Then you get dizzy and may fall down.

Staying right side up is easier for most four-legged animals than it is for people. The center of gravity of a four-legged animal, such as a cat or a horse, is roughly in the middle of its body. Standing, the animal balances its weight among the four legs, which provide solid support. When it walks, a four-legged animal usually lifts only one leg off the ground at a time, leaving the other three on the ground. The animal's body is supported by this tripod, or three-legged stance, just like the legs of a three-legged stool. A four-legged animal's legs also take turns moving when it runs, but the second leg leaves the ground before the first one is back down. So a running horse or cat, for example, balances on two legs at a time. This is more difficult than balancing on a stable tripod of three legs.

A six-legged insect has even more support for its body when it is standing still. When it walks, it typically steps out with three legs (two on one side and one on the other) and then takes the next step with the other three legs. When it is moving, it is always supported by a tripod, just like a four-legged animal is while walking.

In general, larger animals can run faster than smaller ones. The cheetah is the fastest land animal.

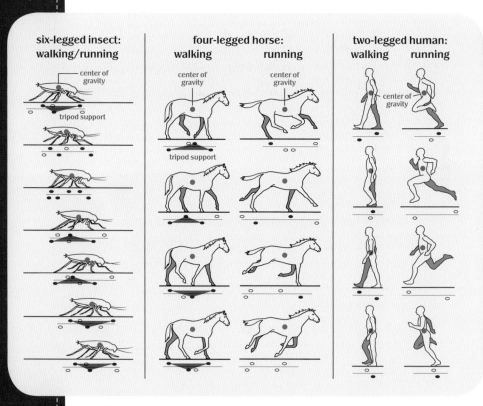

The more legs that touch the ground, the more stable an animal is.

These cats have been clocked at speeds up to 70 to 75 miles (113 to 121 km) per hour, but only in short sprints lasting about fifteen seconds. Very large animals cannot move that fast. Elephants, for example, can't run at all! They weigh so much that their skeletons are not strong enough to support them on just two legs at a time. (If you see a video of elephants "running," look at their feet. They are really just walking very fast, picking up one foot at a time.)

Humans and other two-legged animals have to balance on only two supports when standing still. When they walk, their full weight is supported by just one foot at a time while the other foot is off the ground. In running, part of the time both feet are off the ground at the same time. That is really difficult because it takes more coordination and balance than if we had four or six legs.

Training Wheels

You probably first learned to ride a bike using a tricycle (three-wheeler) or a bicycle with training wheels (two big wheels plus an extra pair of small ones in back). These bikes are much more stable and not as hard to balance because their center of gravity lies midway between three or four supports instead of between just two. Out on the highway, motorcycles—which have only two wheels—are less stable (and more accident-prone) than automobiles, which have four wheels. Big trucks may have more sets of wheels, for even greater stability for balancing a lot of weight while moving.

Some land animals leap when they want to move fast and far. They have very large, strong hind legs that can push them up into the air. Good leapers are found among many groups of animals and include fleas, frogs, and kangaroos. (Kangaroos get some extra jumping help from their long, strong tails, which help them jump and provide tripod support when they are standing.) Animals' jumps can cover quite a distance. The 12-inch (30 cm) leap of a flea may not seem very impressive compared to the 26 feet (8 m) a kangaroo can jump, but consider this: A kangaroo can leap a distance about five times its height. A flea's leap covers two hundred times its body length!

Jumping and leaping involve tremendous forces on the legs and feet. Coming down, the jumper picks

Kangaroos use their strong hind legs and their tail to jump large distances.

Forces and Motion

up kinetic energy due to the acceleration of gravity. When the jumper hits the ground, the ground does not move. It exerts a force strong enough to stop the jumper's motion instantly. This force acts on the jumper's leg and foot bones and the ropy tendons that connect the leg muscles to them. The Achilles tendons, which connect a person's calf muscles to the heels, can withstand a force of more than 1,000 pounds (more than 450 kg). Even so, athletes and ballet dancers, who leap and jump, may suffer painful injuries to these heavy-duty tendons.

Locomotion (moving around) in the water is easier in some ways than moving on land. The buoyancy of the water works against gravity and helps hold you up. You expend less energy and can concentrate on moving in the direction you want to go. Most land animals move through water by paddling (back-and-forth movements of the limbs) or kicking (forceful pushes with strong hind legs) or by a combination of both. The webbed feet of animals that spend a lot of time in the water, such as ducks and frogs, make these

Ducks have webbed feet to help them push more water with each stroke. Scuba divers use flippers to mimic the webbed feet of ducks.

movements more effective by applying the force over a larger surface.

Full-time water dwellers such as fish and dolphins move through the water by waving their streamlined bodies back and forth, propelled by powerful thrusts of a fanlike tail. (Fish tails are generally vertical and flap from side to side. Whales, dolphins, and other sea mammals have tail fins that are horizontal and flap up and down.) Movements of fins or flippers may help in steering. Some sea dwellers, including squids and octopuses, use jet propulsion to move, squirting out a stream of water under pressure in the direction opposite to their movement. The force of the jet may be great enough to blast a squid right out of the water. Some squids can glide through the air for up to 200 feet (61 m) before splashing down.

Copying Nature's Designs

Studying the way animals move can provide ideas on improving our lives as well. People have incorporated some features of animal locomotion into the designs of vehicles that travel on land, through the water, and in the air. Researchers trying to increase the speed of boats and ships, for example, have been studying dolphins for years. There is practically no drag and turbulence as water flows smoothly over a dolphin's body. Yet the streamlining of its body is not enough to explain how it can swim so fast—up to 30 miles (50 km) per hour.

In 2004 a team of Japanese physicists discovered how the dolphin's soft skin greatly decreases friction. Dolphin skin is covered with tiny ripples, small moving folds that run along the length of its body. The constant movement of these little ridges keeps the water around the dolphin calm as it glides through the water, thereby reducing the friction that slows movement.

In addition, its skin produces a kind of lubricant that helps keep it soft. A dolphin constantly sheds flakes of dead skin from its outer surface. (The cells in the outer skin layer last an average of only two hours.) The soft flakes of skin help to break up tiny whirlpools in the water, preventing turbulence. The researchers have built models of dolphin skin, using a soft silicon-rubber plate coated with tiny pieces of film that

Dolphins have skin that flakes off and moves under the pressure of water. This creates very little friction and allows the animals to move easily through water.

gradually peel off. They are working to improve this artificial dolphin skin in order to use it as an outer covering for boats, ocean liners, and submarines.

Velcro fasteners are another practical example of the science of biomimetics—copying devices

Morphing Wings

Some birds change the shape of their wings, depending on how fast they are flying. Scientists at Penn State University in State College, Pennsylvania, used these bird wings as a model for designing a special kind of mechanical wing called a morphing aircraft wing. These wings change shape according to the speed and duration of the flight. To come up with the flexible structure and covering for the wings, scientists borrowed an idea from fish. The surface of the morphing wings is covered with scales that can slide over one another. According to the researchers, morphing aircraft wings will be useful for small surveillance planes, which need to fly rapidly to and from their target site and fly around at slow speed while making observations. Small wings are more efficient for fast flight, but long, narrow wings are better for long flights at slow speeds. With morphing wings, the same plane can do both.

in nature to improve tools and machines. A Swiss engineer invented Velcro in 1948 after looking closely at the burrs he was picking off his dog's fur. The burrs had tiny hooks that clung to the fur. Velcro works similarly. It has two parts: one with stiff hooks like those on the burrs and the other with soft loops like those in cloth. The two parts stick together to hold tightly but can be pulled apart to open the fastener. More recently, researchers discovered that geckos (a lizardlike animal of the tropics) are able to climb smooth surfaces and even walk upside down on the ceiling using tiny Velcro-like hooks on their feet.

Scientists and engineers are using their knowledge of forces and motion to build roads and bridges that are better able to handle increasing traffic. They are also making safer and more efficient vehicles to travel them. They are designing houses that can withstand severe storms and even earthquakes. The sports we play are also being improved by the use of scientific principles of forces and motion. New materials and construction for balls, bats, and other sports equipment bring new challenges for athletes. Better designed helmets and other protective gear help to keep the players safe and healthy. The knowledge of how forces and motion work and interact is basic to almost every part of our modern lives.

Glossary

acceleration: a change in speed or direction of an object

air pressure: the pushing force exerted by the molecules of the atmosphere; also called atmospheric pressure

angular momentum: a measure of the tendency of a turning object to continue turning in a circle

atoms: microscopic particles that make up matter. Atoms contain even tinier particles.

axle: a bar or rod that goes through the center of a wheel

biomimetics: the study and use of methods and devices of natural organisms in designing machines

black hole: a dark region of space caused by the collapse of a massive star. A black hole's gravitational pull is so strong that it sucks in anything that gets too close to it, including light.

buoyancy: the tendency of an object to float or rise when it is placed underwater

center of gravity: the point around which the weight of an object is evenly balanced. In calculations of forces, the object's entire weight may be considered concentrated at this point.

centrifugal force: a force exerted on an object that pulls outward from the center of a circle

centripetal force: a force exerted on an object that pulls in toward the center of a circle

deceleration: reducing speed; slowing down; negative acceleration

density: the amount of matter (mass) in a unit of volume

displaced: pushed aside

drag: resistance of a fluid (such as air or water) to an object moving through it

efficiency: the ratio of the amount of energy a machine uses to the amount of work it does

elastic: able to return back to the original length or shape after being stretched

equilibrium: a situation in which two opposing forces are equal, creating a balance, and no movement takes place

fluid: a substance that flows

force: a push or pull, which can make an object move

friction: the rubbing of one object against another, providing resistance to motion

fulcrum: the fixed point on a surface that supports a lever

gear: a wheel with "teeth," or pegs, on the edges. The teeth of two gears mesh together and can change both force and motion.

gravity: a force of attraction between two objects; the attractive force that holds objects to Earth's surface

hydraulic system: a system that uses fluids under pressure to do work

inclined plane: a simple machine made of a sloping surface with one end raised. It is used to do work with less effort.

inertia: the tendency for an object to stay at rest or continue to move in a straight line at a constant speed unless an outside force acts on it

joule: a unit of work, determined as the amount of force multiplied by the distance in meters

kinetic energy: the energy an object has because of its motion; a form of energy that is actively doing work

lever: a simple machine that consists of a long, rigid bar that can be turned around a fixed point (the fulcrum). It is used to make moving an object easier by transmitting force applied at one point to a load at another point. Depending on the positions of the force, load, and fulcrum, the effect of the force may be increased.

load: the weight of an object that is being moved

locomotion: moving from one place to another

magnetism: a form of energy involving an attraction to objects made of certain metals, such as iron, or to a moving electric current

mass: the amount of matter in an object, which resists being moved

matter: anything that has a definite amount of mass and takes up space

molecules: the building blocks of matter, consisting of atoms joined by chemical bonds

momentum: a measure of an object's inertia; its tendency to keep moving at the same velocity

motion: changing position from one place to another

net force: the combination of all the forces that act on an object

newton: unit of force; the force needed to accelerate a mass of 1 kilogram (2.2 pounds) by 1 meter (3.3 ft) per second per second

pneumatic machine: a device that uses gas under pressure to do work

poles: the regions of a magnet where its magnetic effects are the strongest. On Earth the North Pole and the South Pole are located where the planet's magnetic field is the strongest.

potential energy: stored energy that has the potential to do work

pulley: a simple machine in which a rope or chain is threaded around one or more wheels to increase the force exerted on an object

resistance: opposing force that slows down the movement of an object

screw: a simple machine consisting of a cylindrical body with a spiral groove (thread) around it; used to fasten objects together with less effort and greater holding strength

surface tension: a force exerted on the surface molecules of a liquid by the molecules below them. The force holds the surface molecules so tightly that they form a kind of "skin."

terminal velocity: the point at which the air resistance equals the weight of a falling object

upthrust: upward force

vacuum: space containing no matter; also a space from which all or most of the air has been pumped out

velocity: speed of motion in a particular direction

wedge: a simple machine that tapers to a thin edge. When pressure is exerted on a wedge, it can be used to split an object, to hold objects together, or to tighten objects.

weight: a measure of the force exerted on an object by gravity; used as a synonym for mass in popular speech

work: the amount of energy used when a force is used to move an object

Bibliography

Adair, Robert K. *The Physics of Baseball*. New York: HarperCollins Publishers, 2002.

Brain, Marshall. "How Hydraulic Machines Work." *Howstuffworks*. 1998–2007. http://science.howstuffworks .com/hydraulic.htm (December 5, 2007).

Harris, Tom. "How Hot Air Balloons Work." *Howstuffworks*. 1998–2007. http://travel.howstuffworks.com/ hot-air-balloon.htm (December 7, 2007).

Henderson, Tom. "The Physics Classroom Tutorial." 1996–2007. http://www.glenbrook.k12.il.us/gbssci/phys/ Class/newtlaws/u2l1a.html (December 10, 2007).

Jones, T. Griffith. *Motion, Forces, and Energy*. Upper Saddle River, NJ: Pearson Prentice Hall, 2005.

Krumenaker, Larry, and Pamela J. W. Gore. "Forces and Motion—Newton's Laws of Motion." *Georgia Perimeter College*. May 27, 2007. http://gpc.edu/~pgore/ PhysicalScience/forces-motion.html (December 5, 2007).

Krystek, Lee. "The Speed of Light." *The Museum of UnNatural Mystery*. 1996. http://www.unmuseum.org/speed.htm (January 5, 2008).

Museum of Science. "Inventor's Toolbox: The Elements of Machines." *Museum of Science*. 1997. http://www.mos.org/ sln/Leonardo/InventorsToolbox.html (December 7, 2007).

Reid, David. "Scientists Discover Secret of Dolphin Speed." *Institute of Physics*. May 14, 2004. http://www.eurekalert. org/pub_releases/2004-05/iop-sds051404.php (December 7, 2007).

Robertson, William C. *Force and Motion: Stop Faking It! Finally Understanding Science So You Can Teach It*. Arlington, VA: National Science Teachers Association, 2002.

Russell, Randy. "Elliptical Orbits." *Windows to the Universe*. December 16, 2005. http://www.windows.ucar.edu/tour/link=/physical_science/physics/mechanics/orbit/ellipse.html (January 5, 2008).

Shaw, Robert J. "Dynamics of Flight." *NASA*. May 7, 2004. http://www.ueet.nasa.gov/StudentSite/dynamicsofflight.html (December 7, 2007).

Smithsonian Institution. "Locomotion in Cephalopods." *Smithsonian National Zoological Park*. N.d. http://nationalzoo.si.edu/Animals/Invertebrates/Facts/cephalopods/locomotion.cfm (December 7, 2007).

Westbroek, Glen. "Newton's Laws." *Utah State Office of Education*. August 7, 2000. http://www.schools.utah.gov/curr/science/sciber00/8th/forces/sciber/newtons.htm (December 7, 2007).

Woodford, Chris. "How Hydraulics Works." *Explain that Stuff!* October 10, 2007. http://www.explainthatstuff.com/hydraulics.html (December 6, 2007).

———. "How Jackhammers and Pneumatic Drills Work." *Explain that Stuff!* May 24, 2007. http://www.explainthatstuff.com/jackhammer.html (December 6, 2007).

For Further Information

Books

Cooper, Christopher. *Forces and Motion: From Push to Shove.* Chicago: Heinemann Library, 2004.

DiSpezio, Michael. *Awesome Experiments in Force & Motion.* New York: Sterling Publishing Co., 2000.

Fairley, Peter. *Electricity and Magnetism.* Minneapolis: Twenty-First Century Books, 2008.

Fleisher, Paul. *Objects in Motion.* Minneapolis: Twenty-First Century Books, 2002.

Graham, John. *Hands-On Science: Forces and Motion.* New York: Kingfisher Publications, 2001.

Jones, T. Griffth. *Motion, Forces, and Energy.* Upper Saddle River, NJ: Pearson Prentice Hall, 2005.

Juettner, Bonnie. *Motion.* Farmington Hills, MI: KidHaven Press, 2005.

Lafferty, Peter. *Eyewitness Books: Force and Motion.* New York: Dorling Kindersley, 2000.

———. *Forces and Motion.* Austin, TX: Raintree Steck-Vaughn Publishers, 2001.

Smith, Alastair, and Corinne Henderson. *The Usborne Internet-Linked Library of Science Energy, Force & Motion.* London: Usborne Publishing, 2001.

Stringer, John. *The Science of Gravity.* Austin, TX: Raintree Steck-Vaughn Publishers, 2000.

Websites

Creative Kids at Home Activity Library: Flight
>http://www.creativekidsathome.com/science/flight.html#How%20does
>%20an%20airplane%20take%20off?
>This site contains information on how a plane takes off, experiments, trivia questions, and links to Web pages with more information on flight.

Force and Motion—About the Workshops
>http://www.learner.org/channel/workshops/force/about/
>This website includes brief explanations of falling, friction, collisions, and other aspects of force and motion, with a "minimouse lab" that lets you operate an elevator, and self-tests of your understanding.

Motion & Forces
>http://www.learningscience.org/psc2bmotionforces.htm
>Interactive lessons and learning tools on this site cover simple machines, forces in action, and forces and movement; learning games include Gallileo Drops the Ball; Speed, Eggs, and Slam; and Moov!, which is an online drawing tool for creating drawings that move according to the rules of science.

Scholastic's The Magic School Bus: Motion & Forces
>http://www.scholastic.com/magicschoolbus/games/teacher/motion.htm
>Ms. Frizzle's class helps you understand key concepts about motion and forces, with printable activities.

Your Weight on Other Worlds
>http://www.exploratorium.edu/ronh/weight/index.html
>Fill in your weight for an automatic calculation of your weight on other worlds. There are also links to information about the planets.

Index

levers, 36, 37–41; diagram of, 41
lift, 55
light, 23, 32, 33; speed of, 87
lightbulbs, 51
liquids, 52, 60, 68–71
load, 38–39, 41
locomotion, 90–99
lubrication, 15–16, 37, 97

machines, simple, 36–51
magnetism, 21, 24–26
magnets, 24
mass, 21, 22–23, 78, 79; of Earth, 22
Mercury, 22
metals, 27–28; magnetism of, 25
Milky Way Galaxy, 88
molecules, 53, 57
momentum, 79–83
Moon: gravity on, 23; orbit of, 20–21, 88
motion, 31, 72–83; and gravity, 84–99; laws of, 76–79
movable pulley, 44–45, 46
muscles, 4, 10, 19, 33, 39, 90, 95

nails, 49–50
net force, 6–9
neutrons, 27
Newton, Isaac, 7, 20–21
newtons, 7, 8
Newton's First Law, 76–77
Newton's Second Law, 78
Newton's Third Law, 78–79
nuclear reactions, 32–33, 87
nutcrackers, 40

ocean, water pressure of, 60
octopus, 79
orbits, 20–21, 84, 85–86

outer space, 60

paper-clip chain, 25
parachutes, 76
particles, 26, 53
perception of motion, 73
planets, 85–89; chart of, 89
Pluto, 89
pneumatic drill, 68
poles, magnetic, 24, 25–26
pool, 10–11
potential energy, 31, 32
primaries, 54
propellers, 55–56
protons, 26–27
pulleys, 36, 43–46; diagram of, 46

rabbits, 62
ramps, 47–48
resistance, 52
resistance force, 38–39
rockets, 56
roller-coasters, 74
rubber, 34, 67
rubber bands, 34
running, 73, 92–93

sailboats, 13, 44
scientists, Archimedes, 40, 63; Copernicus, Nicolaus, 84–85; Galileo Galilei, 85–86; Joule, James Prescott, 35; Kepler, Johannes, 86; Newton, Isaac, 7, 20–21
scissors, 40
screw, 36, 43, 50–51
screwdriver, 37–38, 43
second-class lever, 40–41
seesaws, 37–38, 39
sense organs, 91
ships, 65, 96
shoes, 14–15, 61

Photo Acknowledgments

About the Authors

Dr. Alvin Silverstein is a former professor of biology and director of the physician assistant program at the College of Staten Island of the City University of New York. Virginia B. Silverstein is a translator of Russian scientific literature.

The Silversteins' collaboration began with a biochemical research project at the University of Pennsylvania. Since then they have produced six children and more than two hundred published books that have received high acclaim for their clear, timely, and authoritative coverage of science and health topics.

Laura Silverstein Nunn, a graduate of Kean College of New Jersey, began helping with the research for her parents' books while she was in high school. Since joining the writing team, she has coauthored more than eighty books.